Lecture Notes in Artificial Intelligence 6797

Subseries of Lecture Notes in Computer Science

Takashi Onoda   Daisuke Bekki
Elin McCready (Eds.)

New Frontiers in Artificial Intelligence

JSAI-isAI 2010 Workshops
LENLS, JURISIN, AMBN, ISS
Tokyo, Japan, November 18-19, 2010
Revised Selected Papers

 Springer

Series Editors

Randy Goebel, University of Alberta, Edmonton, Canada
Jörg Siekmann, University of Saarland, Saarbrücken, Germany
Wolfgang Wahlster, DFKI and University of Saarland, Saarbrücken, Germany

Volume Editors

Takashi Onoda
CRIEPI
System Engineering Research Lab.
2-11-1, Iwado Kita, Komae-shi
Tokyo 201-8511, Japan
E-mail: onoda@criepi.denken.or.jp

Daisuke Bekki
Ochanomizu University
Graduate School of Humanities and Sciences
Otsuka 2-1-1, Bunkyo-ku
Tokyo 112-8610, Japan
E-mail: bekki@is.ocha.ac.jp

Elin McCready
Aoyama Gakuin University
Department of English
4-4-25 Shibuya, Shibuya-ku
Tokyo 150-8366, Japan
E-mail: mccready@cl.aoyama.ac.jp

ISSN 0302-9743   e-ISSN 1611-3349
ISBN 978-3-642-25654-7   e-ISBN 978-3-642-25655-4
DOI 10.1007/978-3-642-25655-4
Springer Heidelberg Dordrecht London New York

Library of Congress Control Number: 2011941679

CR Subject Classification (1998): I.2, H.3, H.4, H.2.8, C.2

LNCS Sublibrary: SL 7 – Artificial Intelligence

Typesetting: Camera-ready by author, data conversion by Scientific Publishing Services, Chennai, India

Printed on acid-free paper

Springer is part of Springer Science+Business Media (www.springer.com)

Preface

JSAI (The Japanese Society for Artificial Intelligence) is a premier academic society that focuses on artificial intelligence in Japan and was established in 1986. JSAI publishes journals of the JSAI and bimonthly transactions, and hosts 19 special interest groups. The JSAI annual conference attracts several hundred attendees each year. JSAI-isAI (JSAI International Symposia on Artificial Intelligence) 2010 was the Second International Symposium, which hosted four co-located international workshops that were selected by the JSAI-isAI 2010 Organizing Committee. This was in succession to the international workshops co-located with the JSAI annual conferences since 2001. JSAI-isAI 2010 was successfully held during November 18–19 in Tokyo, Japan; 169 people from 15 countries participated in JSAI-isAI 2010. This volume of *New Frontiers in Artificial Intelligence: JSAI-isAI 2010 Workshops* is the proceedings of JSAI-isAI 2010. The organizers of the four workshops, LENLS, JURISIN, AMBN, and ISS, hosted by JSAI-isAI 2010, selected 28 papers. The acceptance rate was about 40%. This resulted in the excellent selection of papers that are representative of some of the topics of AI research both in Japan and in other parts of the world. LENLS (Logic and Engineering of Natural Language Semantics) is an annual international workshop on formal semantics and pragmatics. LENLS hosted by JSAI-isAI 2010 was the seventh event in the series. LENLS focuses on the formal and theoretical aspects of natural language, which demonstrates one of the strengths of Japanese AI studies. The Workshop Chair was Elin McCready (Aoyama Gakuin University). JURISIN (Juris-Informatics) was the fourth event, focusing on juris-informatics among people from various backgrounds such as law, social science, information and intelligent technology, logic and philosophy, including the conventional "AI and law" area. The Workshop Chair was Satoshi Tojo (Japan Advanced Institute of Science and Technology). AMBN (Advanced Methodologies for Bayesian networks) was held for the first time. In this workshop, methodologies for enhancing the effectiveness of Bayesian networks (BNs) including modeling, reasoning, model selection, logic-probability relations, and causality are explored. The exploration of methodologies is complemented by discussions of practical considerations for applying BNs in real-world settings, covering concerns like scalability, incremental learning, parallelization, and so on. The Workshop Chairs were Maomi Ueno (The University of Electro-Communications) and Takashi Isozaki (Sony CSL, Inc.). ISS (Innovating Service Systems) is a workshop of service science. This workshop is motivated by the systems-design dimension of service science and it shares and discusses a progressive vision to develop methods for innovating systems of service resources where novel values are created and supplied sustainably. The Workshop Chairs were Yukio Ohsawa (The University of Tokyo) and Katsutoshi Yada (Kansai University). It is our great pleasure that we were able to share some part of the outcome of these fascinating workshops through this volume. We hope the readers of this book find a way to grasp the state-of-the-art research outcomes of JSAI-isAI 2010, and may be motivated to participate in future JSAI-isAI events.

April 2011   Takashi Onoda
                                                              Elin McCready
                                                              Daisuke Bekki

Table of Contents

LENLS

JURISIN

AMBN

ISS

Logic and Engineering of Natural Language Semantics (LENLS) 7

Elin McCready

Department of English
Aoyama Gakuin University

1 The Workshop

This year's workshop was the seventh LENLS and the second held at the Campus Innovation Center in Mita, Tokyo in November of 2010 as part of the JSAI International Symposia on AI program of the Japanese Society for Artificial Intelligence. The workshop featured invited talks by Alexandru Baltag, on dynamic epistemic logic, and Shunsuke Yatabe, on paradoxes—in particular, paradoxes arising from theories of truth—and coinduction. A paper based on that second talk, "Yablo-like Paradoxes and Co-induction", appears in the present volume. In addition, 18 papers were selected by the program committee (see Acknowledgements) from the submitted abstracts for presentation and as alternates.

As always with the LENLS workshops, the content of the presented papers was rich and varied. This year's theme was salience: its realization in natural language (as well as human reasoning and knowledge representation) and how it should be given a formal representation. In addition to papers on this topic, a wide range of topics were represented, including, on the empirical side, focus phenomena, negative polarity items, reduplication, factivity and vagueness, and, on the theoretical side, variable-free semantics, game-theoretic pragmatics, categorial grammar, and various sorts of dynamic logics. In the remainder of this introduction, I will briefly indicate the content of the papers selected from this wide array of topics to appear in the present volume.

2 Papers

The submitted papers in the LENLS part of the present volume fall into three classes. The first are papers concerned mostly with structural phenomena at the level of the sentence. In this class are the papers by Daisuke Bekki, Alastair Butler and Kei Yoshimoto, and Hiroaki Nakamura. Bekki's paper "Combinatory Categorial Grammar as a Substructural Logic - Preliminary Remarks -" provides a view of CCG from the study of substructural logics and places it within that domain. The paper by Butler and Yoshimoto, "Interpreting Japanese Dependency Structure", analyzes dependency structures in Japanese in a dynamic semantics capable of modeling subsentential phenomena. Finally, the paper by Nakamura, "Binding of Relational Nouns and the Variable-free Semantics", shows how relational nouns (primarily in Japanese) can be given a variable-free analysis.

T. Onoda, D. Bekki, and E. McCready (Eds.): JSAI-isAI 2010, LNAI 6797, pp. 1–2, 2011.
© Springer-Verlag Berlin Heidelberg 2011

The second class of papers is concerned with vagueness and its analysis, though the approaches they take to these phenomena is very different. Satoru Suzuki's paper "Prolegomena to Salient-Similarity-Based Vague Predicate Logic" gives a logical system designed for the analysis of vagueness via a notion of salient similarity. Conversely, the paper by Michael Franke, Gerhard Jäger and Robert van Rooij, "Vagueness, Signaling and Bounded Rationality", analyzes vagueness in a way that crucially involves how communication involving vague predicates takes place, showing that under certain assumptions such communication naturally converges on observed interpretations of vague predicates. The third and final class of papers considers pragmatic phenomena from a formal perspective. The first, by Nicholas Asher and Sylvain Pogodalla, is "SDRT and Continuation Semantics", which shows how SDRT (a formal theory of discourse structure) can be given a continuation-based semantics which preserves many properties of the original dynamic theory while gaining some computational tractability, in line with the current general interest in continuation semantic models for dynamic theories. Finally, Richard Zuber works to characterize intensionality in terms of factivity and presupposition projection in his "Factives and Intensionality".

As the reader will notice, the range of topics addressed by even this subset of the contributed papers is very wide. As a result, the workshop was very stimulating; the participants, with their different perspectives, gave useful and interesting comments on each paper. From the perspective of the organizers at least, the result was very successful. We hope (and believe) that the other participants shared this impression.

Acknowledgements

Let me finally acknowledge some of those who have helped with the workshop. The program committee and organizers, in addition to myself, were Daisuke Bekki, Yoshiki Mori, Yasuo Nakayama, Katsuhiko Yabushita, Tomoyuki Yamada, Alastair Butler, and Kei Yoshimoto; Daisuke Bekki also was liaison with JSAI and organized various aspects of the workshop; properly, though not officially, he was the co-chair of the workshop. I would also like to acknowledge external reviewers Rick Nouwen and Yurie Hara. Finally, the organizers would like to thank JSAI for giving us the opportunity to hold the workshop.

SDRT and Continuation Semantics

Nicholas Asher[1] and Sylvain Pogodalla[2]

[1] IRIT, CNRS
nicholas.asher@irit.fr
[2] LORIA/INRIA Nancy — Grand Est
sylvain.pogodalla@inria.fr

Abstract. Segmented Discourse Representation Theory (SDRT) [2,7] provides a dynamic semantics for discourse that exploits a rich notion of discourse structure. According to SDRT, a text is segmented into constituents related to each other by means of rhetorical relations; the resulting structure, known as a *segmented discourse representation structure* or SDRS has various semantic effects. This theory has shown how discourse structure makes contributions to the interpretation of a variety of linguistic phenomena, including tense, modality, presupposition, the interpretation of anaphoric pronouns and ellipsis. SDRT exploits dynamic semantics [20,14] to interpret SDRSs. We investigate here the advantages of integrating SDRT within continuation style semantics of the sort developed in [17].

Keywords: SDRT, dynamic semantics, continuation semantics.

1 An Introduction to Continuation Semantics

Most versions of dynamic semantics (DS) in linguistics make heavy use of assignment functions as semantic objects. In this SDRT is not different. While this may not be apparent to the casual reader of early work like [20], a compositional semantics for DRT, DPL [14] or more recent developments [11] leads almost inevitably to the introduction of "odd" types whose inhabitants are variables, assignments or other "representational" elements. Dynamic Intensional Logic (DIL)[15,12], following [19]'s work on programming languages, has the virtue of making central the semantic status of assignment functions, as they are the points of evaluation in that model theory. But almost all of extant versions of DS include assignment functions as parts of semantic values. The exploitation of assignment functions as semantic objects plays a crucial role in dynamic semantic approaches to discourse interpretation. This engenders subtle differences in the underlying logic, clouding the logical status of discourse referents in a "top" DRS by making them appear ambiguous between existentially bound variables and free ones (cf. [13]). It also leads to problems of destructive assignment in DPL and with variable clash in DRT or versions of DPL that use partial assignment functions. It is difficult to avoid these problems in a purely compositional environment, leading to cumbersome systems.

T. Onoda, D. Bekki, and E. McCready (Eds.): JSAI-isAI 2010, LNAI 6797, pp. 3–15, 2011.

Continuation style semantics (CS) developed by computer scientists in the 70s and introduced into linguistics by [9,26,17,10] avoid these problems. CS provides a more abstract setting for dynamic logics, abstracting away from assignments that are essential to the formulations of DIL, DPL and DRT. CS, like DS, models the dynamic meaning of a natural language expression as a transition between a left context and a right one. But in CS right contexts are explicitly introduced and are defined in terms of left contexts and sentence denotations. CS exploits the structure of a monad in category theory [23], which specifies the parameters needed to provide a CS: the first is *to specify what a left context is*; the second is to provide a "binder" rule, which tells us *how to combine the semantics of a text with that of subsequent sentences*; the third is *to specify the lexical entries for expressions*. CS thus refocuses semanticists' attention on specifying appropriate lexical entries and discourse contexts. CS permits a wide variety of choices as to what left contexts, binder rules and lexical entries are, a liberalism we exploit below.

As an example, [17]'s CS exploits Montague's homomorphic interpretation of syntactic types and structures into semantic types and terms. But [17] changes Montague's interpretation of the sentence type s, $[\![s]\!]$, from t to $\Omega \stackrel{\Delta}{=} \gamma \to (\gamma \to t) \to t$, where γ is the type of the left context or discourse context already given and $\gamma \to t$ is the type of the right context or discourse "to come"— its *continuation*. If this sentence introduces a new discourse entity x, given an environment i (as *input*) and a continuation k as parameter, it can provide $(x :: i)$ (with $\cdot :: \cdot$ a list constructor of type $e \to \gamma \to \gamma$) as parameter to k, making the value of x available for k.

Other types have standard interpretations. Where $[\![X]\!]$ stands for the λ-term or meaning of X, $[\![np]\!] = (e \to [\![s]\!]) \to [\![s]\!]$ and $[\![n]\!] = e \to [\![s]\!]$. Pronouns have the following interpretation: $[\![it]\!] = \lambda P.\lambda i k.P\,(\mathtt{sel}\,i)\,i\,k$, where $i\colon\gamma$, $k\colon\gamma \to t$, and where $\mathtt{sel}\,i$ is a function that selects a *suitable* discourse antecedent inside i.

A CS like [17]'s must say how a text T combines with a sentence to its right. This is the CS binder issue, which is also an essential part of all dynamical systems—it is the DRS update operation of DRT or relational composition of sentence contents in DPL. Here is the basic binder equation for de Groote's system and ours:

$$(1) \qquad [\![T.S]\!] = \lambda i.\lambda k.[\![T]\!]\,i\,(\lambda i'.[\![S]\!]\,i'\,k)$$

That is, the text to date T takes the meaning of S as its right context, or rather the meaning of S suitably applied and abstracted so that it can be of t type. A quick type check on $\lambda i'.[\![S]\!]\,i'\,k$ confirms that this is indeed the right output: $[\![S]\!] : \gamma \to (\gamma \to t) \to t$ so $\lambda i'.[\![S]\!]\,i'\,k : \gamma \to t$.

Let's look at a sample discourse to see how the theory works.

(2)   A man is sleeping. He is snoring.

Suitable lexical entries provide a completely classical interpretation of these two sentences except that they have both a left and right context and that the second sentence fills in the right context of the first. The entries also make the existential determiner introduce an individual into the right context—a witness that will be "selected" by the pronoun. With this in mind, the interpretation of the first sentence is:

(3) $\qquad \lambda i. \lambda k. \exists x. \; (\textbf{man } x) \wedge (\textbf{sleeping } x) \wedge (k \; (x :: i))$

The second sentence provides the λ-term:

(4) $\qquad \lambda i. \lambda k. (\textbf{snoring } (\textbf{sel } i)) \wedge (k \; i)$

Using the binder rule in (1), these last two λ-terms yield a meaning for (2) :

$\lambda i \; k. [\lambda i \; k. \exists x. (\textbf{man } x) \wedge (\textbf{sleeping } x) \wedge k \; (x :: i)] \, i$
$\qquad\qquad\qquad (\lambda i'. (\lambda i \; k. (\textbf{snoring } (\textbf{sel } i)) \wedge (k \; i)) \; i' \; k)$
$\rightarrow_\beta \lambda i \; k. [\lambda k. \exists x. (\textbf{man } x) \wedge (\textbf{sleeping } x) \wedge (k \; (x :: i))]$
$\qquad\qquad\qquad (\lambda i'. (\textbf{snoring } (\textbf{sel } i')) \wedge (k \; i'))$
$\rightarrow_\beta \lambda i \; k. [\exists x. (\textbf{man } x) \wedge (\textbf{sleeping } x)$
$\qquad\qquad \wedge ((\lambda i'. (\textbf{snoring } (\textbf{sel } i')) \wedge (k \; i')) \; (x :: i))]$
$\rightarrow_\beta \lambda i \; k. [\exists x. (\textbf{man } x) \wedge (\textbf{sleeping } x) \wedge ((\textbf{snoring } (\textbf{sel } (x :: i)) \wedge (k \; (x :: i)))))]$

In selecting the bound variable x, the semantic value of the anaphoric pronoun falls within the scope of the original existential quantifier, reducing anaphoric binding to quantificational binding.

In [8], we show how de Groote's proposal differs from Dynamic Intensional Logic and Dynamic Montague Grammar, which appear to be close cousins. Nevertheless, there are the fundamental differences we have noted above between the two approaches. We argue in this paper that CS in the style of [17,24,8] can profit SDRT in several ways, by generalizing the theory, reducing a dependence on descriptions of representations and integrating syntax and discourse in an interesting way.

2 An Introduction to SDRT in Continuation Semantics

SDRT, as we have said, is a theory that exploits a rich notion of discourse structure. But what is this? For SDRT, as for most theories that investigate discourse structure, such structure involves units or discourse constituents that are linked by discourse relations that define the rhetorical function of the constituent in the discourse. Let us look at some examples.

(5) a. John walked in. • He poured himself a cup of coffee.
   b. John fell. • Mary pushed him.
   c. We bought the apartment, • but we've rented it.
   d. Il commence à dessiner et peindre en 1943 , • fréquente les ateliers de sculpture • puis de peinture de l' école des Beaux-Arts d' Oran , • où il rencontre Guermaz (ANNODIS corpus).

e. Julie had an excellent meal, • beginning with an elegant and inventive truffes du Périgord en première cuisson comme un petit déjeuner,• followed by some wonderful scallops, • then sweetbreads, • a sumptuous cheese plate, • and ending with a scrumptious dessert.

A presumption of relevance leads us to infer some link between *elementary discourse units* or *EDU*s (clauses or subclausal units whose boundaries are marked by • in the examples above). These links involve relations that are familiar even to the non-linguist: some units elaborate or go into more detail concerning something introduced in another constituents (these are Elaboration type relations) as in (5e); some units form a parallel or a contrast with other units (such units are linked by Parallel or Contrast), as in (5c); some units furnish explanations why something described in another unit happened (Explanation) as in (5b); and some units constitute a narrative sequence of events (Narration) (5a) or (5d).

Some discourse relations are encoded grammatically through the use of certain grammatical constructions (like adverbial or purposive clauses, parentheticals or left fronted temporal or spatial adverbials)[1] or through discourse connectors like *as a result, puis* or the choice and sequencing of lexical items. An example of a set of discourse relations triggered by the choice of verb and complement comes in (5e), with the use of *beginning with, followed by* and *ending with*. Sometimes, it is less clear what linguistic source triggers the inference of the discourse relation as in (5a-b)—most likely, an as yet not fully understood mix of lexical semantics and world knowledge. The discourse relations implicated by these devices have impose structural constraints on the discourse context and have truth conditional effects that a number of researchers have explored.[2]

To construct a discourse structure for a text, we must accomplish three tasks:

- to segment a text into EDUs;
- to compute attachment points of EDUs in a discourse structure;
- to compute one or more discourse relations between an EDU and its attachment point(s).

An SDRT discourse structure or SDRS is the result of these computations and may contain complex constituents where several EDUs combine together to make one larger constituent. An SDRS is a logical form for discourse with a well-defined dynamic semantics that has many equivalent formulations— as a first order model like structure consisting of a set of labels and assignments of formulas to labels [7], as a DRS like structure [2] or as we will show below, a λ-term in intensional logic.

To get an idea of what SDRSs look like consider the following text (6) discussed at length in [7]. The model-like SDRS is given in (7).

---

[1] For a discussion of these, see for instance [27].

[2] With regards to temporal structure, see [22]; on pronominal anaphora, see [2,21]; on presupposition see [6]; on sluicing and ellipsis see [2,5,25].

(6) π_1. John had a great evening last night.
       π_2. He had a great meal.
       π_3. He ate salmon.
       π_4. He devoured lots of cheese.
       π_5. He then won a dancing competition.

(7) $\langle A, \mathcal{F}, \mathrm{Last} \rangle$ where:
$$
\begin{cases}
A & = \{\pi_0, \pi_1, \pi_2, \pi_3, \pi_4, \pi_5, \pi_6, \pi_7\} \\
\mathcal{F}(\pi_0) = Elaboration(\pi_1, \pi_6) \\
\mathcal{F}(\pi_6) = Narration(\pi_2, \pi_5) \wedge Elaboration(\pi_2, \pi_7) \\
\mathcal{F}(\pi_7) = Narration(\pi_3, \pi_4) \\
\mathrm{Last} & = \pi_5
\end{cases}
$$

In SDRT we can abstract away from the details of the structure to get a graph representation, which is relevant to computing discourse accessibility (again for details see [7]):

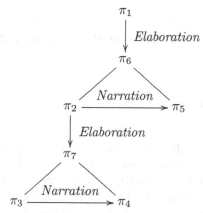

Notice that some discourse relations are represented as vertical lines in the graph whereas others are horizontal arcs; these correspond to two different types of relations—subordinating and coordinating relations, and these two types of relations affect anaphoric and attachment possibilities differently.[3]

Inferring discourse relations to build an SDRS is a matter of defeasible and uncertain inference. Many of the features used to infer discourse relations are only good indications of a particular discourse relation or particular discourse structure; very few are in and of themselves sufficient to deductively infer the relation or structure. Many discourse connectives are for example ambiguous. In addition, many segments may bear discourse relations to other segments despite the lack of discourse connectives or known structural or lexical cues, as in (5a,b) or (6). SDRT uses a nonmonotonic logic, a logic for defeasible inference, tailored to inferring discourse relations. We will appeal to this as an oracle in what follows below.

We now turn to a more logic based representation of discourse structures. As proposed in [4] and then further developed in [7], SDRSs can be represented

---

[3] For a discussion, see for example [3,7].

using a labelled language, where the labels stand for discourse constituents. In such a language every n-ary predicate becomes an $(n+1)$-ary predicate.

In keeping with earlier work, we assume the language is that of IL together with a set of labels $\pi, \pi_1, \pi_2, \ldots$ of atomic type ℓ, representing discourse constituents, and a set of relation symbols of type $\ell \to \ell \to \ell \to t$ that represent discourse relations over constituents. We write $R(\pi_1, \pi_2, \pi) : t$ to state that the discourse relation R holds between π_1 and π_2 in constituent π. These formulas will be introduced during combination process. This process for reasons developed in [7] makes appeal to a separate reasoning module known as the Glue Logic.

An SDRS in CS is a formula or a lambda term of type Ω, the dynamic type of sentences and texts in [17] and [8]. In this framework, we need to specify:

- the nature of γ;
- the binder rule for combining a text and a new constituent;
- and a lexicon.

We define the type γ as records as in [8], the fields of which are:

- a set of Labels;
- a set of Accessible Labels;
- a set of accessible Discourse Entities;
- and a proposition of type t.

The latter, which is redundant with the overall result, is needed to be part of the context so that we can make *inferences* based on the content of the context.[4] SDRT makes the accessibility of a discourse entity dependent upon the discourse structure; we capture this by making the accessible discourse entities for the information to come dependent on the label of attachment—thus our field for discourse entities will be pairs of accessible labels with other variables (for discourse entities). We provide several functions on records that retrieve needed information.

- $\mathtt{sel}_L : \gamma \to \ell$ extracts a label from the left context that is SDRT accessible (for a definition of SDRT accessibility see e.g., [7]).[5]
- $\mathtt{sel}_E : \gamma \to \ell \to e$ extracts a discourse referent from the set of accessible discourse referents associated with a label.
- $\mathtt{sel}_\rho : \gamma \to \ell \to \ell \to \ell \to t$. This function is used to pick a discourse relation (*i.e.* a ternary relation) linking a label chosen from i, the current context, and returns a proposition.

---

[4] We might rather consider a hyperintensional type PROP to make these inferences, but we don't want to focus on that point here. Such inferences may be required in example such as (5b) to get the right temporal order and the right discourse relation which may depend upon the context.

[5] Using the techniques introduced in [24], we could express this function using only an update operator on sets of labels/entities.

– $v: \gamma \to \ell \to \gamma$. This is the update function that changes the left context record in virtue of the information contained in S and the linking of its label to some label in i via a chosen discourse relation. This update function is defined in terms of SDRT's glue logic which operates on fields of a left context. We write the update operation as $v(i, \pi_S)$, where S is the current discourse constituent and i is a left context.

We now present the operation of combining a discourse with a sentence. Several new operations are involved at this level: first an application of sel_L, then an application of sel_ρ, and a use of the update operation v. Note that in order to clearly show how *bound* variables, both for segment labels and discourse referents, can be added to the context during the process, we explicitly use the function :: in the first next examples rather than the v function that somehow "hide" the underlying modifications of the context. This :: function is an overloaded function with type either $\ell \to \gamma \to \gamma$ or $e \to \gamma \to \gamma$. Our binder rule for SDRT is just that of [17][6] which is:

(8) $\qquad [\![D.S]\!] = \lambda io\pi.\exists \pi_1.[\![D]\!](\pi_1 :: i)(\lambda i'.\exists \pi_2.[\![S]\!](\pi_2 :: i') \circ \pi_2) \pi_1$

However, the semantics of a sentence is more complex, since it must attach to the text meaning with one or more discourse relations. Which relations are involved will depend on the structure of the discourse to date and the left context. The discourse relations define a partial order over labels. We say that if $R(\pi_1, \pi_2, \pi_3)$, then $\pi_3 > \pi_1$ and $\pi_2 > \pi_1$. A constraint of well-foundedness says that $>$ always has a unique maximal element and that $>$ is asymmetric and transitive; this ensures that we never have $R(\pi_1, \pi_2, \pi_1)$ or $R(\pi_1, \pi_2, \pi_2)$. The v function should take this into account.

The standard interpretation for a sentence S expressing some predicate P_S in [17] is: $[\![S]\!] = \lambda io\pi.P_S \wedge (o\,i'\,\pi)$, that is, in addition to providing the content P_S to the discourse, it transforms i into i' (*e.g.* adding some new discourse referent with :: or v) and gives its to its continuation. Because discourse relations now come into play, the interpretation we get is in general rather:

(9) $\qquad [\![S]\!] = \lambda io\pi.\exists \pi_S.P_S \wedge \mathsf{sel}_\rho(\mathsf{sel}_L(i), \pi_S, \mathsf{sel}_L(i)) \wedge (o\,i'\,\pi)$

where $i' = v(i, \pi_2)$ consists in i plus the new discourse label and the new discourse relation (plus possible new discourse referents, of course), provided the constraints on $>$ are met. The kind of reasoning done in [7] will tell us how to update i via the Glue Logic and get i'.

There are however some exceptions to this schema. Indeed the rule (9) sometimes results in an inconsistency because the discourse context updated by D has only one label in it (one element in Labels), or even none in the case of the first sentence. In this case, we cannot form a formula $R(\pi_i, \pi_S, \pi_j)$ that is

---

[6] With the slight modification that now $\Omega \overset{\triangle}{=} \gamma \to (\gamma \to \ell \to t) \to \ell \to t$ so that we can anchor a segment using a segment label.

consistent with the constraints on $>$. In these cases, the interpretation also introduces an auxiliary label[7] and we treat this exception to (9) with the following interpretation:

$$(10) \qquad [\![S]\!] = \lambda i o \pi . \exists \pi' . \exists \pi_S . P_S \wedge \mathsf{sel}_\rho(\mathsf{sel}_L(i), \pi_S, \pi') \wedge (o\,i'\,\pi)$$

The case where there is no label at all in the context (starting sentence) is dealt with the same way, except that its semantic representation is limited to the predicate (there is no additional discourse relation).

By adding further constraints about discourse structure, for example those involving complex segments, the nature of discourse relations or topics, (9) may generate other exceptions that we may specify analogously.

2.1 Lexicalized Discourse Relation

Let's illustrate a simple case with a lexicalized discourse relation. We compute the semantic representation of (11) using the lexicon of Table 1. In this lexicon, we integrate the fact that theses sentences occur at the first and the second position directly in the lexicon.

(11) (π_1) A man walked in. (π_2) Then he coughed.

We can then compute the following interpretations:

$$
\begin{aligned}
[\![S_1]\!] &= \lambda i o \pi . \exists x . \mathbf{M}(x, \pi) \wedge \mathbf{W}(x, \pi) \wedge (o\,(x :: i)\,\pi) \\
[\![S_2]\!] &= \lambda i o \pi_2 . \exists \pi . \mathbf{C}(\mathsf{sel}_E(i), \pi_2) \wedge \mathit{Narration}(\mathsf{sel}_L(i), \pi_2, \pi) \wedge (o\,(\pi + i)\,\pi_2) \\
[\![S_1.S_2]\!] &= \lambda i o \pi'' . \exists \pi_1 . [\![S_1]\!]\,(\pi_1 :: i)\,(\lambda i' \pi' . \exists \pi_2 . [\![S_2]\!]\,(\pi_2 :: i')\,o\,\pi_2)\,\pi_1 \\
&= \lambda i o \pi'' . \exists \pi_1 . (\lambda i o \pi . \exists x . \mathbf{M}(x, \pi) \wedge \mathbf{W}(x, \pi) \wedge (o\,(x :: i)\,\pi)) \\
&\qquad\qquad (\pi_1 :: i)\,(\lambda i' \pi' . \exists \pi_2 . [\![S_2]\!]\,(\pi_2 :: i')\,o\,\pi_2)\,\pi_1 \\
\rightarrow_\beta\ &\lambda i o \pi'' . \exists \pi_1 . \exists x . \mathbf{M}(x, \pi_1) \wedge \mathbf{W}(x, \pi_1) \\
&\qquad \wedge ((\lambda i' \pi' . \exists \pi_2 . [\![S_2]\!]\,(\pi_2 :: i')\,o\,\pi_2)\,(x :: (\pi_1 :: i))\,\pi_2) \\
\rightarrow_\beta\ &\lambda i o \pi'' . \exists \pi_1 . \exists x . \mathbf{M}(x, \pi_1) \wedge \mathbf{W}(x, \pi_1) \\
&\qquad \wedge (\exists \pi_2 . [\![S_2]\!]\,(\pi_2 :: (x :: (\pi_1 :: i)))\,o\,\pi_2) \\
\rightarrow_\beta\ &\lambda i o \pi'' . \exists \pi_1 . \exists x . \mathbf{M}(x, \pi_1) \wedge \mathbf{W}(x, \pi_1) \\
&\qquad \wedge (\exists \pi_2 . (\lambda i o \pi_2 . \exists \pi . \mathbf{C}(\mathsf{sel}_E(i), \pi_2) \\
&\qquad\qquad \wedge \mathit{Narration}(\mathsf{sel}_L(i), \pi_2, \pi) \wedge (o(\pi + i)\pi_2)) \\
&\qquad\qquad\quad (\pi_2 :: (x :: (\pi_1 :: i)))\,o\,\pi_2) \\
\rightarrow_\beta\ &\lambda i o \pi'' . \exists \pi_1 . \exists x . \mathbf{M}(x, \pi_1) \wedge \mathbf{W}(x, \pi_1) \\
&\qquad \wedge [\exists \pi_2 . \exists \pi . \mathbf{C}(\mathsf{sel}_E(\pi_2 :: (x :: (\pi_1 :: i))), \pi_2) \\
&\qquad\qquad \wedge \mathit{Narration}(\mathsf{sel}_L((\pi_2 :: (x :: (\pi_1 :: i))), \pi_2, \pi)) \\
&\qquad\qquad \wedge o\,(\pi + (\pi_2 :: (x :: (\pi_1 :: i))))\pi_2]
\end{aligned}
$$

---

[7] For sake of clarity we assume here another kind of interpretation. However, the kind of exception mechanism of [18] for presupposition could be used. Here, the presupposition that needs to be accommodated is the existence of a suitable label π.

Table 1. A simple lexicon

$$\begin{aligned}
[\![man]\!] &= \lambda x.\lambda io\pi.(\mathbf{M}\, x\, \pi) \wedge (o\, i\, \pi)\\
[\![a]\!] &= \lambda P.\lambda Q.\lambda io\pi.\exists x.(P\, x\, (x :: i)\, (\lambda i'\pi'.Q\, x\, o\, i'\, \pi'))\, \pi\\
[\![walked\ in]\!] &= \lambda s.\lambda i'o'\pi'.\exists \pi_1.s(\lambda x.\lambda io\pi.(\mathbf{W}\, x\, \pi) \wedge (o\, i\, \pi'))\, (\pi_1 + i')\, o'\, \pi_1\\
[\![coughed]\!] &= \lambda s.\lambda i'o'\pi'.\exists \pi_1.s(\lambda x.\lambda io\pi.(\mathbf{C}\, x\, \pi) \wedge (o\, i\, \pi'))\, (\pi_1 + i')\, o'\, \pi_1\\
[\![he]\!] &= \lambda P.\lambda io\pi.P\, (\mathbf{sel}_E\, i)\, i\, o\, \pi\\
[\![then]\!] &= \lambda s.\lambda io\pi_2.\exists \pi.s\, i\, (\lambda i'\pi'.Narration(\mathbf{sel}_L(i), \pi_2, \pi) \wedge (o\, (\pi :: i')\, \pi'))\, \pi_2
\end{aligned}$$

2.2 Getting More General

In this section, we don't develop the computation steps anymore. We want to stress here how we can structure the context and how it evolves. Example (12) is very similar to (11) except that there is no lexicalization of the discourse relation.

(12) (π_1) A man walked in. (π_2) He coughed.

Eventually, the discourse relation between π_1 and π_2 is set to *Narration* (meaning $\mathbf{sel}_\rho(\mathbf{sel}_L(i'), \pi_2, \pi)$ gets resolved in $Narration(\pi_1, \pi_2, \pi)$).

The stages in the computation reveal the evolution of the left context as the discourse is processed. Supposing that we have a record i_0 with empty fields for contents, discourse entities and discourse labels, the first sentence provides us with an update to the left context as follows:

(13) $\begin{bmatrix} \text{Labels} = & \{\pi_1\}\\ \text{Available Labels} = & \{\pi_1\}\\ \text{Discourse entities} = & \{(\pi_1, \{x\})\}\\ \text{Content} = & \exists\pi_1.\exists x.\mathbf{M}(x, \pi_1) \wedge \mathbf{W}(x, \pi_1) \end{bmatrix}$

After the update with the second sentence of (12), we assume that

$$\mathbf{sel}_E(\upsilon(\upsilon(i_0, \pi_1), \pi_2), \pi_2) = x$$

and the context is now:

(14) $\begin{bmatrix} \text{Labels} = & \{\pi_1, \pi_2, \pi\}\\ \text{Available Labels} = & \{\pi_2, \pi\}\\ \text{Discourse entities} = & \{(\pi_1, \{x\}), (\pi_2, \{x\})\}\\ \text{Content} = & \exists\pi_1.\exists x.(\mathbf{M}(w, \pi_1) \wedge \mathbf{W}(x, \pi_1)) \wedge \exists\pi.\exists\pi_2.\mathbf{C}(x, \pi_2)\\ & \wedge Narration(\pi_1, \pi_2, \pi) \end{bmatrix}$

(14) provides for a suitable antecedent for the pronoun *he* because the selection function $\mathbf{sel}_E$ can find the appropriate antecedent in the list of discourse entities of the current record. Note that the set of available nodes calculated for a given left context exploits the definition in [7]. Here because *Narration* is a coordinating relation, it makes π_1 not an available label, following [24]. In contrast, the discourse (15a) provides a different picture. Let's suppose that π_2 attaches to π_1 with *Background*, which is a subordinating discourse relation. Intuitively,

we would like to leave open both for the possibility of continuing the elaboration or description of the man or by talking about something that is linked to the first constituent, as in (15b,c). To allow for all these attachments the update of an empty discourse context with (15a) yields the left context in (16) for future continuations.

(15)   a.   (π_1) A man walked in. (π_2) It was raining.
       b.   (π_1) A man walked in. (π_2) It was raining. (π_3) He wanted to buy a new suit.
       c.   (π_1) A man walked in. (π_2) He sported a hat. (π_3) Then a woman walked in. (π_4) She wore a coat.

(16)
$$
\begin{bmatrix}
\text{Labels} = & \{\pi_1, \pi_2, \pi\} \\
\text{Available Labels} = & \{\pi_2, \pi, \pi_1\} \\
\text{Discourse entities} = & \{(\pi_1, \{x\}), (\pi_2, \{x\})\} \\
\text{Content} = & \exists\pi_1.\exists x.\mathbf{M}(x, \pi_1) \wedge \mathbf{W}(x, \pi_1) \wedge \exists\pi.\exists\pi_2.\mathbf{R}(\pi_2) \\
 & \wedge Background(\pi_1, \pi_2, \pi)
\end{bmatrix}
$$

On the other hand, (15c) yields the left context in (17):

(17)
$$
\begin{bmatrix}
\text{Labels} = & \{\pi_1, \pi_2, \pi, \pi_3, \pi', \pi_4\} \\
\text{Available Labels} = & \{\pi', \pi_3, \pi_4\} \\
\text{Discourse entities} = & \{(\pi_4, \{y, c\}), (\pi_3, \{y\})\} \\
 & \exists\pi_1.\exists x.\mathbf{M}(x, \pi_1) \wedge \mathbf{W}(x, \pi_1) \wedge \\
 & \exists\pi.\exists\pi_2.\exists h.\mathbf{S}(\mathbf{sel}_E(x :: \mathbf{nil}, \pi_1), h, \pi_2) \wedge \mathbf{H}(h) \\
 & \wedge Background(\pi_1, \pi_2, \pi) \wedge \\
\text{Content} = & \exists\pi_3.\exists y(\mathbf{Wo}(y, \pi_3) \wedge \mathbf{W}(y, \pi_3)) \\
 & \wedge\exists\pi'.Narration(\pi, \pi_3, \pi') \wedge \\
 & \exists\pi_4.\exists c.\mathbf{Wear}(\mathbf{sel}_E(y :: \mathbf{nil}, \pi_3), c, \pi_4) \\
 & \wedge\mathbf{Coat}(c, \pi_4) \wedge Background(\pi_3, \pi_4, \pi')
\end{bmatrix}
$$

Notice that given the attachments in (15c), the man x and its hat h are no longer an accessible discourse entities for future continuations, even though the existential quantifier introduced in π_1 has scope over the content introduced by π_4 and possible continuations. Our reformulation of SDRT in CS thus makes the right frontier constraint of SDRT, cf. [2,7,1], follow from the semantics, which was not the case in earlier work. A left context specifies an SDRS graph and other more familiar representations of SDRSs used in the literature. Nevertheless, the record formalism is more general and flexible than other specifications of SDRT, and allows the addition of other fields, should they be needed in specifying discourse structure (for example questions under discussion). Further refinements of (8) will allow for multiple attachment points and links with multiple discourse relations, which SDRT allows.

3   A Refinement of the Binder Rule for SDRT

Our continuation style semantics for SDRT allows us to specify more concretely the semantics of discourse relations. For example, consider the distinction made in [7] between veridical and non veridical discourse relations. [7] argues that one cannot have $R(a, b, l) \wedge R'(b, c, l)$, where R is veridical and R' is not veridical but its treatment of the labelled language as a description language did not permit it to really say why such a formula is problematic. For us, this formula is contradictory. We have assigned labels the atomic type ℓ; but in a richer typed framework, we can be more specific: we can take them to be nominalizations of propositions that can be localized—hence some sort of facts or possibilities. We hold that certain discourse relations can affect the type of the labels they relate. We have already made clear that there is a function from labels to their contents (we'll call it $\|.\|$), as discourse related constituents produce an ordinary formula in the labelled language, a formula which has a standard model theoretic content. It is now straightforward to define (left and right) veridical and non veridical discourse relations:

- R is veridical iff $R(a, b, l) \rightarrow \|l\| \subseteq \|a\| \wedge \|l\| \subseteq \|b\|$
- R is non-right and left veridical iff $R(a, b, l) \rightarrow \|l\| \not\subseteq \|a\| \wedge \|l\| \not\subseteq \|b\|$

It is now evident that with a non-left and right veridical relation like Alternation, the following discourse structure is simply inconsistent:

(18) $Contrast(a, b, l) \wedge Alternation(b, c, l)$

We can use the TEST operation of [8] and attempt to use the binder rule in the way above. If the result is consistent, the binder rule can be used as above. However, if the evaluation of the application of the rule yields an inconsistent structure, then we may specify an EXCEPTION condition that explicitly introduces a new constituent for a discourse like

(19)   (π_1) John likes sports but (π_2) Bill doesn't. (π_3) Or Sam doesn't

so that we get the discourse structure in (20):

(20) $Contrast(\pi_1, \pi, l) \wedge Alternation(\pi_2, \pi_3, \pi)$

which is intuitively what is desired.

4   From Syntax to Discourse

Another important reason for exploiting the CS framework is to get a tighter connection between sentential syntax and discourse semantics, something that [7] simply does not treat. The continuation style semantics used in [17,24,8] are all tightly coupled to syntactic theories elaborated in the Abstract Categorial Grammar (ACG) framework [16]. We believe that it will be fruitful to use ACGs to study how syntactic structures can affect discourse semantics, as well as clausal semantics. For example, elements on the left periphery of an IP, parentheticals, can be specified in the syntax semantics interface to generate discourse constituents. Other syntactic and lexical constructions appear useful to analyze in the CS framework:

(21) a. In the thirties, liquor could not be sold in most areas. Speakeasies developed throughout the US *[detached IP adverbial with scope over the subsequent sentence]*

b. Stock shares fell today, partly because of investor anxiety about the weak recovery.

c. John came to the party, only because he couldn't think of anything else to do.

d. He betrayed and then murdered your father *[Obi-Wan Kenobe to Luke Skywalker]*

e. I disagree with the honorable Senator's motion for three fundamental reasons...

All of these examples offer interesting examples of the interplay between syntax, lexical semantics and discourse semantics. Frame adverbials studied in [27] like *in the thirties* and enumeration structures like that announced in (21e) introduce a novel element via lexical and syntactic constructions: they introduce a relation that holds between the label for the material in the adverbial or the clause in (21e) and a label in the discourse to come. Thus, our selection functions must select from future continuations, something that is relatively straightforward in continuation semantics but that requires a heavy-handed use of underspecification in standard formulations of SDRT. Among the various account to handle this case, we could add a new field to the context that, in addition to the content $(\exists \pi_1.\textbf{in\_the\_thirties}(\pi_1))$, could contain (a list of) *pending* relations, introduced by the left adjoined adverbial and that would need to be emptied under some conditions by the next segments, such as:

(22) $\lambda \pi. \lambda i. Elaboration(\pi_1, \pi, \textbf{sel}_L(i)) \wedge o(i)$

In (21b-d), we have examples where syntactic structure incorporates lexical elements like *because* or *and then* that introduce discourse structure. We believe that a framework like CS can treat these cleanly as well.

References

1. Afantenos, S., Asher, N.: Testing SDRT's right frontier. In: 23rd International Conference on Computational Linguistics, COLING 2010 (2010)
2. Asher, N.: Reference to Abstract Objects in Discourse. Studies in Linguistics and Philosophy, vol. 50. Kluwer, Dordrecht (1993)
3. Asher, N.: Troubles on the right frontier. In: Khnlein, P., Benz, A. (eds.) Constraints in Discourse (CID 2005). Pragmatics & Beyond New Series, vol. 172, pp. 29–52. John Benjamins Publishing Company, Amsterdam (2008)
4. Asher, N., Fernando, T.: Effective labeling for disambiguation. In: Bunt, H. (ed.) Second International Workshop in Computational Linguistics, Tilburg, The Netherlands (1997)
5. Asher, N., Hardt, D., Busquets, J.: Discourse parallelism, ellipsis, and ambiguity. Journal of Semantics 18(1), 1–25 (2001)
6. Asher, N., Lascarides, A.: The semantics and pragmatics of presupposition. Journal of Semantics 15(3), 239–299 (1998)

7. Asher, N., Lascarides, A.: Logics of Conversation. Cambridge University Press, Cambridge (2003)
8. Asher, N., Pogodalla, S.: A montagovian treatment of modal subordination. In: Semantics and Linguistic Theory 20, SALT 20 (2010)
9. Barker, C.: Continuations in natural language. In: 4th Continuations Workshop (2004)
10. Bernardi, R., Moortgat, M.: Continuation semantics for the Lambek-Grishin calculus. Information and Computation 208(5), 397–416 (2010); Special Issue: 14th Workshop on Logic, Language, Information and Computation (WoLLIC 2007)
11. Brasoeavnu, A.: Structured anaphora to quantifier domains. Information and Computation (to appear)
12. Dekker, P.: Scopes in discourse. Journal of Language and Computation 1, 7–32 (1999)
13. Fernando, T.: What is a DRS? Tech. Rep. R2.1.B, Dyana deliverable (1994); also in the Proceedings of a Workshop on Computational Semantics, Tilburg, The Netherlands (December 1994)
14. Groenendijk, J., Stokhof, M.: Dynamic predicate logic. Linguistics and Philosophy 14(1), 39–100 (1991)
15. Groenendijk, J., Stokhof, M.: Changing the context: Dynamics and discourse. In: Doron, E., et al. (eds.) 11th Annual Conference and of the Workshop on Discourse (IATL 3). The Israel Association for Theoretical Linguistics, Jerusalem (1996)
16. de Groote, P.: Towards Abstract Categorial Grammars. In: 39th Annual Meeting and 10th Conference of the European Chapter (EACL), Association for Computational Linguistics (ACL), pp. 148–155 (2001)
17. de Groote, P.: Towards a Montagovian account of dynamics. In: Semantics and Linguistic Theory 16, SALT 16 (2006)
18. de Groote, P., Lebedeva, E.: Presupposition accomodation as exception handling. In: 11th Annual SIGdial Meeting on Discourse and Dialogue, SIGDIAL 2010 (2010)
19. Janssen, T.: Foundations and Applications of Montague Grammar. Ph.D. thesis, University of Amsterdam (1983)
20. Kamp, H.: A theory of truth and semantic representation. In: Groenendijk, J.A., Janssen, T., Stokhof, M. (eds.) Formal Methods in the Study of Language. Foris (1981)
21. Kehler, A., Kerta, L., Rohde, H., Elman, J.: Coherence and coreference revisited. Journal of Semantics 25(1), 1–44 (2008); special Issue on Processing Meaning
22. Lascarides, A., Asher, N.: Temporal interpretation, discourse relations and commonsense entailment. Linguistics and Philosophy 16(5), 437–493 (1993)
23. Moggi, E.: Notions of computation and monads. Information and Computation 93(1), 55–92 (1991)
24. Pogodalla, S.: Exploring a type-theoretic approach to accessibility constraint modelling. Journées Sémantique et Modélisation, Toulouse (2008)
25. Romero, M., Hardt, D.: Ellipsis and the structure of discourse. Journal of Semantics 21(4), 375–414 (2004)
26. Shan, C., Barker, C.: Explaining crossover and superiority as left-to-right evaluation. Linguistics and Philosophy 29(1), 91–134 (2006)
27. Vieu, L., Bras, M., Asher, N., Aurnague, M.: Locating adverbials in discourse. Journal of French Language Studies 15(2), 173–193 (2005)

Combinatory Categorial Grammar as a Substructural Logic
— Preliminary Remarks —

Daisuke Bekki*

Ochanomizu University
Faculty of Science, Department of Information Science
2-1-1 Ohtsuka, Bunkyo-ku, Tokyo 112-8610, Japan

Abstract. This paper aims to provide a logical background for Combinatory Categorial Grammar (CCG) and its typological discussions. Based on the Curry-Howard correspondence between Gentzen-style proof systems and Lambek Lamda Calculi, and those between Hilbert-style proof systems and substructural **BCWK**-logic, I define a new class of logic which provides subclasses for each of the substructural combinatory logics, called *Subdirectional Combinatory Logic*, and propose that CCG is a subdirectional logic of a relevance logic (*Combinatory Hypothesis*). This hypothesis allows us to discuss typological parameters in universal grammar in terms of the presence/absence of a certain directional combinators.

1 The Aim: CCG as a Logic of Universal Grammar

Classical Categorial Grammar (CG) [3][4] has long been considered, rightly or wrongly by both theoretical and computational linguists, to be just a toy grammar which only logicians who are not serious about natural language have pursued in relation to proof theories, or just a fragment of grammar as Montague modestly called his version of categorial grammar [21].

However, recent study has revealed that this is not the case for Combinatory Categorial Grammar (CCG) [2][32][34][35], a categorial grammar enriched with *combinators*. It has been proven that CCG is able to provide suitable devices to describe a robust grammar to parse real texts such as those from large-scale corpora and the world-wide web [15][16], and spell out even DRT-style semantic representations [6].

---

* I wish to thank Kenichi Asai, Hideki Aso, Alastair Butler, Sachio Hirokawa, Kristina Liefke, Elin McCready, Hiroakira Ono, Hiroko Ozaki, Ken Shiotani, Shunsuke Yatabe, Kei Yoshimoto and the audiences of the 7th international workshop of Logic and Engineering of Natural Language Semantics (LENLS7, November 18-19th, 2010, Tokyo) and the symposium on Categorial Grammar and Proof Theory (December 23rd, 2010, Tokyo) for their many valuable comments. This research was partially supported by Grant-in-Aid for Young Scientists (A), 22680013, 2010-203, from the Ministry of Education, Science, Sports and Culture, Japan.

T. Onoda, D. Bekki, and E. McCready (Eds.): JSAI-isAI 2010, LNAI 6797, pp. 16–29, 2011.

On the other hand, CCG imposes proper restriction on non-local dependencies such as *wh*-movements so that they obey the island constraints [31] as well as on local dependencies such as control and anaphora binding where the so-called c-command relation is involved[1]. This means that CCG is not a mere overgenerating grammar, and its power to provide a robust grammar comes from the fact that the devices it is equipped with represent some deep aspects of natural language.

This suggests that we had better pay special attention to CCG as a candidate for the proper formalization of human language faculty, or *universal grammar*. Although it is true that CCG still faces many empirical challenges, it is a natural step for us to move on to the study of the conceptual side of CCG; for instance, addressing such questions as "which class of logic/proof system/type theory corresponds to CCG?"

Such questions themselves presuppose the well-known result concerning CG and Lambek calculi [20]: since CG is known to be equivalent to a non-associative Lambek calculus (**NL**) and CCG is an extended categorial grammar, CCG is a stronger system than **NL**. Associative Lambek calculus (**L**) is known to be equivalent to a certain version of CCG with two combinators, **B** and **T** [18].

In order to assess these results correctly, we need some background knowledge about the relation between **L** and **NL**, the Gentzen-style and Hilbert-style proof systems, Curry-Howard isomorphisms between these notions, and *substructural logics*[2], which are summarized in **Fig. 1** and **Fig. 2**.

2   Background: Substructural Logics, Curry-Howard Isomorphisms and Grammars

2.1   Gentzen-style Proofs, Lambek Lambda Calculi and **FL**

Full Lambek calculus (**FL**) is a class of logic obtained by expanding **L** with conjunctions and disjunctions. In other words, **L** is an implicational fragment of **FL**. After the emergence of substructural logics in 1990s, **FL** has been given a major role as the most basic (namely, the weakest) class of Ono's hierarchy [26].

The following rules are structural rules available in **LJ**, which are called *weakening on the left and right* (w), *exchange* (e) and *contraction* (w), respectively. Substructural logics are logics in which one or all of them do not hold.

$$(w)\ \frac{\Gamma \vdash C}{A, \Gamma \vdash C} \qquad (w)\ \frac{\Gamma \vdash}{\Gamma \vdash A} \qquad (e)\ \frac{\Gamma, B, A, \Delta \vdash C}{\Gamma, A, B, \Delta \vdash C} \qquad (c)\ \frac{A, A, \Gamma \vdash C}{A, \Gamma \vdash C}$$

One of the key concepts of substructural logics is that considering variants of proof systems in which a certain structural rule does not hold may lead to new logical operators. For example, under the presence of the exchange rule, the following two introduction rules for implication "$\rightarrow$" are equivalent.

---

[1] In regards to English grammar, see [32], Chapters 2 and 3. In the case of Japanese grammar, refer to [5] for an exhaustive discussion.

[2] The relation between CG and substructural logics are argued in [23] and [9], but they do not mention CCG.

Logic	Type system	Grammar
Gentzen-style proof systems	Typed Lambda Calculi	Lambek Calculi
Hilbert-style proof systems	Combinatory Logics	CCG

Fig. 1. Curry-Howard Isomorphisms and Grammars

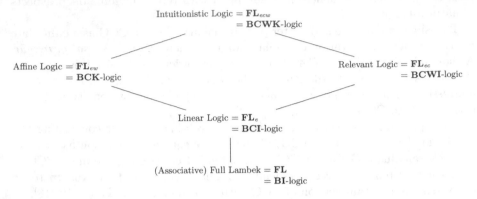

Fig. 2. Ono's hierarchy of Substructural Logics [26]

$$(\to I)\frac{A, \Gamma \vdash B}{\Gamma \vdash A \to B} \qquad (\to I)\frac{\Gamma, A \vdash B}{\Gamma \vdash A \to B}$$

However, this is not the case when the exchange rule is absent, which motivates the system with two distinct implications, which correspond to the respective introduction rules above.

$$(\backslash I)\frac{A, \Gamma \vdash B}{\Gamma \vdash B \backslash A} \qquad (/I)\frac{\Gamma, A \vdash B}{\Gamma \vdash B/A}$$

Under the presence of exchange, $A \backslash B \Leftrightarrow A/B$ is provable; thus, we can give them the same name, "$B \to A$", just as in **LJ**.

Many non-classical logics find their own places in Ono's hierarchy. For example, Relevant logic [29], Affine logic and Linear logic [10] are a *weakening*-free, *contraction*-free and *weakening-and-contraction*-free Gentzen-style proof systems, respectively, and **FL** is a Gentzen system with no structural rules at all (but is still associative).

Through Curry-Howard isomorphism, every Gentzen-style proof system in Ono's hierarchy has a corresponding lambda calculus. In **FL**, each lambda term not only represents a proof for a given judgment, but also a syntactic derivation in linguistic terms. The type theories for **FL**s are called *Lambek lambda calculi* [7][8][19][22][23][24][25][28][30][37].

2.2   Non-associative Lambek Lambda Calculi

Although **FL** is the weakest system in Ono's hierarchy, *Non-associative Full Lambek* **NL** [1][12][13][38] is an even weaker system where associative law does not hold in the premises/contexts of sequents. For example, the following proof of the combinatory rule ($>B$) of CCG in **L** which relies on associativity (namely, $\Gamma, (\Delta, C) = (\Gamma, \Delta), C$) is not a proof of **NL**.

$$
\cfrac{\cfrac{\Gamma \vdash A/B \qquad (/E)\cfrac{\Delta \vdash B/C \qquad (Ax)\overline{C \vdash C}}{\Delta, C \vdash B}}{\Gamma, \Delta, C \vdash A}}{\Gamma, \Delta \vdash A/C} \begin{matrix} (/E) \\ \\ (/I) \end{matrix}
$$

The type theory which corresponds to **NL** is called *Non-associative Lambek Lambda Calculus*.

2.3 Hillbert-Style Proofs, Combinatory Logics and CCG

In the case of Hilbert-style proof systems, all axioms are provided in forms of *combinators*. For example, an implicational fragment of intuitionistic logic consists of the axioms **S** and **K**. Since **S** is equivalent to the combination of **B**, **C** and **W** (see Theorem 1), the axioms for intuitionistic logic can be replaced with **B**, **C**, **W** and **K**. Thus **LJ** is equivalent to the Hilbert system known as **BCWK**-logic. When the deduction theorem is available, the structural rules (e), (c) and (w) in **LJ** correspond to the combinators **C**, **W** and **K**, respectively. Therefore, as indicated in Figure 2, Relevant logic, Affine logic, Linear logic and Full Lambek correspond to **BCWI**-logic, **BCK**-logic, **BCI**-logic and **BI**-logic, respectively, which are **K**-*free*, **W**-*free*, **KW**-*free*, and *all-structural-rules-free* Hilbert systems, respectively.

Theorem 1 (Combinators in CL)

$$
\begin{aligned}
\mathbf{S} &= \mathbf{B(B(BW)C)(BB)} & \mathbf{B'} &= \mathbf{CB} \\
\mathbf{I} &= \mathbf{SKK} & \mathbf{C*} &= \mathbf{CI} \\
\mathbf{B} &= \mathbf{S(KS)K} & \mathbf{\Phi} &= \mathbf{B(BS)B} \\
\mathbf{W} &= \mathbf{SS(KI)} & \mathbf{\Psi} &= \mathbf{B(BW(BC))(BB(BB))} \\
&= \mathbf{SS(SK)} & &= \mathbf{\Phi(\Phi(\Phi B))B(KK)} \\
\mathbf{C} &= \mathbf{S(BBS)(KK)}
\end{aligned}
$$

3 Subdirectional Combinatory Logic

In this paper, I introduce a new class of logic, called *Subdirectional Combinatory Logic*, which provides subclasses for each of the substructural combinatory logics, and define CCG as a certain subclass of **SB**-logic. This allows us to discuss typological parameters systematically in terms of combinatory logics as we will see in Section 5.

3.1 Syntax

Definition 2 (Directed Combinators). *A directional combinator is a combinator in Subdirectional Combinatory Logic which can be obtained by replacing each occurrence of implications that appear in a certain combinator in **CL** with either / or \.*

Example 3 (Directed Combinators for **K***)*

$$\mathbf{K}_{//} : (A/B)/A \qquad \mathbf{K}_{\backslash/} : (A\backslash B)/A$$
$$\mathbf{K}_{/\backslash} : (A/B)\backslash A \qquad \mathbf{K}_{\backslash\backslash} : (A\backslash B)\backslash A$$

A subclass of Subdirectional Combinatory Logic is determined by a set of *ground types* and a set of directional combinators.

Example 4 (CCG). CCG is a Subdirectional Combinatory Logic determined by:

$$\text{the set of ground types} : \{NP, N, S, \overline{S}\}$$
$$\text{the set of directional combinators} : \{\mathbf{B}_{/}, \mathbf{B}_{\backslash}, \mathbf{S}_{/}, \mathbf{S}_{\backslash}\}$$

Definition 5 (Syntax of Subdirectional Combinatory Logic). *Given a set of ground types $\mathcal{GT}$ and a set of directional combinators $\mathcal{C}$, the sets of types (τ) and the sets of raw terms (Λ) for a subdirectional combinatory logic are recursively defined as follows:*

$$\tau ::= \gamma \mid \tau/\tau \mid \tau\backslash\tau \mid$$
$$\Lambda ::= x \mid c \mid \Lambda^{\triangleright}\Lambda \mid \Lambda^{\triangleleft}\Lambda$$

where $\gamma \in \mathcal{GT}$ and $c \in \mathcal{C}$.

I will also use the following notations to describe cases where the direction of a given type/term/rule is underspecified.

Definition 6 (Underspecified notations)

$$\tau \chi \sigma \stackrel{def}{\equiv} \tau/\sigma \quad or \quad \tau\backslash\sigma$$
$$M \overset{\triangleright}{\chi} N \stackrel{def}{\equiv} M \overset{\triangleright}{N} \quad or \quad M \overset{\triangleleft}{N}$$
$$(<>) \stackrel{def}{\equiv} (<) \quad or \quad (>)$$

As for the category $A\backslash B$, we obey the convention standard in CCG in which it takes an object of category B on its left, rather than the convention standard in Lambek calculi or CG in which it takes an object of category A on its left.

The typing rules of Subdirectional Combinatory Logic are defined as follows, which is Curry-Howard correspondent with a substructural Hilbert-style sequent calculus: $(>)$ and $(<)$ are left and right Modus Ponens rules, and the combinators $\mathbf{B}_{/}$, $\mathbf{B}_{\backslash}$, $\mathbf{S}_{/}$ and $\mathbf{S}_{\backslash}$ are axioms.

Definition 7 (Type assignment axioms of Subdirectional Combinatory Logic). *The typing of directional combinators which instantiates one of the following schema is an axiom of Subdirectional Combinatory Logic.*

$$\mathbf{B}_{/} : (A/C)/(B/C)\backslash(A/B)$$
$$\mathbf{B}_{\backslash} : (A\backslash C)\backslash(B\backslash C)\backslash(A\backslash B)$$
$$\mathbf{S}_{/} : (A/C)\backslash(B/C)\backslash(A\backslash B/C)$$
$$\mathbf{S}_{\backslash} : (A\backslash C)/(B\backslash C)\backslash(A/B\backslash C)$$

Definition 8 (Type assignment rules of Subdirectional Combinatory Logic). *Terms in Subdirectional Combinatory Logic are typed by the following rules, where Γ, Δ are any contexts, M, N are any raw terms, and A, B, C are any types.*

$$(VAR)\frac{}{x : A \vdash x : A} \qquad (AX)\frac{}{\text{an axiom in Definition 7}}$$

$$(>)\frac{\Gamma \vdash M : A/B \quad \Delta \vdash N : B}{\Gamma, \Delta \vdash M\overset{\triangleright}{N} : A} \qquad (<)\frac{\Delta \vdash N : B \quad \Gamma \vdash M : A\backslash B}{\Delta, \Gamma \vdash M\overset{\triangleleft}{N} : A}$$

It should be noted that we have to adopt so-called "structural independent forms" for the typing rules, instead of "structural sharing forms", in order to formalize natural language syntax.

3.2 Equational Theory for Subdirectional Combinatory Logic

The equational theory for Subdirectional Combinatory Logic consists of the following axioms and rules.

Definition 9 (Axioms of Subdirectional Combinatory Logic)

$$\mathbf{B}_{/}^{\Diamond}\overset{\triangleright}{f}\overset{\triangleright}{g}\overset{\triangleright}{x} = f^{\triangleright}(g\overset{\triangleright}{x})$$
$$\mathbf{B}_{\backslash}^{\Diamond}\overset{\triangleleft}{f}\overset{\triangleleft}{g}\overset{\triangleleft}{x} = f^{\triangleleft}(g\overset{\triangleleft}{x})$$
$$\mathbf{S}_{/}^{\Diamond}\overset{\triangleleft}{f}\overset{\triangleright}{g}\overset{\triangleright}{x} = (f\overset{\triangleright}{x})^{\triangleleft}(g\overset{\triangleright}{x})$$
$$\mathbf{S}_{\backslash}^{\Diamond}\overset{\triangleright}{f}\overset{\triangleleft}{g}\overset{\triangleleft}{x} = (f\overset{\triangleleft}{x})^{\triangleright}(g\overset{\triangleleft}{x})$$

Definition 10 (Equational rules of Subdirectional Combinatory Logic). *For any term L, M, N, the following inferences are valid.*

$$(=R)\frac{}{M = M} \qquad (=S)\frac{N = M}{M = N} \qquad (=T)\frac{L = M \quad M = N}{L = N}$$

$$(=F\triangleright)\frac{M = N}{F\overset{\triangleright}{M} = F\overset{\triangleright}{N}} \qquad (=F\triangleleft)\frac{M = N}{F\overset{\triangleleft}{M} = F\overset{\triangleleft}{N}}$$

$$(=A\triangleright)\frac{M = N}{M\overset{\triangleright}{A} = N\overset{\triangleright}{A}} \qquad (=A\triangleleft)\frac{M = N}{M\overset{\triangleleft}{A} = N\overset{\triangleleft}{A}}$$

3.3 Deriving Combinatory Rules as Admissible Rules

It is straightforward to deduce from Definition 7 and Definition 8 that the following rules are admissible in Subdirectional Combinatory Logic. The first set of admissible rules are *functional composition rules* and the second set are *crossed functional substitution rules* [32][34].

Theorem 11 (Functional Composition Rules)

$$(>B)\frac{\Gamma \vdash M : A/B \quad \Delta \vdash N : B/C}{\Gamma, \Delta \vdash \mathbf{B}_{/}^{\Phi}M^{\triangleright}N : A/C} \qquad (<B)\frac{\Delta \vdash N : B\backslash C \quad \Gamma \vdash M : A\backslash B}{\Delta, \Gamma \vdash \mathbf{B}_{\backslash}^{\Phi}M^{\triangleleft}N : A\backslash C}$$

Proof

$$(>)\frac{(<>)\dfrac{\vdash \mathbf{B}_{/} : (A/C)/(B/C) \big\backslash (A/B) \quad \Gamma \vdash M : A/B}{\Gamma \vdash \mathbf{B}_{/}^{\Phi}M : (A/C)/(B/C)} \quad \Delta \vdash N : B/C}{\Gamma, \Delta \vdash \mathbf{B}_{/}^{\Phi}M^{\triangleright}N : A/C}$$

$$(<)\frac{\Delta \vdash N : B\backslash C \quad (<>)\dfrac{\Gamma \vdash M : A\backslash B \quad \vdash \mathbf{B}_{\backslash} : (A\backslash C)\backslash(B\backslash C)\big\backslash(A\backslash B)}{\Gamma \vdash \mathbf{B}_{\backslash}^{\Phi}M : (A\backslash C)\backslash(B\backslash C)}}{\Gamma, \Delta \vdash \mathbf{B}_{\backslash}^{\Phi}M^{\triangleleft}N : A\backslash C}$$

Theorem 12 (Crossed Functional Substitution Rules)

$$(>S)\frac{\Gamma \vdash M : A/B\backslash C \quad \Delta \vdash N : B\backslash C}{\Gamma, \Delta \vdash \mathbf{S}_{\backslash}^{\Phi}M^{\triangleright}N : A\backslash C} \qquad (<S)\frac{\Delta \vdash N : B/C \quad \Gamma \vdash M : A\backslash B/C}{\Delta, \Gamma \vdash \mathbf{S}_{/}^{\Phi}M^{\triangleleft}N : A/C}$$

Proof

$$(>)\frac{(<>)\dfrac{\mathbf{S}_{\backslash} : (A\backslash C)/(B\backslash C)\big\backslash(A/B\backslash C) \quad \Gamma \vdash M : A/B\backslash C}{\Gamma \vdash \mathbf{S}_{\backslash}^{\Phi}M : (A\backslash C)/(B\backslash C)} \quad \Delta \vdash N : B\backslash C}{\Gamma, \Delta \vdash \mathbf{S}_{\backslash}^{\Phi}M^{\triangleright}N : A\backslash C}$$

$$(<)\frac{\Delta \vdash N : B/C \quad (<>)\dfrac{\Gamma \vdash M : A\backslash B/C \quad \mathbf{S}_{/} : (A/C)\backslash(B/C)\big\backslash(A\backslash B/C)}{\Gamma \vdash \mathbf{S}_{/}^{\Phi}M : (A/C)\backslash(B/C)}}{\Delta, \Gamma \vdash \mathbf{S}_{/}^{\Phi}M^{\triangleleft}N : A/C}$$

4 Combinatory Hypothesis

Steedman employs the combinators **B**, **T**, **S** and **Φ** for his version of CCG [32][34]. Meanwhile, it is established in combinatory logic that the combinators

S and Φ can be derived from the combinations of **B**, **C** and **W** (see Theorem 1). Thus, if we put **T** aside (we will come back to the status of **T** in Section 5.2), Steedman's version of CCG can be regarded as a subclass of **BCWI**-logic, namely, a Hilbert-style relevance logic, which leads to the following working hypothesis:

Proposition 13 (Combinatory hypothesis for universal grammar). *Universal grammar is a subdirectional logic of* **BCWI**-*logic.*

One of the aims of this paper is to give some preliminary consideration to the status of CCG as a substructural/subdirectional logic under the *Combinatory Hypothesis*. From the linguistic point of view, the discussion of the status of CCG as a substructural/subdirectional logic leads us to new research in which typological discussion can be carried out in terms of substructural/subdirectional logics.

For example, the combinatory rule **B** is the most general syntactic rule among all languages, but languages which have a reflexivization rule such as English may include the combinator **W** [17][36][33], while languages which allow scrambling such as Japanese may include the combinator **C**. This view of the *parameters* (in Chomsky's sense) of individual languages leads to our second working hypothesis:

Proposition 14 (Combinatory hypothesis for individual grammars). *An individual grammar is determined by the parameters whose values are described as a presence or absence of a certain directional combinator, or substructural conditions under which the combinators* **B**, **C**, **W** *and* **I** *are used in the derivation.*

In other words, the parameters of each individual language can be regarded as giving it a status as a certain intermediate logic in Ono's hierarchy of substructural logics.

5   Presence or Absence of Directed Combinators

In this section, I discuss the status of the presence or absence of some directional combinators from the perspective of the two *Combinatory Hypotheses*.

5.1   Absence of K: Universal Grammar is a Relevant Logic

The directional counterparts of **K** combinator ($\equiv \lambda x.\lambda y.x : A \to (B \to A)$ in Combinatory Logic) are not included as the axioms of Subdirectional Combinatory Logic in Definition 9, but we can consider their potential forms as we have seen in Example 3.

For the present purpose, let us consider instead the following forms in which the directions of their first arguments are underspecified.

$$\mathbf{K}_\backslash \stackrel{def}{\equiv} \lambda^{\Phi}\!x.\lambda^{\triangleleft}\!y.x : (A\backslash B)\backslash\!\backslash A$$

$$\mathbf{K}_/ \stackrel{def}{\equiv} \lambda^{\Phi}\!x.\lambda^{\triangleright}\!y.x : (A/B)\backslash\!\backslash A$$

Reduction rules for these directional combinators are as follows:

$$\mathbf{K}_/^{\lhd\,\rhd} x\,y = x$$
$$\mathbf{K}_\backslash^{\lhd\,\lhd} x\,y = x$$

It seems that a grammar of any language must not be equipped with any of the above variations of the combinator $\mathbf{K}$: otherwise, any phrase of any category can appear in any position in a grammatical sentence. For example, in a language in which $\mathbf{K}_\backslash$ and/or $\mathbf{K}_/$ are available, the following set of rules become admissible.

$$(>K)\frac{\Gamma \vdash M : A}{\Gamma \vdash \mathbf{K}_/^{\lhd}M : A/B} \qquad (<K)\frac{\Gamma \vdash M : A}{\Gamma \vdash \mathbf{K}_\backslash^{\lhd}M : A\backslash B}$$

Proof.

$$(<>)\frac{\mathbf{K}_/ : (A/B)\backslash\!\!\backslash A \quad \Gamma \vdash M : A}{\Gamma \vdash \mathbf{K}_/^{\lhd}M : A/B} \qquad (<>)\frac{\Gamma \vdash M : A \quad \mathbf{K}_\backslash : (A\backslash B)\backslash\!\!\backslash A}{\Gamma \vdash \mathbf{K}_\backslash^{\lhd}M : A\backslash B}$$

Then, any word/phrase (for example, *runs* in the following derivation) can be inserted in front of/at the back of any saturated phrase, which is apparently not the case:

$$(<)\frac{\dfrac{runs}{run : S\backslash NP} \quad (<K)\dfrac{(>)\dfrac{\dfrac{John}{\lambda p.p^{\rhd}j : \mathbf{T}/(\mathbf{T}\backslash NP)} \quad \dfrac{runs}{run : S\backslash NP}}{run^{\rhd}j : S}}{\mathbf{K}_\backslash^{\lhd}(run^{\rhd}j) : S\backslash(S\backslash NP)}}{\mathbf{K}_\backslash^{\lhd}(run^{\rhd}j)^{\lhd}run : S}$$

$$(<)\frac{(>K)\dfrac{(>)\dfrac{\dfrac{John}{\lambda p.p^{\lhd}j : \mathbf{T}/(\mathbf{T}\backslash NP)} \quad \dfrac{runs}{run : S\backslash NP}}{run^{\rhd}j : S}}{\mathbf{K}_/^{\lhd}(run^{\rhd}j) : S/(S\backslash NP)} \quad \dfrac{runs}{run : S\backslash NP}}{\mathbf{K}_\backslash^{\lhd}(run^{\rhd}j)^{\rhd}run : S}$$

These effects of adding $\mathbf{K}_\backslash$ or $\mathbf{K}_/$ to our grammar are undesirable not only in the sense that they allow the unexpected phrases to appear elsewhere, but also in the sense that the *meaning* of the unexpected phrases is not reflected at all in the semantic representation, because $\mathbf{K}_\backslash$ and $\mathbf{K}_/$ just discard their second arguments.

$$\mathbf{K}_\backslash^{\lhd}(run^{\rhd}j)^{\lhd}run = run^{\rhd}j$$
$$\mathbf{K}_/^{\lhd}(run^{\rhd}j)^{\rhd}run = run^{\rhd}j$$

There seems to be no language which allows this operation to take place; that is, to adjoin a phrase which has no influence to the meaning of the whole sentence. The reason for the lack of this kind of operation seems to be due to Grice's Maxim of Relevance: "Be relevant" [11]. In other words, we can regard the absence of **K** in universal grammar as a syntactic realization of Grice's Maxim of Relevance.

As indicated in Figure 2, the logical significance of the absence of **K** is the absence of the weakening rule. Thus, universal grammar is a subclass of Relevant logic, in which each premise in a given context must be used at least once.

$$(MP)\dfrac{(ASS)\dfrac{}{\phi \vdash \phi} \quad (MP)\dfrac{\Gamma \vdash \psi \quad {}^{(K)}\dfrac{}{\vdash \psi \to (\phi \to \psi)}}{\Gamma \vdash \phi \to \psi}}{\phi, \Gamma \vdash \psi}$$

The resemblance of denomination between Grice's Maxim and Relevance logic is not a coincidence, because that the restriction that each word in a given sentence must be used at least once means that a word/phrase which is not semantically used and thus does not contribute anything to the resulting meaning of the sentence in the above derivation is not allowed to appear.

5.2 Absence of I: Unavailability of Type Raising

Jäger's version of CCG [18] is **BI**-logic extended with the combinator **T**. While **T** stands for "type raising" [27], it is known as a combinator **C∗** in Combinatory Logic. Since **C∗ = CI** (see Theorem 1), Jäger's system can be regarded as **BCI**-logic.

However, CCG with the combinator **T**, namely, CCG with the type raising operation allows extraction (*wh*-movement) from both complex NPs and subject islands [31].

(1) Complex NP constraint:

   * Who$_i$ does Phineas know [$_{NP}$ a girl who is jealous of t_i]?

The derivations of the phrases "does Phineas know" and "who is jealous of" are as follows.

$$>B\dfrac{>\dfrac{\overset{\text{does}}{S_{inv}/(S_{base}\backslash NP_{nom})/NP^{nom}_{3s}}}{S_{inv}/(S_{base}\backslash NP_{nom})} \quad \overset{\text{Phineas}}{NP_{nom|acc}_{3s}}}{S_{inv}/NP_{acc}} \quad \overset{\text{know}}{S_{base}\backslash NP_{nom}/NP_{acc}}$$

$$>\dfrac{\overset{\text{who}}{N\backslash N/(S_{fin}\backslash NP)} \quad >B\dfrac{\overset{\text{is}}{S_{fin}\backslash NP_{nom}_{3s}/(S\backslash NP)} \quad >B\dfrac{\overset{\text{jealous}}{S\backslash NP/PP_{of}} \quad \overset{\text{of}}{PP_{of}/NP_{acc}}}{S\backslash NP/NP_{acc}}}{S_{fin}\backslash NP^{nom}_{3s}/NP_{acc}}}{N\backslash N/NP_{acc}}$$

Then the application of the type raising rule to "girl" gives rise to the chunking of whole series of phrases and also to an undesirable extraction from the complex NP.

$$
\cfrac{
\text{Who}
}{
\cfrac{\bar{S}_Q/(S_{inv}/NP_{acc})}{}
} \; {}_{>B}
\quad
\cfrac{
\cfrac{\text{does Phineas know}}{S_{inv}/NP_{acc}}
}{
}
\quad
\cfrac{
\cfrac{\text{a}}{NP_{3s}/N}
\quad
\cfrac{
\cfrac{\cfrac{\cfrac{\text{girl}}{N}}{T/(T\backslash N)} {}_{>T} \quad \cfrac{\text{who is jealous of}}{N\backslash N/NP_{acc}}}{N/NP_{acc}} {}_{>B}
}{
}
}{
}
$$

(Derivation tree:)

girl — N; $>T$ $T/(T\backslash N)$; who is jealous of — $N\backslash N/NP_{acc}$; $>B$ N/NP_{acc}

a — NP_{3s}/N; $>B$ NP_{3s}/NP_{acc}

does Phineas know — S_{inv}/NP_{acc}; $>B$ S_{inv}/NP

Who — $\bar{S}_Q/(S_{inv}/NP_{acc})$; $>B$

$\bar{S}_Q$

On the other hand, CCG *without* the type raising operation[3] correctly blocks the extractions from these islands, as the following derivations show.

$$
\cfrac{\text{Who}}{\bar{S}_Q/(S_{inv}\backslash NP_{acc})}
\quad
\cfrac{\text{does Phineas know}}{S_{inv}/NP_{acc}}
\quad
\cfrac{\text{a}}{NP_{3s}/N}
\; * \;
\cfrac{\cfrac{\text{girl}}{N} \quad \cfrac{\text{who is jealous of}}{N\backslash N/NP_{acc}}}{*}
$$

Thus, we are interested in CCG *without* the type raising operation as a candidate for universal grammar. Therefore, we may also conclude that **I** is not available in CCG, assuming that **C** is available in some grammars such as Japanese.

In the combinatory logics in which both **S** and **K** are available, adding **I** to **KS** is redundant since **I** is derivable from **K** and **S** (see Theorem 1). This also applies to Subdirectional Combinatory Logic as follows:

$$
\mathbf{I}^{\triangleleft}x = (\mathbf{S}_{\backslash}{}^{\triangleright}\mathbf{K}_{\backslash})^{\triangleright}\mathbf{K}_{\backslash}{}^{\triangleleft}x
\qquad\qquad
\mathbf{I}^{\triangleright}x = (\mathbf{S}_{/}{}^{\triangleleft}\mathbf{K}_{/})^{\triangleleft}\mathbf{K}_{/}{}^{\triangleright}x
$$

$$
= (\mathbf{K}_{\backslash}{}^{\triangleleft}x)^{\triangleright}(\mathbf{K}_{\backslash}{}^{\triangleleft}x)
\qquad\qquad
= (\mathbf{K}_{/}{}^{\triangleright}x)^{\triangleleft}(\mathbf{K}_{/}{}^{\triangleright}x)
$$

$$
= x
\qquad\qquad\qquad\qquad\qquad
= x
$$

6   Conclusion

Due to space limitations, my discussion could not cover all of the directional combinators. In the future work, I will discuss the status of the other combinators in Subdirectional Combinatory Logic and address the following issues:

1. The presence of the combinator **W** and reflexivization
2. The presence of the combinator **C** and Japanese scrambling
3. The presence of the combinator **Φ** and coordinated structures
4. The presence of the combinator **S** and parasitic gap constructions

---

[3] Here, we have to assign two lexical items of categories $T/(T\backslash NP)$ and $T\backslash(T/NP)$ to every proper name.

References

1. Aarts, E., Trautwein, K.: Non-associative lambek categorial grammar in polynomial time. Mathematical Logic Quarterly 41(4), 485–504 (1995)
2. Ades, A.E., Steedman, M.J.: On the order of words. Linguistics and Philosophy 4, 517–558 (1982)
3. Ajdukiewicz, K.: Die syntaktische konnexitat. Studia Philosophica 1, 1–27 (1935); transl. In: McCall, S. (ed.): Polish Logic in 1929-1939. Clarendon, Oxford (1967)
4. Bar-Hillel, Y.: A quasi-arithmetical notation for syntactic description. Language 29, 47–58 (1953)
5. Bekki, D.: Formal Theory of Japanese Grammar: the conjugation system, categorial syntax, and dynamic semantics. Kuroshio Publisher, Tokyo (2010) (in Japanese)
6. Bos, J., Clark, S., Steedman, M.J., Curran, J.R., Hockenmaier, J.: Wide-coverage semantic representations from a ccg parser. In: COLING 2004, Geneva (2004)
7. Buszkowski, W.: The logic of types. In: Initiatives in Logic, pp. 180–206. Nijhoff, Dordrecht (1987)
8. Buszkowski, W.: Mathematical linguistics and proof theory. In: van Benthem, J., ter Meulen, A.G.B. (eds.) Handbook of Logic and Language, pp. 683–736. Elsevier Science B.V., Amsterdam (1997)
9. Buszkowski, W.: Categorial grammars and substructural logics (2010)
10. Girard, J.-Y.: Linear logic. Theoretical Computer Science 50, 1–102 (1987)
11. Grice, H.P.: Logic and conversation. In: Cole, P., Morgan, J.L. (eds.) Syntax and Semantics 3: Speech Acts, pp. 41–58. Academic Press, London (1975)
12. de Groote, P.: The non-associative lambek calculus with product in polynomial time. In: Automated Reasoning with Analytic Tableaux and Related Methods, pp. 128–139. Springer, Berlin (1999)
13. de Groote, P., Lamarche, F.: Classical non-associative lambek calculus. Studia Logica 71, 355–388 (2002)
14. Hindley, J.R., Seldin, J.P.: Lambda-Calculus and Combinators: an Introduction. Cambridge University Press, Cambridge (2008)
15. Hockenmaier, J.: Data and Models for Statistical Parsing with Combinatory Categorial Grammar. Ph. d. thesis, University of Edinburgh (2003)
16. Hockenmaier, J., Steedman, M.J.: Ccgbank manual. Tech. rep., Department of Computer and Information Science, University of Pennsylvania (2005)
17. Jacobson, P.: Raising as function composition. Linguistics and Philosophy 13, 423–476 (1990)
18. Jäger, G.: Lambek grammars as combinatory categorial grammars. Logic Journal of the IGPL 9(6), 79–781 (2001)
19. Jäger, G.: Anaphora and Type Logical Grammar. In: Trends in Logic. Springer, Heidelberg (2005)
20. Lambek, J.: The mathematics of sentence structure. American Mathematical Monthly 65, 154–169 (1958)
21. Montague, R.: The proper treatment of quantification in ordinary english. In: Hintikka, J., Moravcsic, J., Suppes, P. (eds.) Approaches to Natural Language, pp. 221–242. Reidel, Dordrecht (1973)
22. Moortgat, M.: Categorial type logics. In: van Benthem, J., ter Meulen, A.G.B. (eds.) Handbook of Logic and Language, pp. 93–177. Elsevier Science, Amsterdam (1997)
23. Morrill, G.V.: Type Logical Grammar. Kluwer Academic Publishers, Dordrecht (1994)

24. Morrill, G.V.: Categorial Grammar: Logical Syntax, Semantics, and Processing. Oxford University Press, Oxford (2010)
25. Ogata, N.: Towards computational non-associative lambek lambda-calculi for formal pragmatics. In: The Fifth International Workshop on Logic and Engineering of Natural Language Semantics (LENLS 2008) in Conjunction with the 22nd Annual Conference of the Japanese Society for Artificial Intelligence 2008, Asahikawa, Japan, pp. 79–102 (2008)
26. Ono, H.: Structural rules and a logical hierarchy. In: Petokov, P. (ed.) The Summer School and the Conference 'Heyting'88', pp. 95–104. Plenum Press, New York (1990)
27. Partee, B., Rooth, M.: Generalized conjunction and type ambiguity. In: Bauerle, R., Schwarze, C., Von Stechow, A. (eds.) Meaning, Use and Interpretation of Language, pp. 361–393. Walter De Gruyter Inc., Berlin (1983)
28. Polakow, J., Pfenning, F.: Natural deduction for intuitionistic non-commutative linear logic. In: Girard, J.-Y. (ed.) TLCA 1999. LNCS, vol. 1581, pp. 295–309. Springer, Heidelberg (1999)
29. Priest, G.: An Introduction to Non-Classical Logic. Cambridge University Press, Cambridge (2001)
30. Restall, G.: An Introduction to Substructural Logics. Routledge, London (2000)
31. Ross, J.R.: Constraints on Variables in Syntax. Unpublished ph.d. dissertation, MIT (1967)
32. Steedman, M.J.: Surface Structure and Interpretation. The MIT Press, Cambridge (1996)
33. Steedman, M.J.: Does grammar make use of bound variables? In: The Conference on Variable-free Semantics, Osnabrück (1997)
34. Steedman, M.J.: The Syntactic Process (Language, Speech, and Communication). The MIT Press, Cambridge (2000)
35. Steedman, M.J., Baldridge, J.: Combinatory categorial grammar. In: Borsley, R., Borjars, K. (eds.) Non-Transformational Syntax. Blackwell, Malden (2007)
36. Szabolci, A.: Bound variables in syntax: Are there any? In: Bartsch, R., van Benthem, J., van Emde Boas, P. (eds.) Semantics and Contextual Expression, pp. 295–318. Foris, Dordrecht (1989)
37. Wansing, H.: The Logic of Information Structures. Springer, Berlin (1993)
38. Wansing, H.: A rule-extension of the non-associative lambek calculus. Studia Logica 71, 443–451 (2002)

Appendix A: Abstraction

In Section 5.1, a derivation contains the *lambda abstraction* "$\lambda^{\triangleright} p.p \overset{\triangleleft}{x}$", which is not defined as a term in Subdirectional Combinatory Logic. It is known in the literature (see [14] among others) that in **CL**, lambda-abstraction constructions can be represented solely by the combinators. Following that strategy, we can define lambda abstractions by means of directional combinators as follows.

Definition 15 (Abstraction in Subdirectional Combinatory Logic). *For every term M and every variable x, terms of the form $\lambda^{\triangleright} M$. and $\lambda^{\triangleleft} x.M$ are defined by induction on M:*

$$(1/) \quad \lambda^{\triangleright}x.M \stackrel{def}{\equiv} \mathbf{K}_/{}^{\triangleright}M \qquad\qquad\qquad \text{if } x \notin fv(M).$$

$$(1\backslash) \quad \lambda^{\triangleleft}x.M \stackrel{def}{\equiv} \mathbf{K}_\backslash{}^{\triangleleft}M \qquad\qquad\qquad \text{if } x \notin fv(M).$$

$$(2/) \quad \lambda^{\triangleright}x.x \stackrel{def}{\equiv} \mathbf{I}_/$$

$$(2\backslash) \quad \lambda^{\triangleleft}x.x \stackrel{def}{\equiv} \mathbf{I}_\backslash$$

$$(3/) \quad \lambda^{\triangleright}x.U^{\triangleright}x \stackrel{def}{\equiv} U \qquad\qquad\qquad\quad \text{if } x \notin fv(U).$$

$$(3\backslash) \quad \lambda^{\triangleleft}x.U^{\triangleleft}x \stackrel{def}{\equiv} U \qquad\qquad\qquad\quad \text{if } x \notin fv(U).$$

$$(4/) \quad \lambda^{\triangleright}x.U^{\triangleleft}V \stackrel{def}{\equiv} \mathbf{S}_/{}^{\triangleright}(\lambda^{\triangleleft}x.U)^{\triangleright}(\lambda^{\triangleright}x.V) \qquad \text{if neither } (1/) \text{ nor } (3/) \text{ applies.}$$

$$(4\backslash) \quad \lambda^{\triangleleft}x.U^{\triangleright}V \stackrel{def}{\equiv} \mathbf{S}_\backslash{}^{\triangleleft}(\lambda^{\triangleleft}x.U)^{\triangleright}(\lambda^{\triangleleft}x.V) \qquad \text{if neither } (1\backslash) \text{ nor } (3\backslash) \text{ applies.}$$

Interpreting Japanese Dependency Structure

Alastair Butler[1,2] and Kei Yoshimoto[2]

[1] Japan Science and Technology Agency
[2] Center for the Advancement of Higher Education, Tohoku University

Abstract. This paper details a method of providing interpretations for kakari-uke dependency structures between bunsetsu (phrasal units) for utterances of Japanese. The technique employs a definition of evaluation against a structured assignment to generate meaning representations. An implementation is described which has led to a robust and efficient system for processing unrestricted texts of Japanese. In addition the paper offers a theory for grammatical/valid bunsetsu dependencies in terms of the class of kakari-uke structures combined with case frame information that successfully support evaluation.

Keywords: bunsetsu, dependency structure, semantic evaluation, grammaticality, parsed forms, predicate logic notation.

1 Introduction

Japanese sentence structure can be represented by *kakari-uke* analyses, which detail the modifier (dependence on) relation between *bunsetsus*. Introduced by Hashimoto (1934), a *bunsetsu* is a phrasal unit consisting of one or more adjoining content words (CW; noun, verb, adjective, etc.) and zero or more functional words (FW; copula, postposition, auxiliary verb, etc.). A bunsetsu with a CW that is a verb or an adjective, or whose FW is a copula, works as a predicate, and thus is called a predicative bunsetsu (PB). A bunsetsu whose CW is a noun is called a nominal bunsetsu (NB). The function word or the ending form of a bunsetsu will determine whether the bunsetsu should modify an NB or PB, to give four classes of bunsetsu as follows:

- PB that modifies PB, e.g., *yonde* ('read') - *kara* (particle connection indicating 'after'-clause)
- PB that modifies NB, e.g., *kai* ('to write') - *ta* (past tense auxiliary verb which can indicate a relative clause)
- NB that modifies PB, e.g., *hon* ('book') - *o* (accusative case marker)
- NB that modifies NB, e.g., *watashi* ('I') - *no* (possessive marker)

Constraints on reaching structures for Japanese sentences are the above distinction of four bunsetsu classes, together with two more general conditions, the first of which follows from the exclusively head-final nature of the language:

T. Onoda, D. Bekki, and E. McCready (Eds.): JSAI-isAI 2010, LNAI 6797, pp. 30–44, 2011.

1. Except for the rightmost bunsetsu, each bunsetsu modifies exactly one bunsetsu among those appearing to its right (not necessarily the adjacent bunsetsu).
2. Dependencies do not cross one another.

While the above constraints are often too weak to detect a unique structure of modifier relations between bunsetsu for a sentence, it is possible to introduce heuristics (either manually, e.g., Shirai, Ikehara, Yokoo, and Kimura 1995, Kurohashi and Nagao 2003, or by machine learning, e.g., Utsuro 2000, Kudo and Matsumoto 2002) to thereby reach a unique dependency analysis result which is correct by a high percentage.

Our contribution in this paper is to provide resulting dependency structures with formal semantic interpretations realised by generating meaning representations. To bring about interpretations we have to impose well-formedness constraints which in turn leads to a theory of grammatical kakari-uke analyses, and so an account for why grammatical/valid bunsetsu dependency structures need to be the way they are.

The paper is structured as follows. Section 2 sketches formal details of the procedure of evaluation that underlies the approach. Section 3 gives details for encoding predicates showing how evaluation can either work or fail. Section 4 illustrates the method for reaching an expression that can be evaluated given a kakari-uke structure. Section 5 demonstrates an evaluation. Section 6 concludes.

2   Semantic Evaluation

In this section we detail a generic system based on Scope Control Theory (Butler 2010) for undertaking evaluations of parsed structures to return meaning representations. The method is notable for being able to take as input parsed structures that can in essence be expected conventional natural language parsed forms.

The system provides for a small language a recursive evaluation which is similar to the standard (Tarskian) interpretation of predicate logic in being parameterised against an assignment function that stores accumulated binding information. A difference is that evaluation is used as a mechanism for returning calculated denotations as meaning representations. A further difference is that the assignment has the structure of a *sequence assignment* in which sequences of values are assigned to binding names, a technical innovation due to Vermeulen (1993). This allows for the language of SCT to include primitive operations of scope manipulation that (a) can be extremely fine grained and (b) are frequently inter dependent. In particular bringing about an instance of quantificational binding with SCT might require invoking multiple distinct operations (see below Close together with Use, Hide and Lam for creating quantified bindings, while Rel together with Use and Hide can enforce or prohibit created bindings).

The notations for sequences and operations on sequences we use are listed below: .

- $[x_0, \ldots, x_{n-1}]$: a sequence with n elements, x_0 being frontmost.
- $\boldsymbol{x}$: abbreviation for a sequence.
- nil: the empty sequence.
- $\boldsymbol{x}_i$: the i-th element of a sequence, e.g. $[x_0, \ldots, x_{n-1}]_i = x_i$, where $0 \leq i < n$.
- $|\boldsymbol{x}|$: the sequence length, e.g. $|[x_0, \ldots, x_{n-1}]| = n$.
- $\text{cons}(y, [x_0, \ldots, x_{n-1}]) = [y, x_0, \ldots, x_{n-1}]$.
- $\text{snoc}(y, [x_0, \ldots, x_{n-1}]) = [x_0, \ldots, x_{n-1}, y]$.
- $\text{foldl } f \ b \ [x_0, x_1, \ldots, x_{n-1}] = f(x_{n-1}, \ldots, f(x_1, f(x_0, b)))$.
- $\text{map } f \ [x_0, x_1, \ldots, x_{n-1}] = [f(x_0), f(x_1), \ldots, f(x_{n-1})]$.
- diff (l, l') returns the elements of sequence l that are not in sequence l'.

Primitive relations pop and shift(op) are defined on pairs of assignments (g, h) to move from g to h or vice versa. For shift(op) the operation op needs to be specified, with suitable candidates being cons and snoc to give shift(cons) and shift(snoc).

- $(g, h) \in \text{pop}_x$ iff h is just like g, except that $g(x) = \text{cons}((g(x))_0, h(x))$.
- $(g, h) \in \text{shift}(op)_{x,y}$ iff $\exists k : (h, k) \in \text{pop}_y$ and k is just like g, except that $g(x) = op((h(y))_0, k(x))$.

Relations are iterated n times when augmented with a positive superscript n.

We next introduce a 'usage count' operation $x(e)$. This formally defines the contribution of operators Use and Hide by returning a count of the number of times Use$(x, \#)$ occurs in expression e outside the scope of any Hide$(x, \#)$. For example, "x"(Use("x", Hide("x", Use("x", #)))) $= 1$.

- $x(\text{T}(y, i)) = 0$
- $x(\text{Use}(y, e)) = \begin{cases} x(e) + 1 & \text{if } x = y \\ x(e) & \text{otherwise} \end{cases}$
- $x(\text{Hide}(y, e)) = \begin{cases} 0 & \text{if } x = y \\ x(e) & \text{otherwise} \end{cases}$
- $x(\text{Close}(oper, y, e)) = x(e)$
- $x(\text{Lam}(y, z, e)) = x(e)$
- $x(\text{Garb}(n, \boldsymbol{y}, z, e)) = x(e)$
- $x(\text{Rel}(\boldsymbol{y}, \boldsymbol{z}, r, e)) = \sum_{i=0}^{|e|-1} x(e_i)$

To manipulate the content of an assignment we define the operation $(., ., ., ., .)^{\bullet}$. Utilising ';' as sequential composition, this takes as parameters the assignment to be manipulated g, sequences of bindings names $\boldsymbol{x}$ and $\boldsymbol{y}$, a sequence of expressions $\boldsymbol{e}$ and a number n, where $0 \leq n < |\boldsymbol{e}|$, and outputs a possibly modified assignment.

- $(g, \boldsymbol{x}, \boldsymbol{y}, \boldsymbol{e}, n)^{\bullet} :=$
    if $|\boldsymbol{x}| = 0$ then g
    else
        if $\exists h_0 \ldots h_{|\boldsymbol{x}|} : h_0 = g$ and for $0 \leq i < |\boldsymbol{x}|$,
        $(h_i, h_{i+1}) \in (\text{pop}_{\boldsymbol{x}_i}^{|h_i(\boldsymbol{x}_i)| - \sum_{k=0}^{n} \boldsymbol{x}_i(\boldsymbol{e}_k)}; \text{shift}(\text{snoc})_{\boldsymbol{x}_i, \boldsymbol{y}_i}^{|h_i(\boldsymbol{x}_i)| - \sum_{k=n}^{|\boldsymbol{e}|-1} \boldsymbol{x}_i(\boldsymbol{e}_k)})$
        then $h_{|\boldsymbol{x}|}$
        else $*$

For example, suppose $e = $ [Use("e",T("e",0)),T("c",0),Use("e",T("e",0))], then:

$$\left(\left[\,\text{"e"} \to [y,x]\,\right]\,,\, [\text{"e"}],\, [\text{"c"}],\, e,\, 0\right) = \left[\,\text{"e"} \to [x]\,\right]$$

$$\left(\left[\,\text{"e"} \to [y,x]\,\right]\,,\, [\text{"e"}],\, [\text{"c"}],\, e,\, 1\right) = \left[\,\text{"c"} \to [x]\,\right]$$

$$\left(\left[\,\text{"e"} \to [y,x]\,\right]\,,\, [\text{"e"}],\, [\text{"c"}],\, e,\, 2\right) = \begin{bmatrix} \text{"e"} \to [y] \\ \text{"c"} \to [x] \end{bmatrix}$$

We can now complete the formal definition of evaluation by capturing the contribution of operators T, Close, Lam, Garb and Rel in terms of the recursive definition $(.,.)°$. This takes a sequence assignment, g, and an expression and returns a formula of predicate logic notation that may include predicates taking embedded formulas as arguments.

- $(g, \text{T}(x,i))° :=$
    if $0 \leq i < |g(x)|$ then $(g(x))_i$
    else $*$
- $(g, \text{Use}(x,e))° := (g,e)°$
- $(g, \text{Hide}(x,e))° := (g,e)°$
- $(g, \text{Close}(oper,x,e))° :=$
    if $x(e) = 0$ then $(g,e)°$
    else
        if $\exists h : (h,g) \in \text{pop}_x^{x(e)}$ and $(h,e)° \neq *$
            then $oper(h(x))_0...(h(x))_{x(e)-1}(h,e)°$
        else $*$
- $(g, \text{Lam}(x,y,e))° :=$
    if $\exists h : (g,h) \in \text{shift(cons)}_{x,y}$ then $(h,e)°$
    else $*$
- $(g, \text{Garb}(n,\boldsymbol{x},y,e))° :=$
    if $|\boldsymbol{x}| = 0$ then $(g,e)°$
    else
        if $\exists h_0...h_{|\boldsymbol{x}|} : h_0 = g$ and for $0 \leq i < |\boldsymbol{x}|$,
            $(h_i, h_{i+1}) \in \text{shift(cons)}_{\boldsymbol{x}_i,y}^{|h_i(\boldsymbol{x}_i)|-n}$ then $(h_{|\boldsymbol{x}|},e)°$
        else $*$
- $(g, \text{Rel}(\boldsymbol{x},\boldsymbol{y},r,e))° :=$
    if for $0 \leq i < |e|$, $((g,\boldsymbol{x},\boldsymbol{y},e,i)^\bullet,e_i)° \neq *$ then
        $r(((g,\boldsymbol{x},\boldsymbol{y},e,0)^\bullet,e_0)°,\ldots,((g,\boldsymbol{x},\boldsymbol{y},e,|e|-1)^\bullet,e_{|e|-1})°)$
    else $*$

The following points summarise the consequences of each operator.

- T$(x,\ i)$ returns the i-th value of the sequence assigned to x (a predicate logic variable or constant for the output formula). If there is no i-th value, $*$ is returned.

- Use(x, #) increments and Hide(x, #) ends an x usage count. Their combined contribution signals the overall scope requirements of the expression of which they are a part whenever an x usage count is invoked, specifically with Close(*oper*, x, #) or Rel([...x...], #, #, #). Each has no impact on the evaluation when reached, returning the evaluation of the embedded expression.
- Close(*oper*, x, e) brings about the addition of $x(e)$ new values (predicate logic variables) to the sequence assigned to x and returns the predicate logic notation for *oper* to bind the newly introduced values scoping over the evaluation of e against the adjusted assignment. This allows for the introduction of multiple new bindings depending on the number returned by the usage count $x(e)$.
- Lam(x, y, e) changes the assignment with shift(cons)$_{x,y}$ and returns the evaluation of e against the new assignment state.
- Garb(n, $\boldsymbol{x}$, y, e) modifies the assignment with the shift(cons) operation. Garb differs from Lam by shifting potentially multiple bindings from the binding names of $\boldsymbol{x}$ to y, so that exactly n bindings are left open for each binding name of $\boldsymbol{x}$. The evaluation of e against the new assignment state is returned.
- Rel($\boldsymbol{x}$, $\boldsymbol{y}$, r, e) builds a relation r that has the evaluation of the n-th expression of e as the n-th argument. With evaluation of the entire relation against g, evaluation of the n-th expression of e is determined on the basis of an evaluation against the possibly different assignment $(g, \boldsymbol{x}, \boldsymbol{y}, e, n)^{\bullet}$. In essence this generalises and moreover relativises with parameters $\boldsymbol{x}$ and $\boldsymbol{y}$ the effects of the 'dynamic' conjunction of Dekker (2002) for all relations, providing the mechanism that drives the overall distribution of binding dependencies.

3   Predicates

This section outlines the general approach adopted for encoding predicates. The method involves enforcing fixed grammatical and contextual roles on binding names with the consequence that: (i) semantic evaluation is constrained to accept only the grammatical/valid parsed input of a particular natural language, and (ii) semantic evaluation itself becomes the driving force for the allocation of binding dependencies and so thereby requires less information from the parsed input.

   Grammatical binding roles either (a) provide sources for fresh bindings, that is, available bindings that have yet to actually bind an argument of a predicate, or (b) take on a local binding role in which predicate arguments are bound. Control over binding names to enforce particular roles is gained by making the evaluation sensitive to what should and should not be present as a binding. This is achieved in a general way with the checking operation check, (2). Taking as parameters a binding name y that has a contextual role, either a sequence of fresh or a sequence of local binding names d, a relation name s and a sequence of arguments l, check returns an s relation over l that is sensitive to the names of d.

(2)   check = λy.λd.λs.λl.Rel(d, map (λx.y) d, s, l)

A binding name y takes on a contextual role in virtue of never itself being a checked binding, that is, never being a member of a sequence that is given as the d parameter.

An example of applying check is illustrated in (3). This creates a semantically vacuous relation ("") that is sensitive to the "ga" binding name, such that an evaluation of the embedded expression e against assignment g is only possible when the count value "ga"(e) equals the exact number of bindings open for the "ga" name in g.

(3)   check "c" ["ga"] "" [e] $\longrightarrow$ Rel(["ga"], ["c"], "", [e])

This ability to bring about checks is incorporated into r, (4), which provides a general method for encoding predicates without embeddings. In addition to forming a predicate that places checks on bindings, r also creates support for the bindings required by the predicate. r takes five parameters: lc, fh, args, ext and s. The parameters lc and fh tell two distinct instances of check which binding names they are sensitive to. The first check has vacuous semantic content and checks for the local bindings of concern. This is followed by an application of foldl to create the relevant Use support for the local bindings that need to be present. The second check is made sensitive to the binding names that provide sources for fresh bindings, and has the semantic content of the predicate itself. The remaining parameters are specific to the predicate instance: args gives the binding names for the arguments of the predicate, while ext gives binding names that are not entered into the argument structure of the predicate, but which nevertheless support corresponding bindings for the predicate instance. Finally, s provides the predicate name.

(4)   r = λlc.λfh.λargs.λext.λs.
         foldl (λ(x, e).Hide(x, e)) (
           check "c" lc "" [
             foldl (λ(x, e).Use(x, e)) (
               check "c" fh (foldl (λ(x, s).(s^" +"^x)) s args) (
                 map (λx.(T(x, 0))) args)) (args @ ext)]) lc

In addition to being part of the check for the lc bindings by creating Use requirements from the binding names of args and ext, foldl is used to: (i) add Hide information with the binding names of the lc parameter to ensure that the local use instructions of the predicate do not adversely affect potentially superordinate predicates with their own checks, and (ii) extend the lexical semantics of the predicate name s with the binding names of args, with s^" +"^x returning the string that is the concatenation of s, " +" and x. The predicate itself is created with the second check, taking as arguments terms constructed with map from the binding names of args.

We can see applications of r in (5) with three forms for a predicate: pred1, which supports only a single "ga" binding; pred2 which supports "ga" and "o" bindings; and pred3, which supports a "ga" binding plus an additional vacuous "ga" binding. The effect of case "ga" is to open a "ga" binding with a shift from a supported "e" binding; while case "o" opens an "o" binding, again with a shift from a supported "e" binding. Together with the value for lc which gives "ga" and "o" as the possible local bindings, and the value for fh which gives "e" as the possible source for fresh bindings, we get the evaluation results in (6).

(5) a. case "ga" pred1
    b. case "o" (case "ga" pred1)
    c. case "o" (case "ga" pred2)
    d. case "o" (case "ga" pred3)
    e. case "ga" (case "ga" pred1)
    f. case "ga" (case "ga" pred2)
    g. case "ga" (case "ga" pred3)
        where
        lc = ["ga", "o"]
        fh = ["e"]
        case = λx.λf.Use("e", Lam("e", x, f))
        pred1 = r lc fh ["ga"] nil "pred"
        pred2 = r lc fh ["ga", "o"] nil "pred"
        pred3 = r lc fh ["ga"] ["ga"] "pred"

(6) a. $\exists g : (g,(5a))^\circ = $ pred +ga(x)
    b. $\forall g : (g,(5b))^\circ = *$
    c. $\exists g : (g,(5c))^\circ = $ pred +ga +o(x,y)
    d. $\forall g : (g,(5d))^\circ = *$
    e. $\forall g : (g,(5e))^\circ = *$
    f. $\forall g : (g,(5f))^\circ = *$
    g. $\exists g : (g,(5g))^\circ = $ pred +ga(x)

With (6a) we see that an evaluation with pred1 is possible when there can be only a "ga" binding. We can illustrate the successful evaluation of (6a) with (7), which shows evaluation against an initial assignment that has a single "e" binding, which shifts with case "ga" to a "ga" binding and so furnishes the required support for pred1.

(7)   Use "e"

$\boxed{x}$ ___ ___   Lam "e", "ga"
e   ga₁ at

Hide "o"
Hide "ga"

___ $\boxed{x}$ ___   Rel ["ga", "o"], ["c", "c"], ""
e   ga₁ at

Use "ga"

___ $\boxed{x}$ ___   Rel ["e"], ["c"], "pred +ga"
e   ga₁ at

___ $\boxed{x}$ ___   T("ga", 0)
e   ga   at

With (6b) we see that **pred1** is impossible with an additional "o" binding, while such an environment will support **pred2**, (6c), but not **pred3**, (6d). With (6e) and (6f) we see that **pred1** and **pred2** are impossible with an extra "ga" binding, but that such an environment will support **pred3**, (6g). From these outcomes we can conclude that by saying the dependencies that a predicate supports we are not just saying what the bindings are that the predicate must receive, but also what the bindings are that the predicate must not receive relative to the potential local and fresh bindings. It follows that there will be no need for what is the input syntax to mark the dependency of what opens a checked binding with whatever needs to be bound, as the only valid expressions will have the dependencies that we shall want to see made.

4   Reaching Evaluable Expressions

In this section we sketch how we get to interpretations for kakari-uke structures by demonstrating the process with sentence (9).

(9)   watashi wa   hon   o   yonde kara   terebi   o   mimashita.
      I   book   read after television   watched
      noun   topic noun case verb   coord noun   case verb
      'After I read a book, I watched television.'

Sentence (9) can be parsed to obtain the kakari-uke structure of (10), which details the content of numbered bunsetsu and their dependencies as indicated by marks within a matrix, so e.g., bunsetsu 1 'noun "watashi" topic' is entered into a modifier dependency relation with bunsetsu 5 'verb "mimashita"'. Bunsetsu 5 has no modifee and so is the head bunsetsu of the sentence.

(10)

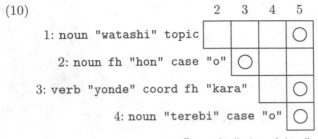

The modifier dependency information of (10) gives the dependency structure of (11).

(11)

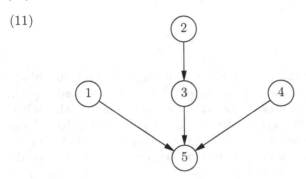

Because of the exclusively head-final nature of the Japanese language, the order of numbering of bunsetsu in a kakari-uke analysis, which is essentially the left-to-right ordering of the bunsetsu within the source utterance, can be interpreted as capturing the hierarchical scoping information of a constituent tree structure with lower numbered modifier bunsetsu receiving wider scoping. Following this convention for determining the scope of the contribution made by bunsetsu the dependency structure (11) can be interpreted as specifying the constituent tree structure (12).

(12)

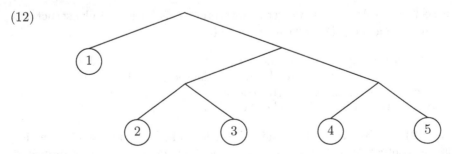

Moreover the functional information of a given modifier bunsetsu can be used to label the parent tree node that connects the bunsetsu with its associated constituent tree structure to the constituent tree structure associated with its head bunsetsu. The arrows in (13) illustrate such an integration of functional information.

(13)

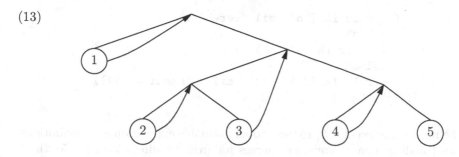

Combining the lexical information of (10) with the structural information of (13) results in the constituent parse tree of (14) in which non-terminal nodes are labelled with functional information.

(14)

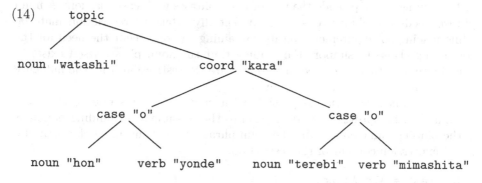

To evaluate (14) with the definitions detailed in section 2 requires one final step of transforming the labelled constituent tree into an expression that consists of the operations T, Use, Hide, Close, Lam, Garb and Rel. This is accomplished by reformulating (14) as the (lambda calculus) representation (15). Representation (15) maintains the constituency of (14), refines node information with operator information, and adds information about possible local binding names (["h", "o", "ga"]).

(15)
```
( λlc.
    ( ( r lc fh ["h"] nil "watashi")
      lslash
      ( kp lc fh "ga" "wa")
      rslash
      ( ( ( r lc fh ["h"] nil "hon")
          lslash
          ( kp lc fh "o" "e")
          rslash
          ( r lc fh ["ga", "o"] nil "yonde"))
        lslash
        ( λe.λe'.check "c" fh "kara" [e, e'])
        rslash
```

```
( ( r lc fh ["h"] nil "terebi")
  lslash
  ( kp lc fh "o" "e")
  rslash
  ( r lc fh ["ga", "o"] nil "mimashita"))))))
["h", "o", "ga"]
```

The representation of (15) reduces to an evaluable expression with definitions for: `fh` (binding names providing sources for fresh bindings; e.g., in (5) `fh` = `["e"]`), `check` (= (2); used to create a coordinating relation with the semantic content of "kara" 'after'), `r` (= (4); used to create predicates), `kp` (case phrase; see below), and `lslash` and `rslash` (guidance for function application to take an argument from the left and right, respectively).

In defining `kp` we provide the role of noun phrases with case markers. A noun phrase needs the ability to support potentially arbitrary restriction material while placing no requirements on its containing clause, except the need for the containing clause to support the binding that the noun phrase itself exists to contribute. It is therefore necessary to insulate the restriction from the influence of the containing clause, while maintaining the binding the noun phrase itself introduces. Such insulation is possible with `rest`, (16). This takes parameters `lc`, `x` and `e`. `lc` sensitises the restriction to the possible local binding names, `x` is the binding name created by the noun phrase in the containing clause, and `e` is the expression content of the restriction.

(16)　rest = λlc.λx.λe.
　　　　Garb(0, ["h"], "c",
　　　　　Lam(x, "h", Garb(0, diff (lc, ["h"]), "c", e)))

Calling `rest` results in the removal of all local bindings, with the exception of the binding given as `x`, which remains open as an "h" binding. The removal of active bindings occurs with two ordered calls of `Garb`. The first shifts any "h" binding to a "c" binding. Such a binding would be open if the restriction calling `rest` was itself embedded inside another noun phrase restriction. This ensures there can be no interference from bindings inherited from another noun phrase. This is followed by the shifting of the binding that the noun phrase itself introduces to an "h" binding. The remaining call of `Garb` acts over the names of `lc` minus the "h" name (removed with `diff`). These operations of `rest` ensure that the binding of the noun phrase itself enters the restriction as the only local binding. It follows that nouns need to take forms that link to the open "h" binding, as demonstrated by, e.g., `r lc fh ["h"] nil "hon"` 'book' in (15). This provides a uniform way of integrating nouns, and indeed any other restriction material (e.g., relative clauses), in a manner that is regardless of the binding name the noun phrase contributes to the containing clause.

The transformation from (14) to (15) relies on the assumption that postpositions, e.g., the topic marker *wa* and case marker *o* are replaced by kp, (18). This has six parameters: lc, fh, x, y, e and a. lc is passed as a parameter to rest; fh tells check the binding names it is sensitive to; x is the local binding name that the noun phrase serves to open; y is used to provide the name for the source of a fresh binding for the noun phrase to shift (and by forming a shift takes on what is essentially the role of case in (5)); e is an expressions passed to rest to form the content of the restriction; and a is the containing clause over which the noun phrase takes scope.

(17) rel = λs.λl.Rel(nil, nil, s, l)

(18) kp = λlc.λfh.λx.λy.λe.λa.
         Use(y,
           Lam(y, x,
             check "c" fh "and" [
               rel "throw_" [rel (y^"_") nil, rest lc x e], a]))

Aside from manipulating the assignment to integrate a fresh binding as a local binding and insulate the restriction, the definition of kp also generates information, notably the presence of "throw_" indexed with (y^"_"), that can be used for the further post-processing of an output formula, as will be sketched in the next section.

5 An Evaluation

To evaluate (15) we need to ensure an environment that contains sufficient fresh bindings to support evaluation. This can be accomplished with env, (20), which will create fresh "wa" and "e" bindings via calls of close, (19). In addition to having the ability to create fresh bindings with the primitive operation of Close, close also generates information, notably with the presence of "catch_" indexed with (x^"_"), that is useful for the further post-processing of an output formula.

(19) close = λx.λa.
         Hide(x, Close(∃, x, rel "catch_" [rel (x^"_") nil, a]))

(20) env = λf.close "wa" (close "e" f)

We are now in a position to evaluate (15) under the scope of env. To get an idea of how evaluation works, we can provide the picture of (14) which offers a (simplified) illustration of the states of an assignment that occur during an evaluation and so reveals the scope manipulations that take place starting from an initially empty assignment state.

(21)

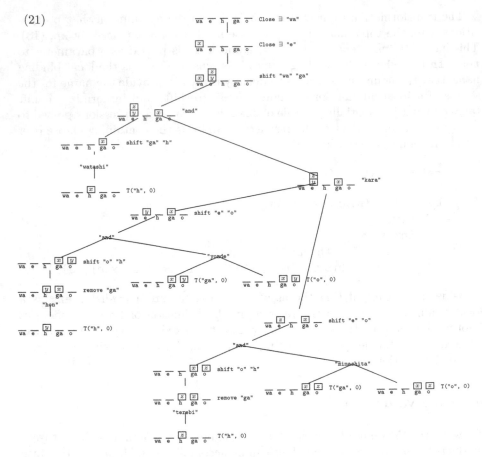

Working through the pictured evaluation of (14) we see that: (i) there are two distinct instances of existential closure (invoked by env), the first of which introduces one sequence value into the assignment as a "wa" binding, and the second of which introduces two sequence values into the assignment as "e" bindings; (ii) the contribution of an instance of kp is encountered that (a) shifts the "wa" binding to an "h" binding where it is able to serve as the binding value for the nominal predicate "watashi" 'I', and (b) shifts the "wa" binding to a "ga" binding from where it is able to serve the subject role for both the main predicate of the sentence "mimashita" 'watched' and the main predicate of the subordinate clause "yonde" 'read'; and so on. What is of special interest to note is that by looking at the terminal nodes we can see that only the correct bindings for the relevant predicates survive.

Following (21) an overall denotation is derived with evaluation returning the formula material of (22).

(22) $\exists x(\text{catch\_}(\text{wa}, \exists yz(\text{catch\_}(\text{e}, \text{throw\_}(\text{wa}, \text{watashi}(x)) \text{ and } \text{kara}(\text{throw\_}(\text{e}, \text{hon}(y)) \text{ and } \text{yonde}(x, y), \text{throw\_}(\text{e}, \text{terebi}(z)) \text{ and } \text{mimashita}(x, z))))))$

The material of (22) contains indexed markers *catch* and *throw*, which are instructions to re-write (22) as the formula (23), with content under the scope of an indexed *throw* taking the scope placement of a correspondingly indexed *catch*.

(23) $\exists x(\text{watashi}(x) \land \exists yz(\text{terebi}(z) \land \text{hon}(y) \land \text{kara}(\text{yonde}(x, y), \text{mimashita}(x, z))))$

Transformation to (23) ensures restriction materials are placed appropriately to align with the instances of quantification restricted. This is notable for ensuring predicates *hon* 'book' and *terebi* 'television' have placement in the meaning representation outside the scope of the coordinator *kara* 'after'. Also *watashi* 'I' in linking as the topic and so taking its binding from "wa" receives widest scope placement, being linked to an instance of quantification that has discourse scope.

6 Conclusion

To sum up, we have demonstrated arriving at a formal semantic interpretation for a kakari-uke analysis of a Japanese sentence. This was achieved by evaluating a re-formatted kakari-uke structure with a recursive routine against the states of a structured assignment with the property of assigning sequences of values to binding names.

The technique can be applied quite generally to thousands of examples when combined with having access to case frame information for main predicates (e.g., the parsed data of the Kyoto Corpus 4.0; Kawahara, Sasano, Kurohashi, and Hashida 2005). This is a significant result given the current state of NLP implementations that are capable of returning kakari-uke analyses with a very high level of precision. Such analyses can now be furnished with a formal semantic treatment involving conventional meaning representations such as predicate logic formulas that make explicit the scopes of quantifiers, connectives and embedding predicates and also capture the inter and intra sentential dependencies and cross-sentential anaphoric dependencies that establish argument values for predicates.

As an additional result we have derived a theory for valid bunsetsu dependencies in terms of the class of kakari-uke structures combined with case frame information that are able to support the completion of a semantic evaluation. As the results of (6) demonstrate, the success of evaluation is far from guaranteed for expressions. That is, by coding sensitivity to binding names we have ended up with expressions that enforce requirements on the states of the assignment against which evaluation is made. This in turn was found to enforce constraints on possible language expressions depending on word class information, as well as being able to contribute to determining the given interpretation for a valid language expression.

Acknowledgement

This research has been supported by the JST PRESTO program (Synthesis of Knowledge for Information Oriented Society).

References

Butler, A.: Semantically restricted argument dependencies. Journal of Logic, Language and Information 20, 69–114 (2011)

Dekker, P.: Meaning and use of indefinite expressions. Journal of Logic, Language and Information 11, 141–194 (2002)

Hashimoto, S.: Essentials of Japanese Grammar (Kokugoho Yousetsu), Iwanami (1934) (in Japanese)

Kawahara, D., Sasano, R., Kurohashi, S., Hashida, K.: Specification for annotating case, ellipsis and coreference. Kyoto Text Corpus Version 4.0 (2005) (in Japanese)

Kudo, T., Matsumoto, Y.: Japanese dependency analysis using cascaded chunking. In: Proceedings of 6th CoNLL, pp. 63–69 (2002)

Kurohashi, S., Nagao, M.: Building a Japanese parsed corpus – while improving the parsing system. In: Abeillé, A. (ed.) Treebanks: Building and Using Parsed Corpora, ch. 14, pp. 249–260. Kluwer Academic Publishers, Dordrecht (2003)

Shirai, S., Ikehara, S., Yokoo, A., Kimura, J.: A new dependency analysis method based on semantically embedded sentence structures and its performance on Japanese subordinate clauses. Journal of Information Processing Society of Japan 36(10), 2353–2361 (1995)

Utsuro, T.: Learning preference of dependency between Japanese subordinate clauses and its evaluation in parsing. In: Proceedings of the 2nd International Conference on Language Resources and Evaluation (2000)

Vermeulen, C.F.M.: Sequence semantics for dynamic predicate logic. Journal of Logic, Language and Information 2, 217–254 (1993)

Vagueness, Signaling and Bounded Rationality

Michael Franke[1], Gerhard Jäger[1], and Robert van Rooij[2],*

[1] University of Tübingen
Tübingen, Germany
[2] Universiteit van Amsterdam & ILLC
Amsterdam, The Netherlands

Abstract. Vagueness is a pervasive feature of natural languages that is challenging semantic theories and theories of language evolution alike. We focus here on the latter, addressing the challenge of how to account for the emergence of vague meanings in signaling game models of language evolution. We suggest that vagueness is a natural property of meaning that evolves when *boundedly rational* agents repeatedly engage in cooperative signaling.

Keywords: vagueness, signaling games, language evolution, bounded rationality, fictitious play, categorization, quantal response equilibrium.

1 Introduction

Much of what is said in natural language is vague, and members of almost any lexical category can be vague. The question that naturally arises is *why* vagueness is so ubiquitous in natural languages. This paper tries to give an answer to this question by investigating under which circumstances evolutionary processes that are traditionally consulted to explain the emergence of linguistic meaning give rise to "vague meanings" as opposed to "crisp ones". Before all, let us first make clear what we mean when we speak of vagueness in natural language meaning.

Traditional truth-conditional semantics assumes a principle of *bivalence*: either a given individual has a given property, or it does not. But vague predicates challenge this appealing picture, in that so-called *borderline cases* seemingly necessitate a third option. For example, even if we are competent speakers of English who know that John's height is precisely 180 cm, we may not know whether the sentence "John is tall" is therefore true or false. It may either be that this sentence has no unique, objective bivalent truth value, or it may be that it does but that we do not know it, and perhaps cannot know it for principled reasons. Although there is no consensus in the literature about the metaphysical status of borderline cases, it is nonetheless widely assumed that the existence of borderline cases, while possibly being a necessary condition for vagueness, is not a sufficient one (c.f. [33,19]): for a predicate to be truly vague it seems that not only should it have borderline cases, but also there should be borderline cases of borderline cases, and so on. In other words, genuine vagueness is constituted not

---

* Author names appear in alphabetical order.

T. Onoda, D. Bekki, and E. McCready (Eds.): JSAI-isAI 2010, LNAI 6797, pp. 45–59, 2011.
© Springer-Verlag Berlin Heidelberg 2011

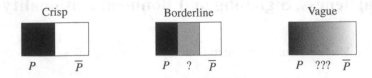

Fig. 1. Crisp and vague denotations, schematically

by *first-order vagueness* alone but by *higher-order vagueness* with completely blurred boundaries. In rough terms, if P is a one-placed predicate and if $\overline{P}$ is its negation, then we would say that these predicates have *crisp denotations* if they split a domain of individuals like shown on the left in Figure 1; existence of a borderline case would look somewhat like in the middle; higher-order vagueness would amount to a gradual blending of categories as depicted on the right.

This paper would like to suggest a *naturalistic explanation* of why and when natural language meanings have vague meanings of this kind. Towards such an explanation, we look at signaling games that were first defined by David Lewis [21] and that have since found good use in modeling the evolution of language (c.f. [29,13,34]). In particular, signaling models are usually employed to demonstrate how linguistic meaning arises from behavioral patterns, which are in turn emerging from repeated interaction in a population of agents. We are interested then in a set of *prima facie* plausible conditions under which a population of signalers converges on a vague code. These conditions would then constitute part of a causal explanation for vagueness: it is *because of* these conditions that (otherwise standard) evolutionary processes lead to vagueness.

Interestingly, a general account of vagueness in terms of the evolution of signaling conventions confronts us with a technical problem. Roughly put, mainstream solution concepts predict that the emerging meaning in adequately defined signaling games will be crisp, because this is *more efficient* and therefore selected for by rationality and evolutionary optimization alike. The main technical question that this paper adresses is therefore: under what reasonable (but conservative) changes to the signaling games framework do vague meanings arise? We focus on models in which signaling agents are *boundedly rational* to some degree, i.e., models which impose some limitations on agents' information processing capabilities. More concretely, we show that vague meanings arise from signaling under two conditions: (i) when agents play rationally but have *limited memory*, and (ii) when agents plays *stochastically rational* due to certain imprecisions in assessing fully optimal play.

The paper is organized as follows. Section 2 introduces the signaling games approach to language evolution and discusses the above mentioned problem that optimization should irrevocably lead to crisp denotations. Section 3 reflects on a number of conceptually plausible explanations for why language might be vague despite this apparent non-optimality. Section 4 then gives a model where the signaling agents play rationally but have only a finite memory of past encounters. Section 5 finally gives a model in which vague meanings arise because the agents' perception of the signaling situation is "noisy" (in a sense to be made clear later on).

2   Signaling Games and the Suboptimality of Vagueness

Signaling Games. A signaling game is an extensive game of imperfect information between a sender S and a receiver R. S observes the actual state $t \in T$, but R only knows that state $t \in T$ occurs with probability $\Pr(t) > 0$. S can send a message $m \in M$ to R, after the observation of which R needs to choose an action $a \in A$. The utilities of players $U_{S,R}: T \times M \times A \rightarrow \mathbb{R}$ map each outcome, i.e., each triple $\langle t, m, a \rangle$ that constitutes one round of playing the game, to a numeric payoff for both players.

We will look in particular at two kinds of signaling games in this paper. The first one is what we call *signaling games for type matching* and will mainly be used to illustrate basic concepts for better understanding. In type-matching games, players are cooperative, signaling is costless and play is successful if and only if the receiver's action matches the sender's private information. More concretely, these games have $T = A$ and utilities $U_{S,R}(t, m, t') = 1$ if $t = t'$ and 0 otherwise. We also conveniently assume throughout that $|M| = |T|$ and $\Pr(t) = \Pr(t')$ for all $t, t' \in T$.

When it comes to explaining how higher-order vagueness can arise in natural language meaning, it is not reasonable to call on signaling games for type matching with their crude all-or-nothing utility structure. Rather we will look at what we call here *signaling games for similarity maximizing*, or, for short, *sim-max signaling games*. In these games, success in communication is a matter of degree, indeed, a matter of *how closely* the receiver's action matches the sender's private information. Technically, we again require $T = A$, but we now assume that the state space T comes with a suitable *objective* similarity measure proportional to which utilities are defined. To keep matters simple, we will assume within this paper that $T \subseteq [0; 1]$ is a (usually: finite) subset of the unit interval, and that $U_{S,R}(t, m, t')$ is identified with the similarity between t and t', which in turn is given by a Gaussian function of their Euclidean distance:

$$\mathrm{sim}(t, t') = \exp\left(\frac{-(t - t')^2}{2\sigma^2}\right). \tag{1}$$

Equilibrium Solutions. Agents' behavior is captured in terms of strategies. A *pure sender strategy s* is a function from T to M that specifies which messages S would send in each state. Similarly, a *pure receiver strategy r* is a function from M to A that specifies how R would react to each message. *Mixed strategies*, denoted by σ and ρ respectively, are functions from choice points to probability distributions over action choices: $\sigma: T \rightarrow \Delta(M)$ and $\rho: M \rightarrow \Delta(A)$. The *expected utility* for $i \in \{S, R\}$ of playing mixed strategies σ and ρ against each other is defined as:

$$\mathrm{EU}_i(\sigma, \rho) = \sum_{t \in T} \sum_{m \in M} \sum_{a \in A} \Pr(t) \times \sigma(m \mid t) \times \rho(a \mid m) \times U_i(t, m, a).$$

A *(mixed) Nash equilibrium* (NE) of a signaling game is a pair of (mixed) strategies $\langle \sigma^*, \rho^* \rangle$ where neither agent would gain from unilateral deviation. Thus, $\langle \sigma^*, \rho^* \rangle$ is an NE iff $\neg \exists \sigma: \mathrm{EU}_S(\sigma, \rho^*) > \mathrm{EU}_S(\sigma^*, \rho^*)$ and $\neg \exists \rho: \mathrm{EU}_R(\sigma^*, \rho) > \mathrm{EU}_R(\sigma^*, \rho^*)$. An NE is *strict* if any unilateral deviation strictly diminishes the deviating agent's expected utility. Strict NEs are stable resting points of gradual processes of bi-lateral optimization.

Emergent Meaning. Lewis famously argued that strict NEs of signaling games for type matching can be seen as endowing initially meaningless signals with a behaviorally-grounded meaning ([21]). In general, any mixed strategy profile $\langle\sigma,\rho\rangle$ for any given signaling game determines how signals are used by the sender to describe states (via σ), and how the receiver interprets these (via ρ). We therefore define the *descriptive meaning* of an expression m, $F_\sigma(m) \in \Delta(T)$, as the likelihood of states given m and σ, and the *imperative meaning* of m, $F_\rho(m) \in \Delta(A)$, as the probability of actions given m and ρ:

$$F_\sigma(m, t) = \frac{\sigma(m \mid t')}{\sum_{t' \in T} \sigma(m \mid t')} \qquad\qquad F_\rho(m, a) = \rho(a \mid m).$$

Of course, we are particularly interested in the (descriptive and imperative) meanings that the strict NEs of a game give rise to. So, for a concrete example, consider a simple signaling game for type matching with two states $T = \{t_1, t_2\}$ and two messages $M = \{m_1, m_2\}$. This game has only two strict NEs, which are given by the only two bijections from T to M as the sender strategy, and the respective inverses thereof as the receiver strategy. In both NEs descriptive and imperative meaning coincide, as each message comes to denote a unique state, both descriptively and imperatively. In other words, we find exactly two stable "languages" here, characterized by: $F_{\sigma,\rho}(m_i) = t_k$ and $F_{\sigma,\rho}(m_j) = t_l$, where $i, j, k, l \in \{1, 2\}$, $i \neq j$ and $k \neq j$.

Emergent Vagueness? In the previous example, evolved meanings are crisp, not vague: there is no overlap between denotations, no borderline cases, just a clear meaning distinction between messages with disjoint denotations. This is generally the case: it is easy to see that the strict NEs of type matching games, as defined here, *never* give rise to vague meanings with (partially, gradually) overlapping denotations. It is tempting to think that this should be different for sim-max games, where the state space is continuously ordered by objective similarity, and where thus continuous category transitions seem *prima facie* plausible. But this is not so. Sim-max games have been studied by, *inter alia*, [18], [16] and [17] where it is shown that in all strict NEs of these games (a) the imperative meanings of the signals are singular *prototypes*, i.e., designated singular *points* of the type space that best represent a signal's meaning, and (b) the indicative meanings are the *Voronoi tesselations* that are induced by these prototypes.

These results for sim-max games are to a large extent very encouraging because they directly correspond to several findings of cognitive semantics (cf. [8]), but it is nowhere near an account of vagueness. For that we would like to see "blurry tesselations" with gradual prototypicality and gradual category membership. Douven et al. ([4]) essentially consider the same problem when they try to integrate vagueness into the conceptual spaces framework of [8]. They do so by constructing tesselations with thick but precise category boundaries from extended but precise prototype *regions*. Our approach is in a sense more ambitious. Firstly, we would also like to include *gradation* in prototypicality and category membership, so as to capture higher-order vagueness. Secondly, we would also like to *derive* "blurry tesselations" —as opposed to mathematical construction— from properties of linguistic interaction.

The Suboptimality of Vagueness. There is, however, a considerable conceptual obstacle: as the above examples already demonstrated, it holds quite in general that standard models of optimal choice preclude vagueness. In a nutshell, the problem is this (Lipman presents a slightly different, more precise formulation in [22]). Firstly, notice that any pure sender strategy will always give rise to a descriptive meaning with sharp, non-vague boundaries. So, in order to see vagueness emerge, we would minimally need a case where a non-degenerate[1] mixed sender strategy is part of a strict NE. But, secondly, it is also easy to see that no non-degenerate mixed strategy is ever *strictly* better than any of the pure strategies in its support. Phrased the other way around, strict NEs will contain only pure strategies. But that means that a vague language, captured in terms a non-degenerate strategies, is never a stable outcome of evolutionary optimization. As Lipman puts it: vagueness cannot have an advantage over precision and, except in unusual cases, will be strictly worse.

3   Re-rationalizing Vagueness

Lipman's argument implies that we need to rethink some of the implicit assumptions encoded in the signaling game approach to language evolution if we want to explain how vague meanings can emerge from signaling interaction. Any changes to the model should of course be backed up by some reasonable intuition concerning the origin and, perhaps, the benefit of vagueness in language. Fortunately, such intuitions abound, and we should review some relevant proposals.

To begin with, it is sometimes argued that it is *useful* to have vague predicates like 'tall' in our language, because it allows us to use language in a *flexible* way. Obviously, 'tall' means something different with respect to men than with respect to basketball players. So, 'tall' has a very flexible meaning. This does not show, however, that *vagueness* is useful: vagueness is not the same as context-dependence, and the argument is consistent with 'tall' having a precise meaning in each context.

Some argue that our vague, or *indirect*, use of language might be *strategically optimal* given that some of our messages be diversely interpretable by cooperative and non-cooperative participants. Indeed, using game theoretical ideas one can show (e.g. [27], [15], [1]) that once the preferences of speaker and listener are not completely aligned, we can sometimes *communicate more* with vague, imprecise, or noisy information than with precise information. Interesting as this might be, we find it hard to believe that speaker-hearer conflicts should have quite *such* deep impact on the semantic structure of natural languages, given that communication as such requires crucially a substantial level of cooperation.

Still, occasionally it may indeed be beneficial for both the speaker *and* the hearer to sometimes describe the world at a more coarse-grained level (see for instance [12] and [20]): for the speaker, deciding which precise term to use may be harder than using an imprecise term; for the listener, information which is too specific may require more effort to analyze. Another reason for not always trying to be as precise as possible is that this would give rise to *instability*. As stressed by [30], for instance, in case one

---

[1] We say that a pure strategy is *degenerate* if it is essentially a pure strategy, i.e., if it puts all probability mass on one pure strategy in its support.

measures the height of a person in all too much detail, this measure might change from day to day, which is not very useful. Though all these observations are valid, none of them make a strong case for vagueness. To economize processing effort, language users could equally well resort to precise but less informative, more general terms whenever conversational relevance allows (and if precision is relevant, processing economy would have to be sacrificed anyway). Similar arguments would also apply to the stability of a precise language.

It is natural to assume that the existence of vagueness in natural language is *unavoidable*. Our powers of discrimination are limited and come with a margin of error, and it is just not always possible to draw sharp borderlines. This idea is modeled in Williamson's [36] epistemic treatment of vagueness, and given a less committed formulation in [32] using Luce's [23] preference theory. This suggests to explain vagueness in terms of a theory of *bounded rationality*: language is vague because its users have *limited information processing capabilities*. In order to fill this general idea with life, we would like to investigate two particular hypotheses. Firstly, we conjecture that vague meanings arise in signaling games if interlocutors have only a finite recollection of previous interactions (Section 4). Secondly, we suggest in Section 5 that vague meanings also show in signaling game models if agents choose actions with a probability proportional to its expected utility. The motivation for this approach is that there might be systematic noise somewhere in the agents' assessment of optimal behavior, be it either in the agents' perception of the game's payoff structure, in the agents' calculation of expected utilities, or yet something we, as modellers, are completely unaware of.

4   Limited Memory Fictitious Play

Fictitious play in normal form games. Humans acquire the meanings of natural language signals (and other conventional signs) by *learning*, i.e., by strategically exploiting past experience when making decisions. A standard model of learning in games is *fictitious play* (see [2]). In its simplest incarnation, two players play the same game against each other repeatedly an unlimited number of times. Each player has a perfect recall of the behavior of the other player in previous encounters, which makes for a loose parallel of this dynamics with exemplar-based theories of categorization (cf. [28]). The players operate under the assumption that the other player is stationary, i.e., he always plays the same —possibly mixed— strategy. The entire history of the other player's behavior is thus treated as a sample of the same probability distribution over pure strategies. Using Maximum Likelihood Estimation, the decision maker identifies probabilities with relative frequencies and plays a best response to the estimated mixed strategy. Most of the research on this learning dynamics has focused on normal form games, where strict NEs are provably absorbing states. This means that two players who played according to a certain strict NE will continue to do so indefinitely. Also, any pure-strategy steady state must be an NE. Furthermore, if the relative frequencies of the strategies played by the agents converge, they will converge to some (possibly mixed strategy) NE. For large classes of games (including 2x2 games, zero sum games, and games of common interest) it is actually guaranteed that fictitious play converges (see [6], Chapter 2, for an overview of the theory of fictitious play and further references).

Limited memory. This result rests on the unrealistic assumption that the players have an unlimited memory and an unlimited amount of time to learn the game. In a cognitively more realistic setting, players only recall the last n rounds of the game, for some finite number n. We call the ensuing dynamics the *limited memory fictitous play* (LMF) dynamics. For the extreme case of $n = 1$, LMF dynamics coincides with so-called Cournot dynamics in strategic games (see Chapter 1 of [6]).

In strategic games LMF dynamics preserves some of the attractive features of fictitious play. In particular, strict NEs are absorbing states here as well. Also, if LMF converges to a pure strategy profile, this is an NE. However, if a game has more than one NE, the memories of the players need not converge at all. To see why, assume that $n = 1$ and the sequence starts with the two players playing different strict NEs. Then they will continue to alternate between the equilibria and never converge to the same NE. Neither is it guaranteed that the relative frequencies of the entire history converge to an NE, even if they do converge. To illustrate this with a trivial example, consider the following coordination game:

	L	R
T	1;1	0;0
B	0;0	2;2

If the dynamics starts with the profile (B, L), the players will alternate between this profile and (T, R) indefinitely. The empirical frequencies will thus converge towards $(\frac{1}{2}, \frac{1}{2})$, which is not an NE of this game.

LMF in Signaling games. There are various ways how to generalize LMF dynamics to signaling games. Observing a single run of an extensive game does not give information about the behavioral strategies of the players in information sets off the path that has actually been played. In some versions of extensive form fictitious play, it is assumed that players also have access to the information how the other player would have played in such unrealized information sets (c.f. [11]). Here we pursue the other option: each player only memorizes observed game histories. We furthermore assume that receivers know the prior probability distribution over types and are Bayesian reasoners. Finally, we assume that both players use the *principle of insufficient reason* and use a uniform probability distribution over possible actions for those information sets that do not occur in memory.

To make this formally precise, let $\bar{s} \in (T \times M)^n$ be a sequence of type-signal pairs of length n. This models the content of the receiver's memory about the sender's past action. Likewise $\bar{r} \in (M \times T)^n$ models the sender's memory about the receiver's past action. We write $\bar{s}(k)$ and $\bar{r}(k)$ for the kth memory entry in $\bar{s}$ or $\bar{r}$. These memories define mixed strategies as follows:

$$\sigma(m \mid t) = \begin{cases} \frac{|\{k \mid \bar{s}(k) = \langle t, m \rangle\}|}{|\{k \mid \exists m' : \bar{s}(k) = \langle t, m' \rangle\}|} & \text{if divisor} \neq 0 \\ \frac{1}{|M|} & \text{otherwise} \end{cases}$$

$$\rho(t \mid m) = \begin{cases} \frac{|\{k \mid \bar{r}(k) = \langle m, t \rangle\}|}{|\{k \mid \exists t' : \bar{r}(k) = \langle m, t' \rangle\}|} & \text{if divisor} \neq 0 \\ \frac{1}{|T|} & \text{otherwise.} \end{cases}$$

When computing the posterior probability $\mu(t \mid m)$ of type t given signal m, the receiver uses Bayes' rule and the principle of insufficient reason. (As before, $\Pr(\cdot)$ is the prior probability distribution over types.)

$$\mu(t \mid m) = \begin{cases} \frac{\sigma(m \mid t)\Pr(t)}{\sum_{t'} \sigma(m \mid t')\Pr(t')} & \text{if divisor} \neq 0 \\ \frac{1}{|T|} & \text{otherwise.} \end{cases}$$

Best response computation is standard:

$$\text{BR}_S(t; \rho) = \arg\max_m \sum_{t' \in T} \rho(t' \mid m) \times U_S(t, m, t'),$$

$$\text{BR}_R(m; \mu) = \arg\max_t \sum_{t' \in T} \mu(t' \mid m) \times U_R(t', m, t).$$

Characterization & Results. How does the LMF dynamic look like in signaling games for type matching? Consider the basic 2-state, 2-message game, with its two strict NEs. It turns out that these equilibria are absorbing states under fictitious play with unlimited memory. However, this does not hold any longer if memory is limited and the game has more than two types. For illustration, assume a signaling game for type matching with three types, t_1, t_2 and t_3, and three forms, m_1, m_2 and m_3. Suppose furthermore that at a certain point in the learning process, both players have consistently played according to the same equilibrium for the last n rounds — say, the one where t_i is associated with m_i for $i \in \{1, 2, 3\}$. With a positive probability, nature will choose t_1 n times in a row then, which will lead to a state where $\bar{s}$ contains only copies of $\langle t_1, m_1 \rangle$, and $\bar{r}$ only copies of $\langle m_1, t_1 \rangle$. If nature then chooses t_2, both m_2 and m_3 will have the same expected utility for the sender, so she may as well opt for m_3. Likewise, t_2 and t_3 have the same expected utility for the receiver as reaction to m_3, so he will choose t_2 with probabilty $1/2$. If this happens, the future course of the game dynamics will gravitate towards the equilibrium where t_2 is associated with m_3, and t_3 with m_2.

Such transitions can occur between any two signaling systems with positive probability. Thus the relative frequencies of actions, if averaged over the entire history, will converge towards the average of all signaling systems, which corresponds to the pooling equilibrium. If the size of the memory is large in comparison to the number of types, this may hardly seem relevant because the agents will spend most of the time in some signaling system, even though they may switch this system occasionally. However, if the number of types is large in comparison to memory size, LMF dynamics will never lead towards the vicinity of a strict equilibrium, even if such equilibria exist.

This observation is not really surprising. In an NE of a signaling game for type matching, the best response to one type does not carry information about the best response to another type (beyond the fact that these best responses must be different). If the agents only have information about a subset of types available in their memory, there is no way how to extrapolate from this information to unseen types. However, if the type space has a topological structure, as in the class of sim-max games, it is actually possible to extrapolate from seen to unseen types to some degree. Similar types lead to similar payoffs. Therefore the information about a certain type is not entirely lost if it intermittently drops out of memory. Likewise, LMF players are able to make informed guesses about

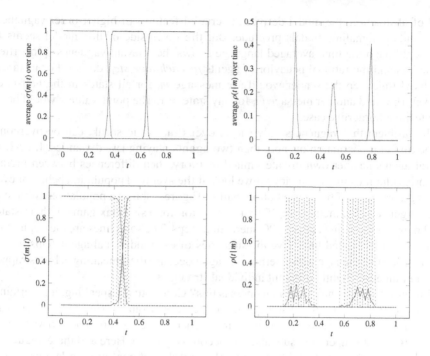

Fig. 2. Results of LMF dynamics

the nature of types that have never been observed before. Consequently, LMF dynamics performs far better in these games. It does not converge towards a strict equilibrium, but somewhere into the proximity of one, thus ensuring a high degree of efficiency.

The top of Figure 2 depicts the outcome of a first simulation of the LMF dynamics. The type space consisted of 500 types that were distributed evenly over the unit interval, and we assumed three signals. The simulation assumed $\sigma = 0.1$ in Equation (1) and a memory size $n = 200$. The graphs show the relative frequencies between the 10,000th and the 20,000th iterations of the game, starting from an initial state where the memories of the agents contain random associations. The sender strategies, shown on the top left of Figure 2, induce a partition of the type space into three categories, one for each message. In the long run, these categories partition the type space into three continuous intervals of about equal size. These intervals are largely stable, but the boundaries shift back and forth somewhat over time. Averaging over a longer period thus leads to categories with blurred boundaries. The prototypes of the categories, i.e., the receiver's interpretation of the three signals as shown on the top right, fall into the center of the corresponding category. Again we observe a certain amount of indeterminacy. Over time, the prototypes are distributed according to a bell shaped curve in the center of the corresponding category.

Interpretation. If we look at the properties of the language that emerges under LMF dynamics over a longer course of time, we find that the emerging categories indeed have non-sharp boundaries, and that they blend seamlessly into one another. On this level of abstraction, the model derives the crucial features of higher-order vagueness that standard signaling models preclude. But the down-side of this model seems to be that although the time-averaged language shows the relevant vagueness properties, the beliefs and the rational behavior of agents *at each time step* do not. For instance, at a fixed time step the sender would use message m_i for all states in the half-open interval $[0; x)$ and another message m_j for any state $> x$. The point-value x would be an infinitesimal borderline case.[2]

The problem that vagueness only shows over time, so to speak, can be overcome by looking at a population of more than two agents playing LMF dynamics. If each of several agents has her own private limited memory, then differences between private memories blur meaning boundaries if we look at the averaged population behavior even at a single moment of time. The bottom half of Figure 2 shows a population average of 60 LMF agents with a memory of 25 past interaction for a sim-max game with 51 states and 2 messages, obtained after 2500 interaction steps. The solid lines are the population averages and the dotted lines give the strategies of each individual agent. This is then an example of a language whose terms are vague because their meaning is bootstrapped from a number of slightly different individual strategies.

How good an explanation of vagueness is this? Conceptually speaking, it is certainly plausible that properties of a language at large emerge from the (limited) power of its users. Moreover, this account is similar in essence to Lewis' approach to vagueness [21], as well as to super- and subvaluation accounts ([5,14]). Here and there vagueness is explained as the result of adding multiple slightly different precise language uses together. But, still, the question is whether memory limitations alone are sufficient to provide a reasonable explanation for vagueness. We do not think so. This is because, although LMF dynamics may explain why language *as such* is vague, each agent's still commands a crisp language at each moment in time. This would leave entirely unexplained the hesitance and insecurity of natural language users in dealing with borderline cases.

The residual problem here is that the notion of a rational best response to a belief —be it obtained from finite observations or otherwise— will *always* yield sharp boundaries and point-level borderline cases. To overcome this problem, and to derive vague meanings also in the beliefs and behavior of individual agents we really need to scrutinize the notion of a rational best response in more detail. The following section consequently discusses a model in which agents play *stochastic best responses*.

5   Quantal Response Equilibria

Stochastic choice rules have been studied extensively in psychology, but have recently also been integrated into models of (boundedly-rational) decision making from economics. We start by providing a sketch of the relevant background on individual choice from psychology, then take this to interactive choices, and finally report on simulation data showing how equilibria of stochastic choices give rise to vague meanings.

---

[2] This is not entirely correct parlor, since the simulation only approximates a continuous state set. But the point should be clear nonetheless.

Individual Stochastic Choice. When faced with a choice among several alternatives, people often not only indecisive, but even inconsistent in that they make different choices under seemingly identical conditions, contrary to the predictions of classical rational choice theory. Choice behavior is therefore often modeled as a probabilistic process. The idea is that people *do* make rational and consistent decisions, but that there is something in their behavior which we cannot name and which our models do not encode explicitly. That unknown something, however, might be rather systematic, and we can therefore often describe empirically observed choice data as rational given a specific probabilistic source of error.

The general idea is this.[3] Suppose we force subjects to repeatedly make *binary choices* between options a and b under identical conditions. This could either be a classical behavioral choice, such as whether to buy a or b, or it could be a *perceptual choice*, such as which of a or b is louder, heavier etc. Even if we knew all physical properties of a and b, it would be ludicrous to assume that we know every single factor that guides a subject's current choice. In order to account for these uncertain factors, probabilistic choice models assume that subjects do not actually treat a and b as they are represented in the model but rather as a' and b' which are systematically related to a and b but not necessarily the same. For example, if $a, b \in [0, 1]$, we would assume that a is treated as if it was $a + \epsilon$ where ϵ is a "tremble" that is drawn from some probability distribution. It is natural to assume that small trembles are likely and large trembles unlikely. In that case, if a and b are nearly identical, confusion is rather likely, but the more a and b differ, the less likely a mix-up. These assumed trembles can have many causes, also depending on the kind of choice situation we are looking at. Among other things, it could be that we, as modelers, are not fully aware of the choice preferences of our subjects, or it may be that subjects make mistakes in perceiving stimuli for what they are. From the modeller's perspective, experimental choice data can then be deemed, if not fully rational, then at least consistent with a particular distribution of trembles.

More concretely, if we assume that "trembles" with which agents perceive the quality of their choices are drawn from an extreme-value distribution (roughly: small trembles very frequent, large trembles highly unlikely), then choice behavior can be modeled by a so-called *logit probabilistic choice rule* which states that the probability $P(a)$ of selecting a is an exponential function of a's utility $u(a)$ (see [25], [26] and [9] for details):

$$P(a) = \frac{\exp(\lambda u(a))}{\sum_b \exp(\lambda u(b))}. \tag{2}$$

Here, $\lambda \geq 0$ captures inversely the influence of the trembles. In other words, λ measures inversely the degree of rationality of the decision maker, where what is rational is defined by the model *without* the trembles. In this sense, $\lambda = 0$ corresponds to a completely irrational agent that picks each action with equal probability regardless of utility. As λ increases to ∞, the probability of non-optimal choices converge to 0, and all optimal choices have equal probability.

---

[3] We do not mean to suggest that we are faithful to the vast statistical literature on this topic, but we merely wish to motivate our modeling approach in accessible terms. The interested reader is referred to the classics, such as [35] or [24].

Quantal Response Equilibrium. This much concerns a single agent's decision. But stochastic choice models of this kind have more recently also been applied in behavioral game theory to model subjects' *interactive choice behavior*. In that case, systematic imperfection in individual decision making may also systematically alter the structure of equilibria that ensue in strategic situations where all players choose with a globally fixed λ.[4] If in a strategic setting all players use rule (2) with the same value for λ, and all players are correct in assessing the probabilities of each other's behavior, the mixed strategies of the players form a so-called *logit equilibrium*. It can be shown that in games with finitely many strategies, such an equilibrium (also called *quantal response equilibrium* (QRE) in this case) always exists [25,26,10].[5]

Consider as an example a 2-state, 2-message signaling game for type-matching. We represent a mixed sender strategy as a 2×2 matrix P, where p_{ij} gives the relative probability that the sender will send signal m_j if she has type t_i. Likewise, a mixed receiver strategy is represented by a 2×2 matrix Q, with q_{ij} being the probability that the receiver will choose action a_j upon observing signal m_i. For (P, Q) to form a QRE, it must hold that:

$$p_{ij} = \frac{\exp(\lambda q_{ji})}{\sum_k \exp(\lambda q_{ki})} \qquad \text{and} \qquad q_{ij} = \frac{\exp(\lambda p_{ji})}{\sum_k \exp(\lambda p_{ki})}.$$

Using these equations and the fact that P and Q are stochastic matrices, it can be shown by elementary calculations that $p_{11} + p_{21} = 1$ and $q_{11} + q_{21} = 1$, and hence that $p_{11} = p_{22}, p_{12} = p_{21}, q_{11} = q_{22}$, and $q_{12} = q_{21}$. From this it follows that $p_{11} = f_\lambda(q_{11})$ and $q_{11} = f_\lambda(p_{11})$, where

$$f_\lambda(x) = \frac{\exp(\lambda x)}{\exp(\lambda x) + \exp(\lambda(1 - x))}. \tag{3}$$

Now suppose $p_{11} < q_{11}$. f_λ is strictly monotonically increasing. Hence $f_\lambda(p_{11}) = q_{11} < p_{11} < f_\lambda(q_{11})$, and vice versa. These are contradictions. It thus follows that $p_{11} = q_{11}$, i.e. $P = Q$. The entire equilibrium is thus governed by a single value α, where $\alpha = p_{11} = p_{22} = q_{11} = q_{22}$. α is a fixed point of f, i.e., $\alpha = f_\lambda(\alpha)$.

For $\lambda \in [0, 2]$, there is exactly one fixed point, namely $\alpha = 0.5$. This characterizes a *babbling equilibrium* where each message is sent with equal probability by each type, and each action is taken with equal probability regardless of the message received. If $\lambda > 2$, $\alpha = 0.5$ continues to be a fixed point, but two more fixed points emerge, one in the open interval $(0, 0.5)$ and one in $(0.5, 1)$. As λ grows, these fixed points converge towards 0 and 1 respectively. They correspond to two *noisy separating equilibria*. Even though each message is sent with positive probability by each type in such a QRE (and each action is induced by each signal with positive probability), there is a statistical correlation between types, messages and actions. In other words, in these QREs information transmission takes place, even though it is imperfect.

Generalization. Already in this simple example there is no longer a sharp delineation in (descriptive and imperative) meanings of signals, and it turns out that if we attend to the more interesting case of sim-max games, logit equilibria also indeed give rise to

---

[4] See [31] for a model that dispenses with the homogeneity of λ among players.
[5] As λ goes to infinity, QREs converge to some NE, the limit cases of perfect rationality.

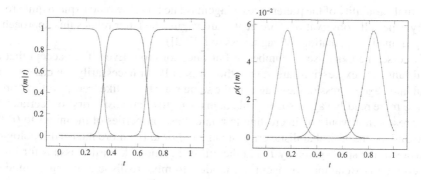

Fig. 3. Separating quantal response equilibrium

continuously blended category boundaries of the relevant kind. We show this by simulation, based on a game with 100 states that are arranged in the unit interval with equal distances. We considered three signals, and chose the value $\sigma = .2$. If λ is small, there is only a (theoretically unappealing) babbling equilibrium in which the sender sends all messages with equal probability in each state. But for values of λ above approximately 4, separating equilibria emerge. Figure 3 shows such an equilibrium for $\lambda = 20$. Here the sender strategy roughly partitions the type space into three categories of about equal size. Crucially, the boundaries between the categories are blurred; category membership smoothly changes from (almost) 1 to (almost) 0 as one moves into a neighboring category. The left half of the figure shows the receiver strategy, i.e., the location of the prototypes. These are not sharply defined points within conceptual space either. Rather, the location of the prototypes can be approximated by a normal distribution with its mean at the center of the corresponding category. In other words, we not only find continuously blended category boundaries in the declarative meaning of signals, but also "graded protoypes" in the imperative meaning.

Interpretation. Vague interpretations of signals emerge with necessity if the perfectly rational choice rule of classical game theory is replace by a cognitively more realistic probabilistic choice rule like the logit choice rule. Unlike for the finite memory model from Section 4, this holds true, also for any momentary belief and behavior of individual agents and even if there are only two agents in a population. The more general reason why this model gives rise to vague meanings is also natural: the sender may only imperfectly observe the state that she wants to communicate, she may make mistakes in determining her best choice, or there may be choice-relevant factors that are not included in the model; similarly for the receiver.

Conceptually, the QRE account of vagueness relates most directly to epistemic accounts of vagueness (e.g. [36]). Since it is natural to assume that players know their opponents' behavior in equilibrium, players should be aware that language is used with a margin of error. Uncertainty about language use is therefore a basic feature of this model. But the QRE model leaves quite some room as to what kind of uncertainty this is. Slack in best responding could come from imprecise observation, but also from contextual variability of the preferences of agents. The former would explain quite readily why especially observational predicates are vague, the latter relates this approach to more pragmatic explanations of vagueness (c.f. [7,3]).

Of course, the QRE raises a number of fair questions too. Even if we accept that all natural language expressions are vague, then it is still not necessarily the case that all natural language expressions are vague in the same way: terms like 'red', 'wet' or 'probable' are more readily vague, so to speak, than terms like 'CD-ROM', 'dry' or 'certain'. In further research it would be interesting to relate these properties of meanings to (i) the source and nature of probabilistic error in QRE, and/or to (ii) more nuanced topological properties of the space given by T and the utility function U. Further issues for future research are to extend the two-agent QRE models to more realistic multi-agent models, to combine LMF and QRE, and to take the step from simulation to analytic results where feasible.

References

1. Blume, A., Board, O.: Intentional vagueness. University of Pittsburgh, Pittsburgh (2010) (unpublished manuscript)
2. Brown, G.W.: Iterative solutions of games by fictitious play. In: Koopmans, T.C. (ed.) Activity Analysis of Production and Allocation. Wiley, New York (1951)
3. Cobreros, P., Egré, P., Ripley, D., van Rooij, R.: Tolerant, classical, strict. Journal of Philosophical Logic (2011)
4. Douven, I., Decock, L., Dietz, R., Egré, P.: Vagueness: A conceptual spaces approach (2009) (unpublished manuscript)
5. Fine, K.: Vagueness, truth and logic. Synthese 30(3-4), 265–300 (1975)
6. Fudenberg, D., Levine, D.K.: The Theory of Learning in Games. MIT Press, Cambridge (1998)
7. Gaifman, H.: Vagueness, tolerance and contextual logic. Synthese 174(1), 5–46 (2010)
8. Gärdenfors, P.: Conceptual Spaces: The Geometry of Thought. MIT Press, Cambridge (2000)
9. Goeree, J.K., Holt, C.A.: Stochastic game theory: For playing games, not just for doing theory. Proceedings of the National Academy of Sciences 96(19), 10564–10567 (1999)
10. Goeree, J.K., Holt, C.A., Palfrey, T.R.: Quantal response equilibrium. In: Durlauf, S.N., Blume, L.E. (eds.) The New Palgrave Dictionary of Economics. Palgrave Macmillan, Basingstoke (2008)
11. Hendon, E., Jacobsen, S.B.: Fictitious play in extensive form games. Games and Economic Behavior 15(2), 177–202 (1996)
12. Hobbs, J.: Granularity. In: Proceedings of the International Joint Conference on Artificial Intelligence (1985)
13. Huttegger, S.M.: Evolution and the explanation of meaning. Philosophy of Science 74, 1–27 (2007)
14. Hyde, D.: From heaps and gaps to heaps and gluts. Mind 106, 641–660 (1997)
15. de Jaegher, K.: A game-theoretic rationale for vagueness. Linguistics and Philosophy 26(5), 637–659 (2003)
16. Jäger, G.: The evolution of convex categories. Linguistics and Philosophy 30(5), 551–564 (2007)
17. Jäger, G., Koch-Metzger, L., Riedel, F.: Voronoi languages (2009), to appear in Games and Economic Behavior

18. Jäger, G., van Rooij, R.: Language stucture: Psychological and social constraints. Synthese 159(1), 99–130 (2007)
19. Keefe, R., Smith, P. (eds.): Vagueness: A Reader. MIT Press, Cambridge (1997)
20. Krifka, M.: Approximate interpretation of number words: A case for strategic communication. In: Bouma, G., Krämer, I., Zwarts, J. (eds.) Cognitive Foundations of Interpretation, pp. 111–126. KNAW, Amsterdam (2007)
21. Lewis, D.: Convention. In: A Philosophical Study. Harvard University Press, Cambridge (1969)
22. Lipman, B.L.: Why is language vague? Boston University (2009) (manuscript)
23. Luce, D.R.: Semiorders and a theory of utility discrimination. Econometrica 24, 178–191 (1956)
24. Luce, D.R.: Individual Choice Behavior: A Theoretical Analysis. Wiley, New York (1959)
25. McKelvey, R.D., Palfrey, T.R.: Quantal response equilibria for normal form games. Games and Economic Behavior 10(1), 6–38 (1995)
26. McKelvey, R.D., Palfrey, T.R.: Quantal response equilibrium for extensive form games. Experimental Economics 1, 9–41 (1998)
27. Myerson, R.B.: Game Theory: Analysis of Conflict. Harvard University Press, Cambridge (1991)
28. Nosofsky, R.M.: Attention, similarity, and the identification-categorization relationship. Journal of Experimental Psychology: General 115(1), 39–57 (1986)
29. Nowak, M.A., Krakauer, D.C.: The evolution of language. PNAS 96, 8028–8033 (1999)
30. Pinkal, M.: Logic and the Lexicon. Kluwer, Dordrecht (1995)
31. Rogers, B.W., Palfrey, T.R., Camerer, C.: Heterogeneous quantal response equilibrium and cognitive hierarchies. Journal of Economic Theory 144(4), 1440–1467 (2009)
32. van Rooij, R.: Vagueness and linguistics. In: Ronzitti, G. (ed.) Vagueness: A Guide. Springer, Heidelberg (2010)
33. Sainsbury, M.: Is there higher-order vagueness? The Philosophical Quarterly 41(163), 167–182 (1991)
34. Skyrms, B.: Signals. Oxford University Press, Oxford (2010)
35. Thurstone, L.L.: Psychophysical analysis. American Journal of Psychology 38, 368–389 (1927)
36. Williamson, T.: Vagueness. Routledge, New York (1994)

Binding of Relational Nouns and the Variable-Free Semantics

Hiroaki Nakamura*

Dept. of Liberal Arts, 5-1, Wakaba-cho,
Kure City, Hiroshima, 737-0832 Japan
hiroaki-nakamura@ax2.mopera.ne.jp
www.jcga.ac.jp

Abstract. This paper examines how the binding relation can be established between discontinuous possessor and possessee NPs in Japanese. Japanese has various peculiar constructions involving relational nouns, in which their possessors seem to appear in positions quite far from their original positions. Without positing empty pronouns as necessary in the standard theory of binding, we adopt the variable-free semantics proposed by Jacobson [3], [4] and [5] to give a unified account to binding phenomena in these constructions. In the binding-without-pronoun approach, we can associate discontinuous possessor and possessee NPs using the type-shift rule for binding, assuming that binding should not be dealt with as relations between linguistic expressions, but as relations between argument slots of functional expressions.

Keywords: relational nouns, binding, type-shift, variable-free semantics, extraction, Combinatory Categorial Grammar.

1 Introduction: Constructions Involving Relational Nouns

In this paper we deal with a wide range of constructions containing so-called relational nouns (nouns denoting relations, not sets of entities, e.g., $[[mother]]$ $= \{\langle x, y \rangle | x$ is the mother of $y\}$) in terms of the tight syntax-semantics relation assumed in a version of categorical grammars, and suggest that some phenomena regarding binding which look syntactic at first blush can be given a unified account from a semantic point of view. There are great differences in distribution of relational nouns between Japanese and English. Their possessive NPs

---

* My work on this paper has benefited tremendously from our lively discussions over the past several years with Kei Yoshimoto, Yoshiki Mori and Masahiko Kobayashi. I am grateful to the participants in LENLS *VII*, who have responded critically and fruitfully to my ideas, in particular, Daisuke Bekki and Chungmin Lee. I am also indebted to Daisuke Bekki for a lot of insightful comments on previous versions of this paper. Remaining errors are my sole responsibility.

T. Onoda, D. Bekki, and E. McCready (Eds.): JSAI-isAI 2010, LNAI 6797, pp. 60–74, 2011.

or pronouns obligatorily appear in the determiner or complement positions in English, whereas they are freely suppressed (notice that Japanese is fully pro-drop) and bare relational nouns can behave like full NPs in Japanese. However, they need to be properly associated with their remote possessors to yield correct interpretations.

When binding of pronominal expressions is discussed, the standard semantic theories assume the presence of variables and the meanings of expressions are treated as functions from assignment functions to something. The necessity of se-mantic variables and assignment functions can be supported from the obligatory presence of pronouns in languages like English. If we assume variables in all the places where pronouns occur in English, we have no choice but to posit phono-logically null elements like pros, PROs or traces in the corresponding positions to deal with binding phenomena in Japanese. In this paper, however, we adopt a completely different view on binding: binding-without-pronoun approach based on the hypothesis of the variable-free semantics proposed in a series of papers by Jacobson ([3], [4] and [5]), who argues that model theoretic-interpretations are directly assigned to syntactic expressions. In her theory of binding, binding is not treated as relations between expressions, but as relations between argu-ment slots (i.e., identification of the two slots). We will address to the binding phenomena involving relational nouns, as illustrated in (1).

(1) a. Subjectivization/Topicalization of the possessor of the following
        subject
        Kono daigaku-dewa   hotondo-no gakusei$_i$-ga/-wa e_i jikka-ga
        this university-at-Top most student-Nom/Top   family-home-Nom
        yuufuku-da.
        rich-be-Pres
        'The family homes of most students of this university are rich.'
     b. Relativization of the possessor of the following subject
        [e_i Jikka-ga   yuufuku-na] hotondo-no gakusei$_i$-wa
                      family-home-Nom rich-be-Pres most-Gen students-Top
        porushe-o   katta.
        porche-Acc buy-Past
        'Most students whose family homes were rich bought cars made by the
        Porche.'
     c. Indirect passive
        John$_i$-wa [sensei-ni e_i siken-no seiseki]-o   homer-are-ta.
        John-Top teacher-BY   exam-Gen score-Acc praise-Pass-Past
        'John's examination results were praised by a teacher.'
     d. (Pseudo) cleft sentence
        John-ga e_i atama-o tataita-no-wa Mary-no kodomo$_i$-da.
        John-Nom   head-Acc hit-Gen-Top   Mary-Gen children-Be-Pres
        'It is Mary's children whose head John hit.'
     e. (Apparent) Parasitic Gap construction

> Yamada-kyoju-ga e_i abusutorakuto-mo yoma-zu-ni e_i
> Yamada-Prof.-Nom   abstract-even   reading-without
> kyakka-sita ronbun$_i$-wa ...
> reject-Past paper-Top
> 'Lit.: the paper which Prof Yamada rejected without reading
> the abstract of ...'

Note that the distribution of the possessor NPs illustrated above is significantly different from that of English. Most Japanese generative linguists assume that the double (or multiple) subject construction in (1a) should be derived via some operation called Possessor Raising (NP-movement) from the specifier position of the following subject. The sentences in (1) seem to indicate that Japanese syntactic structures are more flexible than those in English, allowing unbound dependencies between possessors and possessees. Besides, we will address a difference in extractability between possessor and possessee NPs, as in (2):

(2) a. [e_i jikka-ga   yuufuku-na]   gakusei
                       home-Nom   rich-BE   students
    'the students whose homes are rich'
   b.* [gakusei-ga   yuufuku-na]   jikka

This contrast in extractability can be seen systematically.

We will discuss how binding relation can be established between discontinuous possessors and possesees. For instance, in (1c), which is known as the indirect passive construction, the embedded object *seiseki* 'results' must be associated with the matrix subject, not with the embedded subject. We will present how empty pronouns contained in relational nouns get bound by remote NPs in higher positions to provide correct interpretations step by step, and also offer other various examples which seem to lend some support to the type-shift approach to binding, not to the *binding-as-pronoun-meaning* approach.

2   CCG Formalism and Jacobson's Treatment of Binding

In this section, we will give a brief overview of a version of categorial grammars adopted here, Combinatory Categorial Grammar developed by Steedman ([9], [10]) and his followers, which assumes the tight syntax-semantics relationship and direct compositionality. It is a mildly context-sensitive grammar formalism, which has a limited number of combinatory rules to combine expressions and lexicon which contains a list of lexical entries specified for syntactic categories and meanings. Let us assume that an expression of a language is a triplet of the form <phonological form, syntactic category, meaning>. We represent variables over atomic categories as X, Y, ... In addition to atoms like N, function categories are defined by the use of directional slashes, as in $(X\backslash Y)/Z$, which first seeks an expression of category Z on its right to yield an expression of category $X\backslash Y$, which in turn combines an expression of category X on its left. We use the "result leftmost" notation in which a rightward-combining functor over a domain β into a range α is written α/β, and a leftward-combining function with the same domain and range is written $\alpha\backslash\beta$.

We assume a limited number of combinatory rules to concatenate expressions. The simplest are functional application rules, as defined in (3):

(3) Functional Application
 a. X/Y:f Y:a $\Rightarrow$ X:fa (forward application)
 b. Y:a X\Y:f $\Rightarrow$ X:fa (backward application)

The second set of rules allows functions to compose with other functions to yield new functions.

(4) Functional Composition
 a. X/Y:g Y/Z:f $\Rightarrow_B$ X/Z:gf (forward composition)
 b. Y\Z:f X\Y:g $\Rightarrow_B$ X\Z:gf (backward composition)

In addition, CCG includes type-raising rules, as defined in (5). The type raising rule, for instance, converts a noun phrase, N, which would normally be an argument to a verb phrase, N\S, into a function looking forward for a verb phrase to produce a sentence, S/(S\N), and that the semantics associated with the result,$\lambda P.P(x)$, applies to the verb-phrase argument as a property. Assigning the category S/(S\N) to a noun phrase is in keeping with Lambek's interpretation which turn arguments into functions over functions-over-such-arguments.

(5) Type Raising
 X:a $\Rightarrow_T$ T\(T/X): $\lambda f.fa$ or
        T/(T\X): $\lambda f.fa$

In addition to the rules in (3)-(5), we adopt the following type shift rules, for unary composition and binding, from Jacobson ([3], [4], [5]):

(6) The **g** rule: Let α be an expression of the form $\langle[\alpha]; A/B;\alpha'\rangle$. Then there is an expression β of the form$\langle[\alpha];A^C/B^C; \lambda f\lambda c[\alpha'(f(c))]]\rangle$ (for f of type $<$C',B'$>$ and c of type C').   (Jacobson [5] p. 61)

The **g** rule converts an expression wanting an argument of category A to the one taking an argument of category A^{NP}, which denotes a function from individuals to the type of A, and passes up the information that there is an unbound pronoun within it. The type shift rule for execution of binding is the **z** rule in (7).

(7) The **z** rule: Let α be an expression of the form $\langle[\alpha];(A/NP)/B;\alpha'\rangle$. Then there is an expression β of the form $\langle[\alpha];(A/NP)/B^{NP});\lambda f[\lambda x[\alpha'(f(x))(x)]]\rangle$. (ibid.)

The **z** rule takes an expression looking for an expression of category B and a higher NP argument, and shifts it into a new expression which wants a B-like expression containing a pronoun (or an expression which is a pronoun), i.e., a function from individuals to B-type meaning.

  The **z**-rule binds this individual slot to its higher NP (as the duplicator in the sense of Szabolcsi [12]). The expression A^B is similar to the expression A/B in that both expressions denote functions from B-type meanings to A-type meanings, but syntactically the expression A^B does not combine with an expression of category B. The superscript feature 'records the fact that there is an unbound proform within the expression' (Jacobson [5], p. 60). The category of pronouns is actually the identity function on individuals, so its syntactic category is not N, but rather N^N. In Jacobson's binding theory, there is no identification between linguistic expressions. Binding phenomena are dealt with in terms of merge or identification of two argument slots of (often derived) functional categories. As we have seen above, pronouns are freely (and possessive pronouns often obligatorily) omitted in Japanese, if we use variables for pronouns to establish binding, we must posit phonologically null elements in the positions of the possessors of relational nouns in the constructions as illustrated in (1). If we build binding properties into pronouns as in the radical lexicalist view of binding by putting much of the work in the lexical meanings of expressions, we will reach the same conclusion because requirements of binding should be encoded into the lexical meaning of empty pronouns. In the following sections, we will incorporate Jacobson's binding theory into our CCG framework to give a unified account to binding of 'empty possessors' of relational nouns to distant NPs.

3   Binding of Relational Nouns in Japanese

There have been two approaches to binding of pronouns in the categorial theories. One is to build binding mechanism into the lexical meaning of proforms (which is often referred to as the radical lexicalist approach, as in Szabolcsi [11] and many other type-logical treatments of binding), which encodes binding properties in the type-raised categories of pronouns. The other tries to execute binding 'on the fly' (Szabolcsi [12]; Jacobson [3], [4], [5], etc.), using the type-shift rules (4) and (5) flexibly in the course of derivation/interpretation. The latter approach is more dynamic, capturing a wide range of data including binding of cross-sentential anaphora. We argue that the latter approach has a clear empirical advantage over the former because, as illustrated in (1), Japanese frequently lack and often obligatorily suppress overt possessive pronouns, allowing possessors to move out of their original positions and to behave like independent constituents, but still the syntactically discontinuous possessors and possessees must be associated to derive proper interpretations.

In the generative grammar framework, there is also an attempt to associate binding phenomena with verbs' meanings. Reinhart and Reuland [8], for instance, suggest that reflexivity is a property of predicates and, reflexive pronouns in the object position like *himself* are argued to reflexivize the argument structures of predicates. On this view reflexive pronouns in language do not require to get bound by referential expressions alone but serve as a type shifter of predicates to reduce their arities.

(8) A-binding (logical-syntax based definition) α A-binds β iff α is the sister of a λ-predicate whose operator binds β.   (Reinhart [7])

Let's see how this hypothesis works for binding of Japanese reflexives. Japanese generative linguists generally assume that the complex reflexive *zibunzisin* needs to get bound by its local subject, while the simple counterpart *zibun* can be identified with either a local or higher subject. In the former case, the *zisin*-part of this local anaphora attaches to and reflexivize the theta-grid of a verb selecting it.

(9) a. Taroo$_i$-wa Jiroo$_j$-ga zibun$_{i/j}$-o   syoosan-siteiru-to itta.
        Taroo-Top Jiroo-Nom self   admire-Prog-Comp said
    b. Taroo$_i$-wa Jiroo$_j$-ga zibun-zisin$_{*i/j}$-o syoosan-siteiru-to itta.
        Taroo-Top Jiroo-Nom self   admire-Prog-Comp said
    c. *zisin-shoosan-suru* 'self-admire' : $\lambda x(\text{Admire}'(x,x))$

Forming the reflexivized predicate *jisin-syoosans-* in (9c) results in the reduction of the arity of the verb, suggesting that the local reflexive pronoun is an operator to convert binary predicates to unary predicates. In the radical-lexicalist approach, the pronoun must bear much more responsibility for binding. Non-local anaphor should be given the meaning like $\lambda P \lambda Q[Q(...(P(...x...)), ..., (x)]$, which corresponds to the category which takes a larger structure (potentially surrounding it) to make the pronoun co-referential with an referential NP in a higher clause. It will require a pronoun to combine with a very complex structure to give a proper interpretation of the whole clause.

In the next section, I will show how the identification of higher NPs and possessor slots of relational nouns can be achieved with recourse to the type-shift rules for binding.

4   Discontinuity and Constructions Licensed by Relational Nouns

We will focus on the two points in this section. First, we will show how to associate the discontinuous possessor and possesee NPs in a systematic way, using the z-rule proposed by Jacobson [3]. Then, we will discuss how the constructions we have seen in (1) can be licensed by the presence of relational nouns. The asymmetry in extractability between possessor and possessee NPs will be discussed in the next section.

To present our type-shift approach to binding in Japanese, let us consider the simplest cases involving ordinary and relational nouns.

(10) a. Taroo-wa   sensei-o   keibetsu-sita.
         Taroo-Top   teacher-Acc   disrespect-Past
         'Taroo felt contempt for a teacher.'
     b. Taroo-wa   jibun-o   keibetsu-sita.
                      SELF-Acc
     c. Taroo-wa   titi-o   keibetsu-sita.
                      father-Acc

Keibetsu-suru 'disrespect' is a transitive verb of category $(S \backslash NP_{Sub}) \backslash NP_{Obj}$, which first combines with the object and then combines with the subject on its left to yield a sentence. Though Japanese is a free word order language, let us assume some default order of combination here. In (10a), the predicate *keibetsu-sita* 'disrespect' combines with the arguments in the normal way to yield the sentence with interpretation Disrespect'(Teacher')(Taroo'). *Jibun* 'him/her-self' is a subject-oriented reflexive pronoun, seeking for a local or nonlocal subject as an antecedent. In the binding theory proposed by Jacobson, pronominal expressions are identity functions on individuals, and the category $N\backslash N$ or N^N and the meaning $\lambda x.x$ are assigned to them. Suppose that the type of transitive verbs like *keibetsu-suru* can be shifted to $(S\backslash N)\backslash N^N$ by the z-rule above, which indicates that this verb can take an object with an unbound pronoun, which gets identified with the subject.

(11)

Taroo-ga	jibun-o	keibetsu-sita
N:Taroo'	$N^N:\lambda y[y]$	$(S\backslash N)\backslash N:\lambda y\lambda x(\text{Disrespect'}(y)(x))$

$$\frac{}{(S\backslash N)\backslash N^N:\lambda f\lambda x(\text{Disrespect'}(f(x))(x))}\text{z}$$

$$\frac{}{\begin{array}{c}(S\backslash N):\lambda f\lambda x(\text{Disrespect'}(f(x))(x))(\lambda y[y])\\ = \lambda x(\text{Disrespect'}(x)(x))\end{array}}<$$

$$\frac{}{\text{S:Disrespect'}(\text{Taroo'})(\text{Taroo'})}<$$

In the "binding-without-pronoun" approach, shifted predicates (or other larger derived expressions) are responsible for binding of pronominals, and the z-rule can apply to any functional expression anytime during the course of derivation. Let's turn to sentence (11c) containing the relational noun *titi* 'father' as the object, the category of which should be taken to be of $N\backslash N$ or N^N. In this case, it takes someone to return his or her father, the meaning of which can be represented as $\lambda x\lambda y(\text{Father-of'}(y)(x))$, and we omit the 'inner argument' standing for the 'father' in our representations whenever this does not cause confusion. In Japanese, possessive pronouns of relational nouns can be omitted if they are contextually inferable and the ellipsis of pronouns often looks obligatory (for instance, the sentence $^{??}$*zou-ga sono hana-ga nagai*, 'elephant-Nom its nose-Nom long-Pres' in which the owner of a nose explicitly appears, sounds very awkward). Free ellipsis of relational nouns should be connected with the possibilities of peculiar constructions as exemplified in (1). The derivations of sentence (10c) should proceed in a similar fashion, as in (12):

(12)

Taroo-wa	titioya-o	keibetsu-suru
N:Taroo'	$N^N:$	$(S\backslash N)\backslash N:\lambda y\lambda x(\text{Disrespect'}(y)(x))$
	$\lambda y(\text{Father-of'}(y))$	

$$\frac{}{(S\backslash N)\backslash N^N:\lambda f\lambda x(\text{Disrespect'}(f(x))(x)}\text{z}$$

$$\frac{}{\begin{array}{c}S\backslash N:\lambda f\lambda x(\text{Disrespect}(f(x))(x))(\lambda y(\text{Father-of'}(y)))\\ = \lambda x(\text{Disrespect'}(\text{Father-of'}(x))(x))\end{array}}$$

$$\frac{}{\text{S: Disrespect'}(\text{Father-of'}(\text{Taroo'}))(\text{Taroo'})}$$

We cannot appeal to the reflexivization operation on predicates induced by the pronoun meaning to derive the meaning of (12) because the implicit pronoun does not occupy the argument position of *keibetsu-suru*. Also, it is impossible to attribute the binding requirement of the relational noun to the lexical property of an implicit pronoun because we do not posit any empty category in syntax and variable in semantics, and if the binding property is built into relational nouns, their resulting categories and semantic types must be very complicated. As we have seen in the sentences in (1), binding can be delayed until higher clauses are constructed, so we will need the very complicated category/type of functor expressions with which pronouns combine.

In the type-shift approach, since the **z**-rule is applicable any time in the course of derivation and can operate on complex, derived constituents as well as simple predicates, we can derive any construction in which the possessor and possessee form discontinuous constituency, with a proper interpretation. Let' us consider concrete examples. Japanese and Korean have the so-called multiple subject constructions like (1a) (repeated below) in which more than one nominative subject appears in a simple sentence and Korean has the double object construction in which more than one accusative NP appears in a simple transitive sentence, as shown below:

(13) Kono daigakud-dewa   hotondo-no gakusei-ga   jikka-ga
      this university-at-Top   most student-Nom   family-home-Nom
      yuufuku-da.
      rich-be-Pres

(14) a. Mary-ka   John-uy   tali-lul   cha-ss-ta.
        Mary-NOM   John-GEN   leg-ACC   kick-PAST-DEC
        'Mary kicked John's leg.'
    b. Mary-ka   John-ul   tali-lul   cha-ess-ta.
        Mary-NOM   John-ACC   leg-ACC   kick-PAST-DEC

(15) a. Subeteno-gakuseii-ga   sensei-nii   siken-no seiseki-o
        All students-Nom   teacher-BY   exam-Gen grade-Acc
        homer-are-ta.
        praise-Pass-Past
        'John's examination results were praised by a teacher.'
    b. Kono roojin-home-de-wa   dono dansei-mo   tuma-ni
        this home-for-the-old-In   every man-Nom   wife-Dat
        sakidat-are-teiru.
        die-Pass-Pres
        'In this nursely home for seniors, most men suffered from the death
        of their wife.'

Notice the scope dependency of relational nouns on the subjects in (13) and (15). In the indirect passive (15a), the referent of *seiseki* 'results' must covary with the choice of *gakusei* 'student', never with that of *sensei* 'teacher', and in (15b), the value of *tsuma* 'wife' co-varies with that of *dansei* 'man'. These interpretations result from the obligatory binding of implicit pronouns in the relational nouns, which can be evoked by the shifted meanings of the verbs. Without assuming the presence of phonologically null expressions, we can get the desired interpretations by applying the z-rule to the predicate, as in (16):

(16) <u>Subete-no kodomo-ga</u>   <u>sensei-ni</u>   <u>seiseki-o</u>   <u>homer-are-ta</u>
$\quad$ S/(S\N):$\qquad\qquad$ N:Teacher'$\qquad$ N^N:$\qquad\qquad$ ((S\N)\N)\N:
$\quad$ $\forall x[\text{Child'}(x)\to P(x)]$$\qquad\qquad\qquad\qquad\qquad$ $\lambda y(\text{Achievement-of'}(y))$ Praise-PASS'
$$\qquad\qquad\qquad\qquad\qquad\qquad\qquad\qquad\qquad\qquad\qquad\text{---lexical-z---}$$
$$\qquad\qquad\qquad\qquad\qquad\qquad\qquad\qquad\qquad\qquad\quad ((S\backslash N)\backslash N)\backslash N^N$$

$$((S\backslash N)\backslash N):$$
$$\lambda y\lambda x(\text{Praise-PASS'}(\text{Acheivement-of'}(x))(y)(x))$$

$$(S\backslash N): \lambda x(\text{Praise-PASS'}(\text{Acheivement-of'}(x))(\text{Teacher'})(x))$$

$$S:\forall x[\text{Child'}(x)\to(\text{Praise-PASS'}(\text{Acheivement-of'}(x))(\text{Teacher'})(x))]$$

In (16), the z-rule applies to the three-place predicate *homer-are* 'praise-PASS', and the subject binds the implicit possessor *across* the dative argument *sensei-ni* 'teacher'. Jacobson [3] generalizes the z-rule in (7) so that the NP just before the result category binds *across* NPs or clause-boundaries in the argument slots of z-predicates. We suppress the generalized version of the z-rule, due to space limitations, and would like the interested readers to refer to Jacobson [3]. The resulting category/type incorporates the binding relation between the direct object and matrix subject slots. This account of indirect passive constructions is much more elegant than those given by other approaches, which clearly require empty categories in the possessor positions of relational nouns and some version of binding rule. We can also give an account to the indirect passive with no relational noun in (17), which is interpretable if the proper relation between the higher and lower subjects is given from discourse.

(17) Taroo-wa$\quad$ Hanako-ni$\quad$ totsuzen$\quad$ saki-dat-areta.
$\qquad$ Taroo-Top$\quad$ Hanako-Dat suddenly$\quad$ pass-away-Pass-Past
$\qquad$ 'Taroo was adversely affected by Hanako's sudden death.'

The derived passive verb undergoes the z-rule to yield $\lambda f\lambda x(\text{Die-Pass'}(f(x))(x))$, but in this case the relation between the two individuals is not specified by linguistic expressions. Nonetheless, we frequently encounter sentences like (17) in ordinary texts, so the hearers must be able to infer the relationship somehow. The z-rule must apply in the same way as in (16). So the final meaning of the sentence should be something like $\exists f((f(\text{Taroo'})=\text{Hanako'})\wedge\text{Die-Pass'}$ $(f(\text{Taroo'}))(\text{Taroo'}))$, the truth value of which depends on the relation between *Taroo* and *Hanako* given in discourse. Our approach to binding induced by the type shift can deal with (15b), with only the relation specified, and (17), with the value of the function specified but the relation underspecified.[1]

---

[1] Though referential NPs can also appear in the lower object position, we can derive a proper meaning even for (ib) without any extension.

(18) Taroo-wa   Hanako-ni   sin-are-ta

$$\frac{\overline{\text{N:Taroo'}} \quad \overline{\text{N:Hanako'}} \quad \overline{(S\backslash N)\backslash N^N{:}\lambda f\lambda x(\text{Die-Pass'}(f(x))(x))}}{(S\backslash N)\backslash N{:}\lambda y\lambda x\exists f((f(x){=}y)\wedge\text{Die-Pass'}(f(x))(x))^2}\%$$

$$\frac{S\backslash N{:}\lambda y\lambda x\exists f((f(x){=}y)\wedge\text{Die-Pass'}(f(x))(x))(\text{Hanako'})}{= \lambda x\exists f((f(x){=}\text{Hanako'})\wedge\text{Die-Pass'}(f(x))(x))}$$

$$S{:}\exists f((f(\text{Taroo'}){=}\text{Hanako'})\wedge\text{Die-Pass'}(f(\text{Taroo'}))(\text{Taroo'}))$$

If nothing happens at the step indicated by '%', the passive predicate *sin-are-ta*, which lexically requires a relational noun as the first argument to combine with, cannot combine with the proper noun *Hanako* which can never be interpreted as a relational noun of category N^N, the result of which should be an unacceptable sentence as an indirect passive. Therefore, there should be some pragmatic strategy to save (18) from absolute unacceptability and to construe *Hanako* as a value of the new function created by the **z**-rule as a lexical property of the indirect passive. The exact definition of such a pragmatic strategy remains open at the present stage of our research, but we can say that the resulting sentence (18) , if acceptable, denotes a proposition looking for the function (some relation between *Taroo* and *Hanako*) presupposed or inferable among interlocutors. Note that no plausible explanation can be given to the marginal acceptability of sentence (18) in other binding theories, and if any, it requires completely different explanations for sentences like (1c) or (15b) and for marginal sentences like (18). We have attributed the binding requirement to (shifted) predicates, which we deduce automatically from the assumption that binding should be dealt with as meanings of predicates (and constructions).

Another advantage of the *binding-without-pronoun* approach is the flexible applicability of the **z**-rule. This device is able to apply to potentially discontinuous constituents if proforms are deeply embedded and need to get bound by antecedents in the higher clauses. Observe the sentences in (19):

(19) a. [John-ga   atama-o tatai-ta]   dono kodomo-mo naki-hajime-ta.
        John-Nom head-Acc hit-Past   every child-Nom cry-start-Past
        'Every child whose head John hit started crying.'
    b. [John-ga   atama-o tataita-no]-wa hotondo-no   kodomo-da.
        John-Nom head-Acc hit-Gen-Top   most-Gen   child-Be-Press
        'Lit. It is most children that John hit their heads.'

(i) a. Taroo-wa   sensei-ni   otouto-o   homer-are-ta.
        Taroo-Top teacher-Dat brother-Acc praise-Pass-Past
    b. Taroo-wa   sensei-ni   Jiroo-o   homer-are-ta.
        Taroo-Top teacher-Dat Jiroo-Acc   praise-Pass-Past

(ib) has the interpretaion like $\exists f...(\text{Praise-pass'}(f(\text{Taroo'}){=}\text{Jiroo'}))(\text{Taroo'}))$, where the existence of a function of type $\langle e,e\rangle$ is presupposed.

[2] I thank Daisuke Bekki for suggesting this solution.

In the relative clause in (19a) and the free relative in (19b), the required gaps occupy the possessor position of the embedded relational object NPs, and need to be associated with some elements in the higher structures. Let us assume tentatively that common nouns can directly take open propositions as relative clauses because Japanese has no overt relative pronouns, and open propositions of either category S\N or category S^N can become relative clauses. Though there should be alternative analyses on Japanese relative clauses (see Bekki[1] for the detailed analysis on Japanese relative clauses), these assumptions have no effect on our semantic analysis. We also need to position some version of infixation rule to insert the universal quantifier between the open proposition and common noun in the following derivation.[3] Derivation (20) shows that the flexible inheritance of information resulting from the application of the type-shift rule is possible for any functional constituent anytime.

(20)

John-ga	atama-o	tataita	dono	kodomo-mo ...
N:John'	N^N:Head-of'	(S\N)\N:Hit'	GQ$|_I$CN:	CN\S^N:

$$\frac{\text{N:John'}}{\text{S/(S\textbackslash N):}}\text{t}$$
$$\lambda f(f(\text{j}))$$

$$\frac{N^N\text{:Head-of'} \quad (S\backslash N)\backslash N\text{:Hit'}}{(S\backslash N)^N\backslash N^N\text{:}}\text{g}$$
$$\lambda f\lambda\text{x}(\text{Hit'}(f(\text{x})))$$

$$\frac{S^N/(S\backslash N)^N\text{:}}{\lambda g\lambda\text{x}(g(\text{x})(\text{j'}))}\text{g} \qquad \frac{(S\backslash N)^N}{:\lambda\text{x}(\text{Hit'}(\text{Head-of'}(\text{x})))}$$

$$\frac{S^N:\lambda\text{x}(\text{Hit'}(\text{Head-of'}(\text{x}))(\text{j}))}{\text{CN}:\lambda\text{x}[(\text{Hit'}(\text{Head-of'}(\text{x})(\text{j}))\wedge\text{Child'}(\text{x})]}\langle$$

$$\frac{}{(S/(S\backslash N)):\lambda\text{P}\forall\text{x}[(\text{Head'}(\text{Head-of'}(\text{x})(\text{j}))\wedge\text{Child'}(\text{x}))\rightarrow\text{P}(\text{x})]}\langle_I$$

To derive the proper interpretation for (20), we need to pass up the information on the proform contained in the object onto the resulting category, step-by-step, using the unary composition, **g**-rule. Let us assume that the proper interpretation is composed simply by the rule combining the open proposition with the common noun. Consider a simple example like *John-ga atama-o tataita Mary* 'Mary whose head John hit'. When the open sentence modifies *Mary*, the possessor of the head should be identified with Mary'. Though we have to leave this issue open here, but the point is that we can account for the fact that simple (saturated) sentences containing relational nouns can be relative clauses in Japanese. In our account with the **g**- and **z**-rules, therefore, there is no difficulty in dealing with long distance binding between discontinuous expressions. We do not need, and actually argue against, the application of pied-piping to extract the implicit possessor corresponding to the head of the relative clause. The gap

---

[3] The relevant concatenation rule should be defined as in (i):

(i) Infixation

$$X|_I Y:f \quad Y:a \quad \rightarrow \quad Y_1 XY_2:fa$$

where $Y = [_Y \quad Y_1 \bullet Y_2]$

(i.e., place X at the infixation point indicated by $\bullet$)

occupying the possessor position of the relational noun can be identified later when the relative clause combines with the head-noun.

5 Asymmetry in Extractability

We have shown that the type-shift approach to binding proposed by Jacobson provides an important clue as to a licensing condition of some peculiar constructions in Japanese, which is a full pro-drop language and often systematically omit possessive pronouns if they are inferable from context. The constructions involving discontinuous possessors and possessees illustrated in (1) are quite common in Japanese, so the special mechanism must be necessary to associate these noun phrases, and we have argued that the standard binding theory does not serve to derive these constructions with proper interpretations, without positing phonologically null expressions.

Let us consider here whether we can get an additional empirical support for the type-shift approach to binding. In Japanese, the possessors and possessees behave as if they were independent nominal expressions. For instance, at a first glance, we have two independent nominative NPs in the so-called multiple subject construction, but actually we encounter sharp asymmetries in extractability between these subjects.

(21) a. Tanaka-san-wa   otoosan-ga   okanemoti-da.
       Tanaka-Mr.-Top   father-Nom   rich-Be-Pres
    b. [otoosan-ga   okanemoti-na] Tanaka-san
       'Mr. Tanaka whose father is rich'
    c.* [Tanaka-san-ga   okanemoti-na] otoo-san

It is possible to relativize the major subject, which is NOT an argument of the predicate, while the following thematic subject cannot be extracted. Similarly, in the Korean double object construction in (22), the non-argument possessor object can be extracted, while the argument possessee object cannot.

(22) a. Thalo-ka   meli-lul   simhakey   ttayli-n   Hanakho
       Thalo-Nom head-Acc   hard   hit-PAST Hanakho
       'Hanakho whose head Thalo hit hard'
    b.* Thalo-ka   Hanakho-lul   simhakey   ttayli-n   meli
       Thalo-Nom Hanakho-Acc   hard   hit-PAST head

Again, the matrix subject (i.e., the possessor) can be relativized, while the lower (possessee) subject and object cannot, in the indirect passives, as shown in (23) and (24):

(23) a. [Tsuma-ni   saki-datareta]   Tanaka-san
          wife-Dat   pass-away-Past-Rel. Mr. Tanaka
    b.* [Tanaka-san-ga saki-datareta]   Tsuma
(24) a. [siken-no   seiseki-o   homer-are-ta]   Tanaka-san
          test-Gen   results-Acc   praise-Pass-Past-Rel Mr.Tanaka
    b.*? [Tanaka-san-ga homer-are-ta] siken-no   seiseki

The systematic asymmetries in extractability between the possessors and possessees shown above should be accounted for by any theory of binding because the ungrammaticality of the examples in which the possessees are extracted are very severe. If the possessors and possesees are syntactically licensed just as independent terms, no plausible explanation can be given here.

We can offer a quite simple explanation for the asymmetry observed above. Let's take a indirect passive case as an example.

(25) a. $\underline{\text{Tsuma-ni}}$ $\underline{\text{saki-dat-are-ta}}$ $\underline{\text{Tanaka-san}}$
          N^N:Wife-of'(x) $(S\backslash N)\backslash N^N$: $N\backslash(S\backslash N)$:
                                $\lambda f \lambda x(\text{Die-Pass'}(f(x))(x))$ $\lambda P\iota x(P(x)\wedge x=\text{Tanaka'})$

          $\overline{\hspace{2cm} S\backslash N:\lambda x(\text{Die-Pass'}(\text{Wife-of'}(x))(x)) \hspace{2cm}}$

          $\overline{\hspace{2cm} N:\iota x(\text{Die-Pass'}(\text{Wife-of'}(x))(x)) \wedge x=\text{Tanaka'}) \hspace{2cm}}$

     b. $\underline{\text{Tanaka-san-ga}}$ $\underline{\text{saki-dat-are-ta}}$ $\underline{\text{tsuma}}$
                 N $(S\backslash N)\backslash N^N$: $N^N\backslash(S\backslash N)$:
                         $\lambda f \lambda x(\text{Die-Pass'}(f(x))(x))$ $\lambda P\lambda x(\text{Wife-of'}(x)\wedge P(x))$
        *$\overline{\hspace{8cm}}$

Let us assume that the conjunction of property-denoting expressions is a semantic requirement of the relative-clause formation. In the ungrammatical derivation (25b), the **z**-*sakidat-are* of category $(S\backslash N)\backslash N^N$ cannot combine with *Tanaka-san-ga* of categry N, failing to form a relative clause. On the other hand, in (25a), the function denoted by the relational noun *tsuma* successfully introduces the necessary gap which should be identified with *Tanaka-san*. Note also that the function is extracted in (25b). Cresti [2] suggests that only individual denoting expressions can undergo unbound movement, and the asymmetry in extractability in (25) may give support for her generalization of long-distance *wh*-movement.

It seems that it is almost impossible to recover function meanings once they are extracted. If functions can be extracted, not only nominals but also expressions of any category should be able to be extracted. For instance, in (21b) in which the major subject is relativized, the relative clause *titioya-ga yuufuku-na* can be taken to denote sets of individuals whose father is rich ($\langle$x | x's father is rich$\rangle$), whereas in (21c) where the relational noun is extracted, the resulting relative clause can never denote any property due to the absence of a syntactic gap corresponding to an individual (*$\langle$x | Mr. Tanaka is rich$\rangle$). On the other hand, the standard binding theory which attributes binding to pronoun meanings cannot explain the asymmetries shown above. The other binding theories clearly require the presence of empty prononominal expressions to explain a wide variety of binding phenomena.[4]

---

[4] However, it should be noted here that subjectivization results in a kind of island for extraction, which cannot be accounted for by our theory alone. For instance, in (i), the locative NP can be marked either with locative or with nominative.

Finally let us give a related example to support our account following Jacobson's theory of binding. Compare the following sentences:

(26) a. John$_i$-wa   [daremo$_j$-ga   gendo$_{i/j}$-o   hihan-sita]-to   itta.
     John-Top   everyone-Nom   behavior-Acc criticize-that   say-Past
     'John said that everybody criticized his/her behaviors.'
   b. John$_i$-wa   [everybody$_j$-ga   gendo$_{*i/j}$-o   jiko-hihan-sita]-to   itta.
     John-Top   Mary-Nom   behaviors-Acc self-criticize-that   say-Past
     'John said that Mary criticized *his/her behaviors.'

It appears at a first glance that verbs like *jiko-hihan-suru* 'self-criticize' are formed via the process of reflexivization proposed by Reinhart and Reuland [8], but this is wrong. Japanese lexical reflexive verbs has no function to reduce the arities of original (base) verbs, as seen in (26), and are prone to maintain their argument structures. In (26a), the relational noun *gendo* 'behaviors' can be associated with the matrix subject *John* or bound by the universal quantifier *dare-mo*, both of which can be given proper interpretations in our approach to binding. More interestingly, in (26b), the implicit pronoun of *gendo* cannot get bound by *John*, because the subject of the (lexically) reflexivized lower verb (which we may refer to as a lexical **z**-predicate) unselectively binds all the free variables (including the implicit agent of *gendo* in this case) in the lower clause. It can be said that the advantages of the type-shift approach to binding are highlighted by the contrast in interpretation between the sentences in (26), which should impose another difficulty to the binding-as-pronoun-meaning approach.

6   Conclusion

In this paper, we have argued against the approaches which attempt to attribute binding properties to pronouns as semantic variables, which requires any syntactic theory to posit empty categories wherever we need variables for

---

(i) Tokyo-ni/Tokyo-ga   daikigyoo-ga   ooi.
   Tokyo-Loc/Tokyo-Nom big-company-Nom many-exist-Pres
   'In Tokyo, there are a lot of big companies.'
Once the locative NP is subjectivized, the thematic subject cannot be extracted, as shown in the following contrast:
(ii) a. [Tokyo-ni ooi] daikigyoo-wa ...
    b.* [Tokyo-ga ooi] daikigyoo-wa ...
The ungrammaticality of (iib) is again severe. It may be possible to suggest that the ungrammatical status of (iib) is due to a kind of intervention effect if we posit the null-operator structure for the double subject construction, as in (iii):
(iii) [[$_{CP}$ Tokyo-ga   [$_{CP}$ Op$_i$ [t_i daikigyoo-ga ooi]]
In the structure like (iii), the thematic subject *daikigyoo* 'big companies' cannot use as an escape hatch the lower spec-CP position already occupied by the null operator. The asymmetry does not involve binding, so our type-shift approach, as well as the *binding-as-pronoun-meaning* approach, cannot give a unified account to the subjectivization island phenoma, but I would like to leave this issue as a matter for future research.

interpretation. Japanese avoids pronouns in general and often obligatorily, and this tendency to omit pronouns should permit various language-particular constructions. In Japanese sentences, it seems that open propositions (i.e., clauses with unbound pronouns) can behave as predicates (as in the multiple subject construction), as relative clauses, and as free-relative clauses in the cleft constructions. Possessors and possesees can appear far from each other in the constructions noted in this paper, but they must be associated somehow to derive proper meanings. We propose that the binding theory in which the type-shift rule called the 'z-rule' in Jacobson's work offers an elegant account to establish binding relations between the discontinuous possessors and possesees. We also note the asymmetry in extractability between the possessor NPs and relational nouns, and suggest that it is possible to extract individual-denoting expressions, whereas there is a severe constraint on extraction of function-denoting expressions like relational nouns. This asymmetry can be explained by the type-shift approach to binding in a unified manner, but should pose a great difficulty on the standard approach as well as the binding-as-pronoun meaning approach (see Jacobson [3], [4], and [5] for discussion).

References

1. Bekki, D.: Nihongo-Bunpo-no Keishiki-Riron: Katsuyo-Taikei•Tougo-Kouzo•Imi-Gousei. Kuroshio Publishers, Tokyo (2010)
2. Cresti, D.: Extraction and Reconstruction. Natural Language Semantics 3, 79–122 (1995)
3. Jacobson, P.: Towards a variable-free semantics. Linguistics and Philosophy 22(2), 117–184 (1999)
4. Jacobson, P.: Paycheck pronouns, BachPeters sentenes, and variable-free semantics. Natural Language Semantics 8, 77–155 (2000)
5. Jacobson, P.: Binding without pronouns (and pronouns without binding). In: Kruijff, G.M., Oehrle, R.T. (eds.) Resource-sensitivity, Binding and Anaphora, pp. 57–96. Kluwer Academic Publishers, Dordrecht (2003)
6. Heycock, C.: Syntactic Predication in Japanese. Journal of East Asian Linguistics 2, 167–211 (1993)
7. Reinhart, T.: Strategies of Anaphora Resolution. In: Bennis, H., Everaert, M., Reuland, E. (eds.) Interface Strategies, pp. 295–325. Royal Academy of Sciences, Amsterdam (2000)
8. Reinhart, T., Reuland, E.: Reflexitivity. Linguistic Inquiry 24(4), 657–720 (1993)
9. Steedman, M.: Surface Structure and Interpretation (Linguistic Inquiry Monograph). MIT Press, Cambridge (1996)
10. Steedman, M.: The Syntactic Process. MIT Press, Cambridge (2000)
11. Szabolcsi, A.: Bound variables in syntax: Are there any? In: Bartsch, R., van Benthem, J., van Emde Boas, P. (eds.) Semantics and Contextual Expressions, pp. 295–318. Foris Publications, Dordrecht (1987)
12. Szabolcsi, A.: Binding on the fly. In: Kruijff, G.M., Oehrle, R.T. (eds.) Resource-sensitivity, Binding and Anaphora, pp. 215–227. Kluwer Academic Publishers, Dordrecht (2003)

Prolegomena to Salient-Similarity-Based Vague Predicate Logic

Satoru Suzuki

Faculty of Arts and Sciences, Komazawa University
1-23-1, Komazawa, Setagaya-ku, Tokyo, 154-8525 Japan
bxs05253@nifty.com

Abstract. Vagueness is a ubiquitous feature that we know from many expressions in natural languages. It can invite a serious problem: the Sorites Paradox. The aim of this paper is to proposed a new version of complete logic for vague predicates - salient-similarity-based vague predicate logic (**SVPL**) that can avoid the Sorites Paradox and give answers to all of the Semantic Question, the Epistemological Question and the Psychological Question given by Graff.

Keywords: vagueness, Sorites Paradox, salient similarity, JND, intransitivity, semiorder, measurement theory, representation theorem, epistemicism.

1 Introduction

Vagueness is a ubiquitous feature that we know from many expressions in natural languages. It can invite a serious problem: the Sorites Paradox. The following argument is an ancient example of this paradox:

Example 1 (Sorites Paradox). 1000000 grains of sand make a heap[1].
If 1000000 grains of sand make a heap, then 999999 grains of sand do.
If 999999 grains of sand make a heap, then 999998 grains do.
$\vdots$

If 2 grains of sand make a heap, then 1 grain does.
1 grain of sand makes a heap. □

You can replace the set of conditional premises with a *universally generalised premise*. Hyde ([9]) classified responses to the Sorites Paradox in the following four types:

1. denying that logic applies to soritical expressions,
2. denying some premises,
3. denying the validity of the argument,
4. accepting the paradox as sound.

---

[1] The Sorites Paradox derives its name from the Greek word "σωρός" for heap.

T. Onoda, D. Bekki, and E. McCready (Eds.): JSAI-isAI 2010, LNAI 6797, pp. 75–89, 2011.
© Springer-Verlag Berlin Heidelberg 2011

In this paper we try to pursue response (2) in which the universally generalised premise is denied.

Graff ([[6]: 50]) gives the following three questions to which the theories of vagueness should answer when *the universally generalised premise is not true*:

1. The *Semantic Question*: if the universally generalised premise: $\forall x \forall y (P(x) \wedge R(x,y) \rightarrow P(y))$, where R is a relation that makes this premise seemingly plausible (ex. "is one-grain-of-sand-less than"), is not true, then must its negation, the *Sharp Boundaries Claim*: $\exists x \exists y (P(x) \wedge R(x,y) \wedge \neg P(y))$, be true? If the Sharp Boundaries Claim is true, how is its truth compatible with the fact that vague predicates have borderline cases?
2. The *Epistemological Question*: if it is not true, why are we unable to say which one (or more) of its instances is not true?
3. The *Psychological Question*: if it is not true, why were we so inclined to accept it in the first place?

Graff ([[6]: 50–54]) goes on to provide a brief description of the most popular theories of vagueness: supervaluationism, epistemicism, and degrees-of-truth theories and context-dependent theories. She considers that the first two are incomplete because they cannot give an adequate answer to the Psychological Question, while there is no reason to accept degrees-of-truth theories because they provide no substantial account of what degrees of truth are. She is sympathetic to context-dependent theories which appeal to the context dependence of vague predicates in order to answer the Psychological Question. She ([[6]: 57–64]) proposes the four kinds of constraints on use of vague predicates: Clear-Case Constraints, Relational Constraints, Coordinate Constraints and Salient Similarity Constraint. Although the first three constraints pose no serious problem, the fourth is controversial. This constraint is as follows:

> The *Salient Similarity Constraint*: for any object x and y, if x is saliently similar to y relative to a predicate P and x belongs to the semantic value of P, then y also belongs to it.

According to Graff ([[6]: 59]), if the Salient Similarity Constraint is correct, it provides the resources for answering the Epistemological Question and the Psychological Question. According to Åkerman ([[1]: 5]), the Salient Similarity Constraint is a principle concerning truth, while the Psychological Question is a question concerning belief forming. An alternative to the Salient Similarity Constraint without any straightforward semantic implications seems to answer the Psychological Question in a satisfactory way:

> The *Belief-Forming Constraint*: for any object x and y, if x is saliently similar to y relative to a predicate P, then we tend to form the belief that if x belongs to the semantic value of P, then y also belongs to it.[2]

---

[2] Åkerman's formulation of the Belief-Forming Constraint is as follows:
If two things are saliently similar, we tend to form beliefs according to which one of them falls under a vague predicate iff the other one does ([[1]: 5]).

It is hard to see how the Salient Similarity Constraint could give a satisfactory answer to the Psychological Question without additional premises which would entail the Belief-Forming Constraint. The Belief-Forming Constraint entails the following property.

> The *Revised Salient Similarity Property*: it is possible that there are some object x and y such that x is saliently similar to y relative to a predicate P and x belongs to the semantic value of P but y does not belong to it.

On the other hand, we relabel the property which Graff mistakenly attributes to salient similarity as follows:

> The *Exact Similarity Property*: for any object x and y, if x is exactly similar to y relative to a predicate P and x belongs to the semantic value of P, then y also belongs to it.

In this paper we pursue the *semantic* and *syntactic* concept of salient similarity that entails the Revised Salient Similarity Property and that of exact similarity that entails the Exact Similarity Property. The aim of this paper is to propose a new version of *complete* logic for vague predicates - *salient-similarity-based vague predicate logic* (SVPL) that can avoid the *Sorites Paradox* and give answers to all of the *Semantic Question*, the *Epistemological Question* and the *Psychological Question*.

The structure of this paper is as follows: In Section 2, we define the language $\mathcal{L}_{\mathsf{SVPL}}$ of SVPL, and define a model $\mathfrak{M}$ of SVPL, and provide SVPL with a satisfaction definition and a truth definition, and explain why the Sorites Paradox can be avoided in SVPL, and comment upon a representation theorem for semiorders when the domain is countable, and provide SVPL with a proof system, and touch upon the soundness and completeness of SVPL. In Section 3, we discuss higher-order vagueness. In Section 4, we discuss intransitivity and irrationality.

2   Salient-Similarity-Based Vague Predicate Logic **SVPL**

2.1   Language

We define the language $\mathcal{L}_{\mathsf{SVPL}}$ of SVPL as follows:

Definition 1 (Language)

- *Let $\mathcal{V}$ denote a set of individual variables, $\mathcal{C}$ a set of individual constants, $\mathcal{P}$ a set of one-place vague predicate symbols, $\mathbf{D}_P$ a dissimilarity relation symbol relative to P.*
- *The language $\mathcal{L}_{\mathsf{SVPL}}$ of SVPL is given by the following rule:*

$$t ::= x \mid a,$$
$$\varphi ::= P(t) \mid t_1 = t_2 \mid \mathbf{D}_P(t_1, t_2) \mid \top \mid \neg\varphi \mid \varphi_1 \wedge \varphi_2 \mid \forall x\varphi,$$

where $x \in \mathcal{V}$, $a \in \mathcal{C}$, $P \in \mathcal{P}$. $\bot, \vee, \rightarrow, \leftrightarrow$ and $\exists$ are introduced by the standard definitions.

- $\mathbf{D}_P(t_1, t_2)$ means that t_1 is dissimilar in P-ness from t_2.
- We define a salient similarity relation symbol $\mathbf{S}_P$ relative to P and an exact similarity relation symbol $\mathbf{S}_P^+$ relative to P as follows:

$$\mathbf{S}_P(t_1, t_2) := \neg \mathbf{D}_P(t_1, t_2),$$
$$\mathbf{S}_P^+(t_1, t_2) := \forall x((\mathbf{D}_P(t_1, x) \leftrightarrow \mathbf{D}_P(t_2, x)) \wedge (\mathbf{D}_P(x, t_1) \leftrightarrow \mathbf{D}_P(x, t_2))).$$

- The set of all well-formed formulae of $\mathcal{L}_{\mathsf{SVPL}}$ is denoted by $\Phi_{\mathcal{L}_{\mathsf{SVPL}}}$.   □

Remark 1. The definition of $\mathbf{S}_P^+(t_1, t_2)$ depends upon the later definition of a weak order $\succeq$ (Definition 11).   □

2.2 Semantics

Model One possible explanation for the Sorites Paradox is that the *intransitivity* of salient similarity results from the fact that we cannot generally discriminate *very close quantities*. The psychophysicist Fechner ([5]) explained this inability by the concept of a *threshold of discrimination*, that is, *just noticeable difference (JND)*. Given a *measure function* f that the *experimenter* assigns to the *subject* and an object a, its JND δ is the *lowest intensity increment* such that $f(a) + \delta$ is recognised to be higher than $f(a)$ by the subject. We formalise *dissimilarity* in terms of a JND and then define *salient similarity* and *exact similarity* in terms of dissimilarity. We define a model $\mathfrak{M}$ of SVPL as follows:

Definition 2 (Model). $\mathfrak{M}$ is a sequence $(\mathcal{I}, a_1^{\mathfrak{M}}, \ldots, P_1^{\mathfrak{M}}, \ldots, f_{P_1}, \ldots, \delta_{P_1}, \ldots)$, where:

- $\mathcal{I}$ is a nonempty set of individuals, called the universe of $\mathfrak{M}$,
- $a_1^{\mathfrak{M}} \in \mathcal{I}, \ldots$,
- $P_1^{\mathfrak{M}} \subseteq \mathcal{I}, \ldots$,
- δ_{P_1} is a JND relative to P_1 that the experimenter assigns to the subject, $\ldots$,
- f_{P_1} is a measure function from $\mathcal{I}$ into $\mathbb{R}$ that the experimenter uses in order to measure the ability of the subject for discrimination relative to P_1, satisfying the following condition:
  For any $t_1^{\mathfrak{M}}$ and $t_2^{\mathfrak{M}}$, if $f_{P_1}(t_1^{\mathfrak{M}}) > f_{P_1}(t_2^{\mathfrak{M}}) + \delta_{P_1}$ or $f_{P_1}(t_2^{\mathfrak{M}}) > f_{P_1}(t_1^{\mathfrak{M}}) + \delta_{P_1}$ and $t_1^{\mathfrak{M}} \in P_1^{\mathfrak{M}}$, then $t_2^{\mathfrak{M}} \notin P_1^{\mathfrak{M}}$, (Dissimilarity Property).
    □

Truth. We define an (extended) assignment function as follows:

Definition 3 (Assignment Function)

- We call $s : \mathcal{V} \to \mathcal{I}$ an assignment function.
- We call $\tilde{s} : \mathcal{V} \cup \mathcal{C} \to \mathcal{I}$ an extended assignment function.   □

We provide SVPL with the following satisfaction definition relative to $\mathfrak{M}$:

Definition 4 (Satisfaction). *What it means for $\mathfrak{M}$ to satisfy $\varphi \in \Phi_{\mathcal{L}_{\mathsf{SVPL}}}$ with s, in symbols $\mathfrak{M} \models_{\mathsf{SVPL}} \varphi[s]$ is inductively defined as follows:*

- $\mathfrak{M} \models_{\mathsf{SVPL}} P(t)[s]$ *iff* $\tilde{s}(t) \in P^{\mathfrak{M}}$,
- $\mathfrak{M} \models_{\mathsf{SVPL}} t_1 = t_2[s]$ *iff* $\tilde{s}(t_1) = \tilde{s}(t_2)$,
- $\mathfrak{M} \models_{\mathsf{SVPL}} \mathbf{D}_P(t_1, t_2)[s]$ *iff* $f_P(t_1^{\mathfrak{M}}) > f_P(t_2^{\mathfrak{M}}) + \delta_P$ *or* $f_P(t_2^{\mathfrak{M}}) > f_P(t_1^{\mathfrak{M}}) + \delta_P$,
- $\mathfrak{M} \models_{\mathsf{SVPL}} \top$,
- $\mathfrak{M} \models_{\mathsf{SVPL}} \neg\varphi[s]$ *iff* $\mathfrak{M} \not\models_{\mathsf{SVPL}} \varphi[s]$,
- $\mathfrak{M} \models_{\mathsf{SVPL}} \varphi \wedge \psi[s]$ *iff* $\mathfrak{M} \models_{\mathsf{SVPL}} \varphi[s]$ *and* $\mathfrak{M} \models_{\mathsf{SVPL}} \psi[s]$,
- $\mathfrak{M} \models_{\mathsf{SVPL}} \forall x\varphi[s]$ *iff*   *for any* $\mathfrak{d} \in \mathcal{I}$, $\mathfrak{M} \models_{\mathsf{SVPL}} \varphi[s(x|\mathfrak{d})]$,

  where $s(x|\mathfrak{d})$ is the function that is exactly like s except for one thing: For the individual variable x, it assigns the individual $\mathfrak{d}$. This can be expressed as follows:

$$s(x|\mathfrak{d})(y) := \begin{cases} s(y) & \text{if } y \neq x \\ \mathfrak{d} & \text{if } y = x. \end{cases}$$ □

Remark 2. We can provide the satisfaction clauses of $\mathbf{S}_P(t_1, t_2)$ and $\mathbf{S}_P^+(t_1, t_2)$ in terms of that of $\mathbf{D}_P(t_1, t_2)$.   □

We define the truth in $\mathfrak{M}$ by means of satisfaction and then define validity as follows:

Definition 5 (Truth and Validity)

- *If $\mathfrak{M} \models_{\mathsf{SVPL}} \varphi[s]$ for all s, we write $\mathfrak{M} \models_{\mathsf{SVPL}} \varphi$ and say that φ is true in $\mathfrak{M}$.*
- *If φ is true in all models of* SVPL, *we write $\models_{\mathsf{SVPL}} \varphi$ and say that φ is valid.*   □

Our Answer to Semantic Question. Now we can give an answer to the Semantic Question.[3] Our answer is "Yes". Because in SVPL the *bivalence* holds, the fact that vague predicates have borderline cases does not imply the truth value gap or so. Both this fact and the truth of the Sharp Boundaries Claim result from the fact that, like the subject in focus, we have only limited ability of discrimination. In this sense SVPL has a position of *epistemicism*. According to epistemicism, vagueness is a type of *ignorance*. Because vague predicates have extensions with sharp boundaries, *bivalence* can be retained. We cannot know where those boundaries lie. The Stoics were supposed to hold this type of position. It has been recently revived by Williamson ([27] and [28]). Our position in this paper can be considered to be a kind of epistemicism for two reasons:

---

[3] The Semantic Question was as follows: if the universally generalised premise: $\forall x \forall y (P(x) \wedge R(x, y) \rightarrow P(y))$, where R is a relation that makes this premise seemingly plausible (ex. "is one-grain-of-sand less than"), is not true, then must its negation, the Sharp Boundaries Claim: $\exists x \exists y (P(x) \wedge R(x, y) \wedge \neg P(y))$, be true? If the Sharp Boundaries Claim is true, how is its truth compatible with the fact that vague predicates have borderline cases?

First, the semantic values of vague predicates in the model $\mathfrak{M}$ of Definition 2 have sharp boundaries. Second, JNDs $\delta_{P_1}, \ldots$ reflect ignorance. The merit of epistemicism is expressed best by Williamson ([[27]: 162]) when he says:

> The epistemic view (epistemicism) involves no revision of classical logic and semantics; its rivals do involve such revisions. Classical logic and semantics are vastly superior to the alternatives in simplicity, power, past success, and integration with theories in other domains. In these circumstances it would be sensible to adopt the epistemic view in order to retain classical logic and semantics even if it were subject to philosophical criticisms in which we could locate no fallacy; not every anomaly falsifies a theory.

Our Answer to Epistemological Question. Next we give an answer to the Epistemological Question.[4] Our Answer is that we are unable to one (or more) of its instances is not true, because, like the subject in focus, we have only limited ability of discrimination.

Semiorder. Luce ([12]) introduced the concept of a *semiorder*[5] [6] that can provide a *qualitative* counterpart of a JND that is *quantitative*. Scott and Suppes ([[17]: 117]) defined a semiorder as follows:

Definition 6 (Semiorder). $\succ$ on $\mathcal{I}$ is called a semiorder if, for any $w, x, y, z \in \mathcal{I}$, the following conditions are satisfied:

1. $x \not\succ x$. (Irreflexivity),
2. If $w \succ x$ and $y \succ z$, then $w \succ z$ or $y \succ x$. (Strong Intervality),
3. If $w \succ x$ and $x \succ y$, then $w \succ z$ or $z \succ y$. (Semitransitivity). □

There are two main problems with *measurement theory*[7]:

1. the representation problem–justifying the assignment of numbers to objects,
2. the uniqueness problem–specifying the transformation up to which this assignment is unique.

A solution to the former can be furnished by a *representation theorem*, which establishes that the specified conditions on a qualitative relational system are

---

[4] The Epistemological Question was as follows: if the universally generalised premise is not true, why are we unable to say which one (or more) of its instances is not true?

[5] Van Rooij ([25] and [26]) also argued the relation between the Sorites Paradox and semiorders from a different point of view that does not focus on a representation theorem.

[6] In [22] and [23] we proposed a new version of complete and decidable preference logic based on a semiorder on a Boolean algebra.

[7] [15] gives a comprehensive survey of measurement theory. The mathematical foundation of measurement had not been studied before Hölder developed his axiomatisation for the measurement of mass ([8]). [10], [19] and [13] are seen as milestones in the history of measurement theory.

(necessary and) sufficient for the assignment of numbers to objects that represents (or preserves) all the relations in the system. Scott and Suppes ([17]) proved a representation theorem for semiorders when $\mathcal{I}$ is *finite*. The Scott-Suppes theorem was first extended by to *countable* sets by Manders ([14]). Because $\mathcal{I}$ of the model $\mathfrak{M}$ of SVPL may be countable, the Manders theorem must be considered. A condition ($\sim^*$-Connectedness) is necessary for $\succ$ to have a *positive threshold* even when $\mathcal{I}$ is countable. We define $\sim$ by $\succ$ as follows:

Definition 7 ($\sim$). *For any $x_1, x_2 \in \mathcal{I}$, $x_1 \sim x_2 := x_1 \not\succ x_2$ and $x_2 \not\succ x_1$.* ☐

$\sim^*$ is defined by $\sim$ and $\succ$ as follows:

Definition 8 ($\sim^*$)

> *For any $x, y \in \mathcal{I}$, $x \sim^* y := x \sim y$,*
>
> > *or $x \succ y$ and for any $z \in \mathcal{I}$, not ($x \succ z$ and $z \succ y$),*
> >
> > *or $y \succ x$ and for any $z \in \mathcal{I}$, not ($y \succ z$ and $z \succ x$).* ☐

A $\sim^*$-chain is defined by $\sim^*$ as follows:

Definition 9 ($\sim^*$-Chain). *Let $a_0, \ldots, a_n \in \mathcal{I}$ be such that for any $k < n, a_k \sim^* a_{k+1}$. Then we call $(a_0, \ldots, a_n)$ a $\sim^*$-chain between a_0 and a_n.* ☐

$\sim^*$-Connectedness is defined by a $\sim^*$-chain as follows:

Definition 10 ($\sim^*$-Connectedness). *$\sim^*$ on $\mathcal{I}$ is connected if for any $x_0, x_n \in \mathcal{I}$, there is a $\sim^*$-chain between x_0 and x_n.* ☐

The Manders theorem can be stated by means of $\sim^*$-Connectedness as follows:

Theorem 1 (Representation for Semiorders, Manders ([14])). *Suppose that $\succ$ is a binary relation on a countable set $\mathcal{I}$ and that $\sim^*$ is defined by Definition 8 and that δ is a positive number. Then $\succ$ is a semiorder and $\sim^*$ is connected iff there is a function $f : \mathcal{I} \to \mathbb{R}$ satisfying*

$$a_1 \succ a_2 \text{ iff } f(a_1) > f(a_2) + \delta.$$
☐

From Semiorder to Weak Order We define $\succeq$ as follows:

Definition 11 ($\succeq$). *For any $x_1, x_2 \in \mathcal{I}$, $x_1 \succeq x_2 :=$ for any $x_3 \in \mathcal{I}$, (if $x_2 \succ x_3$, then $x_1 \succ x_3$ and if $x_3 \succ x_1$, then $x_3 \succ x_2$).* ☐

The next proposition concerning $\succ$ and $\succeq$ obtains.

Proposition 1 (From Semiorder to Weak Order, Roberts ([15])). *If $\succ$ is a semiorder and $\succeq$ is defined by Definition 11, $\succeq$ is a weak order (transitive and connected).* ☐

Cantor ([3]) proved the representation theorem for weak orders.

Theorem 2 (Representation for Weak Orders, Cantor ([3])). *Suppose $\mathcal{I}$ is a countable set and $\succeq$ is a binary relation on $\mathcal{I}$. Then $\succeq$ is a weak order iff there is a function $f : \mathcal{I} \to \mathbb{R}$ such that for any $x, y \in \mathcal{I}$,*

$$x \succeq y \text{ iff } f(x) \geq f(y).$$

☐

Global Rationality and Bounded Rationality. The standard model of economics is based on *global rationality* that requires an *optimising behavior*. But according to Simon ([18]), cognitive and information-processing constrains on the capabilities of agents, together with the complexity of their environment, render an *optimising behavior* an *unattainable ideal*. He dismissed the idea that agents should exhibit global rationality and suggested that they in fact exhibit *bounded rationality* that allows a *satisficing behavior*. Because the truth condition of the *Revised Salient Similarity Property* concerning $\mathbf{S}_P$ implies that the subject in focus has a *positive* threshold (only limited ability) of discrimination, she or he is considered to be only *boundedly rational*. On the other hand, because the truth condition of the *Exact Similarity Property* concerning $\mathbf{S}_P^+$ implies that the subject in focus has a *zero* threshold (perfect ability) of discrimination, she or he is considered to be *globally rational*.

Sorites Paradox Revisited. We now return to the Sorites Paradox. Assume that $\mathfrak{U} := (\mathcal{I}, a_1^{\mathfrak{U}}, \ldots, a_{1000000}^{\mathfrak{U}}, H^{\mathfrak{U}}, f_H, \delta_H)$ is given, where:

- $\mathcal{I} := \{a_1, \ldots, a_{1000000}\}$, where a_i denotes i grain(s) of sand, for any $i(1 \leq i \leq 1000000)$,
- H denotes making a heap,
- f_H is a measure function for H that satisfies the Dissimilar Property of Definition 2,
- δ_H is a JND relative to H,
- $a_{1000000} \in H^{\mathfrak{U}}$,
- $f_H(a_i^{\mathfrak{U}}) \not> f_H(a_{i+1}^{\mathfrak{U}}) + \delta_H$ and $f_H(a_{i+1}^{\mathfrak{U}}) \not> f_H(a_i^{\mathfrak{U}}) + \delta_H$, for any $i(1 \leq i \leq 999999)$,
- $f_H(a_{1000000}^{\mathfrak{U}}) > f_H(a_1^{\mathfrak{U}}) + \delta_H$.

Then we have the following proposition:

Proposition 2 (Revised Salient Similarity Property)

$\mathfrak{U} \not\models_{\mathsf{SVPL}} ((\mathbf{S}_H(a_{1000000}, a_{999999}) \wedge H(a_{1000000})) \to H(a_{999999})) \wedge \cdots \wedge ((\mathbf{S}_H(a_2, a_1) \wedge H(a_2)) \to H(a_1)).$ □

From this proposition we obtain the following result:

Corollary 1 (Avoidance of Sorites Paradox)

$\not\models_{\mathsf{SVPL}} (H(a_{1000000}) \wedge ((\mathbf{S}_H(a_{1000000}, a_{999999}) \wedge H(a_{1000000})) \to H(a_{999999})) \wedge \cdots \wedge ((\mathbf{S}_H(a_2, a_1) \wedge H(a_2)) \to H(a_1))) \to H(a_1).$ □

On the other hand, we have the following proposition:

Proposition 3 (Exact Similarity Property)

$\models_{\mathsf{SVPL}} ((\mathbf{S}_H^+(a_{1000000}, a_{999999}) \wedge H(a_{1000000})) \to H(a_{999999})) \wedge \cdots \wedge ((\mathbf{S}_H^+(a_2, a_1) \wedge H(a_2)) \to H(a_1)).$ □

From this proposition we obtain the following result:

Corollary 2 (Invitation of Sorites Paradox)

$\models_{\mathsf{SVPL}} (H(a_{1000000}) \wedge ((\mathbf{S}_H^+(a_{1000000}, a_{999999}) \wedge H(a_{1000000})) \to H(a_{999999})) \wedge \cdots \wedge ((\mathbf{S}_H^+(a_2, a_1) \wedge H(a_2)) \to H(a_1))) \to H(a_1).$ □

Our Answer to Psychological Question. Now we can give an answer to the Psychological Question.[8] Our Answer is that we tend to form the belief that the *only boundedly rational* subject is *globally rational* and attribute to him the *Exact Similarity Property* instead of the *Revised Salient Similarity Property*.

2.3   Syntax

Semiorder and Proof System. The Manders theorem relates *JNDs* to *semiorders*, which enables us to propose the following proof system of SVPL based on semiorders that is an extension of a proof system of *first-order logic with an equality symbol*.[9]

Proof System. We extend it in such a way as to add the syntactic counterparts of *Irreflexivity*, *Strong Intervality*, *Semitransitivity*, the *Dissimilarity Property* and $\sim^*$-*Connectedness*. We define $\mathbf{S}_P^*$ that is the syntactic counterpart of $\sim^*$ as follows:

Definition 13 ($\mathbf{S}_P^*$)

$$\mathbf{S}_P^*(t_1, t_2) := \mathbf{S}_P(t_1, t_2)$$
$$\vee (\mathbf{D}_P(t_1, t_2) \wedge \forall x \neg (\mathbf{D}_P(t_1, x) \wedge \mathbf{D}_P(x, t_2))). \qquad \square$$

The proof system of SVPL consists of the following:

Definition 14 (Proof System)

1. *all tautologies of first-order logic with an equality symbol,*
2. $\forall x \neg \mathbf{D}_P(x, x)$ *(Syntactic Counterpart of Irreflexivity),*
3. $\forall w \forall x \forall y \forall z ((\mathbf{D}_P(w, x) \wedge \mathbf{D}_P(y, z)) \rightarrow (\mathbf{D}_P(w, z) \vee \mathbf{D}_P(y, x)))$
   (Syntactic Counterpart of Strong Intervality),
4. $\forall w \forall x \forall y \forall z ((\mathbf{D}_P(w, x) \wedge \mathbf{D}_P(x, y)) \rightarrow (\mathbf{D}_P(w, z) \vee \mathbf{D}_P(z, y)))$
   (Syntactic Counterpart of Semitransitivity),
5. $\forall x \forall y ((\mathbf{D}_P(x, y) \wedge P(x)) \rightarrow \neg P(y))$
   (Syntactic Counterpart of Dissimilarity Property 1),
6. $\forall x \forall y ((\mathbf{D}_P(x, y) \wedge \neg P(x)) \rightarrow P(y))$
   (Syntactic Counterpart of Dissimilarity Property 2),

---

[8] The Psychological Question was as follows: if the universally generalised premise is not true, why were we so inclined to accept it in the first place?

[9] Beja and Gilboa proposed another condition necessary for $\succ$ to have a positive threshold when $\mathcal{I}$ is countable as follows:

Definition 12 (Positivity). *For any* $x \in \mathcal{I}$ *and any* $y_1, y_2, y_3, \ldots \in \mathcal{I}$, *if* $y_1 \succ y_2, y_2 \succ y_3, \ldots$, *then for some* n $x \succ y_n$, *and if* $y_2 \succ y_1, y_3 \succ y_2, \ldots$, *then for some* n $y_n \succ x$.
$\square$

In $\mathcal{L}_{\mathsf{SVPL}}$ the syntactic counterpart of Positivity is not expressible, for it contains *infinite* quantifier sequence and conjunctions. It is possible to propose an incomplete *infinitary logic* that adopts as an axiom the syntactic counterpart of Positivity.

7. $\forall x_0 \forall x_n \exists x_1 \ldots \exists x_{n-1}(\mathbf{S}_P^*(x_0, x_1) \wedge \ldots \wedge \mathbf{S}_P^*(x_{n-1}, x_n))$
   (Syntactic Counterpart of $\sim^*$-Connectedness),
8. *Modus Ponens.* □

We define the provability in SVPL as follows:

Definition 15 (Provability)

- *A proof of $\varphi \in \Phi_{\mathcal{L}_{\text{SVPL}}}$ is a finite sequence of $\mathcal{L}_{\text{SVPL}}$-formulae having φ as the last formula such that either each formula is an instance of an axiom, or it can be obtained from formulae that appear earlier in the sequence by applying an inference rule.*
- *If there is a proof of φ, we write $\vdash_{\text{SVPL}} \varphi$.* □

Then we have the following propositions:

Proposition 4 (Syntactic Counterpart of Revised Salient Similarity Property)

$$\not\vdash_{\text{SVPL}} \forall x \forall y ((\mathbf{S}_P(x, y) \wedge P(x)) \rightarrow P(y)).$$ □

Proposition 5 (Syntactic Counterpart of Exact Similarity Property)

$$\vdash_{\text{SVPL}} \forall x \forall y ((\mathbf{S}_P^+(x, y) \wedge P(x)) \rightarrow P(y)).$$ □

2.4   Metalogic of SVPL

We prove the metatheorems of SVPL. It is easy to prove the soundness of SVPL.

Theorem 3 (Soundness). *For any $\varphi \in \Phi_{\mathcal{L}_{\text{SVPL}}}$, if $\vdash_{\text{SVPL}} \varphi$, then $\models_{\text{SVPL}} \varphi$.* □

We can also prove the completeness of SVPL by the *Manders theorem*, Lindenbaum Lemma and Truth Lemma.

Theorem 4 (Completeness). *For any $\varphi \in \Phi_{\mathcal{L}_{\text{SVPL}}}$, if $\models_{\text{SVPL}} \varphi$, then $\vdash_{\text{SVPL}} \varphi$.*
□

3   Discussion 1: Higher-Order Vagueness

3.1   Higher-Order Vagueness Is Per Se Paradoxical

Wright ([[30]: 129–132]) argues that "higher-order vagueness is *per se* paradoxical"([[30]: 139]) as follows.[10] What can cause the *first-order* Sorites Paradox is that the vagueness of "F" implies the truth of the form:

(1) $\neg\exists x(F(x) \wedge \neg F(x'))$,

where x' is the immediate successor of x. In order to avoid the first-order Sorites Paradox, Wright introduces an operator Def expressing *definiteness* or

---

[10] [[30]: 129–132] summarises the argument of [[29]: 228–235].

determinacy. The introduction of Def implies that the vagueness of "F" does not consist in the truth of (1). Instead, what is required is the truth of the form:

(2) $\neg \exists x(Def(F(x)) \wedge Def(\neg F(x')))$.

But this merely postpones the difficulty. For if the distinction between things which are F and borderline cases of F is *itself* vague, then assent to

(3) $\neg \exists x(Def(F(x)) \wedge \neg Def(F(x')))$

would seem to be compelled even if assent to (1) is not. If (2) rather than (1) express the vagueness of "F", then

(4) $\neg \exists x(Def(Def(F(x))) \wedge Def(\neg Def(F(x'))))$

rather than (3) should express that of $Def(F(x))$. It is very natural to adopt as a rule of inference the following:

(DEF) $\dfrac{\{Def(\varphi_1), \ldots, Def(\varphi_n)\} \vdash \psi}{\{Def(\varphi_1), \ldots, Def(\varphi_n)\} \vdash Def(\psi)}$

The definitisation of (4):

(5) $Def(\neg \exists x(Def(Def(F(x))) \wedge Def(\neg Def(F(x')))))$

is as plausible as (4). But from (5) and so on, by means of (DEF), one can derive

(6) $\forall x(Def(\neg Def(F(x'))) \rightarrow Def(\neg Def(F(x))))$.

(6) can entail that F has no definite instances if it has definite borderline cases of the first-order, which is absurd. From (2), on the other hand, one can only derive

(7) $\forall x(Def(\neg F(x')) \rightarrow Def(\neg Def(F(x))))$,

which is innocuous. The trouble is thus distinctively at higher-order.[11]

3.2 Operator versus Predicate Symbol

The introduction of the operator Def enables us to avoid the *first-order* Sorites Paradox. But it has such a harmful consequence as (6) in *higher-order* vagueness. Since Def is an operator, we can apply it iteratively. This strong expressive power leads us to derive (6). What is required is a logic for vague predicates that is *strong* in expressive power enough to avoid the *first-order* Sorites Paradox and *weak* enough not to have such a harmful consequence as (6) in *higher-order* vagueness. SVPL is such a logic. In SVPL, the dissimilarity symbol $\mathbf{D}_P$ relative to a one-place vague predicate symbol P is a device to avoid the first-order Sorites Paradox that corresponds to Def. Since $\mathbf{D}_P$ is a *predicate symbol*, we cannot it iteratively. So SVPL is weak in expressive power enough not to have such a consequence as (6).

---

[11] Heck ([7]) blocks Wright's derivation by prohibiting the discharge of a premise φ within conditional proof or reductio ad absurdum, when φ occurs as a premise of a line obtained by (DEF). But Heck does not justify this restriction.

4   Discussion 2: Intransitivity and Irrationality

4.1   Intransitivity and Money Pump Argument

In this paper we have proposed a version of complete logic for vague predicates - SVPL that can avoid the Sorites Paradox. In SVPL the transitivity of *salient similarity* is not provable, which enables SVPL to avoid the paradox. Tversky ([[24]: 455]) says on the relation between the transitivity of preference and the Money Pump Argument as follows:

> Transitivity, however, is one of the basic and the most compelling princi-
> ples of rational behavior. For if one violates transitivity, it is a well-known
> conclusion that he is acting, in effect, as a "money-pump." [12]

Tversky ([[24]: 455–456]) goes on to say on a form of the Money Pump Argument:

> Suppose an individual prefers y to x, z to y, and x to z. It is reasonable
> to assume that he is willing to pay a sum of money to replace x by y.
> Similarly, he should be willing to pay some amount of money to replace
> y by z and still a third amount to replace z by x. Thus, he ends up with
> the alternative he started with but with less money.

Lehrer and Wagner ([[11]: 249]) give an example of the Money Pump Argument against the intransitivity of indifference:

> Let us consider the case of a buyer of wine. This individual, after exten-
> sive tasting, finds that he is equally attracted to wines A and B, and
> to wines B and C, yet prefers A to C. While he discerns no difference
> between A and B in a paired comparison and none between B and C in
> a similar comparison, he does discern a difference between A and C in
> such a comparison, and in favor of A.

Lehrer and Wagner ([[11]: 250]) go on to say:

> But suppose that our wine buyer wishes to purchase a case of wine in
> the following situation: His wine merchant informs him that these wines
> will be available for purchase in a certain sequential fashion. Two of the
> wines, say x and y, will be available on Monday (and determined only
> then) and the remaining wine, z, may or may not be available on Tuesday.
> The merchant requires instructions from the buyer as to how to reserve
> for him a case of wine. The rules of this transaction require that the mer-
> chant make for the buyer a provisional choice of x or y, whatever they
> turn out to be. If z turns out not to be available on Tuesday, the buyer
> receives Monday's choice. If z is available, the merchant must choose z
> or Monday's choice. Suppose that the buyer informs the merchant of his
> preferences and indifferences, as described above, and instructs him to
> be guided by these, i.e., if the buyer is indifferent, the merchant may

---

[12] We can trace the origin of the Money Pump Argument back to [4].

choose (provisionally or finally) either, and if he has a preference, the merchant must follow it. It turns out that wines A and B are available on Monday and wine C on Tuesday. As the buyer is indifferent between A and B, the merchant provisionally chooses B for him, and since the buyer is indifferent between B and C, the merchant makes for him the final choice of C. Thus, although A was available and preferred to C, the buyer receives C, in full compliance with his instructions.

Does the intransitivity of indifference, salient similarity and so on always lead to irrationality?

4.2 Diachronic Independence

This Lehrer and Wagner's argument is considered to assume "diachronic independence (additivity)" ([[16]: 117]). Diachronic independence is as follows:

··· that the arrangements are value-wise independent, that if the agent knew of the arrangements he had already accepted, this would not affect the value he set on the arrangement just offered him ([[16]: 117]).

We agree with Schick ([[16]: 117]) when he says:

Again, the additivity/independence assumption cannot be taken for granted. Indeed, in typical cases it is false, and the obvious reasons: the gradual depletion of the agent's funds, his awareness of being exploited, and the like.

So because the independence assumption is not valid, the Lehrer and Wagner's argument does not imply that the intransitivity of indifference, salient similarity and so on is irrational.

5   Conclusion

In this paper we have proposed a new version of *complete* logic for vague predicates - salient-similarity-based vague predicate logic (SVPL) that can avoid the *Sorites Paradox* and give answers to all of the *Semantic Question*, the *Epistemological Question* and the *Psychological Question* given by Graff. This paper is only a part of our larger *measurement-theoretic* study. We are now trying to construct such logics as *dynamic epistemic preference logic* ([20]), *dyadic deontic logic* ([21]), *threshold utility maximiser's preference logic* ([22] and [23]) and *logic of questions and answers* by means of measurement theory.

Acknowledgements. We would like to thank an anonymous reviewer for his helpful comments.

References

1. Åkerman, Y.: Vagueness, Belief Forming, and Similarity Constraints. In: Oxford 11th Graduate Conference (2007)
2. Beja, A., Gilboa, I.: Numerical Representations of Imperfectly Ordered Preferences (A Unified Geometric Exposition). Journal of Mathematical Psychology 36, 426–449 (1992)
3. Cantor, G.: Beiträge zur Begründung der Transfiniten Mengenlehre I. Mathematische Annalen 46, 481–512 (1895)
4. Davidson, D., McKinsey, J.C.C., Suppes, P.: Outline of a Formal Theory of Value, I. Philosophy of Science 22, 140–160 (1955)
5. Fechner, G.T.: Elemente der Psychophysik. Breitkopf und Hartel, Leipzig (1860)
6. Graff, D.: Shifting Sands: An Interest-Relative Theory of Vagueness. Philosophical Topics 28, 45–81 (2000)
7. Heck Jr., R.G.: A Note on the Logic of (Higher-Order) Vagueness. Analysis 53, 201–208 (1993)
8. Hölder, O.: Die Axiome der Quantität und die Lehre von Mass. Berichte über die Verhandlungen der Königlich Sächsischen Gesellschaft der Wissenschaften zu Leipzig. Mathematisch-Physikaliche Classe 53, 1–64 (1901)
9. Hyde, D.: Sorites Paradox. In: Stanford Encyclopedia of Philosophy (2005)
10. Krantz, D.H., et al.: Foundations of Measurement, vol. I. Academic Press, New York (1971)
11. Lehrer, K., Wagner, C.: Intransitive Indifference: The Semi-order Problem. Synthese 65, 249–256 (1985)
12. Luce, D.: Semiorders and a Theory of Utility Discrimination. Econometrica 24, 178–191 (1956)
13. Luce, R.D., et al.: Foundations of Measurement, vol. III. Academic Press, San Diego (1990)
14. Manders, K.L.: On JND Representations of Semiorders. Journal of Mathematical Psychology 24, 224–248 (1981)
15. Roberts, F.S.: Measurement Theory. Addison-Wesley, Reading (1979)
16. Schick, F.: Dutch Bookies and Money Pump. The Journal of Philosophy 83, 112–119 (1986)
17. Scott, D., Suppes, P.: Foundational Aspects of Theories of Measurement. Journal of Symbolic Logic 3, 113–128 (1958)
18. Simon, H.A.: Models of Bounded Rationality. The MIT Press, Cambridge (1982)
19. Suppes, P., et al.: Foundations of Measurement, vol. II. Academic Press, San Diego (1989)
20. Suzuki, S.: Prolegomena to Dynamic Epistemic Preference Logic. In: Hattori, H., Kawamura, T., Idé, T., Yokoo, M., Murakami, Y. (eds.) JSAI 2008. LNCS (LNAI), vol. 5447, pp. 177–192. Springer, Heidelberg (2009)
21. Suzuki, S.: Measurement-Theoretic Foundation of Preference-Based Dyadic Deontic Logic. In: He, X., Horty, J., Pacuit, E. (eds.) LORI 2009. LNCS (LNAI), vol. 5834, pp. 278–291. Springer, Heidelberg (2009)
22. Suzuki, S.: Measurement-Theoretic Foundation of Threshold Utility Maximiser's Preference Logic. In: van Benthem, J., Yamada, T. (eds.) Electronic Post-Proceedings of the Second International Workshop on Philosophy and Ethics of Social Reality (SOCREAL 2010), pp. 83–214 (2010)
23. Suzuki, S.: Prolegomena to Threshold Utility Maximiser's Preference Logic. In: Electronic Proceedings of the 9th Conference on Logic and the Foundations of Game and Decision Theory (LOFT 2010), Paper No. 44 (2010)

24. Tversky, A.: Intransitivity of Preferences. Psychological Review 76, 31–48 (1969); Rpt. in: Shafir, E. (ed.): Preference, Belief and Similarity: Selected Writings / by Amos Tversky, pp. 433–461. The MIT Press, Cambridge (2004)
25. Van Rooij, R.: Revealed Preference and Satisficing Behavior. In: Electronic Proceedings of 8th Conference on Logic and the Foundations of Game and Decision Theory (LOFT 2008), Paper No. 48 (2008)
26. Van Rooij, R.: Vagueness and Linguistics. In: Ronzitti, G. (ed.) The Vagueness Handbook (forthcoming)
27. Williamson, T.: Vagueness and Ignorance. Proceedings of the Aristotelian Society, Supplementary Volumes 66, 145–162 (1992)
28. Williamson, T.: Vagueness. Routledge, London (1994)
29. Wright, C.: Further Reflections on the Sorites Paradox. Philosophical Topics 15, 227–290; Rpt. In: Keefe, R. and Smith, P.: Vagueness: A Reader. The MIT Press, Cambridge (1997)
30. Wright, C.: Is Higher Order Vagueness Coherent? Analysis 52, 129–139 (1992)

Yablo-Like Paradoxes and Co-induction

Shunsuke Yatabe

Collaborate Research Team for Verification
National Institute of Advanced Industrial Science and Technology, Japan
shunsuke.yatabe@aist.go.jp

Abstract. We review three pairwise similar paradoxes, the modest liar paradox, McGee's paradox and Yablo's paradox, which imply the ω-inconsistency. We show that is caused by the fact that co-inductive definitions of formulae are possible because of the existence of the truth predicate.

1 Introduction

Recently, co-induction plays a very important role in computer science to represent behaviors of non-terminate automatons [MT91][Cq93]. Now philosophers begin to study languages whose formulae are constructed co-inductively, i.e. these languages are allowed to have sentences of infinite length [L04]. However, such languages are not so new: they have already appeared in the study of truth theories, for example. In this paper, we review such an appearance of co-inductive sentences which causes famous paradoxes, the modest liar paradox [Rs93][HPS00], McGee's paradox [Mc85] and Yablo's paradox [Yb93] (they imply the ω-inconsistency) for instance.

First let us explain what truth theories are. They are logical theories to formalize the notion of truth by using *Tarskian T-schema*:

$$\varphi \equiv \mathbf{Tr}(\lceil \varphi \rceil)$$

for any formula φ where $\lceil \varphi \rceil$ is a name (or Godel code) of φ, $\mathbf{Tr}(x)$ is a predicate whose domain is the set of names of formulae and $\equiv$ is an equivalence relation [T33]. Implicitly to say, T-schema is of the form "Snow is white" is true if and only if snow is white. And a logical theory whose language contains $\mathbf{Tr}(x)$ and whose axiom contains some fragment of T-schema together with some machinery, such as arithmetic, to name its sentences is called a *truth theory*.

It is well known that the full form of T-schema implies a contradiction in truth theories (whose arithmetic is enough strong to do diagonalization argument) in classical logic even though it is seemingly-harmless. It is because we can define the liar sentence: "*This sentence is false*", $\mathbf{\Lambda} \equiv \neg\mathbf{Tr}(\lceil \mathbf{\Lambda} \rceil)$. There are two ways out: the classical approach and the non-classical approach. The former is to sustain classical logic and to abandon full T-schema not to prove the T-schema for the the liar sentence, and the latter is the other way round, to sustain full T-schema and to abandon classical logic. They are approximations of *the*

T. Onoda, D. Bekki, and E. McCready (Eds.): JSAI-isAI 2010, LNAI 6797, pp. 90–103, 2011.
© Springer-Verlag Berlin Heidelberg 2011

ideal classical truth theory with full T-schema by consistent weakened theories. Therefore, the theory closer to the ideal theory is better: it is desired that the restriction to T-schema is not so strict in the classical approach, and the base logic is desired to be close to classical logic in non-classical logic case. And, it is often desired that the notion of truth should be as *transparent,* i.e. no theoretical restriction on T-schema (as "T-schema cannot be applied to the liar sentence") is made, as possible [BG08].

However it turns out that both classical and non-classical truth theories are not as transparent as we hoped: McGee's paradox shows the classical theory Γ is *ω-inconsistent,* i.e. any its model contains non-standard natural numbers, and the modest liar paradox shows that so is the fuzzy truth theory $\mathbf{PA\Lt Tr_2}$. Since the base arithmetic (as $\mathbf{Q}$ or $\mathbf{PA}$) has a standard model, adding a truth predicate "entails a drastic deviation from the intended ontology of the theory" [L01]. Therefore, there are some objections for ω-inconsistent truth theories. For example, McGee rejected the truth theory Γ because of its ω-inconsistency, and Field [F08] concluded that $\mathbf{PA\Lt Tr_2}$ is not enough conservative because of ω-inconsistency.

It is not an aim of this paper to discuss whether non-transparent truth theories should be abandoned. Rather, we discuss what aspect of the notion of truth causes such ω-inconsistency. Roughly speaking, it is caused by the fact that truth predicate enables to define formulae *co-inductively.* Such co-induction defines the paradoxical formulae which look like the result of infinitely operations on formulae, as λ which is the limit of $\neg\lambda$, $\lambda \to \neg\lambda$, $\lambda \to \lambda \to \neg\lambda$, $\cdots$, in the modest liar paradox. It is possible because we can define operations over Godel codes of formulae recursively, and they are interpreted as real operations on formulae by the truth predicate in truth theories.

The ideal truth theory with full T-schema involves the bare circularity, hence it implies a contradiction in classical logic. By weakening such theories not to imply a contradiction, we find the possibility of co-induction behind closed doors of the liar paradox. It is focused because they imply the ω-inconsistency, but this fact should not be considered as a fault but be investigated positively and seriously.

2   Preliminaries

In this section, we introduce the background of this paper: axiomatic truth theories. A key problem on axiomatic theories of truth is how to overcome the liar paradox, and it is well-known that there are two ways out: classical approach and non-classical approach. We explain classical truth theories in section 2.1, and non-classical truth theories in section 2.2.

2.1   Truth Theories within Classical Logic

In this section, we introduce the first way out. In this approach, the priority of sustaining classical logic is higher than that of sustaining full T-schema. The basic strategy to exclude the inconsistency is to restrict T-schema not to imply a contradiction. For example, in McGee's truth theory Γ, the right-to-left direction of T-schema is not generally allowed [Mc85]:

$$\mathbf{Tr}(\lceil \varphi \rceil) \not\rightarrow \varphi \qquad \cdots (*)$$

Such the restriction prevents that the theory implies T-schema for the liar sentence as a theorem[1]. More precisely, let us give a definition.

Definition 1 (McGee's truth theory Γ). *McGee's truth theory Γ [Mc85] consists of the following axioms:*

- *Γ contains Robinson's arithmetic **Q**,*
- *Γ is closed first order consequence,*
- *Γ contains $\mathbf{Tr}(\lceil \varphi \rceil)$ if Γ contains φ (i.e. $\varphi \rightarrow \mathbf{Tr}(\lceil \varphi \rceil) \in \Gamma$ for any $\varphi \in \Gamma$),*
- *Γ contains all instances of the following schemata:*
  - **K**: $\mathbf{Tr}(\lceil \varphi \rightarrow \psi \rceil) \rightarrow (\mathbf{Tr}(\lceil \varphi \rceil) \rightarrow \mathbf{Tr}(\lceil \varphi \rceil))$,
  - **D**: $\mathbf{Tr}(\lceil \neg\varphi \rceil) \rightarrow \neg\mathbf{Tr}(\lceil \varphi \rceil)$,
  - **Barcan**: $\forall x(\mathbf{Tr}(sub(\lceil y \rceil, \lceil \varphi \rceil, nam(x))) \rightarrow \mathbf{Tr}(\lceil \forall y\varphi \rceil))$.

  where, for any natural number n, $nam(n)$ denotes the numeral $\bar{n}$ in any standard model.

We note that Γ is a subsystem of Halbach's truth theory **CT** [Hl05] and Friedman-Sheard's truth theory **FS** [FS87].

2.2   Truth Theories with the Full T-Schema within a Fuzzy Logic

It is well-known that full T-schema does not imply a contradiction without the contraction rule in classical logic. In this section, we introduce a truth theory **PAŁTr₂** in Łukasiewicz infinite-valued logic $\forall$Ł with full T-schema as an example of non classical truth theories[2].

We work within $\forall$Ł, Łukasiewicz infinite-valued predicate logic with its standard semantics. It is known that $\forall$Ł is not recursively axiomatizable[3], therefore, for simplicity, we introduce $\forall$Ł by defining its models. Given $\mathbf{M} = \langle M, (r_P)_{P\,\mathrm{predicate}}, (m_c)_{c\,\mathrm{constant}} \rangle$ where $M \neq \emptyset$, $m_c \in M$, $r_P : M^n \rightarrow [0,1]$ (if P is n-ary relation) and a valuation v i.e. v : (object variables) $\rightarrow M$, let $\|\varphi\|_{M,v}$ be the truth value of φ in M, v iff

---

[1] From the philosophical viewpoint, to restrict T-schema as $(*)$ seems to be problematic because it is too ad hoc. There are many arguments to justify such the restriction, but none of them is successful [F08].

[2] We note that there are many non-classical logics (e.g. para-consistent logics [B08]) in which full T-schema does not imply a contradiction. Among them, it is known that $\forall$Ł is one of the strongest logics in which full T-schema does not imply a contradiction: "strongest" is used in the sense that full T-schema implies a contradiction in any Łukasiewicz finite valued logic. Therefore studying **PAŁTr₂** gives us an approximation of a consistent ideal classical truth theory with full T-schema, and this is a reason why we focus on **PAŁTr₂**.

[3] M. Ragaz showed that it is Π_2-complete. For details about fuzzy logics, see [CH10].

- $\|P(x,\cdots,c\cdots)\|_{M,v} = r_P(v(x),\cdots,m_c,\cdots)$,
- $\|A \to B\|_{M,v} = \|A\|_{M,v} \Rightarrow \|B\|_{M,v}$ and $\|A\&B\|_{M,v} = \|A\|_{M,v} * \|B\|_{M,v}$,
- $\|(\forall x)\varphi\|_{M,v} = \inf\{\|\varphi\|_{M,v'} : v'(y) = v(y)$ for all variable y except possibly $x\}$,

where $x \Rightarrow y = \min(1, 1 - x + y)$ and $x * y = \max(0, x + y - 1)$. Other connectives are defined by using $\to$ and constant $\bar{0}$ (for example $\|\neg A\|_{M,v} = \|A\|_{M,v} \Rightarrow 0$ and $\|A \wedge B\|_{M,v} = \|\neg(A \to \neg(A \to B))\|_{M,v}$, $(\exists x)\varphi(x)$ by $\neg(\forall x)\neg\varphi(x))$.

Set $\|\varphi\|_M = \inf\{\|\varphi\|_{M,v} : v$ is a valuation on $\mathbf{M}\}$. We note that $\|(\forall x)\varphi(x)\|_M = \inf\{\|\varphi(a)\|_M : a \in M\}$ holds for any closed formula $(\forall x)\varphi(x)$.

Definition 2. *For T a theory within $\forall L$, $\mathbf{M} = \langle M, (r_P)_{P\ predicate}, (m_c)_{c\ constant}\rangle$ is a model of T (or a natural Tarskian semantics for T) if $\|\varphi\|_M = 1$ for any axiom $\varphi \in T$.*

We call φ is valid in T when φ has truth value 1 in any model of T.

Next we introduce a typical truth theory in a fuzzy logic:

Definition 3. PAŁTr$_2$ *[HPS00] is a truth theory in $\forall \mathbf{L}$*

- *whose axioms are all axioms of classical* **PA**,
- *the induction scheme for formulae possibly containing* **Tr**,
- *full T-schema: for any formula φ (which may include* **Tr***), $\varphi \equiv \mathbf{Tr}(\lceil\varphi\rceil)$ where $\lceil\varphi\rceil$ is the Gödel code of φ.*

As we mentioned, full T-schema is not contradictory in **PAŁTr$_2$** [HPS00]. For example, the liar sentence Λ does not imply a contradiction in $\forall \mathbf{L}$: $\|\Lambda\| = 0.5$.

3 Yablo-Like Paradoxes

In this section, we introduce three paradoxes, the modest liar paradox, McGee's paradox, and Yablo's paradox which imply ω-inconsistency. Their construction of the paradoxical sentence are very similar since they use the same machinery. Here, we only introduce how these paradoxes are implied in truth theories. In section 3.1, we explain the modest liar paradox and ω-inconsistency proof of **PAŁTr$_2$**. Similar result, McGee's paradox which shows the ω-inconsistency of Γ, is in section 3.2. Yablo's paradox, which is closely related to the former paradoxes with respect to the non-standardness, is introduced in section 3.3.

3.1 The Modest Liar Paradox

As we explained, non classical truth theories are expected to be transparent, however the notion of truth in **PAŁTr$_2$** is not as transparent as we hoped.

Theorem 1. PAŁTr$_2$ *is ω-inconsistent[4] [Rs93][HPS00].*

---

[4] The formal definition of the ω-inconsistency is as follows: there is a formula φ such that $\varphi(n)$ is proved for any numeral $n \in \mathbb{N}$ but $\exists x \neg\varphi(x)$ is also proved. Therefore, it involves that some of non-standard numbers can be distinguished from standard numbers by a definable predicate.

Proof. Let's see **PAŁTr₂** is ω-inconsistent by using so-called *the modest liar paradox*. To show that, let us introduce a new connective $\uparrow$ which is recursively definable in **PAŁTr₂**:

Definition 4. $-\ 0 \uparrow \varphi \equiv \varphi,$
- $(n+1) \uparrow \varphi \equiv \neg\varphi \to (n \uparrow \varphi),$

Precisely to say, $\uparrow$ is recursively defined (as arithmetical function f) as follows:

(a) $f_0(0, x) = x,$
(b) $f_0(n+1, x) = \dot{\neg}x \dot{\to} f_0(n, x)^5.$
(c) $n \uparrow A$ is just an abbreviation of $\mathbf{Tr}(f_0(n, \lceil A \rceil)).$

We note that the following lemma is trivial:

Lemma 1. $\|n \uparrow \varphi\| = \min\{(n+1) \times \|\varphi\|, 1\}$ *for any standard* n.

By using $\uparrow$, we can define *the modest liar sentence*: I am at least a little false [CH10]. Formally it is defined by using the diagonalization lemma as follows:

$$\lambda \equiv \exists x \mathbf{Tr}(\lceil x \uparrow \neg\lambda \rceil)$$

Next let us consider the truth value of λ. If $\|\lambda\| < 1$, then there is some m such that $\|\mathbf{Tr}(\lceil m \uparrow \neg\lambda \rceil)\| = 1$ by lemma 1; so $\|\lambda\| = 1$, contradiction. Therefore $\|\lambda\| = 1$. This means that **PAŁTr₂** is ω-inconsistent. For, $\|\exists x \mathbf{Tr}(\lceil x \uparrow \neg\lambda \rceil)\| = 1$ though $\|\mathbf{Tr}(\lceil n \uparrow \neg\lambda \rceil)\| = 0$ for any standard natural number n.   □

The ω-inconsistency involves the non-standardness: there is some d such that $\mathbf{Tr}(\lceil d \uparrow \neg\lambda \rceil) \neq 0$ in the proof of ω-inconsistency. This means that d must be a *non-standard natural number*, e.g. there is no numeral $\bar{n}$ such that $\bar{n}^{\mathrm{M}} = d$. Therefore **Form**, which is a set of Godel codes of formulae of **PAŁTr₂**, contains a non-standard member because $\lceil d \uparrow \neg\lambda \rceil$ is in **Form**.

3.2   McGee's Paradox

The modest liar paradox is often said to be similar to the proof of ω-inconsistency of Γ [Mc85]. Here we omit the proof: for more details, see [Mc85] and [L01]. We only introduce how the paradoxical sentence, e.g. λ in the modest liar paradox, is constructed. To show that, let us introduce a new connective $\mathbf{T}^n$ which is recursively defined as follows:

Definition 5. $-\ \mathbf{T}^0\varphi \equiv \varphi,$
- $\mathbf{T}^{n+1}\varphi \equiv \mathbf{Tr}(\lceil \dot{\mathbf{T}}^n(\lceil \varphi \rceil) \rceil)^6.$

Precisely to say, it is defined $\mathbf{T}^x\varphi \equiv \mathbf{Tr}(f(x, \lceil \varphi \rceil))$ where

$$f(n, \lceil \varphi \rceil) = \lceil \underbrace{\mathbf{Tr}(\lceil \cdots \mathbf{Tr}(\lceil \varphi \rceil) \cdots)}_{n \text{ times}} \rceil$$

Then the sentence is defined by using the diagonalization lemma as follows:

$$\sigma \equiv \neg\forall x \mathbf{T}^x \sigma$$

---

[5] $\dot{\to}$ is an arithmetical function such that $\lceil A \rceil \dot{\to} \lceil B \rceil = \lceil A \to B \rceil$. Similarly, for any connective $\circ$, $\dot{\circ}$ is an arithmetical function such that $\lceil A \rceil \dot{\circ} \lceil B \rceil = \lceil A \circ B \rceil$.

[6] As in the previous footnote, $\dot{\mathbf{T}}^n$ is an such that $\dot{\mathbf{T}}^n \lceil A \rceil = \lceil \mathbf{T}^n A \rceil$.

3.3 Yablo's Paradox

Leitgeb pointed out that the previous McGee's paradox is very similar to Yablo's paradox [L01].

Definition 6 (Yablo's sequence). $\langle \mathbf{Y}(n) : n \in \omega \rangle$ *is an Yablo sequence if*

- $\mathbf{Y}(i)$ *says "for all $j > i$, $\mathbf{Y}(j)$ is false",*
- $\mathbf{Y}(i) \equiv \forall x > i \neg \mathbf{Tr}(\lceil \mathbf{Y}(x) \rceil)$.

We note that $\mathbf{Y}(i) \equiv \neg \mathbf{Tr}(\lceil \mathbf{Y}(i+1) \rceil) \wedge \mathbf{Y}(i+2)$ holds for any $i \in \omega$. Technically speaking, we can construct a Yablo sequence in truth theories with (nearly) full T-schema in a quite complicated way [Co06]:

- define the satisfaction predicate $\mathbf{Sat}(\lceil \varphi(x) \rceil, z) \equiv \varphi(z)$,
- define a 2-ary predicate $P(x, y) \equiv \forall z [z > x \rightarrow \neg \mathbf{Sat}(y, z)]$,
- define a unary predicate $\mathbf{Y}(x)$ by taking a diagonalization of $P(x, y)$ with respect to y: $\mathbf{Y}(x) \equiv P(x, \lceil \mathbf{Y}(x) \rceil)$.

We note that the diagonalization lemma is used to define $\mathbf{Y}(x)$ [P97].

Theorem 2. *Yablo's sequence is not definable in any consistent and ω-consistent truth theory in classical logic.*

Proof. Suppose it is definable. If $\mathbf{Y}(0)$ is true, then for all $j > 0$, $\mathbf{Y}(j)$ is false unless the theory is ω-inconsistent, so see the next case. If $\mathbf{Y}(0)$ is false, there is some $\mathbf{Y}(j)$ ($j > 0$) such that $\mathbf{Y}(j)$ is true. Therefore all $\mathbf{Y}(k)$'s ($k > j$) are false. However, since $\mathbf{Y}(j+1)$ is false, there is $\mathbf{Y}(n)$ ($n > j+1$) such that $\mathbf{Y}(n)$ is true; this contradicts that $\mathbf{Y}(k)$'s ($k > j$) are false. Therefore, that implies a contradiction[7]. □

We note that, in many consistent truth theories with full (or nearly full) T-schema, all $\mathbf{Y}(j)$'s are definable and not contradictory. For example, in $\mathbf{PALTr_2}$, the truth value of any Yablo sentence is 0.5. But this involves that the truth theory is ω-inconsistent[8].

4 Co-induction

In this section, we investigate the common machinery which enables to define the paradoxical sentences. The keyword is *co-induction* which enables to define *potentially infinite objects*. It is not generally allowed in arithmetics such

---

[7] Any sentence $\mathbf{Y}(i)$ does not refer to itself, but refer to $\mathbf{Y}(i+1), \mathbf{Y}(i+2), \cdots$. Therefore Yablo himself insisted that this paradox does not use any self-referential or circular machinery [Yb93]. On the other hand the diagonalization lemma (self-referential!) plays a key role to construct the Yablo sentence, therefore Priest objected Yablo's proposition [P97]. This remains a controversial topic in some quarters.

[8] Any finite collection of Yablo sentences, $\{S_{i_\nu} : \nu < n\}$ for some n, cannot imply a contradiction in case any S_i does not contain quantifiers[Hd95]. Leitgeb proved the ω-inconsistency in a different formulation[L01].

as **PA**, but its variants are possible in many truth theories with the help of the truth predicate. It also set off the ω-inconsistency. In section 4.1, we explain two notions, co-induction and *productivity*. We give detailed analysis of three paradoxes, in particular how the paradoxical sentences are constructed, in terms of co-induction in section 4.2. We also discuss what makes possible to define formulae co-inductively and how we can represent co-inductive formulae in **PAŁTr$_2$**.

4.1 Co-induction and Productivity

We introduce co-induction together with productivity here. As for the notation, we use the algebraic notation such as that of [Rt00].

First let us introduce a typical example of an inductive definition to compare with the co-inductive definition.

Example 1. Let A be any set. Then "the list of A" is of the type $\langle A^{<\omega}, \gamma :$ $(1 + (A \times A^{<\omega})) \to A^{<\omega} \rangle$ such that

- (the initial step of the construction) 1 consists of the empty list $\langle \rangle$,
- (the successor step) for any $a_0 \in A$ and $\langle a_1, \cdots, a_n \rangle \in A^{<\omega}$,

$$\gamma(a_0, \langle a_1, \cdots, a_n \rangle) = \langle a_0, a_1, \cdots, a_n \rangle \in A^{<\omega}$$

Next we introduce co-inductive definition. The basic idea behind co-induction is called the *productivity* (γ represents the productivity in example 2):

even though the value is conceptually infinite, it should always be possible to compute the next unit of information in finite time [D10].

Co-induction is a way to construct *potentially* infinite objects by delaying to construct the main body of the object forever.

Definition 7. *For any set A, a co-inductive type over A is of the type $\langle A^{\infty}, \gamma :$ $A^{\infty} \to (A \times A^{\infty}) \rangle$. The co-induction principle over A guarantees the existence of co-inductive type over A.*

A typical example of co-inductive definitions is as follows.

Example 2. For any set A, "*streams* of A" is of the type $\langle A^{\infty}, \gamma : A^{\infty} \to (A \times A^{\infty}) \rangle$. Intuitively speaking, this definition describes that, for any $\langle a_0, a_1, \cdots \rangle \in A^{\infty}$, γ takes the first element of the infinite stream

$$\gamma(\langle a_0, a_1, \cdots \rangle) = (a_0, \langle a_1, \cdots \rangle) \in (A \times A^{\infty})$$

From now on, we write $\mathbf{head}(\langle a_0, a_1, \cdots \rangle) = a_0$ and $\mathbf{tail}(\langle a_0, a_1, \cdots \rangle) = \langle a_1, \cdots \rangle$.

The type which is defined as A^{∞} is called a *co-inductive type*[9]. The construction, which only consists of the successor steps, does not contain the initial step; one only constructs the first element, a_0, of the infinite stream $\langle a_1, a_2, \cdots \rangle$, and the construction of the main body of the stream is *delayed one step after*: such the postponement can be continued forever.

---

[9] We note that A^{∞} is isomorphic to *the greatest fixed point* $\nu X.A \times X$ (i.e. $A^{\infty} \simeq A \times A \times \cdots$), and the existence of such co-inductive types needs a very strong type-existence principle.

4.2   Paradoxes of Co-induction

Form now on, we work in **PAŁTr**$_2$, and we investigate the machinery which enables to construct the paradoxical sentences. We give detailed analysis of three paradoxes, in particular how the paradoxical sentences are constructed, in terms of co-induction, what makes possible to define formulae co-inductively and how we can represent co-inductive formulae in **PAŁTr**$_2$ which only has induction and the truth predicate in this section.

Our strategy is, first we define virtual co-inductive languages in which certain sentences can be defined co-inductively. Second, we really want to construct an interpretation of that as **Form**, but it is impossible because **Form** is constructed not purely co-inductively. Therefore, we introduce a co-inductive language **Form**$^\infty$ whose domain is "co-inductive formulae" **Form**$^\infty$ in meta-theory, and we interpret co-inductive sentences to some member of **Form**$^\infty$. Third, we see that such co-inductive objects can be interpreted as the paradoxical sentences, which are defined by the fixed point argument and by using $\mathbf{Tr}(x)$, by thinking the intuitive meaning. In this sense, we can say co-induction-like construction is available in the truth theories. We note that, such co-inductively-defined sentences involves non-standardness as in the case of λ.

The definition of $\mathcal{F}^\infty$ is as follows:

Definition 8.   – **Form** *is a set of natural numbers which consists of Godel codes of formulae in* **PAŁTr**$_2$ *and some natural number which represents* **T**,
   – $\mathcal{F}^\infty = \langle \mathbf{Form}^\infty, \gamma_0, \eta_0, \eta_1, \eta_2, \eta_3, \eta_4 \rangle$ *where* $\gamma_0, \eta_0, \eta_1, \eta_2, \eta_3, \eta_4 : \mathbf{Form}^\infty \to (\mathbf{Form} \times \mathbf{Form}^\infty)$, *is a co-inductive language whose domain is* **Form**.

For the simplicity, we write "A is $a \Rightarrow B$" if $\eta_0(A) = (a, B)$. Similarly, we write "A is $a \bigwedge B$" if $\eta_1(A) = (a, B)$, "A is $a \bigvee B$" if $\eta_2(A) = (a, B)$, "A is $\sim B$" if $\eta_3(A) = (\lceil \bot \rceil, B)$ and "A is **T** B" if $\eta_4(A) = (\mathbf{T}, B)$.

We remark that we can define the identity relation over co-inductive formulae by using *bi-simulation* [10] in $\mathcal{F}^\infty$.

---

[10] Let us define an equation relation over co-inductive objects, those of $\mathcal{A}_0$ in the modest liar paradox for example, by using the *bi-simulation*.

Definition 9. $\sim$ *is an equality relation over* $\mathcal{A}_0$ *of* $\mathcal{A}_0$ *defined by: for any* $\Delta, \Xi \in \mathcal{A}_0$,

$$\Delta \sim \Xi \text{ iff } \mathbf{head}(\Delta) \equiv \mathbf{head}(\Xi) \wedge \mathbf{tail}(\Delta) \sim \mathbf{tail}(\Xi)$$

Sometimes the identity defined by the bi-simulation behaves strangely. For example, let $\Delta \in \mathcal{A}_0^\infty$ be such that $\mathbf{head}(\Delta) = \neg\lambda$ and $\mathbf{tail}(\Delta) = \Lambda$. Then, it is easy to see that $\Delta \sim \Lambda$ where Λ appears after definition 11. Implicitly to say, $(\neg\lambda, \Lambda)$ is equal to Λ in the sense of the bi-simulation.

On the other hand, we have not known any problem when we assume $\mathbf{Tr}(\lceil \delta \to \xi \rceil)$ is equivalent to $\mathbf{Tr}(\lceil \xi \rceil)$ when $(\delta, \Xi) \sim \Xi$ and Ξ's intuitive meaning is ξ: the proof of theorem 3 cannot be directly applied to prove a contradiction from $\mathbf{Tr}(\lceil \mathbf{Tr}(x \dot{\to} y) \rceil) \equiv \mathbf{Tr}(\lceil \mathbf{Tr}(x) \to \mathbf{Tr}(y) \rceil)$. Therefore, bi-simulation between co-inductive objects is *seemingly* able to be interpreted as the equivalence relation between formulae of the form $\mathbf{Tr}(\lceil \varphi \rceil)$ in this case.

The modest liar paradox. Let us remember that the modest liar sentence is

$$\lambda \equiv \exists x \mathbf{Tr}(\lceil f_0(x, \lceil \neg \lambda \rceil) \rceil)$$

where f_0 is a recursive function such that $f_0(n+1, \lceil A \rceil) = \lceil \neg A \to f_0(n, \lceil A \rceil) \rceil$. Then the intuitive meaning of λ is $\lambda \to (\lambda \to (\cdots))$ which is an infinite stream.

Let us define the co-inductive language $\mathcal{A}_0$ as follows:

Definition 10. $\mathcal{A}_0 = \langle A_0^\infty, \gamma_0 : A_0^\infty \to (A_0 \times A_0^\infty) \rangle$ *is a co-inductive language whose domain A_0 is* $\{\neg \lambda\}$.

Intuitively speaking, this definition describes that γ_0 takes the first element of the infinite stream $\gamma(\langle \neg \lambda, \neg \lambda, \cdots \rangle) = (\neg \lambda, \langle \neg \lambda, \cdots \rangle) \in (A_0 \times A_0^\infty)$. Next let us think about the productivity γ_0. We define a mapping which maps the productivity over $\mathcal{A}_0$ to $\mathbf{Form}^\infty$.

Definition 11. $\pi_0 : A_0^\infty \to \mathbf{Form}^\infty$ *is defined by*

- $\pi_0(\alpha) = \lceil \neg \alpha \rceil$ *for any $\alpha \in A_0$,*
- $\pi_0(\Gamma) = \pi_0(\mathbf{head}(\Gamma)) \Rightarrow \pi_0(\mathbf{tail}(\Gamma))$.

It is easy to see that π_0 corresponds to the operation by f_0. Let Λ be a co-inductively defined object whose intuitive meaning is $(\neg \lambda, \neg \lambda, \neg \lambda, \cdots)$. Here Λ generates (or unfolds) an infinite stream which is equal to the intuitive meaning of λ, therefore we may identify Λ to λ.

McGee's paradox. Similarly, let us define the co-inductive language $\mathcal{A}_1$ as follows:

Definition 12. $\mathcal{A}_1 = \langle A_1^\infty, \gamma_1 : A_1^\infty \to (A_1 \times A_1^\infty) \rangle$ *is a co-inductive language whose domain A_1 is* $\{\mathbf{T}, \mathbf{N}\}$.

The paradoxical sentence is

$$\sigma \equiv \neg \forall x \mathbf{Tr}(f_1(x, \lceil \sigma \rceil))$$

where $f_1(n, \lceil \sigma \rceil) = \underbrace{\lceil \mathbf{Tr}(\lceil \cdots \mathbf{Tr}(\lceil \sigma \rceil) \cdots) \rceil}_{n \text{ times}}$. Then the intuitive meaning of σ is $\mathbf{Tr}(\lceil \mathbf{Tr}(\lceil \cdots \rceil) \rceil)$ which is an infinite stream. Let us define a stream Σ whose intuitive meaning is $(\mathbf{N}, \mathbf{T}, \mathbf{T}, \cdots)$. By the similar argument to the modest liar case, we may identify Σ to σ.

Yablo's paradox. Similarly, let us define a co-inductive language $\mathcal{A}_2$ as follows:

Definition 13. $\mathcal{A}_2 = \langle A_2^\infty, \gamma_2 : A_2^\infty \to (A_2 \times A_2^\infty) \rangle$ *is a co-inductive language whose domain A_2 is* $\{\mathbf{Y}(1), \mathbf{Y}(2), \cdots\}$.

This time the domain is a countable set (rather to say, it is a range of some recursive functions). The paradoxical sentence $\mathbf{Y}(0)$ is

$$\forall z[z > 0 \to \neg \mathbf{Sat}(\lceil \mathbf{Y}(x) \rceil, z)]$$

(roughly speaking it is $(\forall z)\neg\mathbf{Tr}(\lceil\mathbf{Y}(z)\rceil)$). The intuitive meaning of $\mathbf{Y}(0)$ is $\neg\mathbf{Tr}(\lceil\mathbf{Y}(1)\rceil) \wedge \neg\mathbf{Tr}(\lceil\mathbf{Y}(2)\rceil) \wedge \neg\mathbf{Tr}(\lceil\mathbf{Y}(3)\rceil) \wedge \cdots$.

Let us define a stream Δ whose intuitive meaning is $(\mathbf{Y}(1), \mathbf{Y}(2), \mathbf{Y}(3), \cdots)$. By the similar argument to the modest liar case, we can define the mapping π_2 by $\pi_2((\mathbf{Y}(1), \mathbf{Y}(2), \mathbf{Y}(3), \cdots)) = \lceil\neg\mathbf{Y}(1)\rceil \wedge \pi_2((\mathbf{Y}(2), \mathbf{Y}(3), \cdots))$ (corresponding to the productivity). Therefore we may identify Δ to $\mathbf{Y}(0)$.

We note that, this construction suggests that a very general form of co-inductive construction, whose domain is a recursively enumerable countable set actually, can be done in $\mathbf{PA\mathL Tr}_2$.

4.3   The Machinery and Non-standardness

Now we focus on what makes possible to define formulae co-inductively[11].

Let us remember co-inductive definitions are not generally possible in **PA**. Therefore the truth predicate plays a key role to define formulae co-inductively (this means that it expands definability of operations of formulae): **Tr** interprets *arithmetical operations on Godel codes* (as f_0) as actual *operations on formulae* (as $\uparrow$, $\mathbf{T}^x$). Because of the existence of full T-schema, we can identify Godel codes as formulae themselves. So we can apparently define recursive operations on formulae by defining a recursive function. In this way, the recursive operations allow the co-inductive definition of formulae (with some exception on non-standardness: see the next section).

We note that there might be many co-inductively defined formulae which cannot be defined in $\mathbf{PA\mathL Tr}_2$, because the cardinality of $\mathbf{Form}^\infty$ is greater than that of $\mathbf{Form}$ in many case[12]. However many of members of $\mathbf{Form}^\infty$ can be represented by a some member of $\mathbf{Form}$.

Example 3. Let $\langle\varphi_i : i \in \omega\rangle$ be a member of $\mathbf{Form}^\infty$ such that it is a recursive enumeration, i.e. there is a recursive function g such that $g(i) = \lceil\varphi_i\rceil$. Then, the co-inductive formulae $\bigwedge_{i\in\omega}\varphi_i \in \mathbf{Form}^\infty$ is represented by $\forall x\mathbf{Tr}(g(x))$.

As for non-standardness, roughly speaking, co-induction involves it (they were closely related in origin[Ml88]): any model of $\mathbf{PA\mathL Tr}_2$ instantiates a non-standard natural number d s.t.

$$\mathbf{Tr}(\lceil[\underbrace{(\neg\lambda \to (\neg\lambda \to (\neg\lambda \to \cdots)))}_{d\text{-many }\neg\lambda\text{'s}}]\rceil)$$

This is a model theoretic representation of *infinite streams*; since we have co-inductive formulae, we also have their correspondences in the model.

---

[11] Here, we concentrate on the definability of recursive operation, but the diagonalization lemma also plays very important role.

[12] For example, if we define $\mathbf{Form}^\infty$ in the meta-theory (as **ZFC**), then they can be identified to the infinite sequences of natural numbers, therefore $\mathbf{Form}^\infty$ is an uncountable set though $\mathbf{Form}$ is countable if we work in a countable model of $\mathbf{PA\mathL Tr}_2$. Contrary, $\mathbf{Form}^\infty$ is countable if it is the set of all recursively definable sequences in $\mathbf{PA\mathL Tr}_2$ (see example 3), and then almost all non-standard natural numbers might be nothing to do with co-inductive definition in an uncountable model of $\mathbf{PA\mathL Tr}_2$.

5   Conflict to Induction

In this section, we explain another unexpected consequence[13], namely *the failure of the formalized commutation scheme,* and discuss the conflict between them. We explain that failure in section 5.1, and we interpret it in terms of *the mixture of induction and co-induction* together with *guarded co-recursion* in section 5.2.

5.1   Another Unexpected Result

First let us introduce the failure of the formalized commutation scheme [HPS00].

Definition 14. *The formalized commutation scheme is as follows*[14]:

$$\forall x, y(\mathbf{Form}(x)\&\mathbf{Form}(y) \rightarrow [\mathbf{Tr}(x \dot{\rightarrow} y) \equiv (\mathbf{Tr}(x) \rightarrow \mathbf{Tr}(y))])$$

Theorem 3. *The theory* **PAŁTr**$_3$ *extending* **PAŁTr**$_2$ *by the formalized commutation scheme is contradictory.*

For the proof, see [HPS00]: let us introduce its sketch. Recall that $\lambda \equiv \exists x \mathbf{Tr}(\ulcorner x \uparrow \neg\lambda \urcorner)$ where $(n + 1) \uparrow A$ is $\neg A \rightarrow (n \uparrow A)$. Since λ is provable, $\neg \mathbf{Tr}(\ulcorner 0 \uparrow \neg\lambda \urcorner)$ is of truth value 1. And, if, $\|\neg\mathbf{Tr}(\ulcorner n \uparrow \neg\lambda \urcorner)\| = 1$, then λ and the formalized commutativity imply $\neg\mathbf{Tr}(\ulcorner (n + 1) \uparrow \neg\lambda \urcorner)$. Therefore, induction proves $\|\forall x \neg\mathbf{Tr}(\ulcorner x \uparrow \neg\lambda \urcorner)\| = 1$, i.e. $\|\neg\lambda\| = 1$.   □

We note that T-schema shows that the following axiom schema, *the axiom schema of commutativity of truth,*

$$\mathbf{Tr}(\ulcorner \varphi \rightarrow \psi \urcorner) \equiv (\mathbf{Tr}(\ulcorner \varphi \urcorner) \rightarrow \mathbf{Tr}(\ulcorner \psi \urcorner))$$

is provable in **PAŁTr**$_2$ for each pair of formulae φ, ψ of **PAŁTr**$_2$ ($\ulcorner \varphi \urcorner, \ulcorner \psi \urcorner$ are standard elements of **Form**). This seems to suggest that, the paradox is not about *real* connectives such as $\rightarrow$, rather *about recursive definitions* of $\uparrow$: the commutativity holds for formulae which are not defined by recursive definition[15].

---

[13] This result seems to cause a feeling of anxiety, since the commutativity has been regarded as one of the desired properties of **Tr**. Therefore Field rejected **PAŁTr**$_2$ because of this unprovability of the formal commutativity [F08].

[14] where **Form**(x) is a predicate which says that $x \in \mathbf{Form}$.

[15] In other words, the failure of the formalized commutation scheme is not enough to reject **PAŁTr**$_2$ on the ground that **Tr** does not satisfy the formal commutativity, therefore the failure of the formalized commutativity is not a serious problem on truth conceptions. We note that this argument is suggested by Hajek and this can be interpreted as being along the lines of Halbach [Hl05]. This is against the suggestion of Field [F08].

5.2   The Mixture of Induction and Co-induction

In this section, we interpret theorem 3 from the viewpoint of the mixture of induction and co-induction together with *guarded co-recursion*.

First, we give a rough picture of theorem 3. The key idea is a conflict between induction and co-induction. As a matter of course, there is *no* conflict between induction principle in *object level* and co-inductive definition in *object level* in non-standard arithmetic. That is due to the fact that Godel codes of potentially infinite objects are related to non-standard natural numbers which are infinite objects from the viewpoint of meta-theory, but they are finite object from the viewpoint of object theory. However, in the case of theorem 3, there is no way-out. It is because, roughly speaking, inductive definition of formulae by using *real* connectives is done in *meta-level*: if A, B are formulae, then $A \to B$ is a formula. On the other hand, there are co-inductively defined formulae, which are of the form $\mathbf{Tr}(\cdots)$, in *object theory*. They, e.g. $\neg\lambda \to \neg\lambda \to \cdots$, are infinite objects in the sense of meta-theory, however the inductive definition of formulae in meta-theory requires they should be finite object in the sense of meta-theory. Therefore the correspondence between inductively defined formulae and co-inductively formulae should not be perfect.

However, explicitly to say, the situation is more complicated. It is because, formulae of $\mathbf{PALTr}_2$ are not purely inductively defined: if $\mathbf{Tr}(d)$ is co-inductively defined formula, then $\mathbf{Tr}(d) \to \mathbf{Tr}(d)$ is inductively defined in meta-level. Therefore, the definition of formulae is an example of the mixture of inductive and co-inductive definition. Such mixture sometimes appears in the study of co-induction: for example, $\langle B^\infty, \beta : B^\infty \to (1 + (B \times B^\infty)) \rangle$ represents the finite and infinite words over B.

We should be careful when we talk about the mixture: it is well-known that an inadvertent and unrestricted form of co-induction is contradictory to induction in many case [Cq93] [D10]. Let us give an example of Martin-Lof's Intuitionistic Type Theory (MLITT) case. By using co-induction, we can define functions *whose computation does not terminate* in finite steps in the sense of meta-theory. However, MLITT's basic principle, which is based on induction, is that "computations of any definable functions must terminates eventually": so this contradicts to the above. Therefore, in the language of Agda[16] which is an extension of MLITT, only a restricted form of co-induction, *guarded co-recursion*, are allowed in an extension: recursive definition over co-inductive objects are only allowed in case it is *guarded*, i.e. it is inside a special constructor $\sharp$. For example, roughly speaking, co-recursive definition of $\mathbf{map} : (A \to B) \to A^\infty \to B^\infty$ is defined as

$$\mathbf{map}\, f\, \langle x, x_0, \cdots \rangle = \langle f(x) \rangle \frown (\sharp\, \mathbf{map}\, f\, \langle x_0, x_1, \cdots \rangle)$$

where $\frown$ means the concatenation of two sequence. Here recursive call of **map** only appears inside $\sharp$. The important thing is that the inside and outside of $\sharp$ are essentially different as if the those of modal operators are different, e.g. $\Box(\varphi \wedge \psi)$ and $(\Box\varphi) \wedge \psi$ are different.

---

[16] Agda is a proof assistant based on MLITT and implemented by Haskell[A10].

The idea of guarded co-recursion seems to be a good analogy to understand theorem 3. Actually, in $\mathbf{PA\pounds Tr_2}$, if the commutativity fails then it is of the form $\mathbf{Tr}(d)$ and d is a non-standard natural number[Yt09]. As we saw, the paradoxical sentences are defined co-inductively *inside the truth predicate*. In case of λ, when d is a nonstandard number, it is easy to see that $\mathbf{Tr}(d+1 \uparrow x) \equiv \mathbf{Tr}(\lceil \neg \mathbf{Tr}(x) \rceil \dot{\rightarrow} (d \uparrow x))$ holds because of the definition of $\uparrow$, however the truth value of the following might *not* be 1:

$$\mathbf{Tr}(\lceil d+1 \uparrow \lambda \rceil) \equiv \neg \mathbf{Tr}(\lceil \lambda \rceil) \rightarrow \mathbf{Tr}(\lceil d \uparrow \lambda \rceil)$$

This can be interpreted as follows: the definition of λ is a guarded co-recursion of formula with respect to a special constructor $\mathbf{Tr}$, i.e. the recursive call of the co-inductive object, λ, should be *guarded* by $\mathbf{Tr}$. In case of $\mathbf{Tr}(\lceil \neg \mathbf{Tr}(\lceil \lambda \rceil) \rceil \dot{\rightarrow} \lceil d \uparrow \lambda \rceil)$, all λs are guarded because all recursive call of λ are inside the same $\mathbf{Tr}$. But in case of $\mathbf{Tr}(\lceil \lambda \rceil) \rightarrow \mathbf{Tr}(\lceil d \uparrow \lambda \rceil)$, the recursive calls of λ are not inside the same $\mathbf{Tr}$, therefore they are not guarded.

6   Conclusion

In this paper, we analyzed the computational content of truth theories. We reviewed three paradoxes, the modest liar paradox, McGee's paradox and Yablo's paradox, which are pairwise similar and imply the ω-inconsistency for instance, and we show that is caused by the fact co-inductive definitions are possible because of the existence of the truth predicate.

Roughly speaking, ω-inconsistency is caused by the fact that the truth predicate enables to define formulae *co-inductively*. Such co-induction defines objects which seems to be the result of infinitely operations on formulae such as λ which is the limit of $\neg\lambda$, $\lambda \rightarrow \neg\lambda$, $\lambda \rightarrow \lambda \rightarrow \neg\lambda$, $\cdots$. It is possible because we can define operations over Godel codes of formulae recursively, and they are interpreted as real operations on formulae by the truth predicate in truth theories. Therefore we could recursively define formulae which causes paradoxes. The existence of non-standard natural numbers is a direct consequence of the fact that such results of infinitely operations are definable in the language: the fact that "finite" formula represents such results force the conception of finiteness against permitting non-standard numbers.

This analysis on ω-consistency, together with the fact that adding the truth predicate makes the theory's proof theoretic strength very high [FS87], reconfirms the fact that the truth predicate increases the expression power of language. That is based on the very nature of truth predicate, and non-standardness is its direct consequence (the ontology is secondary problem in this sense). This seems to suggest that the notion of truth is no sense transparent if the transparency is interpreted as "it does not have a major impact on the expression power of the language". ω-inconsistent truth theories are intrinsically equipped the machinery, co-induction, which is widely used in computer science and enables to represent infinite processes. Rejecting them involves rejecting co-induction at a time though it is very useful and natural, therefore we need to balance the profits and losses of rejecting co-induction before we reject them.

Acknowledgement

The author would like to thank the following people for their kind advice and discussions: Ryota Akiyoshi, Alexandru Baltag, J.C. Beall, Libor Behounek, Daisuke Bekki, Kengo Okamoto, John Power, Graham Priest, Greg Restall, Kentaro Sato, Takeshi Yamada, and in particular Petr Hájek.

References

[A10]   The Agda Team. The Agda Wiki (2010),
          http://wiki.portal.chalmers.se/agda/
[B08]   Beall, J.: Spandrels of Truth. Oxford University Press, Oxford (2008)
[BG08]   Beall, J., Glanzberg, M.: Where the paths meet: remarks on truth and para-
          dox. In: Truth. Notre Dame University Press (2008)
[CH10]   Cintula, P., Hajek, P.: Triangular norm based predicate fuzzy logic. Fuzzy
          Sets and Systems 161, 311–346 (2010)
[Cq93]   Coquand, T.: Infinite Objects in Type Theory. Types, 62–78 (1993)
[Co06]   Cook, R.T.: There are non-circular paradoxes (but Yablo's isn't one of
          them!). The Monist 89(1), 118–149 (2006)
[D10]   Danielsson, N.A.: Beating the Productivity Checker Using Embedded Lan-
          guages (2010) (preprint)
[F08]   Field, H.: Saving Truth From Paradox. Oxford (2008)
[FS87]   Friedman, H., Sheard, M.: An axiomatic approach to self-referential truth.
          Annals of Pure and Applied Logic 33, 1–21 (1987)
[HPS00]   Hájek, P., Paris, J.B., Shepherdson, J.C.: The Liar Paradox and Fuzzy Logic.
          Journal of Symbolic Logic 65(1), 339–346 (2000)
[Hl05]   Halbach, V., Horsten, L.: The Deflationist's Axioms for Truth. In: Deflation-
          ism and Paradox, pp. 203–217. Oxford University Press, Oxford (2005)
[Hd95]   Hardy, J.: Is Yablo's paradox liar-like? Analysis 55, 197–198 (1995)
[L01]   Leitgeb, H.: Theories of truth which have no standard models. Studia Log-
          ica 68, 69–87 (2001)
[L04]   Leitgeb, H.: Circular languages. Journal of Logic, Language and Informa-
          tion 13, 341–371 (2004)
[Ml88]   Martin-Lof, P.: Mathematics of infinity. In: Conference on Computer Logic,
          pp. 146–197 (1988)
[Mc85]   McGee, V.: How truthlike can a predicate be? A negative result. Journal of
          Philosophical Logic 17, 399–410 (1985)
[MT91]   Milner, R., Tofte, M.: Co-induction in relational semantics. Theoretical Com-
          puter Science 87, 209–220 (1991)
[P97]   Priest, G.: Yablo's paradox. Analysis 57, 236–242 (1997)
[Rs93]   Restall, G.: Arithmetic and Truth in Łukasiewicz's Infinitely Valued Logic.
          Logique et Analyse 36, 25–38 (1993)
[Rt00]   Rutten, J.J.M.M.: Universal co-algebra. Theoretical Computer Science 249,
          3–80 (2000)
[T33]   Tarski, A.: The concept of truth in the languages of the deductive sciences
          (1933) (polish); expanded English translation in Logic, Semantics, Meta-
          mathematics, (Hackett) pp. 152–278
[Yb93]   Yablo, S.: Paradox Without Self-Reference. Analysis 53, 251–252 (1993)
[Yt09]   Yatabe, S.: The revenge of the modest liar. Non-Classical Mathematics (2009)

Factives and Intensionality

Richard Zuber

Rayé des cadres du CNRS, Paris, France
Richard.Zuber@linguist.jussieu.fr

Abstract. Notions of normal intensionality and intensionality preserving negation are introduced. Both these notions apply to intensional sentential operators. When applied to factive operators they allows us to understand the way these operators give rise to presuppositions and their duals, assertions. They allow us also to distinguish semantically emotive factives from non-emotive ones.

1 Introduction

Factives are verbs of propositional attitudes. As is well-known verbs of propositional attitudes and operators formed from them are traditionally considered as posing special problems in formal semantics of natural languages on the one hand and as giving rise to particular questions in the philosophy of language and of knowledge. The difficulties that are encountered in formal semantics when approaching these verbs and constructions in which they occur are usually related to the fact that these verbs form intensional contexts and thus violate in various ways some general principles accepted in formal semantics (Partee 1979). In particular their strong intensionality, roughly speaking is not easily compatible with a compositional treatment of their semantics (Pelletier 1994)). In this paper I want to discuss something which, as far as I can tell, not has been explicitly discussed in the context of verbs of propositional attitudes: these are, roughly speaking, specific entailment like relations which hold between sentences (expressions) formed from verbs of propositional attitudes or their arguments and which are caused precisely by the intensionality of these verbs. Thus I will discuss the well-known relation of presupposition of factive verbs and the less discussed, but related relation of assertion. As we will see both these relations are easily obtainable in the context of some sub-set of verbs of propositional attitudes and a specific but natural negation of them.

Two warnings are needed at the outset. First, though I will discuss some semantic properties of sentential operators formed from verbs of propositional attitudes, I will not, strictly speaking, discuss the semantics of these verbs themselves. Their semantics has many sides and probably is not separable from various pragmatic aspects. I will discuss those semantic aspects of sentential operators formed from verbs of propositional attitudes which are essential for presuppositions and the assertions which can be associated with them. This means in particular that I will treat such operators as syntactically and semantically non-decomposable wholes. Thus I will mostly ignore the fact that such verbs usually

T. Onoda, D. Bekki, and E. McCready (Eds.): JSAI-isAI 2010, LNAI 6797, pp. 104–114, 2011.

take grammatical subjects referring to human beings. I will also ignore the fact that such verbs can take quantificational noun phrases as grammatical subjects. This does not seem to be harmful since usually the subject position is considered as not giving rise to intensionality. Consequently I will only analyse sentential operators of the form *A V that* where *A* is a proper name and V a verb of propositional attitudes.

The second warning concerns the notion of presupposition. I want to stress that this paper does not offer any general theory of presuppositions. There is a huge literature concerning presuppositions from both the theoretical and empirical points of view. An important topic in these considerations concerns the problem of presupposition projection, that is the way the presuppositions of more complex expressions are obtained from presuppositions of their simpler components. Again, this will not be considered here. The presuppositions that we will discuss are presuppositions of factives only. As will be seen, the way the existence of presuppositions of factives is explained does not easily generalise to other presupposing constructions. The reason is that the notion of normal intensional negation which plays an essential role in the understanding of the presuppositions of factives does not apply to cases in which intensionality is not involved.

As indicated above, I will discuss various entailments between sentences formed from sentential operators (which are formed from the verbs of propositional attitudes). The notion of entailment is taken in rather an intuitive sense. It takes for granted the notion of a possible world. Thus, simply, sentence S is said to entail a sentence T iff T is true in every possible world in which S is true. No more sophisticated notion of a logical model will be used.

There are at least three cases of entailments, or more generally of implications, under intensional operators interesting from the semantic point of view. The first is the case of factives predicates presupposing their sentential complements, the second is the entailment between two similar sentences with the same factive predicate in both sentences and differing only by the complementizer (*that* vs *whether*) of the factive. Finally there is a case of "neg-transportation" entailments (implications) to which some intensional predicates give rise. I will only mention this third type of entailment since it does not involve factive verbs. In the next section I recall more specifically these three cases with particular intention paid to the first two types involving factive verbs. Then in the next section I propose a specific notion of negation applicable to verbs of propositional attitudes which allows us to understand both types of entailments to which factives give rise.

2   Factives

Since the publication of Kiparsky and Kiparsky 1970) the term factive refers in linguistic semantics to verbs and predicates like *to know, to forget, to regret, be sad, be strange*, etc. when they take sentential complements. These predicates have an interesting semantic property : when completed by the grammatical subject referring to a human (which is usually the most natural case for them) they form sentential operators which presuppose the truth of the sentential complement that they take as argument. More specifically (positive forms of) sentences formed from factive predicates and their (natural) negations both entail the complement sentence. Thus (1a) and (1b)

(1a) Leo knows/regrets that P
(1b) Leo does not know/not regret that P

both seem to entail, on the most natural and generally accepted reading, that the sentence P is true.

Although before Kiparsky's article some philosophers also have tried to analyse certain verbs taking sentential complements with the help of the notion of presupposition (cf. Filmore 1963, Odegard 1965), their work was much more complete, empirically rich and gave rise to the renewal of the research on presuppositions. Indeed, sentences with factives represented a new set of presupposing constructions, different from those traditionally studied in the context of definite descriptions for instance. These new constructions showed that, as in the case of existential presuppositions, the notion of negation needed in the definition of presupposition must be different from the classical negation. This is because, as often has been pointed out, the sentence *Leo does not know that P* can be considered as true in the case when P is false (cf. *Leo does not know that P because not-P*).

Kiparsky's distinguish, in part by syntactic means, two type of factive predicates: non-emotive and emotive ones. The first class includes verbs like *know, remember, realise* and to emotive factives belong verbs like *regret, resent* or predicates like *be sad, be strange, be interesting* etc, when they take impersonal subjects.

It is not clear to what extent the syntax alone is sufficient to distinguish clearly emotive from non-emotive factive predicates. Some of criteria for such a distinction seem to be language dependent. Let me mention here the differences which are important for the purposes of this article. One difference between those two classes is that, informally, emotive factives seem to be sensitive to more, contingent and non-contingent, sentences than non-emotive ones. Consequently emotive factives presuppose "more" than non-emotive ones. Consider the following examples:

(2a) Leo knows that the bottle is half empty.
(2b) Leo knows that the bottle is half full.
(3a) Leo regrets that the bottle is half empty.
(3b) Leo regrets that the bottle is half full.

Very likely sentences in (2) have both the same truth value whereas those in (3) have different truth values. We express this by saying that *Leo regrets that* is intensionally stronger than *Leo knows that*. The notion of the "strength of intensionality" will be made more precise in what follows.

The second difference between emotive and non-emotive factives is that emotive, but not non-emotive, seem to presuppose in addition "knowledge" of the truth of the complement sentence (Zuber 1977). For instance (4a) presupposes (4b) and (5a) presupposes (5b) :

(4a) Leo regrets that P.
(4b) Leo knows that P.
(5a) It is strange that P.
(5b) It is known that P.

Obviously sentences with non-emotive factives do not have such a presupposition. For instance (4b) does not presuppose itself nor (5b). Neither do these sentences presuppose a belief of any kind by the human beings denoted by the subject noun phrases occurring in them.

Finally, non-emotive factives differ from emotive ones by the fact that only non-emotive can take in addition the complementizer *whether*. Thus we have *know whether* and *remember whether* but not **regret whether* or **it is sad whether*.

The fact that intensional verbs forming non-emotive factives can take two complementizers (*that* vs *whether*) can be related to another semantic relation to which non-emotive factives give rise. This relation will be called *assertion* (in opposition to presupposition). It can be illustrated by the following examples:

(6a) Leo knows that P.
(6b) Leo knows whether P.
(7a) Leo does not know that P.
(7b) Leo does not know whether P.

As already has been indicated, it is generally accepted, also by logicians, that (6a) entails (6b). Although it has not been often claimed so, it is also true that (7a), taken as presupposing P, entails (7b). Indeed, suppose *a contrario* that (7a) is true and (7b) is false. The falsity of (7b) means that either (1) Leo knows that P or (2) Leo knows that not-P. This is, however, impossible: (1) cannot be true because (7a) is true and (2) cannot be true because (7a) presupposes the truth of P. Notice that the negation in (7a) and (7b) cannot be interpreted by the classical propositional negation (obviously syntactically it is not) and in particular it must be a presupposition preserving negation in (7a). Thus (8a) can be true and (8b) false in the situation in which Leo knows that not-P is true:

(8a) It is not true that Leo knows that P.
(8b) Leo knows whether P.

The last case of intensional sentence-embedding predicates giving rise to specific entailments concerns the so-called Neg-raising predicates. As I said I will not discuss them in detail but I only indicate their main property. These predicates have the following property: when negated sentences with such predicates imply a corresponding sentence in which the negation takes scope in the embedded clause. Thus, intuitively (9a) implies (9b):

(9a) Leo does not think that life is sad.
(9b) Leo thinks that life is not sad.

Notice that the negation in (8a) cannot be interpreted as just the metalinguistic or classical propositional negation. Indeed it is easy to see that (10) does not imply (9b):

(10) It is not true that Leo thinks that life is sad.

For instance in most cases when Leo is sleeping (10) is true and (9b) is false.

Concerning the relation between (9a) and (9b) one could also ask whether these two sentences are equivalent: should one consider that (9b) also implies (9a). We will not discuss this possibility since it does not concern factive operators.

We can thus see that in the all three cases of entailments (or implications) presented above we need a special negation. The purpose of this paper is to show that we have the same negation in the case of presupposition of factives and in the case of assertion of factives..

3   Intensionality Preserving Negation

Obviously entailments and implications concerning presuppositions, assertions and neg-transportation essentially involve a negation. Moreover the cases we are considering involve intensional functional expressions (intensional sentential operators). This means that defining the negation we have to take into account precisely the fact that it has to apply to intensional functional expressions. So first we have to precise the notion of intensionality of such expressions and then define the appropriate negation of them.

Intensionality of functional expressions that we will use is characterised by the fact that the Leibniz' law does not hold in their context. Since we are basically interested in intensional operators taking sentences as arguments, the failure of Leibniz' law just means that the substitution of sentential arguments by logically equivalent sentences does not preserve truth-value. Since we are interested in sentential operators formed from verbs of propositional attitudes which take as grammatical subjects NPs referring to human beings it is preferable to relativise he notion of intensionality to a possible world. More precisely we will adopt the following definition:

Definition 1. *A sentential operator O (an expression of the category S/S) is normally intensional iff for some sentence P $O(P)$ is true in some world w and for every sentence P and every possible world w, if $O(P)$ is true in w, then there exists a sentence P' such that P and P' have the same truth-value in w and $O(P')$ is false in w.*

Few remarks about the definition. First, as already indicated, we will treat syntactically complex expressions consisting of a grammatical subject and a verb of propositional attitude as operators having syntactically non complex form. This maybe be a simplification. Second, as we will see, definition D1 does not make directly the difference between the intensionality of classical modal operators and the intensionality of operators formed from verbs of propositional attitudes. Indeed we know that modal operators display weaker intensionality than the propositional attitude verbs (Creswell 1975). In addition they do not give rise to semantic relations discussed above. In particular the necessity operator does not presuppose, but only entails, the truth of its argument. One could make the indicated difference by imposing the condition of contingency on sentences used in substitution; none of the sentences which substitute the other can be a necessary sentence. We will see that it is also possible to make the difference by the appropriate notion of negation of normally intensional operators.

Finally, it follows from definition 1 that for a sentential operator to be normally intensional it must be possible to show that the appropriate substitution never preserves truth-value (and not only in some cases as it is the case for "classical" intensionality). This feature can be related to the fact that intensional operators we consider here are strictly speaking syntactically complex being composed of a subject NP and a verb phrase. The subject NP usually refers, directly or indirectly, to human beings, which are non omniscient and sensitive to different ways of presentation of the same semantic content. Different logically equivalent sentences can be considered as different ways of presentation of the same (logical) content.

One can check that the sentential operators formed with verbs of propositional attitudes (not only factive predicates) are normally intensional. This is true not only of predicates whose subject NPs refers to human beings but also of predicates whose subject NP is the impersonal pronoun *it*. The classical modal operator of necessity is also normally intensional. the possibility operator is not normally intensional.

Although we will not be interested in (Booleanly) complex intensional operators nor in the problem of calculating presuppositions and assertions of complex sentences notice the following simple facts concerning some compositions of normally intensional operators:

Proposition 1. *Let O_1 and O_2 be two normally intensional operators such that $O_1 \neq \neg O_2$ (where $\neg$ is the classical negation), T the classical truth operator and N the classical propositional negation. Then:*
(i) $O_1 \wedge O_2$ and $T \wedge O_1$ are normally intensional.
(ii) $O_1 \vee O_2$ and $N \vee O_1$ are not normally intensional.

We want now to define a natural negation of intensional operators. We observe that some of such intensional operators can be considered as being related to other intensional operators by a specific lexical negation making them contrary to each other. This is the case for instance with *believe that* vs *doubt that* or *remember that* vs *forget that*. Notice that both members of these pairs are normally intensional. So we can suppose that there not only lexical but also a syntactic (and semantic) way to negate normally intensional operators. This can be done by the normal negation n whose semantics is defined as follows:

Definition 2. *Let O be a normally intensional operator. Then n-O is the normal negation of O iff for any sentence P, n-$O(P)$ has the same truth value as $\neg(O(P))$ and n-O is a normally intensional operator (where $\neg$ is the classical negation, and, since O is of the category S/S, n is of the category $(S/S)/(S/S)$).*

Thus n does the job of ordinary negation, but in addition it preserves the intensionality of the operator to which is applies.

Obviously normal intensional negation n entails the "ordinary" extensional negation but not the other way around. In addition the ordinary negation $\neg$ does not preserve the normal intensionality. We can show this with the following example. Let O be a factive operator *Leo knows that* (which is normally intensional) and consider the complex propositional operator $\neg O$: *It is not true that Leo knows that*. Clearly, if P is false $\neg O(P)$ is true. However since P is false there is no sentence P_1 equivalent to P such that $\neg O(P_1)$ would be false. Thus $\neg O$ is not normally intensional even though O is.

Notice also that definition 2 does not guarantee that all normally intensional operators have a normal negation. For instance the modal operator of necessity does not have a normal negation.

The importance of the normal negation is shown in the following proposition which indicates that normal negation is precisely the negation which is used when factives give rise to presuppositions:

Proposition 2. *If O is a normally intensional operator such that for any P, $O(P)$ entails P, then n-$O(P)$ also entails P.*

Proof. (Zuber 1980): Suppose *a contrario* that there exists a world w such that n-$O(P)$ is true in w and P is false. This means, given definition 2, that there exists P' with the same truth value as P in w and such that $O(P')$ is true in w. But this is impossible since $O(P')$ entails P'.   □

Thus factives are verbs of propositional attitudes which, roughly speaking, etail the sentential complement to which they apply. Consequently we are justified in calling factives verbs of propositional attitudes which entail their sentential argument because their normal negation also entails it.

As indicated there are two types of factives, emotive and non-emotive ones. Examples like (2) and (3) above, and like the following ones, suggest that emotive factives distinguish a "stronger semantic equivalence" than the equivalence distinguished by non-emotive factives:

(11a) Leo knows that Bill bought a car from Sam.
(11b) Leo knows that Sam sold a car to Bill.
(12a) Leo regrets that Bill bought a car from Sam.
(12b) Leo regrets that Sam sold a car to Bill.

For our purposes we can assume, at least for some possible world w, that (11a) and (11b) have the same truth value (in w) whereas (12a) and (12b) differ in their truth value (in w). This supposition means that the emotive factive operators (*Leo regrets that*) are in some sense intensionally stronger than the non-emotive ones.

It follows from the above examples that *A regrets that* is intensionally stronger than *A knows that* in the sense that is is sensitive to more arguments. Similarly it has been noticed (Creswell 1975) that verbs of propositional attitude are more strongly intensional than for instance the classical modal operator of necessity. On way to show this difference is to point out that intensionality of verbs of propositional attitudes can be tested by a pair of materially equivalent sentences such that both members of the pair are contingent sentences. This is not the case with the operator of necessity: we can show that this operator is intensional only using a pair of equivalent sentences such that one of the sentences is contingent and the other one non-contingent (necessarily true). So our definition of the strength of intensionality has to take into account these facts. Furthermore we want also that if O is normally intensional then O and $n\text{-}O$ should have the same intensional strenght. These observations lead to a series of a new notions. First we define a *detector of intensionality*:

Definition 3. *The set of two sentences P, P' is a detector of intensionality of the operator O (in the world w), iff P and P' have the same truth value in w, but $O(P)$ and $O(P')$ have different truth-values in w.*

Obviously extensional propositional operators do not have detectors of intensionality (in no possible world). Furthermore, any detector of intensionality of the modal operator of necessity contains a necessarily true sentence as a member. Normally intensional operators formed from verbs of propositional attitudes can have detectors of intensionality which contain only sentences.

With the help of the detector of intensionality we define the notion of the degree of intensionality of a given sentential operator, which needs not to be normally intensional:

Definition 4. *Degree of intensionality of the sentential operator O in the possible world w, noted $DI(w, O)$, is the set of the detectors of intensionality of O in w.*

For instance the degree of intensionality of an extensional sentential operator (in any possible world) is the empty set.

We can now precise how to compare the intensional strength of two sentential operators:

Definition 5. *The sentential operator O is intensionally stronger than the intensional operator O' iff for any possible world w the set $DI(w, O')$ is strictly included in the set $DI(w, O)$. If these sets are equal then O and O' have the same intensional strength.*

Notice that since the set-inclusion constitutes a partial order there are normally intensional operators which cannot be compared from the point of view of their strength of intensionality.

Concerning normally intensional operators and their normal negation the following fact is true:

Proposition 3. *For any possible world w and any normally intensional operator O the following equality holds: $DI(w, O) = DI(w, n\text{-}O)$.*

Thus normal intensional negation preserves the degree of intensionality of a given intensional operator. This means in particular that normal intensional negation is not intensional operator. In fact in some sense it is even "stronger" than the clasical extensional negation. This observation will be used when discussing some properties of assertions.

Definitions 2 and 5 allow us to prove the following proposition which accounts for the presuppositions of emotive factives (Zuber 1982):

Proposition 4. *If O is a sentential operator which is intensionally stronger than O' and for any P, $O(P)$ entails $O'(P)$ then $n\text{-}O(P)$ entails $O'(P)$.*

Proof. Suppose *a contrario* that there exists a world w such that $n\text{-}O(P)$ is true in w and $O(P)$ is false (in w). Since O is intensionally stronger than O' this means, given definition 5 and proposition 3, that there exist sentences P_1 and P_2 which are detectors of intensionality of O but are not detectors of intensionality of O' (in w). Consider now the following two sets of sentences $\{P, P_1\}$ and $\{P, P_2\}$ as possible detectors of intensionality of O and O' (in w). Suppose first that $\{P, P_1\} \in DI(O, w)$. It follows from this supposition that $\{P, P_1\} \notin DI(O', w)$ and thus that $O'(P_1)$ is false in w. This is impossible, however, because $O(P_1)$ is true in w (since $n\text{-}O(P)$ is true in w). Suppose now that $\{P, P_1\} \notin DI(O, w)$. It is easy to show that in this case $\{P, P_2\} \in DI(O, w)$ and $\{P, P_2\} \notin DI(O', w)$. But this is again impossible because in this case $O(P_2)$ would be true and $O'(P_2)$ false in w. Thus *a contrario* supposition leads to a contradiction. $\square$

Notice that proposition 4 is a generalisation of proposition 2, if we suppose that any sentence P is equivalent to $T(P)$, where T is the classical truth operator. The reason is that T can be considered, according to definition 5, as intensionally weaker than any normally intensional operator.

Concerning the relation of assertion one can show that it is related to the identical intensionality strength of sentential operators. More precisely the following proposition is true (Zuber 1982):

Proposition 5. *If O and O' have the same intensional strength and $O(P)$ entails $O(P')$ then $n\text{-}O(P)$ entails $n\text{-}O'(P)$.*

Proof. Suppose *a contrario* that there exists a world w such that $n\text{-}O(P)$ is true in w and $n\text{-}O'(P)$ is false (in w). Since $n\text{-}O$ is normally intensional there is a sentence P' which forms with P a detector of intensionality of O and $n\text{-}O$ in w. Given the hypothesis of the proposition the set $\{P, P_1\}$ is also the detector of intensionality of O' and $n\text{-}O'$. But then $O(P_1)$ would be true and $O'(P_1)$ false in w which is impossible. $\square$

Proposition 5 can be illustrated by examples in (6) and (7): since (6a) entails (6b) and *Leo knows that* and *Leo knows whether* have the same intensional strength, we have to conclude, given proposition 5, that (7a), the intensional negation of (6a) entails (7b), the intensional negation of (6b). Thus we can say, roughly, that *know that* asserts *know whether*. And this is true of many other non-emotive factives.

4   Conclusions

A negation-preserving intensionality applying to verbs of propositional attitudes has been introduced in order to explain the mechanism producing in particular presuppositions of factive prdicates. Though the idea of such a negation is intuitively clear its precise rendering, I must say, is not obvious. It is quite possible that another non-equivalent definition of intensional negation, in which partial functions are used, is necessary.

The machinery proposed for the explication of factive presuppositions have also been used to justify semantically the distinction between emotive and non-emotive factives. It is well-known that there is no general agreement concerning the observed data relating to emotive factive. I considered, following Zuber 1977, that they presuppose knowledge. According to some researches they only presuppose belief. Still others consider that they are not even veridical (for a review of different stands see Egré 2008). It seems to me that one can reach the final conclusion in these matters after considering other syntactic and semantic factors (cf. Egré 2008, Zuber 1982).

The above analyses cannot be generalised to implicative verbs (Karttunen 1971). The reason is that they are not normally intensional (at the predicate level). More specifically it is not true that given an implicative verb (*to manage, to forget, etc.*) and the predicate to which it applies, one can always find another co-extensional predicate such that the substitution of the one predicate for the other one will (systematically) lead to the change of the extension of the whole complex (modified by the implicative verb) predicate. In fact it is often very difficult to decide whether different VPs have the same denotation. The reason is that that VPs with implicative modifiers probably denote events. Sharvit 2003 shows that the verb *try* lexically related to many implicative modifiers is not intensional (though not exactly in the sense used here). And indeed implicatives give rise to different implications than factives do. This is in particular true with negated implicatives.

References

Cresswell, M.: Hyperintensional logic. Studia Logica 34, 25–38 (1975)

Egré, P.: Question-Embedding and Factivity. Philosophische Studien 77, 85–125 (2008)

Fillmore, C.: Entailments rules in a semantic theory. Project on Linguistic Analysis Report N 10 (1965); reprinted in Rosenberg and Travis (eds.) Readings in the Philosophy of Language. Prentice Hall, Englewood Cliffs (1972)

Karttunen, L.: Implicative verbs. Language 47, 340–358 (1971)

Kiparsky, P., Kiparsky, C.: Fact. In: Bierwisch, M., Heidolph, K.E. (eds.) Progress in Linguistics, pp. 143–173. Mouton, The Hague (1970)

Odegard, D.: On defining 'S knows that p'. Philosophical Quarterly 15 (1965)

Partee, B.H.: Semantics - Mathematics or Psychology? In: Bauerle, R., et al. (eds.) Semantics from Different Points of View, pp. 1–14. Springer, Heidelberg (1979)

Pelletier, F.J.: The Principle of Semantic Compositionality. Topoi 13, 11–24 (1994)

Sharvit, Y.: Trying to be Progressive: the Extensionality of Try. Journal of Semantics 20, 403–445 (2003)

Zuber, R.: Decomposition of factives. Studies in Language 1:4, 407–421 (1977)

Zuber, R.: Note on why factives cannot assert what their complement sentences express. Semantikos 4-2 (1980)

Zuber, R.: Some universal constraints on the semantic content of complex sentences. In: Dirven, R., Radden, G. (eds.) Issues in the Theory of Universal Grammar, pp. 145–157. Gunter Narr Verlag, Tubingen (1982)

Zuber, R.: Semantic restrictions on certain complementizers. In: Proc. of the 12th International Congress of Linguists, Tokyo, pp. 434–436 (1983)

The Fourth International Workshop on Juris-Informatics

Satoshi Tojo

Japan Advanced Institute of Science and Technology

The Fourth International Workshop on Juris-Informatics (JURISIN 2010) was held on November 18–19, 2010 at Campus Innovation Center in Tokyo, Japan, as a part of the second JSAI International Symposia on AI (JSAI-isAI 2010), with supports of Japan Advanced Institute of Science and Technology (JAIST) and National Institute of Informatics (NII).

The main purpose of the JURISIN workshop is to discuss both the fundamental and the practical issues in juris-informatics among researchers from diverse backgrounds such as law, social science, information and intelligent technology, logic and philosophy, including the conventional 'AI and law' area. In our 'call for papers' the following topics are mentioned: legal reasoning, argumentation/argumentation agent, legal term ontology, formal legal knowledge-base, intelligent management of legal knowledge-base, translation of legal documents, computer-aided law education, use of informatics and AI in law, legal issues on ubiquitous computing/multi-agent system/the Internet, social implications of use of informatics and AI in law, and so on.

According to the diversity of topics, the members of Program Committee (PC) are leading researchers in various fields: Phan Minh Dung (AIT, Thailand), Guido Governatori (University of Queensland, Australia), Tokuyasu Kakuta (Nagoya University, Japan), Luong Chi Mai (IOIT, Vietnam), Makoto Nakamura (Japan Advanced Institute of Science and Technology, Japan), Katsumi Nitta (Tokyo Institute of Technology, Japan), Shozo Ota (University of Tokyo, Japan), Henry Prakken (University of Utrecht and Groningen, The Netherlands), Seiichiro Sakurai (Meiji Gakuin University, Japan), Giovanni Sartor (European University Institute, Italy), Ken Satoh (National Institute of Informatics and Sokendai, Japan), Hajime Sawamura (Niigata University, Japan), Akira Shimazu (Japan Advanced Institute of Science and Technology, Japan), Nuanwan Soonthornphisaj (Ksetsart University, Thailand), Fumihiko Takahashi (Meiji Gakuin University, Japan), Satoshi Tojo (Japan Advanced Institute of Science and Technology, Japan), Katsuhiko Toyama (Nagoya University, Japan), Radboud Winkels (University of Amsterdam, the Netherlands), and John Zeleznikow (Victoria University, Australia).

Despite of the short announcement period, twenty papers were submitted, each of which was reviewed by three members of PC. This year, we have allowed a double submission to JURIX 2010 and six papers were withdrawn because of the multiple acceptance, and thus twelve papers were accepted in our workshop. The collection of papers covers such themes as legal reasoning, argumentation theory,

T. Onoda, D. Bekki, and E. McCready (Eds.): JSAI-isAI 2010, LNAI 6797, pp. 115–116, 2011.
© Springer-Verlag Berlin Heidelberg 2011

legal ontology, computer-aided law education, application of AI and informatics to law, application of natural language processing and so on.

After the workshop, ten papers were submitted for the post proceedings. They were reviewed by PC members again and four papers were finally selected. Followings are their synopses.

Marina de Vos et al. present a methodology to support legal reasoning using institutions that specify the normative behaviour of participants, as well as a corresponding computational model. They illustrate the use of their framework by modelling contract cancellation under Japanese contract law. Yasuhiro Ogawa et al. describe how to analyze Japanese statutory sentences. They propose a new design of syntactic tags for statutory sentences and develop a support tool that corrects the output of a parser, focusing on dependency structure of sentences. Also they present an overview of the design and compilation of the corpus. Davide Cameiro et al. present Online Dispute Resolution tools, aimed at supporting mediation between two or more parties. Specifically, this tool looks at past known mediation processes and tries to guide the process into a successful outcome. Specifically, they target scenarios in which one or more party exhibits avoiding or uncooperative conflict styles. Ken Satoh et al. propose a legal reasoning system called PROLEG (PROlog based LEGal reasoning support system) based on the Japanese 'theory of presupposed ultimate facts' (JUF), which is used for decision making by judges under incomplete information, so that it reflect lawyers' reasoning more adequately.

Finally, we wish to express our gratitude to all those who submitted papers, PC members, discussant and attentive audience.

April 2011
Satoshi Tojo
JAIST

Improving Mediation Processes with Avoiding Parties

Davide Carneiro[1], Paulo Novais[1], Francisco Andrade[2], and José Neves[1]

[1] Department of Informatics, University of Minho, Braga, Portugal
{dcarneiro,pjon,jneves}@di.uminho.pt
[2] Law School, University of Minho, Braga, Portugal
fandrade@direito.uminho.pt

Abstract. With the advent of the telecommunication technologies, a new form of disputes taking place in virtual environments started to emerge. In order to settle these disputes, Online Dispute Resolution tools appeared. In this paper we present such a tool, aimed at supporting mediation between two or more parties. Specifically, this tool looks at past known mediation processes and tries to guide the process into a successful outcome. Moreover, this tool places an emphasis on providing useful information for the parties before the resolution process actually starting, helping them take more rational decisions. Specifically, in this work we target scenarios in which one or more party exhibits avoiding or uncooperative conflict styles, i.e., the party cannot or is not willing to generate valid proposals for dispute resolution.

Keywords: Case-based Reasoning, Multi-agent Systems, Online Dispute Resolution, Mediation.

1 Introduction

In recent years the changes caused by technological evolution have been overwhelming. This has effects in every aspect of our lives. Namely, we can now easily engage into electronic transactions or contracts with virtually anyone in the world. One thing that did not change is the fact that, despite the nature of the contract, disputes are likely to arise. In traditional contracts the process followed to solve the dispute usually consists in going into court. There are however some known drawbacks in this method. Generally, litigation in court is seen as costly and slow. Moreover, it is a win-lose or even a lose-lose process. This means that one party wins what the other loses or both parties will be worst at the end of the process than they were at the beginning. Litigation thus results in a highly competitive approach to solve disputes. Moreover, it is also a public process in which the parties have a high level of exposure to the media, which is usually undesirable.

In order to address some of these drawbacks alternative approaches emerged that aimed at solving disputes in a more cooperative fashion. The so-called Alternative Dispute Resolution (ADR) methods include mediation [1], negotiation [2], arbitration [3], among others. Essentially, these methods aim at creating a private environment in which the parties cooperate to solve the dispute in a cheaper and faster way. Nevertheless, we easily conclude that these methods are outdated when considering the new nature of disputes.

T. Onoda, D. Bekki, and E. McCready (Eds.): JSAI-isAI 2010, LNAI 6797, pp. 117–128, 2011.
© Springer-Verlag Berlin Heidelberg 2011

In fact, nowadays disputes are not only increasing in number but have also new characteristics. The most evident is that the two disputant parties are no longer in the geographical proximity of each other but can be anywhere in the world. Traditional litigation is not suited anymore to deal with these disputes as, in order to settle it, the parties would have to meet in a physical place that is, probably, distant from their respective home locations. Being a slow process, it is also not suited to deal with the increasing amount of disputes. Likewise, ADR methodologies are outdated, namely because of the question of the location.

A new trend thus emerged that aims at bringing the advantages of ADR methodologies into virtual spaces, the so-called Online Dispute Resolution (ODR) methodologies [4]. These are similar to the ones of ADR but can be used by parties scattered around the world through the use of the new telematic means. Moreover, these methodologies can be supported by intelligent software agents that can automate processes and support the parties involved [5, 6]. In fact, increasing the efficiency of the processes is paramount in order to deal with the rising amount of disputes.

The work presented in this paper builds on a pre-existing ODR platform: UMCourt. Specifically, we are looking at ways to improve the efficiency of mediation processes in which one or more parties exhibit an avoiding behavior by providing guidance and meaningful information. Such parties are not willing or cannot generate potential solutions, thus constituting an impediment for the effective resolution of the dispute. In that sense, our approach consists in letting the system assume the responsibility of proposing solutions for the resolution of the dispute rather than asking the parties for them. Thus, parties have only to express how they feel about each proposal that the system provides. This is then used by the system as an input to decide about the next solution to propose with the aim to achieve a solution that can satisfy all the parties. Moreover, in order to decide about the following outcome, the system also considers a list of previous successful similar mediation processes. Instead of having to explicitly plan a strategy and propose a solution in each step, parties have only to answer to proposals of the system. In that sense, we expect to increase the acceptation and use rate of these platforms among parties that show an avoiding behavior. The application scenario is in the context of the Portuguese Labor Law, in line with the application scenario of UMCourt. In that sense, the disputes addressed by the platform deal essentially with the issue of an employee being fired. In that sense, a significant amount of legal parameters are considered, including the possibility of a "just cause for dismissal" being declared by the Court, the existence (or not) of a valid and legal procedure of dismissal, the validity (or not) of the dismissal, the antiquity of the worker in the company, supplementary work, night work, justified or unjustified absence from work, the possibility of dismissal being accepted without indemnities or of it being accepted but accompanied by indemnities that could range from a very low to a very high amount of money.

2 Conflict Resolution

Conflict resolution is the action by means of which two entities use a method for alleviating or eliminating sources of conflict. These methods generally include negotiation, mediation or arbitration, most of the times with the assistance or supervision of a neutral third party. In any case, conflict resolution aims at solving the dispute outside of courts, i.e. it aims at avoiding traditional litigation in court. Conflicts can arise in the most different scenarios and they are present in our day-to-day life. In 1974, Kenneth Thomas and Ralph Kilmann formalized the way we respond to conflict situations into five different modes in terms of individual's assertiveness and cooperativeness [7]. In this context, assertiveness denotes the extent to which the person attempts to satisfy his/her own interests while cooperativeness denotes the extent to which the person attempts to satisfy the other person's interests. The conflict styles are:

- Competing - This is an uncooperative style by means of which an individual aims at maximizing his/her own gain at the other's expenses. This is a power-oriented style in which an individual will use whatever power seems appropriate to win his/her position (e.g. ability to argue, rank, economic sanctions);
- Accommodating – This style is the opposite of competing, i.e., it is cooperative. When an individual shows an accommodating behavior, he/she neglects his/her own gain to maximize the gain of the other. Under this behavior one founds an element of self-sacrifice. Accommodating includes well-known behaviors such as selfless generosity or charity, obeying another individual's order when we may prefer not to do so or accepting another's point of view;
- Avoiding - The individual that shows an avoiding style of conflict tries to satisfy neither his/her own interests nor those of the other individual. It can be said that he/she is not dealing with the conflict. This style may be evidenced by behaviors such as diplomatically sidestepping an issue, postponing an issue until a better opportunity arises, or simply withdrawing from a threatening situation;
- Collaborating – This cooperative style is the complete opposite of avoiding. When an individual collaborates, he/she attempts to work with the other party to find some solution that fully satisfies the interests of both parties. In this process, the individual explores an issue to discover the underlying desires and fears of the two individuals. An individual that is collaborating might try to explore a disagreement to learn from other's insights;
- Compromising – When an individual has a compromising style of dealing with a conflict, he/she tries to find some expedient, mutually acceptable solution that can partially satisfy both parties. This style is somewhat an intermediate one between competing and accommodating. Generally, compromising can mean splitting the differences between the two positions, exchanging concessions, or seeking a quick middle-ground solution.

Whether it is because of the practice or because of our temperament, each of us is capable of using all of these conflict-handling styles. Moreover, none of us can be characterized as having one single style of dealing with a conflict. Nevertheless, certain individuals rely on some modes more than others and, therefore tend to use them more often. It is therefore important, in the first place, to determine the style of the parties towards the conflict resolution process in an attempt to define how to guide it. One way of determining this style is by taking the TKI test (Thomas-Kilmann Conflict-Mode Instrument), a test designed specifically by Thomas and Kilmann.

Once the styles are identified there are several strategies that can be used for conflict resolution. One of them is the well-known Interest-Based Relational (IBR). This approach is characterized by respecting peoples' individuality while at the same time helping each party to avoid to become too entrenched in a fixed position.

3 UMCourt

UMCourt is an agent-based platform for the development of ODR services. This platform implements a wide range of functionalities that can be used to build complex services. The key component of UMCourt is a Case-based Reasoning (CBR) module that allows to develop services such as retrieving similar cases, retrieving most likely solutions, retrieve similar solutions, retrieve similar mediation processes, among others. This work essentially builds on this module. As the architecture of UMCourt has already been presented previously, we will here only briefly describe the agents that build it and their high level roles. For a more detailed description see [8].

In UMCourt agents run inside an instance of a Jade agent platform [9] and are organized in two groups. The *Main Agents* group is populated by agents that have a major and autonomous role in the CBR process. These are detailed in Table 1. In Table 2 the agents of the *Secondary Agents* group are listed. These have no autonomy, having as its foremost objective to support the actions of the main agents. This departure between main and secondary agents has been performed in order to simplify the first ones. Following this line of attack, we not only simplify the main agents but also increase code (thus functionalities) reuse.

Table 1. The Main Agents and their functionalities

Name	Functionalities
Coordinator	Receive task requests from other agents (e.g. external agents, interface agents) and take the necessary steps (requesting tasks to other agents) in order to perform them. This agent maintains a list of active tasks and has access to a list of finite state automata that define the next action for each task, provided by the FSA agent.
Retriever	Retrieve the cases more similar to a given one. This agent has the autonomy to change the search settings, the similarity parameters and the retrieve algorithms in order to perform a better selection of cases.
Reuse	When requested by the Coordinator, performs the necessary actions to adapt a given case so that it can be used.
Reviser	Looks at a group of cases in order to select an outcome/solution for a given case. Proposes the outcome to the coordinator as well as a justification and waits for the outcome. If the outcome does not comply with the one suggested provides a list of more probable reasons for the failure.
Learning	Has the autonomy to make changes to the knowledge base and to the rules according to the each proposed outcome and real outcome. This agent embodies the ability to acquire new experiences and learn with failed ones.

Table 2. The Secondary Agents that support the lifecycle of the Main ones

Name	Functionalities
FSA	Contains a list of Jade FSM behaviours that describe the guidelines or steps necessary for an agent to implement specific actions.
Selector	Multiple instances of this agent exist that implement different pre-selected algorithms (e.g. Template Retrieval, Clustering).
Similarity	This agent is able to compute the values of similarity between two cases, according to the desired rules.
Settings	Defines several search and similarity settings according to which retrieve parameters can be changed.
Database	Implements an application layer that surrounds the database of cases, that caters for all the actions to be applied to the cases stored.
Rules	Embodies rules of type if *condition* then *action* that provide the basic reactive actions for guiding some of the remaining agents.
ATNA	Computes the BATNA and WATNA in a given context using a set of logical rules defined after the Portuguese labour law.
Loader	Loads the information of cases from XML files and provides it as a Java object maintaining and updating loaded cases.
Indexer	Indexes each new case in the database according to the rules defined.
Parser	Checks the validity and parses XML files according to the defined schemas.
Process Validity	Verifies the validity of a case in terms of the dates and the corresponding statutory periods.
Roles	Contains information about the roles of registered external agents. This is used to decide which actions each external agent can perform.

4 The Mediation Process Model

4.1 Compilation of Initial Information

As mentioned, the mediation process depicted in this work builds on the previously existing UMCourt architecture. Namely, UMCourt is used to compile some initial information that is useful for both the mediation tool and the disputant parties. Using this information, we aim at achieving better outcomes by: (1) providing the parties with more knowledge about the dispute and (2) potentiating the role of the parties throughout all the process. In fact, parties that have poor access to important information generally end making bad choices or, at least, they hardly make the best choice. Moreover, parties usually have a reduced role on the resolution process, resulting in suspicion about the outcome, mostly because they do not understand how it was achieved.

This information includes the BATNA or Best Alternative to a Negotiated Agreement [10]. In fact, when parties enter into a dispute resolution process, they expect to achieve better results than would otherwise occur. It is of utter importance that, during this process, parties are aware of the possible results if the negotiation is unsuccessful. In fact, failing to do so may drive the parties into accepting an agreement that they would do better or rejecting one that they would do better of fall into. Likewise, the WATNA, or the Worst Alternative to a Negotiated Agreement is equally important. Looking at these two elements, parties can definitively improve their outcome by looking at the whole picture. ODR platforms that embody such concepts can help parties take better decisions [11]. In order to determine these two values, we are using a rule-based approach. Considering the parallel between rule-based system and legal systems, one can picture the development of rule-based systems that describe rules of specific legal fields that can then be used to determine which rules apply in a given case. Thus, software agents formalize the computation of the BATNA and WATNA in the form of IF-THEN rules.

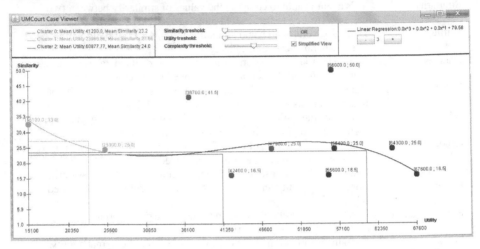

Fig. 1. A detail of the graphical representation of the information compiled, including past cases, the value of similarity and utility of each case, BATNA, WATNA, MLATNA (the region in which the curve of the linear regression is green) and some clusters with respective mean similarity and utility. The X axe represents the Utility while the Y axe represents the Similarity.

Although these two values are important, they may not be enough for the parties to take the best decision possible. In that sense, UMCourt also provides the MLATNA - Most Likely Outcome for a Negotiated Agreement [12] for a given case. This perception takes us to the most likely scenario if the dispute resolution process fails. It represents therefore a good starting point for the process to start. When using these details, parties are aware of the possible and potential consequences of solving the dispute in court. In this sense, parties are able to take their decisions while encompassing the whole picture.

The last information that the mediation tool uses is a list of past successful mediation processes that happened in the past and concerned a similar dispute. This list is compiled by the Case-based Reasoning module of UMCourt and is based on the similarity of the current dispute with past known disputes. In that sense, UMCourt will select the most similar cases and the corresponding mediation processes that led to the solution, as detailed in [13]. To compute the similarity, UMCourt uses a hybrid approach, combining a template algorithm with a nearest neighbor one: the template retrieval narrows the search space so that the nearest neighbor algorithm performs quicker. In this sense, template retrieval works much like SQL queries: a set of cases, with given characteristics, is retrieved from the database. In the next step, the nearest neighbor algorithm has only to be applied to this set of cases instead of applying it to all the cases in the case memory.

$$\frac{\sum_{i=1}^{n} W_i * fsim_i(Arg_i^N, Arg_i^R)}{\sum_{i=1}^{n} W_i} \tag{1}$$

In equation 1, our closest neighbor algorithm is shown. In this equation,

- n – number of elements to consider to compute the similarity;
- W_i – weight of element i in the overall similarity;
- Fsim – similarity function for element i;
- Arg – arguments for the similarity function representing the values of the element i for the new case and the retrieved case, respectively N and R.

The information the similarity between cases will then be used by the system to try to guide the dispute into a successful end as will be seen below. Moreover, this information can be provided to the parties by means of a graphical interface in order for them to take more informed and rational decisions (Figure 1).

4.2 New Agents

A software agent can be a complex entity and can thus be defined from several points of view. However, independently of the type of agent, there are some abstract notions that are common and can be used to define it. Namely, we define an agent according to their roles, services and world description.

Definition 4.1. An agent is defined as a 4-tuple:

$$A:=(Id, R, S, WD)$$

where Id is the unique identifier of the agent, R a set of roles, S a set of services that are provided by the agent and WD a set of additional descriptors of the world in which the agent exists.

Definition 4.2. The world is defined as a 3-tuple:

$$WD:=(WId, OD, ACLD)$$

where WId uniquely identifies the world, i.e., an instance of the dispute resolution platform, OD is an ontology description and ACLD is an agent communication language description. The OD allows increasing the semantic richness of the system by defining the vocabulary and a domain-specific ontology, allowing agents to exchange messages containing complex concepts (e.g. proposal, solution, case, norm) (Figure 2). It also defines all the agent actions.

In order to implement the mediation tool, UMCourt has been extended with two new agents that implement the concept of blackboard. In this paradigm, there is a shared space, the blackboard, to which the participants can publish their messages as well as read messages from the others participants or external entities taking part in the process. In this context, these messages essentially contain outcome proposals from the mediator or the parties. Specifically, this environment is built on top of instances of two different agents: *blackboard* and *party*. The former is responsible for controlling the whole process, while the second facilitates the interaction of the parties with the blackboard. In a few words, the process model implemented by these

```
//Case
cs = (ConceptSchema) getSchema(CASE);
cs.add(CASE_ID, (PrimitiveSchema) getSchema(BasicOntology.STRING), ObjectSchema.MANDATORY);
cs.add(CASE_EMPLOYEE_ID, (PrimitiveSchema) getSchema(BasicOntology.STRING), ObjectSchema.MANDATORY);
cs.add(CASE_EMPLOYER_ID, (PrimitiveSchema) getSchema(BasicOntology.STRING), ObjectSchema.MANDATORY);
cs.add(CASE_EMPLOYEE_NORMS, (ConceptSchema) getSchema(NORM), 0, ObjectSchema.UNLIMITED);
cs.add(CASE_EMPLOYER_NORMS, (ConceptSchema) getSchema(NORM), 0, ObjectSchema.UNLIMITED);
cs.add(CASE_PARTY1WINS, (PrimitiveSchema) getSchema(BasicOntology.BOOLEAN), ObjectSchema.MANDATORY);
```

Fig. 2. An excerpt from the ontology containing a simplified definition of the concept Case. Here, a case is defined by a unique identifier, the identifiers of the parties, a list of norms addressed by each party and a variable denoting the party that won the case.

two types of agents consists in iteratively send proposals for outcomes until an agreement is reached or the process ends by another reason. The roles and services of these two agents are presented in table 3 and table 4.

4.3 The Mediation Process Model

The mediation process starts with the system providing the information mentioned before to the parties. Basically, the mediation develops as follows: the platform goes on suggesting solutions until one party leaves the process, all agree on the proposed solution or the platform runs out of solutions. A solution consists on a list of steps detailing specific actions that parties must comply with. Each step is described by a unique identifier, the identifier of the party to whom the step refers to, a structured description of the step (e.g. "give up, 20%, night_work", "demand, 100%, indemnity") and the monetary value (if applicable) involved in the step. Each solution may have one or more steps. The structured nature of the solution allows for parties to easily understand and change the information contained.

In order to implement the mediation algorithm, a list of previous negotiation sessions is needed. This list is provided by UMCourt. It contains mediation sessions that happened in the past and have a given degree of similarity with the current case. Moreover, they have already been applied successfully in the past so they may constitute a valid solution for the current dispute. Each of these mediation sessions contains a list of solutions. These solutions describe the several steps that the mediation session took, i.e., how the mediation evolved until the final outcome was achieved. In order for UMCourt to build this list of past mediation sessions, it looks at similarity of the current case with past known cases. It will select the mediation sessions that were used to solve similar cases. To implement this, UMCourt makes use of the CBR module, as depicted in [13]. Moreover, the mediation sessions are sorted according to the decreasing degree of similarity of the corresponding cases so it is a sorted list.

The mediation process model is implemented as a cycle. In each step of this cycle the platform suggests a possible solution and waits for the answers of the parties. When the process starts, the platform proposes the first solution of the most similar mediation process known. This is also the MLATNA computed by UMCourt, i.e., the system starts by proposing the most likely outcome to the parties. A solution will then be worked out from this point on. After publishing this proposal on the blackboard, the system waits for the parties to read it and answer. As this approach is focused on parties that exhibit avoiding behaviors, the system does not expect them to answer

Table 3. The information about the roles and services of agent *blackboard*

Roles	Services
Request Initial Information	Get Information
Initiate Mediation	Get Status
Accept Register	Register
Refuse Register	Unregister
Build new Outcome	
End Mediation	

Table 4. The information about the roles and services of agent *party*

Roles	Services
Register	Get Message
Exit	Edit Message
Propose new Outcome	Send Message
Accept	
ReplyTo	
Ignore	
Refuse	

with an alternative suggestion for a solution. Parties can rather reply to the proposal in one of three ways: they can either agree, disagree or simply ignore it.

Once all the parties published their answers on the blackboard, the platform will analyze them. If at least one party leaves the mediation, the process ends. If all the parties agree on the solution, the process ends with success as one consensual outcome has been achieved. Otherwise, there are two possible paths.

If the majority of the parties agree with the solution proposed by the system, it means that the mediation is following a promising path. In that sense, the platform will propose the following solution of the mediation session being considered. However, if there are no more solutions on the current session, the system will move on to the first solution of the following mediation session, if any.

On the other hand, if the majority of the parties does not agree with the proposed solution, the platform will drop the mediation session being used and advance into the following one, if any. The platform does so because it interprets this configuration of replies as indicating that the mediation path being followed is not promising. It will thus start following the next known mediation session in the following round.

The high-level algorithm that implements the mediation process model presented in this paper

```
Algorithm Mediation is
   input:  List of previous mediation processes, L
           List of parties, P
   output: A solution for the dispute
```

```
round := 0          (identifies the round)
msgSet := []        (a list of received messages)
agree := 0          (the number of agents that agree)
exit := 0           (the number of agents that exit)
proposal := []      (the current proposal)
i := 0              (index of the mediation process in use)
j := 0              (index of the step being proposed)
mediation := []     (lists of steps from past mediations)


while (agree < length(P) and exit < 1)
      mediation := Lᵢ
      solution := mediationⱼ
      publish proposal
      for each party in P
          msg := receive from party or timeout
          msgSet := msgSet ∪ msg
      agree = count "agree" in msgSet
      exit  = count "exit" in msgSet
if (exit > 0)
    return null
if (agree = Length(P))
    return solution
else if (agree > Length(P)/2)
          j++    (majority agrees, advance to next step)
      else i++   (minority agrees, select next mediation)
          j := 0 (start in first step of new mediation)
if (j = Length(mediation)) (reached last step in
    j := 0                          current mediation)
    i++
if (i = Length(L)) (reached last selected mediation)
    return null
round++
```

To better follow the evolution of this process, several user interfaces have been developed. In Figure 3 the interface for the *blackboard* agent is shown. Essentially, this interface shows the state of the mediation. It provides information about the current round, the number of parties currently registered, the answers already received in this round, and the amount of solutions that have already been proposed. Moreover, it shows some statistics for the current round. It is also possible to select each party and see, in detail, the corresponding messages in another interface.

In figure 4 it is shown a message from agent Party2 stating that it agrees with the proposal published by agent *BlackBoard@TIARAC-1:1099/JADE*, with id 1279539858546. This specific proposal is made up by only one step in which party 1 will gave up 20% of the night work, evaluated in a total amount of 4523.0.

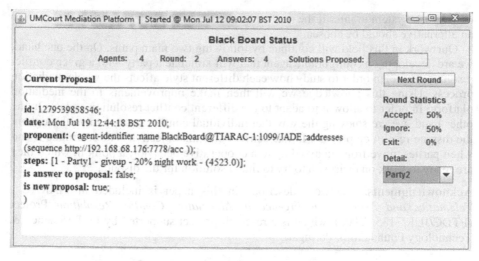

Fig. 3. The interface for the *blackboard* agent

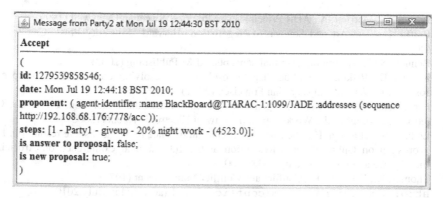

Fig. 4. An interface with a message from a party denoting the acceptation of a given proposal

5 Conclusions and Future Work

Parties that cannot effectively generate solutions and strategies for dispute resolution can be a major obstacle. In such scenarios it is necessary the existence of an external entity, with the ability to generate valid potential solutions. In this paper we have presented such an entity. Particularly, we have developed a mediation platform that is able to propose valid solutions to parties that are not willing or cannot do so. Moreover, the solutions proposed are potential solutions as they are selected from previous successful mediation processes. In order to do this, the system uses a previously developed Case-based Reasoning algorithm that retrieves mediation processes based on the similarity of the cases addressed. The key idea in the whole process model is that the system has the responsibility to suggest potential outcomes while the parties have only to state whether they agree with it or not. This way, although parties cannot generate valid solutions, they can still solve their dispute with the help of an electronic mediator. Moreover, the feedback from the parties will be used by the system to infer if the mediation process is going in the correct direction or an alternative should be chosen.

Our work in this field will continue by following two main paths. On the one hand, we are developing a configurable agent that will simulate a party with a given conflict resolution style, in order to study how each different style affects the whole mediation process. Using this knowledge we will then make improvements to the mediation platform in order to allow it to adapt to the different conflict resolution styles. On the other hand, we are studying the way that individual conflict styles evolve throughout the dispute resolution process. In that sense, our main objective is to determine if and when parties move from an avoiding to a cooperative behavior, a point in which they are ready to work on their own to try to find a solution for the dispute.

Acknowledgments. The work described in this paper is included in TIARAC - *Telematics and Artificial Intelligence in Alternative Conflict Resolution* Project (PTDC/JUR/71354/2006), which is a research project supported by FCT (Science & Technology Foundation), Portugal.

References

1. Brown, H., Marriott, A.: ADR Principles and Practice. Sweet and Maxwell (1999)
2. Raiffa, H.: The Art and Science of Negotiation. Harvard University Press, Cambridge (2002)
3. Bennett, S.C.: Arbitration: essential concepts. ALM Publishing (2002)
4. Katsch, E., Rifkin, J.: Online dispute resolution – resolving conflicts in cyberspace. Jossey-Bass Wiley Company, San Francisco (2001)
5. Peruginelli, G.: Artificial Intelligence in Alternative Dispute Resolution. In: Sartor, G. (ed.) Proceedings of the Workshop on the Law of Electronic Agents (2000)
6. Lodder, A., Thiessen, E.: The role of artificial intelligence in online dispute resolution. In: Workshop on Online Dispute Resolution at the International Conference on Artificial Intelligence and Law, Edinburgh, UK (2003)
7. Thomas, K., Kilmann, R.: Conflict and Conflict Management (1974), http://www.kilmann.com/conflict.html (accessed in: July 2010)
8. Andrade, F., Novais, P., Carneiro, D., Zeleznikow, J., Neves, J.: Using BATNAs and WATNAs in Online Dispute Resolution. In: Nakakoji, K., Murakami, Y., McCready, E. (eds.) JSAI-isAI 2009. LNCS (LNAI), vol. 6284, pp. 5–18. Springer, Heidelberg (2010) ISBN 978-3-642-14887-3
9. Bellifemine, F., Poggi, A., Rimassa, G.: Developing Multi-agent Systems with JADE. In: Intelligent Agents VII Agent Theories Architectures and Languages, pp. 42–47 (2001)
10. Notini, J.: Effective Alternatives Analysis In Mediation: "BATNA/WATNA" Analysis Demystified, http://www.mediate.com/articles/notini1.cfm (accessed in February 2011)
11. De Vries, B.R., Leenes, R., Zeleznikow, J.: Fundamentals of providing negotiation support online: the need for developing BATNAs. In: Proceedings of the Second International ODR Workshop, pp. 59–67. Wolf Legal Publishers, Tilburg (2005)
12. Guasco, M.P., Robinson, P.R.: Principles of negotiation. Entrepreneur Press (2007)
13. Carneiro, D., Novais, P., Andrade, F., Zeleznikow, J., Neves, J.: The Legal Precedent in Online Dispute Resolution. In: Legal Knowledge and Information Systems, ed. Guido Governatori (proceedings of the Jurix 2009 - the 22nd International Conference on Legal Knowledge and Information Systems), pp. 47–52. IOS Press, Amsterdam (2009) ISBN 978-1-60750-082-7

Legal Modelling and Reasoning Using Institutions

Marina De Vos[1], Julian Padget[1], and Ken Satoh[2]

[1] Department of Computer Science, University of Bath
{mdv,jap}@cs.bath.ac.uk
[2] National Institute of Informatics
ksatoh@nii.ac.jp

Abstract. To safeguard fairness for all parties involved and proper procedure, actions within a legal context are heavily constrained. Detailed laws determine when actions are permissible and admissible. However, these restrictions do not prevent participants from acting. In this paper we present a methodology to support legal reasoning using institutions—systems that specify the normative behaviour of participants—and a corresponding computational model. We show how it provides a useful separation between the identification of real world actions, if and how they affect the legal model and how consequences *within* the legal model can be specified and verified. Thus, it is possible to define a context, introduce a real-world event and examine how this changes the state of the legal model: hence, the modeller can explore both model adequacy and that of the legal framework from which it is derived, as well as offering a machine-usable legal 'oracle' for software components. We illustrate the use of our framework by modelling contract cancellation under Japanese contract law.

Introduction

The concept of normative frameworks, or institutions, and organizational modelling is gaining acceptance in the multi-agent systems (MAS) as a potential solution to the challenge of governing open systems. Modelling frameworks typically provide a method for the formalization of norms, thus capturing some statement of the designer's intentions for how participants *should* behave: which actions they are allowed to perform and which ones are not permitted. That does not necessarily ensure compliant behaviour: violation detection is generally feasible, as long as agents' actions are somehow observable, but enforcement is a separate issue, which has many implementations on the spectrum between social and legal punishment.

For the last four years, we have been developing a modelling framework and toolset, based on the logic programming language of Answer Set Programming [3], that addresses the governance of multi-agent systems. The aim is to express the range of actions, and constraints, on software agents in a machine processable form. The designer can (exhaustively) explore the reachable states of the model as a means to validate it and in a running system, the model can be used to compare agent behaviour against expectations. It may also function as an oracle service for agents to query at run time.

The preoccupations of just building a system that behaves as desired tends to occlude the precept that agents, the actors, are *situated* and that situation does not include just the physical environment that agents can sense and act upon [13], but should also

T. Onoda, D. Bekki, and E. McCready (Eds.): JSAI-isAI 2010, LNAI 6797, pp. 129–140, 2011.

take account of the (multiple) legal contexts in which such systems may be deployed. An essential aspect of our modelling framework is its support for the distinction—and connection—that the designer can make between real world events and institutional events, following the principle of "counts-as" established by Jones and Sergot [11]. This "counts-as" relation, effective on events, is different from the count-as relations discussed in [6] that operate on facts and are context dependent. Since this institutional interpretation of events is a declarative program, it can be a formal representation of some fragment of a legal code, thus building a connection between agents and a situating legal framework. In this paper we use Japanese contract law as a case study.

1   Institutions

1.1   Formal Model

Our formal model has been described in detail in [1], but to make this paper self-contained we provide a brief overview here.

The premise of our model is that events trigger the creation of institutional facts, inspired by Jones and Sergot' [11] account of institutional power and the notion of 'counts-as', to explain the connection between exogenous events and institutional events—this is our *generation* relation. An event may change the institutional state by initiating or terminating fluents—this is our *consequence* relation. The state consists of brute domain facts [9] and institutional facts specifying permission and power, of events and of obligations to perform an action. Thus, given an event and an institutional model state, represented as a set of (institutional) facts, the next state is determined by the transitive closure of the generation and consequence relations. The analogy we make for legal reasoning is that the generation relation models actions of individuals in the real world, creating institutional events in the pertinent legal context, consequently initiating and terminating domain and institutional facts by means of the consequence relation.

The formal institutional model is necessarily more detailed and precise than the sketch above. The essential elements are: (i) events ($\mathcal{E}$), that bring about changes in state, and (ii) fluents ($\mathcal{F}$), that characterise the state at a given instant, where a fluent is a term whose presence in the institutional state indicates it is true, and absence implies falsity. We distinguish two kinds of events: institutional ($\mathcal{E}_{inst}$), that are the events defined by the model and exogenous ($\mathcal{E}_{ex}$), that are outside its scope, but whose occurrence triggers institutional events reflecting the counts-as principle. We partition institutional events into institutional actions ($\mathcal{E}_{act}$) that denote changes in institutional state and violation events ($\mathcal{E}_{viol}$), that signal the occurrence of violations. Violations may be generated explicitly, or through the occurrence of a non-permitted event, or from the failure to fulfil an obligation. We distinguish two kinds of fluents: *institutional* that denote institutional properties of the state such as permissions $\mathcal{P}$, powers $\mathcal{W}$ and obligations $\mathcal{O}$, and *domain* $\mathcal{D}$ that correspond to institutional framework specific properties. The set of all fluents is denoted as $\mathcal{F}$.

The evolution of the state of the framework is achieved through the definition of two relations: (i) the generation relation: that specifies how the occurrence of one (exogenous or institutional) event generates another (institutional) event, subject to the empowerment of the actor. Formally, this can be expressed as $\mathcal{G} : \mathcal{X} \times \mathcal{E} \rightarrow 2^{\mathcal{E}_{inst}}$, where $\mathcal{X}$ denotes a formula over the (institutional) state and $\mathcal{E}$ an event, whose confluence results in an institutional event, and (ii) the consequence relation, that specifies the initiation and termination of fluents subject to the performance of some action in a state matching some expression, or formally $\mathcal{C} : \mathcal{X} \times \mathcal{E} \rightarrow 2^{\mathcal{F}} \times 2^{\mathcal{F}}$.

Again, for the sake of context, we summarize the semantics of our framework and cite [1] for an in-depth discussion. The semantics is defined over a sequence, called a trace, of exogenous events. Starting from the initial state, each exogenous event is responsible for a state change, through initiation and termination of fluents, that is achieved by a two-step process: (i) the transitive closure of $\mathcal{G}$ with respect to a given exogenous event determines all the (institutional) events that result from this event, including violations of events that where not permitted and violations events of unfulfilled obligations, while excluding events that are not empowered. (ii) the application of $\mathcal{C}$ to this set of events, identifies all fluents to initiate and terminate with respect to the current state in order to obtain the next state; this also includes the termination of obligations that have been fulfilled or violated. So for each trace, we can obtain a sequence of states that constitutes the model of the institutional framework.

1.2   InstAL

While the formal framework has its value, from a designer's point of view it is not very convenient and forces technical/mathematical details to intrude into the modelling process. Consequently, we designed a simple domain-specific language for institutional frameworks called Inst*AL* . We give a brief introduction through examples of the language features taken from the case study on Japanese contract law which features later in this paper:

- institution *name* declares the name of the institutional framework, such as institution legal
- type *identifier* declares a type, such as type Agent. Type declarations establish a disjoint set of mono-morphic types.
- exogenous event *event-name(type$^+$)* declares a new physical world event and the types of its parameters, such as exogenous event sale(Agent, Agent)
- inst event *event-name(type$^+$)* declares a new legal world event and the types of its parameters, such as inst event intSale(Agent, Agent).
- violation event *event-name(type$^+$)* declares a new violation event, such as violation event contractViolationBuyer(Agent)
- fluent *fluent-name(type$^+$)* declares a new institutional fact—that is, an object that can be an element of the institutional state, such as fluent contract(Agent, Agent)
- *event-name* generates *legal-world-event$^+$* [*if state-condition*] adds a new pair to the generation relation with domain event (physical or legal) and range legal world event, subject to an optional condition on the state. For example: sale(Seller, Buyer) generates intSale(Seller, Buyer) if hasGood(Seller), hasMoney(Buyer), where the condition is the presence of the fluents hasGood and hasMoney with the corresponding Seller and Buyer (these variables are unified) in the institutional state.

- *event-name* initiates *legal-world-fluent*+ [*state-condition*] adds a new pair to the consequence (addition) relation, with event (physical or legal) and fluent. Thus, sale(Seller, Buyer) initiates contract(Seller, Buyer) adds the corresponding fluent to the institutional state.
- *event-name* terminates *legal-world-fluent*+ [*condition*] adds a new pair to the consequence (deletion) relation, with event (physical or legal) and fluent. Thus, transfer(Seller) terminates hasGood(Seller) deletes the corresponding fluent from the institutional state.
- perm(*event*) is a special fluent whose presence indicates that the event is permitted, such as perm(transfer(Seller)), and is typically the subject of an initiates or terminates rule.
- pow(*event*) is a special fluent whose presence indicates that the event is empowered (has an effect), such as pow(transfer(Seller)), and is typically the subject of an initiates or terminates rule.
- obl(*event*, *event*, *event*) is a special fluent whose presence indicates the existence of an obligation, such as obl(transfer(Seller), handOverDeadline, contractViolationSeller(Seller)), indicating that the first event needs to occur before the second. If this is not the case, the third event, normally a violation event will take place. In either case, the obligation is terminated. Typically the subject of an initiates rule.

We realize a computational model of the above specification by translation to a (nonmonotonic) logic programming language call Answer Set Programming (ASP) [3]. This translation includes code to take care of inertia of fluents and removal of satisfied or violated obligations. Again the full details can be found in [1], including a proof of the soundness and completeness of the translation. The result of the translation is a computational model that can generate sequences of all possible states of the institutional framework (these are the answer sets of program), given some initial conditions. The development, execution and visualization of institutions is supported by the IDE Inst*Suite* [8].

1.3 Methodology

Our institution terminology refers to *exogenous* and *institutional* events. From the perspective of a legal domain, the first represent the actions of the participants: e.g. signing a contract, while institutional events are a mechanism for the legal interpretation of these actions. For example, a signature of a minor is not recognised or stating that one cancels a contract does not automatically mean that the contract has indeed been cancelled; certain conditions must be fulfilled for a contract to be cancelled. Institutions make explicit this separation of concerns and allow reasoning on both levels.

In our model, each exogenous event of concern has a corresponding institutional event, that functions as a gatekeeper to the legal model. If the actor of an exogenous event does not have the necessary credentials or certain conditions are not met, the institutional event does not occur and nothing changes within the model, so the exogenous event is of no consequence. The credentials are modelled by assigning institutional power to the the gatekeeper events. Without institutional power, these events are not

```
Case:
Contract:
        – X had a contract to buy a piece of jewellery from Y for 1 million yen.
        – X was supposed to pay 1 million yen on Sep 30 2009 at Y's residence and
        – Y was supposed to give the jewellery to Y on the same day.
2007 Sep 30:
        – X gave 1 million yen to Y, but Y did not give the jewellery to X, so X demanded to Y to give the
          jewellery J by Oct 14
2007 Oct 14:
        – Y did not give the jewellery to X
2007 Oct 15:
        – X cancels the contract

Question: Is the cancellation of the contract by X valid?
```

Fig. 1. Contract Cancellation Scenario

triggered. Permission of exogenous events and gatekeeper events is determined by the legal rules that are modelled.

Each institutional event can generate further institutional events to allow for the specification of special or alternative cases, e.g. buyers and sellers have different obligations when a contract is established.

Obligations are used to express when future events have to take place, e.g. the contract requires that the goods are transferred before a certain date. To make the model as abstract as possible, dates are not encoded in the model instead we use exogenous events that act as deadlines, i.e. the obligation has to satisfied before the deadline occurs. This deadline can be generated by an agent action as a timekeeper.

Dedicated violation events can be introduced to indicate not only that an event has taken place without permission but also that an obligation was not fulfilled or that an undesirable event has taken place given the current state of affairs.

The domain fluents are used to describe the non-institutional state of the world. They keep track of what has happened in the system; i.e. a contract was signed, money was transferred, relevant details of the participants, etc..

2   Modelling Contract Law: A Case Study

2.1   Contract Cancellation under Japanese Law

We take our case study from Japanese contract law, within which we look at contract cancellation. The question we aim to be able to answer is "When is it permissible to cancel a contract?". Although the specification is more general, the objective is to answer the question for the scenario presented in Figure 1 against the Articles presented in Figure 2.

2.2   InstAL Specification

Contract execution and cancellation consists of various stages: (i) first a contract has to be established, (ii) then, if all parties adhere to it, the contract is executed (iii) a reminder can be sent if one of the parties misses a deadline (iv) if a party breaks the contract, the other party can cancel the contract, after which the transactions have to be undone. The

- **Article 412 (Time for Performance and Delay in Performance)**
  1. If any specified due date is assigned to the performance of an obligation,
     the obliger shall be responsible for the delay on and after the time of
     the arrival of such time limit.
  2. If any unspecified due date is assigned to the performance of a claim,
     the obliger shall be responsible for the delay on and after the time when
     he/she becomes aware of the arrival of such time limit.
  3. If no time limit is assigned to the performance of an obligation, the
     obliger shall be responsible for the delay on and after the time he/she
     receives the request for performance.
- **Article 540 (Exercise of Right to Cancel)**
  1. If one of the parties has a right to cancel in accordance with the
     provisions of the contract or law, the cancellation shall be effected
     by manifestation of intention to the other party.
  2. The manifestation of intention under the preceding paragraph may not be
     revoked.
- **Article 555 (Sale)**
  1. A sale shall become effective when one of the parties promises to transfer
     a certain real rights to the other party and the other party promises to
     pay the purchase money for it.
- **Article 541 (Right to Cancel for Delayed Performance)**
  1. In cases where one of the parties does not perform his/her obligations,
     if the other party demands performance of the obligations, specifying a
     reasonable period and no performance is tendered during that period, the
     other party may cancel the contract.

Fig. 2. Related Civil Law on contract cancellation (translated provided by Japanese Law Translation http://www.japaneselawtranslation.go.jp)

InstAL specification of these five phases, set-up, execution, reminding, cancellation and transaction reversal, can be found in Figures 3-8.

We discuss these stages in more detail later, but before doing so we need to declare the types, events and fluents needed in the specification. Their full declaration can be found in Figure 3. We name our institutional framework legal (Line 1). Our specification has only needs one type (Line 4) to represent the participants. The participant actions are represented as exogenous events (Lines 7-13). The contract institutions has five deadlines (dates) by which certain actions have to be performed. They are modelled as exogenous events (Line 15 -19). Each institutional framework has a special event that will initialise it: for legal, we name this creation event start (Line 22). As described in section 1.3, for each exogenous events for which the model should account, we define a corresponding institutional event (Lines 25-32). Here, this means all the actions of the participants except for the reminder. Setting up the contract, intSale, results in two further institutional events, transferReq and paymentReq, whose purpose is to differentiate between buyers and sellers (Lines 26-27). The model also distinguishes four violation events, different from unpermitted events, to indicate that the buyer or the seller has not fulfilled their obligation with respect to the contract or its return policy (Lines 35-38). Apart from keeping track of power and permission for each of the events, the model also monitors the contract, the goods and the money involved in the transactions. This is done by the domain fluents defined in Lines 41-46.

The next step is to define the rules of the institutional framework, starting with setting up the contract (see Fig. 4). The triggering event of this phase is sale. A contract between buyer and seller (Line 53) is set up if intSale is empowered and permitted and if the seller has the goods and the buyer has the money (Line 53). The generation of intSale generates transferReq and paymentReq (Line 57) and initiates the

```
1   institution legal;
2
3   % Types
4   type Agent;
5
6   % exogeneous events
7   exogenous event sale(Agent,Agent);  % Seller, Buyer
8   exogenous event giveGoods(Agent);
9   exogenous event makePayment(Agent);
10  exogenous event reminder(Agent);
11  exogenous event cancel(Agent);
12  exogenous event repayBuyer(Agent);
13  exogenous event returnSeller(Agent);
14
15  exogenous event handOverDeadline;
16  exogenous event paymentDeadline;
17  exogenous event handOverDeadline2;
18  exogenous event paymentDeadline2;
19  exogenous event returnDeadline;
20
21  % creation
22  create event start;
23
24  % institutional events
25  inst event intSale(Agent,Agent);    % Seller, Buyer
26  inst event transferReq(Agent);
27  inst event paymentReq(Agent);
28  inst event transfer(Agent);
29  inst event payment(Agent);
30  inst event cancellation(Agent);
31  inst event intrepayBuyer(Agent);
32  inst event intreturnSeller(Agent);
33
34  % violation
35  violation event contractViolationBuyer(Agent);
36  violation event contractViolationSeller(Agent);
37  violation event contractReturnViolationBuyer(Agent);
38  violation event contractReturnViolationSeller(Agent);
39
40  % fluents
41  fluent contract(Agent,Agent);  % Seller, Buyer
42  fluent cancelledContract(Agent,Agent);  % Seller, Buyer
43  fluent hasGood(Agent);
44  fluent hasMoney(Agent);
45  fluent paid;
46  fluent transferred;
```

Fig. 3. Declaration of types and events in the model

contract fluent (Line 58). In turn, the two generated events set up the contractual obligations for the buyer and seller and give them the necessary power and permission to do so (Lines 61–70). The contractual obligations are automatically removed when the participants fulfil them or when the deadlines expire.

The next phase details the normal execution of a contract (see Fig. 5). When the seller (giveGoods) or the buyer (makePayment) satisfies their part of the contract (Lines 75–76), the corresponding institutional events change the owner of the money or goods and removes the power and permission of the execution events (Lines 78–84). If either participant fulfils their contractual obligations, irrespective of the deadline, it should be impossible for the other party to cancel the contract (Lines 87–90). The occurrence of the deadlines handOverDeadline and PaymentDeadline permits the occurrence of reminders and terminates the permission for the deadline to occur again (Lines 92–96).

```
48   %-----------------------------------------------------------------
49   % Establish Contract
50   %-----------------------------------------------------------------
51   % the sale proceeds if sale is empowered and both participants have
52   % the correct assests
53   sale(Seller,Buyer) generates intSale(Seller,Buyer) if hasGood(Seller),
54                                hasMoney(Buyer);
55
56   % sale split between buyer and seller responsibilities
57   intSale(Seller,Buyer) generates transferReq(Seller), paymentReq(Buyer);
58   intsale(Seller,Buyer) initiates contract(Seller,Buyer);
59
60   % obligations for buyer and seller specified
61   transferReq(Seller) initiates obl(transfer(Seller),handOverDeadline,
62                                contractViolationSeller(Seller));
63   paymentReq(Buyer) initiates obl(payment(Buyer),paymentDeadline,;
64                                contractViolationBuyer(Buyer));
65
66   % appropriate permission and power given
67   transferReq(Seller) initiates pow(transfer(Seller)),perm(transfer(Seller)),
68                                perm(handOverDeadline);
69   paymentReq(Buyer) initiates pow(payment(Buyer)),perm(payment(Buyer)),
70                                perm(paymentDeadline);
```

Fig. 4. Setting up a contract in Inst*AL*

```
72   %-----------------------------------------------------------------
73   % Executing Contract
74   %-----------------------------------------------------------------
75   giveGoods(Seller) generates transfer(Seller) if hasGood(Seller);
76   makePayment(Buyer) generates payment(Buyer) if hasMoney(Buyer);
77
78   transfer(Seller) initiates transferred, hasGood(Buyer)
79                                if contract(Seller,Buyer);
80   transfer(Seller) terminates hasGood(Seller);
81   payment(Buyer) initiates paid, hasMoney(Seller) if contract(Seller,Buyer);
82   payment(Buyer) terminates hasMoney(Buyer);
83   transfer(Seller) terminates pow(transfer(Seller)),perm(transfer(Seller));
84   payment(Buyer) terminates pow(payment(Buyer)),perm(payment(Buyer));
85
86   % transfer or payment retracts permission to cancel for opposite party
87   transfer(Seller) terminates pow(cancellation(Byer)),perm(cancellation(Buyer)),
88                                perm(cancel(Buyer)) if contract(Seller,Buyer);
89   payment(Buyer) terminates pow(cancellation(Seller)),perm(cancellation(Seller)),
90                                perm(cancel(Seller)) if contract(Seller,Buyer);
91
92   handOverDeadline initiates perm(reminder(Buyer));
93   paymentDeadline initiates perm(reminder(Seller));
94
95   handOverDeadline terminates perm(handOverDeadline);
96   paymentDeadline terminates perm(paymentDeadline);
```

Fig. 5. Executing a contract in Inst*AL*

```
98   %-----------------------------------------------------------------
99   % Reminder
100  %-----------------------------------------------------------------
101  % give the agents a second change
102  reminder(Seller) initiates obl(transfer(Seller),handOverDeadline2,
103                                contractViolationSeller(Seller)),
104                                perm(handOverDeadline2) if not transferred;
105
106  reminder(Buyer) initiates obl(payment(Buyer),paymentDeadline2,
107                                contractViolationBuyer(Buyer)),
108                                perm(paymentDeadline2) if not paid;
```

Fig. 6. Reminders in the model

```
110  %-------------------------------------------------------------------
111  % Cancelling the contract
112  %-------------------------------------------------------------------
113  % Cancellation procudure: cancellation only empowered when violation
114  % occured and  only given to grieved agent
115
116  cancel(Agent) generates cancellation(Agent);
117  cancellation(Agent) terminates contract(Seller,Buyer);
118  cancellation(Agent) initiates cancelledContract(Seller,Buyer)
119      if contract(Seller,Buyer);
120
121  cancellation(Agent1) terminates pow(cancellation(Agent)),
122                               perm(cancellation(Agent)), perm(cancel(Agent));
123
124  % power and permission to cancel is given to appropriate agent
125  contractViolationSeller(Seller) initiates pow(cancellation(Agent)),
126                                     perm(cancellation(Agent)),
127                                     perm(cancel(Agent))
128                                     if contract(Seller,Agent), paid;
129  contractViolationBuyer(Buyer) initiates pow(cancellation(Agent)),
130                                     perm(cancellation(Agent)),
131                                     perm(cancel(Agent))
132                                     if contract(Agent,Buyer), transferred;
```

Fig. 7. Cancelling the contract in Inst*AL*

```
134  %-------------------------------------------------------------------
135  % Return Policy
136  %-------------------------------------------------------------------
137  % if goods or money has changes owner they need to be returned when the
138  % contract is cancelled
139  cancellation(Agent) initiates perm(repayBuyer(Seller)),
140                                pow(intrepayBuyer(Seller)),
141                                perm(intrepayBuyer(Seller)),
142                                obl(repayBuyer(Seller),returnDeadline,
143                                    contractReturnViolationSeller(Seller))
144                                if contract(Seller,Buyer), hasMoney(Seller);
145  cancellation(Agent) initiates perm(returnSeller(Buyer)),
146                                pow(intreturnSeller(Buyer)),
147                                perm(intreturnSeller(Buyer)),
148                                obl(returnSeller(Buyer), returnDeadline,
149                                    contractReturnViolationBuyer(Buyer))
150                                if contract(Seller,Buyer), hasGood(Buyer);
151
152  repayBuyer(Seller) generates intrepayBuyer(Seller);
153  intrepayBuyer(Seller) initiates hasMoney(Buyer)
154                          if cancelledContract(Seller,Buyer);
155  intrepayBuyer(Seller) terminates hasMoney(Seller)
156                          if cancelledContract(Seller,Buyer);
157
158  returnSeller(Buyer) generates intreturnSeller(Buyer);
159  intreturnSeller(Buyer) initiates hasGood(Seller)
160                          if cancelledContract(Seller,Buyer);
161  intreturnSeller(Buyer) terminates hasGood(Buyer)
162                          if cancelledContract(Seller,Buyer);
```

Fig. 8. Modelling the return policy in Inst*AL*

```
164  %-------------------------------------------------------------------
165  % initial state
166  %-------------------------------------------------------------------
167  initially pow(transferReq(seller)), pow(paymentReq(buyer)),
168            perm(transferReq(seller)), perm(paymentReq(buyer)),
169            perm(sale(seller,buyer)), perm(makePayment(buyer)),
170            perm(giveGoods(seller)),hasGood(seller), hasMoney(buyer),
171            pow(intSale(seller,buyer)), perm(intSale(seller,buyer));
```

Fig. 9. The initial state

The reminder phase is specified in Fig. 6. From the previous phase we know that this phase can only occur without causing violation (from the reminder perspective) when the deadline for the contractual obligation has lapsed for one of the participants.

The cancellation phase specification is given in Fig. 7. Whenever one of the participants tries to cancel a contract (cancel) it is the status of the empowerment of the institutional event cancellation that determines whether the contract cancellation is valid or not (Line 116). The state of the contract may be changed from contract to cancelled (Lines 117–119). Once the contract is cancelled power and permission to cancel the contract is no longer required (Line 121). The power and permission to cancel the contract is given to a party in the contract when the other party fails to satisfy their part of the contract. In our model, failure is represented by a contractViolation event (Lines 125–132).

The final phase, the return policy, appears in Fig. 8. When a contract is cancelled, transferred goods and money must be returned to the original owner. Therefore, the occurrence of cancellation generates the permission and the obligation for the participants to return what they have received (Lines 139–150). When the buyer and seller return/repay the goods/money, ownership is adjusted accordingly (Lines 152–162).

With the five phases now specified, we just need the initial state to complete the model. In this case, this is the power and permission for the events that make up the first phase of the model (see Fig. 9).

2.3   Running the Model

Before we can run the model, we must declare the participating agents, by means of: Agent: buyer seller. The resulting ASP program can be used in a variety of ways, such as: finding all valid traces, providing a partial trace for completion, filtering traces for certain properties or examining a complete trace in detail. From a legal reasoning perspective, the last two are probably the most useful: constraints on traces permit looking for unusual situations or flaws in the model, while full traces enable closer examination of specific cases and reaching legal decisions. Without any constraints, the model computes all the possible ways exogenous events can take place and their consequences. From a more practical point of view, the model can be used to answer specific questions about the validity of an action/event given a sequence of events. While in most cases a complete set of events would be given, e.g. representing a specific case, the model is capable of reasoning about an incomplete sequence of events. Another use of the model is to verify the current state of affairs, e.g. is the contract still in place or has it been cancelled. Also, one can query the model for legal loopholes by asking if it is possible for a certain situation to occur.

While in litigation one often only takes the current status of rights and obligation between parties into account, there are situations, from example in tort or when reasoning about a prescription, where past and future statuses do matter. The model presented in paper, due the tracking the various states and partial sequences of events, allows for reasoning not only in the present but past and future as well.

ASP facts of the form observed(event, time) are added to represent complete or partial traces. A complete trace matching the scenario in Fig 1 displayed in Fig 10. It starts with the creation event followed by setting up the contract. After payment and the

```
1   observed(start,i00).                    6   observed(reminder(seller),i05).
2   observed(sale(seller,buyer),i01).       7   observed(handOverDeadline2,i06).
3   observed(makePayment(buyer),i02).       8   observed(cancel(buyer),i07).
4   observed(paymentDeadline,i03).          9   observed(repayBuyer(seller),i08).
5   observed(handOverDeadline,i04).
```

Fig. 10. The complete trace of our contract example

expiry of deadlines the seller (y) is reminded about his/her obligations. After that deadline expires the buyer cancels the contract. The trace finishes with seller repaying the buyer. The textual output from running the model is rather hard for humans to process. To make examining the model more user friendly Inst*Suite* provides trace diagrams that graphically represent the events and state changes over time.

The trace visualization is omitted here, due to space limitations. However, in this case, the only violation that occurs is `contractViolationSeller(seller)`. No `viol(cancel(buyer))` occurred indicating that it was legal for buyer to cancel the contract.

3   Summary, Related and Future Work

In this paper we have demonstrated that is possible to use the concept of an institutional framework for the representation of and reasoning about legal state. We have shown that the same tools can be usefully employed to make machine processable equivalents of legislation available for the governance of and reference by software components.

The formal representation of legal frameworks by normative systems has been a subject of research for several decades: a comprehensive discussion appears in [10]. Contracts, specifically, have received much attention using different formalisms, although defeasible logic [4,5] is considered particularly appropriate, along with various executable representations, such as RuleML in [4].

Herrestad in [7] argues that Sergot's formalisation of the library regulations is confronted with Chisholm's paradox and that logic programming is ill-suited for modelling such of knowledge. Herrestad's claim is based on the assumption that implication can be rewritten as disjunction. In answer set programming, this is not the case as it uses negation as failure whose semantics differs from classical negation (see [2] for more information). Furthermore, with our approach there is no need to express that no disciplinary action is taken when books are returned on time. This is supported implicitly.

Prakken and Sergot [12] present the concept of contrary-to-duty, where two obligations conflict each other and a mechanism is need to determine which of two should be followed. They illustrate this with the dog and fences example: one should have not a fence, one should not have a dog, if there is a dog there needs to be a fence which is council approved. While this model is fluent based, we could assume that "construct a fence", "take dog" and "obtain approval" would be the corresponding actions. We could model the first two with an initial absence of the permission to construct a fence and the other with taking a dog. Depending on what the designer would wish to model, the latter rule could be implemented as taking a dog initiates the obligation to construct a fence by a certain date and to obtain approval. At the same time, permission for taking a dog and constructing a fence could be initiated.

At this stage, we have completed an off-line specification that can be used to answer the question posed in section 2.1. While this is "just another model", we observe that conventionally in litigation, only the current status of rights and obligations between parties is usually considered. However, a potential benefit of the approach taken is the capacity to reason about not only the current status, but also the past (postdiction) and future status (prediction) [8]. Furthermore, the tools demonstrated (and under development—see below) may offer a way to bridge the practical gap between legal modelling and software agents.

Future work is proceeding on five fronts: (i) **contract recision:** this extends the case described here (ii) **on-line reasoning:** (in the context of a different problem) we are developing the means for agents to reason about institutional facts using the same computational model (iii) **model refinement:** as models become more complicated, they are harder to write and to debug: consequently, we are developing an inductive logic programming approach that, given test cases and desired outcomes suggests new, and revises old, rules. (iv) **extend the formal modal:** Currently we only deal with violations of not permitted actions or unfulfilled obligations. We are extending the model to reason about the state of the institutions and to represent obligations that do not just have to be satisfied by the occurrence of an action but by a certain state.

References

1. Cliffe, O., De Vos, M., Padget, J.: Specifying and reasoning about multiple institutions. In: Noriega, P., Vázquez-Salceda, J., Boella, G., Boissier, O., Dignum, V., Fornara, N., Matson, E. (eds.) COIN 2006. LNCS (LNAI), vol. 4386, pp. 67–85. Springer, Heidelberg (2007)
2. Denecker, M.: What's in a model? Epistemological analysis of logic programming. In: Principles of Knowledge Representation and Reasoning: Proceedings of the Ninth International Conference (KR 2004), pp. 106–113 (2004)
3. Gelfond, M., Lifschitz, V.: Classical negation in logic programs and disjunctive databases. New Generation Computing 9(3-4), 365–386 (1991)
4. Governatori, G.: Representing business contracts in RuleML. International Journal of Cooperative Information Systems 14(2-3), 181–216 (2005)
5. Governatori, G., Rotolo, A.: Defeasible logic: Agency, intention and obligation. In: Lomuscio, A., Nute, D. (eds.) DEON 2004. LNCS (LNAI), vol. 3065, pp. 114–128. Springer, Heidelberg (2004)
6. Grossi, D., Meyer, J.-J.C., Dignum, F.: The many faces of counts-as: A formal analysis of constitutive rules. J. Applied Logic 6(2), 192–217 (2008)
7. Herrestad, H.: Norms and formalization. In: ICAIL 1991: Proceedings of the 3rd International Conference on Artificial Intelligence and Law, pp. 175–184. ACM Press, New York (1991)
8. Hopton, L., Cliffe, O., De Vos, M., Padget, J.: Instql: A query language for virtual institutions using answer set programming. In: ClimaX, pp. 87–104 (2009)
9. Searle, J.R.: The Construction of Social Reality. The Penguin Press, Allen Lane (1995)
10. Jones, A.J.I., Sergot, M.: On the characterization of law and computer systems: the normative systems perspective. In: Deontic Logic in Computer Science: Normative System Specification, pp. 275–307. John Wiley and Sons Ltd., Chichester (1993)
11. Jones, A.J.I., Sergot, M.: A Formal Characterisation of Institutionalised Power. ACM Computing Surveys 28(4es), 121 (1996) (Read November 28, 2004)
12. Prakken, H., Sergot, M.J.: Contrary-to-duty obligations. Studia Logica (SLOGICA) 57(1), 91–115 (1996)
13. Wooldridge, M.: An Introduction to MultiAgent Systems. Wiley, Chichester (2010)

Design and Compilation of Syntactically Tagged Corpus of Japanese Statutory Sentences

Yasuhiro Ogawa, Masayuki Yamada,
Ryuta Kato, and Katsuhiko Toyama

Graduate School of Information Science, Nagoya University
Furo-cho, Chikusa-ku, Nagoya, 464-8603 Japan
{yasuhiro,toyama}@is.nagoya-u.ac.jp
http://www.kl.i.is.nagoya-u.ac.jp/

Abstract. This paper describes how to analyze Japanese statutory sentences. Although statutory sentences have many technical terms and characteristic structures, the design of the general Japanese corpus has no tags to handle such structures and usual Japanese parsers cannot analyze them correctly. Thus, we propose a new design of syntactic tags for statutory sentences and develop a support tool that corrects the output of a parser. In this paper, we focus on dependency structure of sentences and present an overview of the design and compilation of the corpus of Japanese statutory sentences.

Keywords: legal corpus, statutory text processing, dependency structure, statute document.

1 Introduction

Dependency structure of sentences plays an important role in NLP, and there is no exception in statutory text processing. The dependency structure of statutory sentences offers, for example, reading support for understanding their complicated structure and writing support based on exemplar search.

In addition, acquiring lexical knowledge such as synonyms, hypernyms, and hyponyms is important for advanced statutory text processing. Today, acquiring such knowledge from large corpora is a major issue in NLP and many of such acquisition methods are based on the distributional hypothesis, where the word relatedness is measured by the commonality of the contexts of words. For example, an algorithm called *monaka*[2] automatically acquires important terms in Japanese statutory documents by bootstrapping with character n-gram context.

Although *monaka* requires only simple n-gram context, other methods usually use richer contexts such as dependency path[3, 11]. These methods assume a corpus where sentences are correctly annotated with syntactic information. Therefore, we need a large annotated statutory corpus for advanced acquisition of legal lexical knowledge.

To compile such a corpus, we need a parser for statutory sentences. However, statutory sentences are usually so long that they require large search spaces for

T. Onoda, D. Bekki, and E. McCready (Eds.): JSAI-isAI 2010, LNAI 6797, pp. 141–152, 2011.

dependency analysis. In addition, we focus on Japanese statutes. Expressions peculiar to Japanese statutes have so complicated syntactic structures that the parser must deal with many ambiguous structures, which causes analysis errors. For these reasons, the existing parsers do not have sufficient performance to analyze Japanese statutory sentences, so we need a new one tailored to them.

How to make such a parser? The popular method is based on machine learning techniques such as CaboCha[4] based on SVM, and it requires correctly annotated training data. This implies that we need an annotated corpus in order to compile a larger one.

In this paper, therefore, we compile a certain size of Japanese statutory corpus with syntactic information, whose compilation design is based on the one for the Kyoto Text Corpus (KTC). Since it was designed for ordinary sentences such as the ones in newspapers and does not assume dealing with statutory sentences, we extended its construction method; that is, we designed additional tags for statutory sentences and compiled a statutory corpus with such tags.

This paper is organized as follows: in Sect. 2, we briefly describe Japanese dependency structure and KTC. Section 3 shows the problems that arise when we compile the Japanese statutory corpus and the design of tags to solve them. In Sect. 4, we show how to compile our statutory corpus and to correct parsing errors, and Sect. 5 summarizes this paper.

2   Japanese Dependency Structure

Since Japanese is a free word order language and allows the omission of various components in a sentence, dependency structure is more suitable than phrase structure for dealing with syntactic structure[6].

2.1   Characters of Japanese Dependency Structure

Japanese dependency structure is usually defined on *bunsetsu* units, which are linguistic units in a Japanese sentence and consist of a word alone, or a word with some particles or other suffixes[8]. The English equivalents for bunsetsus would be a small noun phrase, a prepositional phrase, a verb phrase consisting of auxiliary verbs and a main verb, and so on.

Japanese dependency usually keeps the following three constraints[6, 10]:

1. No dependency is directed from right to left, since Japanese is a head-final language.
2. Dependencies do not cross each other.
3. Each bunsetsu, except the last one, depends on only one other bunsetsu. The last bunsetsu depends on none.

2.2   Tags in the Kyoto Text Corpus

The Kyoto Text Corpus (KTC) is syntactically annotated in dependency formalism, and consists of 40,000 Japanese newspaper sentences. The information assigned in the corpus is as follows[8]:

Morphological Information:
- boundaries between words,
- pronunciation, basic form, part-of-speech, conjugation type, conjugation form of each word.

Syntactic Information:
- boundaries between bunsetsus,
- governor bunsetsu of each bunsetsu, and one of the following three relations between the bunsetsu and the governor bunsetsu:

  D: predicate-argument/adjunct relation or head-modifier relation,

  P: coordination relation,

  A: appositive relation.

Coordination and appositive relations are special cases. Other relations are included in D tag, so we call a relation indicated by D tag a "normal relation."

3   Tags in Japanese Statutory Corpus

We designed a Japanese statutory corpus based on KTC. Since it cannot handle some characteristics in statutory texts, we introduce a new design to solve them. In this section, we discuss the following three problems and propose solutions to them:

1. parenthesized phrases,
2. parallel structure,
3. technical terms in statutory sentences.

3.1   Parenthesized Phrases

Japanese statutory sentences very often have parenthesized phrases. In fact, their occurrence ratio in 194 laws and regulations is 24.7% $(18,503/75,024)$, while that in the EDR Japanese corpus version 1.5, which is collected from newspaper and magazine articles, is 0.755% $(1,569/207,832)$.

We show examples of parenthesized phrases in statutory sentences as follows.

(S1) 内閣府に、統計委員会 (以下「委員会」という。) を置く。 / The Statistics Commission (hereinafter referred to as "the Commission") shall be established in the Cabinet Office. [1]

(S2) 一組合員の出資口数は、出資総口数の百分の二十五 (信用協同組合にあつては、百分の十) を超えてはならない。 / The number of units of contribution per member shall not exceed twenty-five percent (ten percent in the case of a credit cooperative) of the total number of units of contribution. [2]

---

[1] Art. 44, para. (1) of Statistics Act (Act No. 53, 2007).

[2] Art. 10, para. (3) of Small and Medium Sized Enterprise, etc., Cooperatives Act (Act No. 181, 1949).

Fig. 1. Normal relation between inside and outside parentheses

(S3) 民事訴訟法第百五十四条（通訳人の立会い等）の規定は、審判に準用する。 /
Article 154 (Attendance of Interpreter, etc.) of the Code of Civil Procedure
shall apply mutatis mutandis to a trial. [3]

It is generally not easy to analyze a sentence including parenthesized phrases.
In addition, excluding the phrases, the sentence has the same structure regarding
morphological and syntactic information in many cases. Therefore, KTC does
not include parenthesized phrases; that is, if an original text has such phrases,
they have been excluded. However, parenthesized phrases play a prescribed role
and include information that should not be omitted in statutes. Thus, we have
to analyze and annotate statutory sentences including parenthesized phrases.

To annotate tags to parenthesized phrases, we should consider the relations
between phrases inside and outside parentheses. To solve this problem, we assume that *each of the phrases inside and outside parentheses forms a sentence*.
This assumption can allow us to independently annotate parenthesized phrases
and the remaining part of the sentence after excluding them (hereafter we call
the latter a *parenthesized-phrase-free sentence (PPFS)*).

Here, we define three types of dependency relations between a parenthesized
phrase and its PPFS, since they originally form one sentence and all bunsetsus
have some relation to some other bunsetsus in a sentence. These definitions are
a reclassification of relation types classified by legal experts[9]. Our definition
considers a parenthesis to be a special bunsetsu that links a parenthesized phrase
to its PPFS, and the dependency relation between them is established through
the right parenthesis.

Normal Relation. The parenthesized phrases used for definition, abbreviation,
as well as expansion or restriction of meaning include a predicate ending with
the punctuation mark "。" corresponding to an English period. Since such a
parenthesized phrase is considered as a modifier to the bunsetsu in its PPFS, we
define that the last bunsetsu in a parenthesized phrase depends on the bunsetsu
just before the left parenthesis with a normal relation.

For example, the dependency structure of (S1) is shown in Fig. 1. In this
paper, "A → B" indicates "A depends on B" and the arcs without tags indicate
their relations are normal; that is, D tags are usually omitted.

---

[3] Art. 146, para. (1) of Patent Act (Act No. 121, 1959).

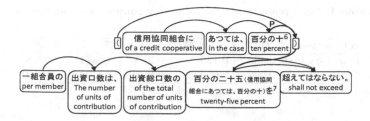

Fig. 2. Coordination relation between inside and outside parentheses

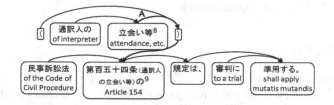

Fig. 3. Appositive relation between inside and outside parentheses

Notice that we tag a connection between a bunsetsu "いう"[4] and a right parenthesis ")" instead of between "いう"[4] and another bunsetsu "統計委員会を"[5] in order to keep the non-crossing dependency constraint. In Fig. 1, the D tag on the arc between "いう"[4] and ")" indicates that "いう"[4] depends on "統計委員会を"[5] with normal relation.

Coordination Relation. The parenthesized phrases that indicate whether to replace the words just before the phrases with the words in the phrases under some conditions include a conditional phrase and replacing words that have the same part-of-speech as the replaced one. Since such replacing words and the replaced words are considered as coordinates, we define that the last bunsetsu in a parenthesized phrase depends on the bunsetsu just before the left parenthesis with a coordination relation.

For example, the dependency structure of (S2) is shown in Fig. 2. As with the case of the normal relation, the P tag on the arc between "百分の十"[6] and ")" indicates that "百分の十"[6] and "百分の二十五を"[7] have a coordination relation.

Appositive Relation. The parenthesized phrases used for supplementation such as a law number or a summary include only a noun phrase. Since such a noun phrase refers to the same person or thing as the words just before the phrases, we define that the last bunsetsu in a parenthesized phrase depends on the bunsetsu just before the left parenthesis with an appositive relation.

---

[4] "いう" is equivalent to "referred to" in English.

[5] "統計委員会を" is equivalent to "The Statistics Commission."

[6] "百分の十" is equivalent to "ten percent."

[7] "百分の二十五を" is equivalent to "twenty-five percent."

Table 1. Occurrence ratio of coordinating conjunctions per sentence

conjunction	又は[10]	若しくは[11]	及び[12]	並びに[13]	かつ[14]
statutory text	0.439	0.129	0.255	0.0374	0.0278
EDR corpus[†]	0.00287	0.000250	0.00507	0.000279	0.00101

† *Hiragana* notations are included.

For example, the dependency structure of (S3) is shown as Fig. 3 and the A tag on the arc between "立会い等"[8] and ")" indicates that "立会い等"[8] and "第百五十四条の"[9] have an appositive relation.

3.2 Parallel Structure

Five coordinating conjunctions "又は,"[10] "若しくは,"[11] "及び,"[12] "並びに,"[13] and "かつ"[14] are very often used in Japanese statutory sentences (Table 1). The conjunctions "又は"[10] and "若しくは"[11] present options, alternates or substitutes and are equivalent to "or." The conjunctions "及び,"[12] "並びに,"[13] and "かつ"[14] are used to connect words, phrases or clauses and are equivalent to "and." There are few differences between "又は"[10] and "若しくは,"[11] or "及び"[12] and "並びに"[13] in ordinary Japanese usage, while there is clear differentiation in Japanese statutory sentences according to legislative custom, which indicates hierarchical parallel structure clearly.

Parts of Speech and Bunsetsu Boundary. KTC classifies coordinating conjunctions into two types of part-of-speech as follows.

(S4) 競争関係にある他人の営業上の信用を害する虚偽の事実を告知し、又は 流布する行為 / acts of making or circulating a false allegation that is injurious to the business reputation of another person in a competitive relationship [15]

(S5) 外国の政府 又は 地方公共団体の公務に従事する者 / a person who engages in public services for a foreign state or local government [16]

If a coordinating conjunction follows the previous words with a punctuation mark "、" as in (S4), it is classified as a conjunction. On the other hand, if it follows without the punctuation mark as in (S5), it is classified as a conjunctive

---

[8] "立会い等" is equivalent to "attendance, etc."

[9] "第百五十四条の" is equivalent to "Article 154."

[10] "又は" is equivalent to "or."

[11] "若しくは" is equivalent to "or."

[12] "及び" is equivalent to "and."

[13] "並びに" is equivalent to "and."

[14] "かつ" is equivalent to "and."

[15] Art. 2, para.(1), item (xiv) of Unfair Competition Prevention Act (Act No. 47, 1993).

[16] Art. 18, para.(2), item (i) of Unfair Competition Prevention Act (Act No. 47, 1993).

Fig. 4. Parallel structures based on KTC

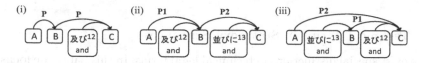

Fig. 5. Parallel structures based on the statutory corpus

particle. Note that the Japanese punctuation mark "、" sometimes does not correspond to an English comma in translation; that is, we cannot distinguish this difference in the English translation.

KTC defines that a coordinating conjunction and its previous word form one bunsetsu in both cases. However, a bunsetsu usually consists of a word alone or a word with some particles or other suffixes, and Japanese coordinating conjunctions are considered as a word, not as a particle or a suffix. Therefore, we considered that the definition of KTC is unnatural.

In the statutory texts, the punctuation mark "、" is inserted when both words before and after a coordinating conjunction are verbs, adjectives or adverbs. That is to say, the occurrence of the punctuation mark depends on legal orthography and the role of coordinating conjunctions is independent of the occurrence.

Thus, we define that a coordinating conjunction constantly forms one bunsetsu and its part-of-speech is a conjunction in the statutory sentences.

Hierarchical Parallel Structure. According to Japanese legislative customs, the use of "又は"[10] and "若しくは"[11] and the use of "及び"[12] and "並びに"[13] indicate strength of parallel structure in statutory sentences. For example, in the following phrases, three words A, B and C have right-side relations, respectively, where words in the inside parentheses have stronger connection.

(i) A, B 及び[12] C   → (A, B 及び[12] C)
(ii) A 及び[12] B 並びに[13] C → ((A 及び[12] B) 並びに[13] C)
(iii) A 並びに[13] B 及び[12] C → (A 並びに[13] (B 及び[12] C))

KTC prepares only a P tag for coordination relation, and it can distinguish only two types of parallel structures as shown in Fig. 4. Hence, the design of KTC cannot distinguish the above three structures.

To overcome this problem, we attach a number to P tags that indicates the strength of parallel relation, where the smaller number indicates the stronger connection. We can annotate the structures in the above example as shown in Fig. 5, where the parallel structure of "及び"[12] tagged with P1 is stronger than that of "並びに"[13] tagged with P2. Notice that, when all parallel relations have the same strength, P tags are annotated.

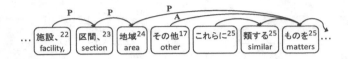

Fig. 6. Dependency relations in the statutory sentence with "その他"

3.3   Technical Terms in Statutory Sentences

There exist special distinctions in technical legal terms. In this paper, we focus on the distinction between "その他"[17] and "その他の,"[18] which have few differences in ordinary Japanese usage. The following examples (S6) and (S7) illustrate the distinction. However, since both "その他"[17] and "その他の"[18] are equivalent to "other" in English, it is difficult to make the distinction in English translation.

(S6) 法律の規定に基づき施設、区間、地域 その他 これらに類するものを指定する
命令又は規則 / Orders or rules which provide for, pursuant to the provisions of Acts, the designation of facility, section, area and other similar matters. [19]

(S7) 公務員の給与、勤務時間 その他の 勤務条件について定める命令等 / Administrative Orders, etc. about the salaries, working hours and other working conditions of public officers [20]

"その他"   KTC considers that "その他"[17] depends on the following words with an appositive relation in the same way as "など."[21]

On the other hand, in the statutory texts, "その他"[17] is used for parallel exemplification and has a clear distinction from "など."[21] In (S6), "施設,"[22] "区間,"[23] "地域"[24] and "これらに類するもの"[25] are ranked equally and "これらに類するもの"[25] includes none of "施設,"[22] "区間,"[23] or "地域."[24] That is, in this case, "その他"[17] indicates the elements in a set of something without "施設,"[22] "区間"[23] and "地域."[24] Therefore, it indicates the same things indicated by "これらに類するもの."[25]

From this, we defined that the part-of-speech of "その他"[17] is a pronoun and it depends on the following appropriate bunsetsu with an appositive relation as shown in Fig. 6.

"その他の"   KTC considers that "その他の"[18] depends on the following appropriate words with normal relation.

---

[17] "その他" is equivalent to "other."

[18] "その他の" is equivalent to "other." and consists of "その他"[17] and a particle "の."

[19] Art. 3, para. (2), item (iv) of Administrative Procedure Act (Act No. 88, 1993).

[20] Art. 3, para. (2), item (v) of Administrative Procedure Act (Act No. 88, 1993).

[21] "など" is equivalent to "etc."

[22] "施設" is equivalent to "facility."

[23] "区間" is equivalent to "section."

[24] "地域" is equivalent to "area."

[25] "これらに類するもの" is equivalent to "similar matters."

Fig. 7. Dependency relations in the statutory sentence with "その他の"

On the other hand, in the statutory texts, "その他の"[18] indicates that the words before it are subordinate concepts of the word after it. In (S7), "給与"[26] and "勤務時間"[27] denote equally ranked concepts and both are subordinate to "勤務条件."[28] That is, in this case, "その他の"[18] indicates the "勤務条件"[28] except for "給与"[26] and "勤務時間."[27] Therefore, it is considered to be equivalent to "給与"[26] and "勤務時間"[27] in structure.

From this, we define that the part-of-speech of "その他"[17] is a pronoun and it has a coordination relation with the preceding appropriate words. In addition, the bunsetsu "その他の"[18] depends on the following appropriate bunsetsu with an appositive relation as shown in Fig. 7.

4 Compilation of Statutory Corpus

In this section, we describe how to compile a statutory corpus based on our design mentioned in Sect. 3. First, we describe the entire process briefly, then show the problems caused by Japanese analyzers. In particular, the structures peculiar to Japanese statutory sentences cause analysis errors. To overcome these problems, we construct an automatic correction tool for parsing results.

4.1 Compilation of Corpus

The project to compile KTC used a Japanese morphological analyzer, JUMAN[7], and a Japanese dependency structure analyzer, KNP[6], to annotate the corpus.

Although the information annotated to our statutory corpus is based on KTC, we used other analyzers: a morphological analyzer, ChaSen[1], and a dependency structure analyzer, CaboCha[4, 5]. The practical reason we chose them is the part-of-speech systems of the morphological analyzers. JUMAN adopts a special part-of-speech system that is unfamiliar to many people. On the other hand, the part-of-speech system of ChaSen is almost the same as that which most Japanese people learned in school. Thus, we adopted ChaSen for our project. In addition, since KNP uses JUMAN's result for input, we adopted CaboCha, which can analyze the output of both JUMAN and ChaSen.

However, these analyzers sometimes output incorrect results. Statutory texts including long sentences and many technical terms cause analysis errors. In addition, the analyzers cannot deal with structures such as parenthesized phrases and

---

[26] "給与" is equivalent to "salaries."
[27] "勤務時間" is equivalent to "working hours."
[28] "勤務条件" is equivalent to "working conditions."

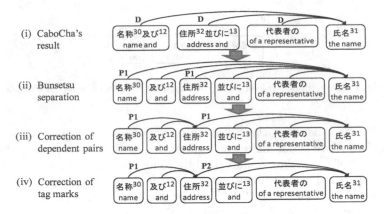

Fig. 8. Example of correcting dependency

parallel structure, for which we proposed solutions in Sect. 3. Therefore, human annotators should correct such errors. Through such correction, we classified the errors into several types and made an automatic correction tool for some of them. To stay within page limits, we describe an example of error correction instead of showing correction methods in detail. In the following example, we focused on the parallel structures.

4.2   Correction of Dependency Relations

Since the parallel structures in statutory texts differ from those in ordinary texts mentioned above, CaboCha cannot analyze them correctly. Figure 8 illustrates the correction procedure for the sentence "名称及び住所並びに代表者の氏名." [29]

Separation of conjunctions. Figure 8(i) is the output of CaboCha, and it contains four bunsetsus. CaboCha often concludes that a conjunction and its preceding noun form one bunsetsu as shown in the figure, where the first bunsetsu includes "及び" [12] and the second bunsetsu includes "並びに." [13] However, a single conjunction forms one bunsetsu in our design as we mentioned in Sect. 3.2. Thus, we separate the conjunctions from each bunsetsu. Both bunsetsus are broken up and dependency tags are also corrected as shown in Fig. 8(ii).

Correcting dependency relations. In Fig. 8(ii), the first bunsetsu "名称" [30] depends on the last bunsetsu "氏名" [31] beyond other bunsetsus. However, since the conjunction "及び" [12] connects the two words before and after it, it is wrong

---

[29] "名称及び住所並びに代表者の氏名" is from Art. 14, para. (1), item (i) of Consumer Contract Act (Act No. 61, 2000) and equivalent to "Name and address and the name of a representative."

[30] "名称" is equivalent to "name."

[31] "氏名" is equivalent to "name."

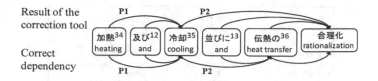

Fig. 9. Example of correction error

that "名称"[30] just before the conjunction depends on some bunsetsu beyond another conjunction. Thus, the tool makes both "名称"[30] and "及び"[12] depend on "住所,"[32] which follows "及び."[12]

There are other patterns of parallel structures in statutory texts. We analyzed these patterns and made nine correction rules for them.

Correcting dependency tags. In Fig. 8(iii), there are two P1 tags. Since the two conjunctions "及び"[12] and "並びに"[13] have different strength as mentioned in Sect. 3.2, we correct the tags. In this case, the second P1 tag is replaced with P2 since the "並びに"[13] has a weak relation.

Finally, we can get the correct dependency structure as shown in Fig. 8(iv), where "名称,"[30] "住所"[32] and "氏名"[31] are coordinate.

4.3 Limit of Automatic Correction

In the case of Fig. 8, our automatic correction tool works correctly. In the case of another example, "加熱及び冷却並びに伝熱の合理化,"[33] our tool outputs the above dependency in Fig. 9. However, it is wrong and the correct dependency is shown below, where "加熱,"[34] "冷却"[35] and "伝熱"[36] are coordinate.

When the morphological analyzer ChaSen analyzes both examples, they have the same sequences as part-of-speech tags. Therefore, we need more advanced information such as semantics in order to distinguish them. In our study, we do not automatically correct them and relegate the task to human experts.

5 Conclusion

We proposed the design of a syntactically tagged corpus of Japanese statutory sentences and implemented a support tool to compile the corpus. We have already tagged 12 acts and regulations containing 2,052 sentences. Figure 10 shows part of our corpus, and we continue to compile other statutes.

---

[32] "住所" is equivalent to "address."

[33] "加熱及び冷却並びに伝熱の合理化" is from Art. 5, para. (1), item (ii) of Act on the Rational Use of Energy (Act No. 47, 2008) and equivalent to "Rationalization of heating and cooling as well as heat transfer."

[34] "加熱" is equivalent to "heating."

[35] "冷却" is equivalent to "cooling."

[36] "伝熱" is equivalent to "heat transfer."

* 0 2P1 加熱	カネツ	加熱	名詞-サ変接続
(heating	*kanetsu*		Noun - Sa-hen)
* 1 2D 及び	オヨビ	及び	接続詞
(and	*oyobi*		Conjunction)
* 2 4P2 冷却	レイキャク	冷却	名詞-サ変接続
(cooling	*reikyaku*		Noun - Sa-hen)
* 3 4D 並びに	ナラビニ	並びに	接続詞
(and	*narabini*		Conjunction)
* 4 5D 伝熱	デンネツ	伝熱	名詞-一般
(heat transfer	*den'netsu*		Noun - Common)
4 5D の	ノ	の	助詞-連体化
(	*no*		Particle - Attributive)
* 5 -1O 合理化	ゴウリカ	合理	名詞-サ変接続
(rationalization	*gourika*		Noun - Sa-hen)

Fig. 10. Example of statutory corpus with morphological and syntactic information

The recall of the output of CaboCha, i.e. the ratio of bunsetsus correctly separated and annotated, is 67.0%, while the one of our support tool is 76.6%. The improvement of the tool using feedback from human annotators remains for future work. In addition, we are planning to apply machine learning techniques to our statutory sentences to improve the parser. The acquisition of lexical knowledge from the corpus also constitutes future work.

References

1. Asahara, M., Matsumoto, Y.: Extended models and tools for high-performance part-of-speech tagger. In: Proc. COLING 2000, pp. 21–27 (2000)
2. Hagiwara, M., Ogawa, Y., Toyama, K.: Effective Use of Indirect Dependency for Distributional Similarity. Journal of Natural Language Processing 14(5), 119–150 (2008)
3. Hagiwara, M., Ogawa, Y., Toyama, K.: Bootstrapping-based Extraction of Dictionary Terms from Unsegmented Legal Text. In: Hattori, H., Kawamura, T., Idé, T., Yokoo, M., Murakami, Y. (eds.) JSAI 2008. LNCS, vol. 5447, pp. 213–227. Springer, Heidelberg (2009)
4. Kudo, T., Matsumoto, M.: Japanese Dependency Analysis using Cascaded Chunking. In: Proc. CoNLL 2002, pp. 63–69 (2002)
5. Kudo, T., Matsumoto, M.: Fast Methods for Kernel-based Text Analysis. In: Proc. ACL 2003, pp.24–31 (2003)
6. Kurohashi, S., Nagao, M.: KN Parser: Japanese Dependency/Case Structure Analyzer. In: Proc. Workshop on Sharable Natural Language Resources, pp. 48–55 (1994)
7. Kurohashi, S., Nakamura, T., Matsumoto, Y., Nagao, M.: Improvements of Japanese morphological analyzer JUMAN. In: Proc. Workshop on Sharable Natural Language Resources, pp. 22–28 (1994)
8. Kurohashi, S., Nagao, M.: Building a Japanese Parsed Corpus. In: Abeille, A. (ed.) Treebanks: Building and Using Parsed Corpora, pp. 249–260. Kluwer, Dordrecht (2003)
9. Maeda, M.: Workbook Hosei Shitsumu (revised ed.), Gyosei, Tokyo (2005)
10. Ohno, T., Matsubara, S., Kawaguchi, N., Inagaki, Y.: Robust Dependency Parsing of Spontaneous Japanese Spoken Language. IEICE Trans. E88-D(3), 545–552 (2005)
11. Padó, S., Lapata, M.: Dependency-Based Construction of Semantic Space Models. Computational Linguistics 33(2), 161–199 (2007)

PROLEG: An Implementation of the Presupposed Ultimate Fact Theory of Japanese Civil Code by PROLOG Technology*

Ken Satoh, Kento Asai, Takamune Kogawa, Masahiro Kubota, Megumi Nakamura, Yoshiaki Nishigai, Kei Shirakawa, and Chiaki Takano

National Institute of Informatics and Sokendai
ksatoh@nii.ac.jp

Abstract. In this paper, we propose a legal reasoning system called *PROLEG* (PROlog based LEGal reasoning support system) based on the Japanese "theory of presupposed ultimate facts" (called "Yoken-jijitsu-ron" in Japanese, the JUF theory, in short). The theory is used for decision making by judges under incomplete information. Previously, we proposed a translation of the theory into logic programming. However, it turns out that the knowledge representation in logic programming is difficult for lawyers to understand. So, in this paper, we change knowledge representation of rules in the JUF theory in PROLEG so that we reflect lawyers' reasoning using the idea of "openness" proposed by a judge who is a main investigator of the JUF theory.

1 Introduction

The Japanese Presupposed Ultimate Fact Theory[3](JUF theory we call in this paper and called *"Yoken-jijitsu-ron"* in Japanese) is a decision making tool used in civil litigation. The JUF theory attaches a burden of proof[6] to each conditions in civil code in order for a judge to enable to make a judgement even if truth values of some facts are not known because of a lack of enough evidence.

Previously, we proposed a mathematical semantics of the JUF theory in [7] based on logic programming with "negation as failure". However, from the experience of giving explanation of our formalization in logic programming to lawyers, it turns out that a semantics of logic programming with "negation as failure" is difficult for lawyers to understand. Since the aim of our research is to give a support system of lawyers and a computer-aided learning system of the JUF theory for law school students and scholars who seek their interpretations of civil code, it is necessary for us to propose a system which is understandable to lawyers. Fortunately, in legal domain, Ito, who is one of the main investigator of the JUF theory as a lawyer, explains the JUF theory using *openness* of the ultimate facts[3]. He divides ultimate facts in a condition of a rule into two

---

* This work has been done partially while Kento Asai, Masahiro Kubota, Megumi Nakamura, Kei Shirakawa and Chiaki Takano were with NII.

T. Onoda, D. Bekki, and E. McCready (Eds.): JSAI-isAI 2010, LNAI 6797, pp. 153–164, 2011.

categories; one category corresponds with facts which normally lead to the conclusion of a rule and the other category corresponds with facts which represent exceptional situations. Ito argues that a fact in the latter category is regarded as "open" so that the truth value is not decided until the counterpart explicitly alleges and proves the fact. Therefore, it is sufficient for a judge to make a deduction using normal rules in order to draw a conclusion when exceptional facts are not explicitly known. So, we decide to change the knowledge representation of the JUF theory into the one which simulates Ito's explanation of the JUF theory and propose *PROLEG* (PROlog based LEGal reasoning support system) in this paper. Specifically, we separate a positive condition part and a "negation as failure" part in order to familiarize a rule form with a lawyer in PROLEG.

PROLEG consists of two knowledge bases; a *rulebase* and a *factbase*. A rulebase stores rules and exceptions defined in the JUF theory and a factbase stores information about actions in the court performed by both parties and judgement of truth values by judge for ultimate facts in a given legal case (see Appendix A). Then, PROLEG automatically applies a rule or exceptions which matches true ultimate facts and gives an answer whether a conclusion of a case is derived or not together with a trace of derivation (see Appendix B).

In this sense, it is related with "rule-based legal expert systems" many of which have been developed so far[4,8,9]. However, we believe that none of the work incorporates burden of proof in their system. On the other hand, PROLEG is based on the JUF theory so that burden of proof is incorporated into the system and correctly handles uncertainty as shown in [7]. Moreover, while previous approaches considered more specific legal domains such as Tax law[4], British Nationality Act[8], and the United Nations Convention on Contracts for the International Sale of Goods (CISG)[9], PROLEG considered civil code in general since PROLEG is based on the JUF theory which has been developed by judges in the Japanese Legal Training and Research Institute for civil litigation in general. In addition to this generality, the JUF theory has been taught to all trainees of lawyers at the Institute for many years and proved its usefulness. Therefore, we believe that generality and usefulness of the JUF theory ensures the generality and the usefulness of PROLEG.

Moreover, PROLEG can represent actions by both parties in the court and judgements of the ultimate facts by a judge in a factbase. These actions and judgements actually corresponds with actions and judgement of civil procedure law so these representation also enhances familiarity of PROLEG to lawyers.

PROLEG outputs a trace of derivation. This trace is represented in the form of an argument between plaintiff and defendant. In this sense, PROLEG relates with argumentation systems[1,5,2]. As shown in[7], the JUF theory itself can be translated into a logic program with negation as failure and therefore the semantics of PROLEG may be formalized by Dung's argumentation semantics[1] since Dung's semantics was originally aimed at giving a semantics of a logic program. However, the main function of PROLEG is not to give an argumentation system, but to simulate the judge's decision process and a derivation trace is only a by-product of legal reasoning performed by a judge in the form of argument.

However, there might be a possibility of using PROLEG indirectly as an argumentation system. That is, in stead of using PROLEG by a judge, a plaintiff and a defendant provide ultimate facts according to a burden of proof so an argument between a plaintiff and a defendant is constructed during the court activity. However, rules in the JUF theory is fixed so both parties can provide only ultimate facts to create an argument. Therefore, PROLEG has less freedom of making arguments compared with other argumentation system such as Carneades system [2] which has a function of making rules to produce new arguments.

2   The JUF Theory

We explain the JUF theory using the following working example.

- Suppose that a plaintiff claims that a lease contract for his house between him and the defendant ended by his cancellation of the contract[1] because the defendant let his sister use a room in the house. The plaintiff alleged that the contract was concluded [2], and his house was handed over to the defendant by the lease contract[3], and the sublease contract between the defendant and his sister was concluded [4], and the room in his house was handed over to his sister by the sublease contract[5], and she used the room or make profit by using the room[6], and the plaintiff manifested the intention of cancellation of the lease contract[7].
- In turn, the defendant alleged that
  - the plaintiff approved the sublease[8], and the approval was before the cancellation[9].
  - his subleasing a room to her does not cause any abuse of confidence with the plaintiff because the time of use was very short[10].
- In turn, the plaintiff alleged that neighbors' complaints about noise from piano lessons during subleasing abused the confidence with the plaintiff[11].

To handle the above case, we took into account the Japanese Civil Code Article 612,

---

[1] In this paper, this fact is represented as `cancellation_due_to_sublease`. Note that in this paper, we only considers propositional case for the sake of simplicity. But our system can handle the first-order case with variables.

[2] This fact is represented as `agreement_of_lease_contract`.

[3] This fact is represented as `handover_to_lessee`.

[4] This fact is represented as `agreement_of_sublease_contract`.

[5] This fact is represented as `handover_to_sublessee`.

[6] This fact is represented as `using_leased_thing`.

[7] This fact is represented as `manifestation_cancellation`.

[8] This fact is represented as `approval_of_sublease`.

[9] This fact is represented as `approval_before_cancellation`.

[10] This fact is represented as `fact_of_nonabuse_of_confidence`.

[11] This fact is represented as `fact_of_abuse_of_confidence`.

- Paragraph 1 states that a lessee may not assign the lessee's rights or sublease a leased thing without obtaining the approval of the lessor, and
- Paragraph 2 states that if the lessee allows any third party to make use of or take profits from a leased thing in violation of the provisions of the preceding paragraph, the lessor may cancel the contract.

However, according to the previous Supreme Court case[12], paragraph 2 is not applicable in exceptional situations where the sublease does not harm the confidence between a lessee and a lessor.

So from these rules, it firstly must be shown that the contract with the defendant was concluded and then that the contract is terminated by cancellation because of the sublease to the defendant's sister based on paragraph 2. If there were no counter-arguments, we can conclude that the lease contract is canceled. However, there are two possible counter-arguments. One counter-argument is that the plaintiff had given approval of the subleasing to the defendant according to paragraph 1, whereas the other counter-argument is that the defendant had not abused the confidence of the plaintiff according to the case rule above. Suppose that we can not conclude that the approval was given or not because of a lack of evidence. In this case, we cannot deductively prove that the counter-argument is true or not. However, the decision has to be made by the court, so we have to find a way to solve the above problem. In order to solve the problem, a judge use the idea of *burden of proof*. The idea of burden of proof is that if a party which has a burden of proof of a fact fails to prove that the fact is true, then the fact is considered to be false. In the above case, since the burden of showing the existence of approval resides in the defendant, if the defendant fails to prove that there was an approval, no approval was considered to be made.

However, in order to use this idea, we must decide to which party the burden of proof of each ultimate fact is assigned. Therefore, there has been a high demand for deciding to assign the burden of proof in each civil law code. In Japan, a group of judges has been developing just such an assignment of the burden of proof and this theory of assignment is called the "Presupposed Ultimate Fact Theory" (called "*Yoken-jijitsu-ron*" in Japanese).

3 Reflexion of Lawyers' Reasoning

3.1 Rule Format

In our previous logic programming translation[7], we explicitly introduce "negation as failure" in order to express exceptions. In the above example, the rule is formalized using "negation as failure" as follows:

```
cancellation_due_to_sublease :-
agreement_of_lease_contract,
handover_to_lessee,
agreement_of_sublease_contract,
```

---

[12] Supreme Court Case:1966.1.27,20-1 Minsyu 136.

```
handover_to_sublessee,
using_leased_thing,
manifestation_cancellation,
not (approval_of_sublease,approval_before_cancellation),
not fact_of_nonabuse_of_confidence.
```

In this representation, a user must understand the semantics of "negation as failure" in logic programming and it would prevent a user from understanding the behavior of the system. Especially, if "negation as failure" is nested, semantics becomes too complicated to understand. Fortunately, in legal domain, Ito, who is one of the main investigator of the JUF theory as a lawyer, explains the JUF theory using *openness* of the ultimate facts[3]. He divides ultimate facts in a condition of a rule into two categories; one category corresponds with facts which normally lead to the conclusion of a rule and the other category corresponds with facts which represent exceptional situations. Ito argues that a fact in the latter category is regarded as "open" so that the truth value is not decided until the counterpart explicitly prove the fact. Therefore, it is sufficient for a judge to make a deduction using normal rules in order to draw a conclusion when exceptional facts are not explicitly known. So, we decided to change the syntax of the above rules into new knowledge representation call *PROLEG* rules to simulate Ito's inference. That is, we separate a positive condition part and a "negation as failure" part in order to familiarize a rule form with a lawyer. The above example is represented in PROLEG as follows:

```
cancellation_due_to_sublease <=
agreement_of_lease_contract,
handover_to_lessee,
agreement_of_sublease_contract,
handover_to_sublessee,
using_leased_thing,
manifestation_cancellation.

exception(cancellation_due_to_sublease,get_approval_of_sublease).
exception(cancellation_due_to_sublease,nonabuse_of_confidence).
get_approval_of_sublease <=
approval_of_sublease,approval_before_cancellation.
nonabuse_of_confidence<=
fact_of_nonabuse_of_confidence.
```

We then introduce "exception" predicate which takes two arguments, the former of which is the head of default rule [13] and the latter of which is an exception of the rule. This is used for the check of existence of exceptions by the meta-interpreter.

Moreover, we introduce *intermediate concept* which aggregates some ultimate facts or intermediate concepts in order to summarize meaningful sets of these or if

---

[13] Let $H \Leftarrow B_1, ..., B_n$ be a PROLEG rule. We call H as a head of the rule and $B_1, ..., B_n$ a body of the rule. $H, B_1, ..., B_n$ are atoms which have the same syntax as PROLOG terms so they have the same representation power as PROLOG terms.

some concepts will be used for a higher level concept. Although the intermediate concept is not proposed in the JUF theory, we believe that it also enhances readability of knowledge representation in PROLEG.

As an example of intermediate concept which aggregates some of the conditions, we could introduce `effective_lease_contract` and a rule

```
effective_lease_contract <=
    agreement_of_lease_contract,handover_to_lessee.
```

in order to summarize how to make a lease contract effective and replace `agreement_of_lease_contract` and `handover_to_lessee` in the above rule by `effective_lease_contract`.

As an example of intermediate concept which is used for a higher level concept, "the cancellation of lease contract due to sublease without approval" can be one of causes for ceasing the lease contract[14] and there are other causes, for example, "expiring the term of lease contract"[15]. In this case, `contract_end` is a higher level concept over `cancellation_due_to_sublease` and `expiration_of_the_term_of_the_lease_contract`, so we can use these concept as an intermediate concept for `contract_end` and introduce the following rules:

```
contract_end <= cancellation_due_to_sublease.
contract_end <= expiration_of_the_term_of_the_lease_contract.
```

We show a complete rule set for the above example in the Appendix A.

3.2   Fact Handling

To check the truth of fact in conditions, we introduce four kind of predicates "allege", "provide_evidence", "plausible", "admission".

"allege", "provide_evidence", "admission" are actions performed by each party during argument at the court and "plausible" represents judgement about the fact performed by judge.

- "allege(F,P)" is an action of allegement of truth value of a fact F by a party P.
- "provide_evidence(F,P)" is an action of providing some evidence to support the truth of a fact F performed by a party P.
- "admission(F,P)" is an action of admission of the truth of a fact F asserted by a party P.
- "plausible(F)" means that the standard of proof for F is satisfied and F is regarded as true.

In civil litigation, each party must firstly allege a fact to the judge which the party would like to prove. Otherwise, the fact will not be considered by the judge. This is called a burden of production. allege(F,P) predicate is used to express such allegement. We also consider a burden of providing evidence. If either of

---

[14] Ceasing the lease contract is represented as "contract_end" in this paper.
[15] This fact is represented as "expiration_of_the_term_of_the_lease_contract" in this paper.

the burden of production and providing evidence is not fulfilled, the fact will not be considered by the judge. `provide_evidence(F,P)` predicate represents this action. If `allege(F,P)` and `provide_evidence(F,P)` are satisfied then the judge will consider the truth value of the fact F and if `plausible` is true then F is considered to be true. Moreover, in civil litigation, even if neither `allege(F,P)` nor `provide_evidence(F,P)` is performed by a party P, if the opposite party O admits the fact F, F must be considered to be true. `admission(F,O)` expresses this situation.

We show an example of such fact information for the cancellation example in the Appendix A[16].

4   Execution of PROLEG

In this section, we explain the main function of PROLEG. The function is to check whether the conclusion is proved or not according to rules and facts. However, for the sake of understanding reasoning process, PROLEG will show a trace of reasoning by adding printing function along with reasoning in the form of an argument between a plaintiff and a defendant.

The detail of the meta-interpreter can be found in Fig. 1. Given a goal G which represents a conclusion, the meta-interpreter calls prove($\{G\},P$). Then, the meta-interpreter checks whether there is a rule whose head is unifiable with G. Then we try to prove the body of the rule. If all the B_i's are proved, we check exceptions. If there is no exception, then the execution succeeds, that is, the plaintiff wins. If there exist exceptions for the rule, that is, there is exception(A,E) s.t. A is unifiable with H, then we have to check whether each exception(A,E) fails by checking whether prove($\{E\}$,opposite(P)) fails where opposite(P) is a counter party of P. If there exists an exception(A,E) which succeeds then the execution fails.

In the step of derivation of G, we replace a goal by literals in the body of the rule which matches a goal until we encounter an ultimate fact. If we encounter an ultimate fact F, the meta-interpreter checks if plausible(F) or admission(F,opposite(P)) is not in the factbase.

Note that before checking truth of a new body of the rule, we check for all the ultimate facts F to satisfy the rules, if (allege(F,P) and provide_evidence(F,P)) or admission(F,opposite(P)) is in the factbase. Otherwise,

---

[16] In the factbase, we assume that the defendant admits all the conditions of cancellation rule due to sublease without approval, `agreement_of_lease_contract`, `handover_to_lessee`, `agreement_of_sublease_contract`, `handover_to_sublessee`, `using_leased_thing`, `manifestation_cancellation`. In turn, the defendant makes a counter-arguments of `get_approval_of_sublease` and `nonabuse_of_confidence` but fails to persuade the judge about `get_approval_of_sublease` and `approval_before_cancellation`(expressing by the non-existence of `plausible(approval_of_sublease)` and `plausible(approval_before_cancellation)` in the factbase), and in turn a plaintiff make a counter-counter-argument of `fact_of_abuse_of_confidence`.

```
prove(S,P) goal set S; party P;
begin
  if S == ∅ return(true);
  select an atom A ∈ S;
  if A is an ultimate fact s.t. plausible(F) or admission(F,opposite(P))
    is in a factbase and F is unifiable with A then
  begin
    S := S − {A}; return(prove(S,P))
  end
  else if A is an intermediate concept then
  begin
    select a rule H ⇐ B₁, ..., Bₙ
      whose head matches A with H by most general unifier θ;
    if such a rule does not exist then return(false);
    select δ s.t. alleged_and_having_evidence((B₁, ..., Bₙ)θ,P) returns δ;
    S := (S − {A} ∪ {B₁, ..., Bₙ})θδ;
    if prove(S,P)==true then
    begin
      for every exception(G,E) s.t. Aθδ is unified with G by most general unifier η
        if prove({Eθδη},opposite(P))==true then return(false)
      return(true)
    end
  end
  else return(false);
end

alleged_and_having_evidence(S,P) goal set S; party P;
begin
  if S == ∅ return(ε); /* ε is an empty substitution. */
  select an atom A ∈ S;
  if A is an ultimate fact s.t.
      (allege(F,P) and provide_evidence(F,P)) or admission(F,opposite(P))
      is in a factbase and F is unifiable with A by most general unifier θ then
  begin
    S := S − {A};
    δ = alleged_and_having_evidence(S,P);
    return(θδ)
  end
  else if A is an intermediate concept then
  begin
    select a rule H ⇐ B₁, ..., Bₙ
      whose head matches A with H by most general unifier θ;
    if such a rule does not exist then return(false);
    S := (S − {A} ∪ {B₁, ..., Bₙ})θ;
    δ = alleged_and_having_evidence(S,P);
    return(θδ)
  end
end
```

Fig. 1. Algorithm of PROLEG Meta-Interpreter

the meta-interpreter does not check the satisfaction of the body. Along with this checking, applicable rules will be instantiated so the instantiated rules will be shown in a trace of reasoning and it makes the reasoning process more intuitive.

A trace of execution of cancellation of leasing contract defined in the Appendix A can be found at the Appendix B. Note that although there is a rule about expiration_of_the_term_of_the_lease_contract is in Appendix A, the rule is not applied since there is no allegement of the fact in the condition of the rule. Therefore, no trace about applying the rule is shown in the Appendix B.

5 Conclusion

We presented PROLEG which simulates a process of reasoning about civil code with a burden of proof based on the JUF theory. The characteristic of PROLEG are as follows.

- PROLEG reflects lawyers' reasoning about law where exceptions are ignored unless it is explicitly stated.
- PROLEG handles legal actions at the court facts such as allegement, evidence production, plausibility and admission.

We have already wrote several examples in civil code in terms of the JUF theory such as contract law and property rights and checked the correctness of behavior of PROLEG using derivation traces. As future research, we plan the following.

- We will evaluate our claim that PROLEG is more familiar with lawyers than other legal representation language.
- We will develop a legal knowledge representation which has a syntax closer to natural language to enhance readability.
- We will develop a unified method of naming predicates and deciding predicate arguments.
- We will develop a diagrammatic representation of reasoning in the JUF theory.
- We will show that the JUF theory is applicable not only for the Japanese civil code, but any other laws such as foreign civil code or criminal laws.

References

1. Dung, P.M.: On the Acceptability of Arguments and its Fundamental Role in Nonmonotonic Reasoning, Logic Programming and n-Person Games. Artif. Intell. 77(2), 321–358 (1995)
2. Gordon, T.F., Prakken, H., Walton, D.: The Carneades Model of Argument and Burden of Proof. Artif. Intell. 171(10-15), 875–896 (2007)
3. Ito, S.: Lecture Series on Ultimate Facts. Shojihomu (2008) (in Japanese)
4. McCarty, L.T., Sridharan, N.S., Sangster, B.C.: The Implementation of TAXMAN II: An Experiment in Artificial Intelligence and Legal Reasoning. Report LRP-TR-2, Rutgers University (1979)

5. Prakken, H.: Logical Tools for Modelling Legal Argument: A Study of Defeasible Reasoning in Law. Law and Philosophy Library 32 (1997)
6. Prakken, H., Sartor, G.: Formalising Arguments about the Burden of Persuasion. In: Proc. of ICAIL 2007, pp. 97–106 (2007)
7. Satoh, K., Kubota, M., Nishigai, Y., Takano, C.: Translating the Japanese Presupposed Ultimate Fact Theory into Logic Programming. In: Proc. of JURIX 2009, pp. 162–171 (2009)
8. Sergot, M.J., Sadri, F., Kowalski, R.A., Kriwaczek, F., Hammond, P., Cory, H.T.: The British Nationality Act as a Logic Program. CACM 29(5), 370–386 (1986)
9. Yoshino, H.: On the Logical Foundations of Compound Predicate Formulae for Legal Knowledge Representation, vol. 5(1-2), pp. 77–96 (1997)

Appendix A: Example of PROLEG Program

```
%========================= PROLEG rulebase =========================
contract_end <= cancellation_due_to_sublease.
contract_end <= expiration_of_the_term_of_the_lease_contract.

cancellation_due_to_sublease<=
      agreement_of_lease_contract, handover_to_lessee,
      agreement_of_sublease_contract, handover_to_sublessee,
      using_leased_thing,
      manifestation_cancellation.

exception(cancellation_due_to_sublease,get_approval_of_sublease).
exception(cancellation_due_to_sublease,nonabuse_of_confidence).

get_approval_of_sublease <=
      approval_of_sublease,
      approval_before_cancellation.

nonabuse_of_confidence <= fact_of_nonabuse_of_confidence.

exception(nonabuse_of_confidence,abuse_of_confidence).
abuse_of_confidence <= fact_of_abuse_of_confidence.

expiration_of_the_term_of_the_lease_contract<=
          end_of_the_term_of_the_lease_contract,
          notice_of_renewal_refusal_between_12month_and_6month,
          justifiable_reason.
% ====================== PROLEG factbase =========================
admission(agreement_of_lease_contract,defendant).
admission(handover_to_lessee,defendant).
admission(agreement_of_sublease_contract,defendant).
admission(handover_to_sublessee,defendant).
admission(using_leased_thing,defendant).
admission(manifestation_cancellation,defendant).
```

```
allege(approval_of_sublease,defendant).
provide_evidence(approval_of_sublease,defendant).

allege(approval_before_cancellation,defendant).
provide_evidence(approval_before_cancellation,defendant).

allege(fact_of_nonabuse_of_confidence,defendant).
provide_evidence(fact_of_nonabuse_of_confidence,defendant).
plausible(fact_of_nonabuse_of_confidence).

allege(fact_of_abuse_of_confidence,plaintiff).
provide_evidence(fact_of_abuse_of_confidence,plaintiff).
plausible(fact_of_abuse_of_confidence).
```

Appendix B: Example of PROLEG Execution Trace

```
1    plaintiff tried to prove "contract_end".
2    To prove "contract_end",
3      we need to prove the following requisites:
4
5        requisite1: cancellation_due_to_sublease
6
7      plaintiff tried to prove "cancellation_due_to_sublease".
8      To prove "cancellation_due_to_sublease",
9        we need to prove the following requisites:
10
11          requisite1: agreement_of_lease_contract
12          requisite2: handover_to_lessee
13          requisite3: agreement_of_sublease_contract
14          requisite4: handover_to_sublessee
15          requisite5: using_leased_thing
16          requisite6: manifestation_cancellation
17
18        defendant admitted "agreement_of_lease_contract".
19        defendant admitted "handover_to_lessee".
20        defendant admitted "agreement_of_sublease_contract".
21        defendant admitted "handover_to_sublessee".
22        defendant admitted "using_leased_thing".
23        defendant admitted "manifestation_cancellation".
24        defendant alleges "get_approval_of_sublease"
25          as a defense against "cancellation_due_to_sublease".
26          defendant tried to prove "get_approval_of_sublease".
27          To prove "get_approval_of_sublease",
28            we need to prove the following requisites:
29
30              requisite1: approval_of_sublease
31              requisite2: approval_before_cancellation
32
```

```
33              defendant tried to prove "approval_of_sublease".
34              defendant failed to prove "approval_of_sublease".
35            defendant failed to prove "get_approval_of_sublease".
36          defendant failed to prove
37            "get_approval_of_sublease" as a defense
38              against "cancellation_due_to_sublease".
39          defendant alleges "nonabuse_of_confidence"
40            as a defense against "cancellation_due_to_sublease".
41            defendant tried to prove "nonabuse_of_confidence".
42            To prove "nonabuse_of_confidence",
43              we need to prove the following requisites:
44
45                requisite1: fact_of_nonabuse_of_confidence
46
47              defendant tried to prove "fact_of_nonabuse_of_confidence".
48                "fact_of_nonabuse_of_confidence" is determined to be plausible.
49              defendant successfully proved "fact_of_nonabuse_of_confidence".
50              plaintiff alleges "abuse_of_confidence"
51                as a defense against "nonabuse_of_confidence".
52                plaintiff tried to prove "abuse_of_confidence".
53                To prove "abuse_of_confidence",
54                  we need to prove the following requisites:
55
56                  requisite1: fact_of_abuse_of_confidence
57
58                plaintiff tried to prove "fact_of_abuse_of_confidence".
59                  "fact_of_abuse_of_confidence" is determined to be plausible.
60                plaintiff successfully proved "fact_of_abuse_of_confidence".
61              plaintiff successfully proved "abuse_of_confidence".
62            plaintiff successfully proved "abuse_of_confidence"
63            as a defense against "nonabuse_of_confidence".
64          defendant failed to prove "nonabuse_of_confidence".
65        defendant failed to prove
66          "nonabuse_of_confidence" as a defense
67            against "cancellation_due_to_sublease".
68      plaintiff successfully proved "cancellation_due_to_sublease".
69    plaintiff successfully proved "contract_end".
```

First International Workshop on Advanced Methodologies for Bayesian Networks

Maomi Ueno[1] and Takashi Isozaki[2]

[1] The University of Electro-Communications
[2] Sony Computer Science Laboratories, Inc.

The First International Workshop on Advanced Methodologies for Bayesian Networks (AMBN 2010) was held on November 18–19, 2010, at the Campus Innovation Center in Tokyo, Japan. It was part of the second JSAI International Symposium on AI (JSAI–isAI 2010), and was co-hosted by the Minato Discrete Structure Manipulation System Project on Exploratory Research for Advanced Technology (ERATO) of the Japan Science and Technology Agency (JST). It was supported by Mathematical Systems Inc.

AMBN is a workshop focusing on Bayesian Networks (BNs). Over the last few decades, BNs have become an increasingly popular AI approach for treating uncertainty around random variables. In AMBN 2010, we concentrated on exploring methodologies for enhancing the effectiveness of BNs, including modeling, reasoning, model selection, logic-probability relations, and causality. The exploration of methodologies was complemented by discussions of practical considerations for applying BNs in real-world settings, covering concerns such as scalability, incremental learning, and parallelization.

The members of Program Committee (PC) are leading researchers in BNs field:

Hei Chan (The Institute of Statistical Mathematics, Japan)
Arthur Choi (UCLA, USA)
Koichi Hirata (Kyusyu Institute of Technology, Japan)
Axel Hochstein (Stanford University, USA)
Burton H. Lee (Stanford University, USA)
Chao Lin-Liu (National Chengchi University, Taiwan)
Jian-Qin Liu (National Institute of Information and Communications Technology, Japan)
Robert Mateescu (Microsoft Research, USA)
Neil Rubens (The University of Electro-Communications, Japan)
Changhe Yuan (Mississippi State University, USA)
Yi Wang (The Hong Kong University of Science and Technology, China)

The workshop had a competitive acceptance rate of 56% (out of 30 submitted papers, 17 papers were accepted); notwithstanding the short announcement period. The topics of the latter included the following: probabilistic reasoning using BNs, combination of probabilistic reasoning and logic in BNs, learning BNs, causal discovery, causal inference, and advanced application of BNs.

T. Onoda, D. Bekki, and E. McCready (Eds.): JSAI-isAI 2010, LNAI 6797, pp. 165–166, 2011.
© Springer-Verlag Berlin Heidelberg 2011

We were very pleased to have four distinguished invited speakers: Arthur Choi (UCLA), Adnan Darwiche (UCLA), Seiya Imoto (University of Tokyo), and Petri Myllymäki (University of Helsinki).

The AMBN workshop had over 70 participants and many lively and interesting discussions over the course of its duration. After the workshop, eight papers were submitted for the post-proceedings. Each paper was reviewed by one meta-reviewer and three reviewers. Five papers were selected for publication. This chapter includes these papers.

We would like to express our gratitude for the contributions and support of the JST ERATO Minato project and Mathematical Systems Inc., which allowed us to make AMBN 2010 a successful and interesting event. In addition, we gratefully acknowledge the support of Dr. Neil Rubens of the University of Electro-Communications (UEC) for administering the submission/review system, and Yoshimitsu Miyasawa of UEC for managing the workshop website: http://www.ai.is.uec.ac.jp/ambn2010/. Finally, we are grateful to the JSAI-isAI committee members, all those who submitted papers, the PC members, the reviewers, and all other participants.

Relax, Compensate and Then Recover

Arthur Choi and Adnan Darwiche

Computer Science Department,
University of California, Los Angeles, USA
{aychoi,darwiche}@cs.ucla.edu

Abstract. We present in this paper a framework of approximate probabilistic inference which is based on three simple concepts. First, our notion of an approximation is based on "relaxing" equality constraints, for the purposes of simplifying a problem so that it can be solved more readily. Second, is the concept of "compensation," which calls for imposing weaker notions of equality to compensate for the relaxed equality constraints. Third, is the notion of "recovery," where some of the relaxed equality constraints are incrementally recovered, based on an assessment of their impact on improving the quality of an approximation. We discuss how this framework subsumes one of the most influential algorithms in probabilistic inference: loopy belief propagation and some of its generalizations. We also introduce a new heuristic recovery method that was key to a system that successfully participated in a recent evaluation of approximate inference systems, held in UAI'10. We further discuss the relationship between this framework for approximate inference and an approach to exact inference based on symbolic reasoning.

1 Introduction

In this survey-style paper, we highlight two frameworks for probabilistic inference, one for exact probabilistic inference and the second for approximate probabilistic inference.

The framework for *approximate probabilistic inference* is based on performing exact inference on an approximate model, which is obtained by *relaxing* equivalence constraints in the original model. The framework allows one to improve the resulting approximations by *compensating* for the relaxed equivalences, which can be realized through the enforcement of weaker notions of equivalence. One can improve the approximations even further by *recovering* equivalence constraints in the relaxed and compensated model. Interestingly, the influential algorithm of loopy belief propagation [33,36] can be characterized in terms of relaxing and compensating for equivalence constraints [7,9]. The third step of recovery can be used here to find even better approximations, which correspond to some forms of generalized belief propagation.

The framework for *exact probabilistic inference* that we shall survey is based on reducing probabilistic inference into a process of enforcing certain properties

T. Onoda, D. Bekki, and E. McCready (Eds.): JSAI-isAI 2010, LNAI 6797, pp. 167–180, 2011.

on propositional knowledge bases. In particular, if we encode the Bayesian network into an appropriate logical form [17], the problem of exact probabilistic inference can be reduced to one of compiling the knowledge base into a tractable form that satisfies two properties, known as *decomposability* and *determinism* [14,16,20]. The resulting framework has an ability to perform exact probabilistic inference on models that are beyond the reach of more traditional algorithms for exact inference [18,4,3]. Moreover, this framework can significantly increase the effectiveness of the framework for approximate inference that we mentioned earlier, which requires an exact inference engine, although such integration has not been realized in practice yet.

These two frameworks for exact and probabilistic inference have been validated in practice: notably, they have formed the basis of systems successfully employed in (respectively) exact and approximate inference evaluations conducted by the Uncertainty in Artificial Intelligence (UAI) community in 2006, 2008 and 2010 [2,19,23]. We survey these two frameworks in this paper, highlighting some of the relevant results along the way. Moreover, we shall introduce a new recovery heuristic that was particularly key to the success of a solver employed in the UAI'10 approximate inference evaluation. We finally conclude with a discussion on the pending advances that are needed to allow one to effectively use the framework for exact inference as a basis for the one on approximate inference, which we call *relax, compensate and then recover.*

2   Exact Probabilistic Inference

Consider the Bayesian network in Figure 1(a). There are a variety of algorithms available for performing exact inference in such networks, including variable elimination [38,21], the jointree algorithm [27,30] and recursive conditioning [15], which have running time complexities that are generally exponential in a model's treewidth. In the first part of this paper, we will be more concerned with another approach to exact probabilistic inference that is based on *knowledge compilation*, which among other advantages, can be used to tackle networks having large treewidth.

Consider Figure 1(b) where we "encode" the Bayesian network of Figure 1(a) as a propositional knowledge base, in conjunctive normal form (CNF), augmented with weights. Figure 1(c) further shows an equivalent, but more useful, representation in negation normal form (NNF), which is a DAG whose internal nodes are labeled with disjunctions and conjunctions, and whose leaf nodes are labeled with literals or the constants true and false.

Previous work has shown that if one has an ability to convert CNF to an NNF satisfying two key properties, *decomposability* and *determinism*, then one has the ability to perform probabilistic inference efficiently on a wide range of probabilistic representations [18,4,3]. Moreover, the latter can be performed in time *linear* in the NNF size, assuming the NNF satisfies decomposability and

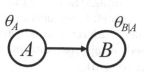
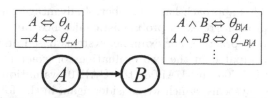

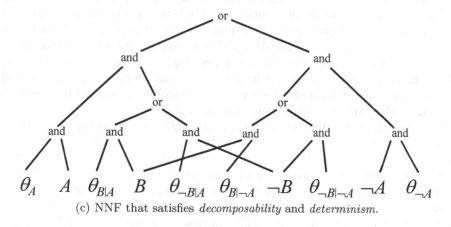

(a) A simple Bayesian network.   (b) A Bayesian network as a weighted CNF (weights on literals θ not shown). We use $\alpha \Leftrightarrow \beta$ as shorthand for the two clauses $\neg \alpha \vee \beta$ and $\alpha \vee \neg \beta$.

(c) NNF that satisfies *decomposability* and *determinism*.

Fig. 1. Bayesian network inference as weighted model counting

determinism, such as the NNF in Figure 1(c).[1] In this case, the NNF represents an *arithmetic circuit* for the Bayesian network: the leaf nodes input the network parameters and any given evidence, the or-nodes represent additions, and the and-nodes represent multiplications. A simple upward evaluation pass then computes the probability of evidence.

To illustrate this formulation more concretely, we note that the CNF Δ in Figure 1(b) "encodes" the Bayesian network of Figure 1(a) as follows. For any event α, the weighted model count of $\Delta \wedge \alpha$ equals the probability of event α according to the Bayesian network. Since the NNF in Figure 1(c) is equivalent to the CNF Δ, probabilistic inference on the Bayesian network can now be performed through weighted model counting on the NNF (a linear-time operation). Hence, to implement probabilistic reasoning, all one needs computationally is an ability to enforce decomposability and determinism, since Bayesian networks can be easily encoded as CNFs [4,3].

---

[1] An NNF is *decomposable* (called a DNNF) iff each of its conjunctions is decomposable, i.e., its conjuncts share no variables. A DNNF is *deterministic* (called a d-DNNF) iff each of its disjunctions is deterministic, i.e., if each pair of its disjuncts is mutually exclusive. For more on decomposability and determinism, and knowledge compilation in general, see [14,16,20].

This approach has a number of advantages, as compared to more traditional approaches to exact probabilistic inference, and these advantages have been realized in practice. For example, systems based on this approach have successfully participated in the two evaluations of exact probabilistic inference conducted for UAI'06 and UAI'08 (the UAI'10 evaluation focused on approximate inference systems, which we consider again in the following section).

A system that utilizes the approach we described was submitted to UAI'06 by the Automated Reasoning Group at UCLA, and was the only system to solve all given benchmarks [2]. At UAI'08, it was again the only one to solve a large class of very difficult networks that are synthesized from relational models [19].

The key advantage of the described approach is that it *exploits local structure* (i.e., the structure of parameters that quantify the network) in addition to the *global structure* (i.e., network topology). The relational network suite mentioned earlier in connection to UAI'08 has an average clique size that is greater than 50. Given the current state of the art in exact probabilistic inference, any method that does not exploit local structure would have to be exponential in treewidth [4,3] and is therefore not feasible on such networks.

We remark that the above approach to exact inference applies equally to different probabilistic representations, such as Bayesian networks, Markov networks, and factor graphs. The only difference between all these representations is that each requires its own "encoding" into a propositional knowledge base. Hence, to apply this approach practically to a new probabilistic representation all one needs to do is provide an "encoder" of that representation into an appropriate propositional knowledge base. This approach has been successfully applied in other domains as well. For example, it has been recently used by database researchers to identify tractable classes of probabilistic databases, by showing that the knowledge bases they lead to have tractable compilations that satisfy decomposability and determinism [28].

Finally, the ACE system, which was successfully employed at the UAI'06 and UAI'08 inference evaluations as we just described, is available online.[2] It is based on two components: An encoder of Bayesian networks into CNFs, and a compiler called C2D which converts CNFs into NNFs that satisfy decomposability and determinism.[3] Indeed, these are two of the key dimensions of applying this approach to exact probabilistic inference in practice: (1) efficiently encoding the probabilistic representations to CNF, and (2) developing more efficient compilers for enforcing decomposability and determinism. More recently, a new open-source compiler, called DSHARP, was released by the University of Toronto,[4] which is claimed to be one-to-two orders of magnitude more efficient than C2D on some benchmarks.

3   Approximate Probabilistic Inference

Consider now the problem of *approximate* probabilistic inference. In particular, consider formulating approximate inference as *exact* inference in an *approximate*

---

[2] The ACE system is available at http://reasoning.cs.ucla.edu/ace/

[3] The C2D compiler is available at http://reasoning.cs.ucla.edu/c2d/

[4] The DSHARP system is available at http://www.haz.ca/research/dsharp/

model.[5] In this section, we shall present a particular perspective on this approach that we call *relax, compensate and then recover*, which is quite special in a number of ways:

- It defines the approximate model specifically as the result of *relaxing* equivalence constraints in the original model and then *compensating* for the relaxed equivalences.
- It subsumes a number of well-known approximation schemes, including the influential algorithm of loopy belief propagation [33,36,7,9].
- It was successfully employed in the UAI'10 evaluation of approximate probabilistic inference, where it was the leading system in two of the most time-constrained categories evaluated [23].

We will now provide a concrete description of each part of this relax, compensate and then recover framework. We further conclude this section by introducing a critical technique that was introduced for the UAI'10 evaluation.

3.1 Relax

Relaxations are often used to tackle many types of problems, where a tractable but relaxed problem is used to approximate the solution of an intractable one. Here, we will be considering a specific type of relaxation, that is based on relaxing *equivalence constraints*. Here, we examine relaxations (and compensations) in pairwise Markov random fields [9], although this framework is easily applied to models such as Bayesian networks [7], factor graphs and even symbolic models [13]. We shall highlight a few of these examples, later.

Consider Figure 2(a), which depicts a pairwise MRF with an edge that represents an equivalence constraint between variables X and Y. Relaxing this equivalence constraint amounts to dropping this edge and its corresponding potential from the model. The resulting model in Figure 2(b) is sparser (a tree in particular) and, hence, is more amenable to exact inference algorithms.

More generally, any pairwise MRF can be made as sparse as needed by relaxing enough equivalence constraints. Namely, if the original model does not contain equivalence constraints, one can always introduce them, as shown in Figure 3(b), to relax them later, as in Figure 3(c). For example, we can replace an edge X—Y with a chain X—$\hat{Y}$—Y where the original potential $\psi(X, Y)$ is now over variables X and $\hat{Y}$, and where potential $\psi(Y, \hat{Y})$ represents an equivalence constraint $Y \equiv \hat{Y}$ (where variable Y and $\hat{Y}$ have the same states).

In sum, one has fine control over the sparsity (treewidth) of a given model through only the relaxation of equivalence constraints, which in turn translates to fine control over the amount of work that exact inference algorithms will need to perform on the relaxed model. Again, this is a general technique for controlling the difficulty of exact inference on all kinds of models, whether probabilistic or even symbolic as shown in [12,13].

---

[5] This approach includes mean-field and other variational approximations [29,26,25], but as we shall highlight, it also includes approximations such as loopy belief propagation [33,36] and mini-buckets [22] as well.

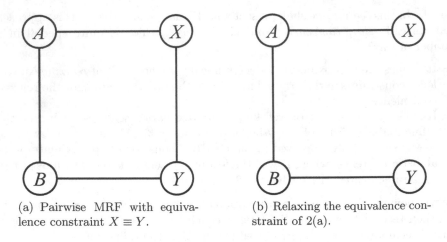

(a) Pairwise MRF with equivalence constraint $X \equiv Y$.

(b) Relaxing the equivalence constraint of 2(a).

Fig. 2. Relaxing an equivalence constraint in a pairwise MRF

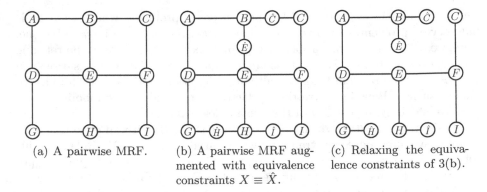

(a) A pairwise MRF.

(b) A pairwise MRF augmented with equivalence constraints $X \equiv \hat{X}$.

(c) Relaxing the equivalence constraints of 3(b).

Fig. 3. Introducing and then relaxing equivalence constraints

3.2 Compensate

We have shown in [6] that performing exact inference on *relaxed* models leads to approximations that coincide with those computed by the mini-bucket elimination algorithm [22].

One can obtain better approximations, however, by *compensating* for a relaxed equivalence $X \equiv Y$. Broadly defined, compensation refers to imposing a weaker notion of equivalence in lieu of the relaxed equivalence (for example, ensuring that X and Y have the same probability in the approximate model). In pairwise MRFs, compensating for an equivalence constraint $X \equiv Y$ is done by adding additional potentials $\psi(X)$ and $\psi(Y)$, while choosing the values of these potentials carefully. Other models, such as Bayesian networks, suggest different mechanics for compensation, but the goal is always the same: Imposing a

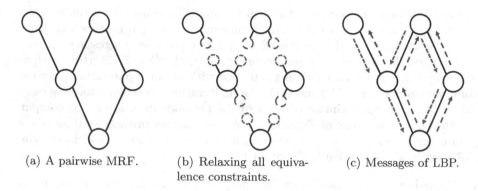

(a) A pairwise MRF.   (b) Relaxing all equiva-   (c) Messages of LBP.
                        lence constraints.

Fig. 4. Compensating for relaxations, and loopy belief propagation

weaker notion of equivalence between variables X and Y. We have proposed a number of compensation schemes in previous work and with respect to different representations [5,7,8,13,12].

One particular scheme, however, stands out. This scheme is derived while assuming that relaxing the equivalence constraint $X \equiv Y$ will split the model into two independent components, one containing variable X and another containing variable Y. Under this assumption, one can find unique values of potentials $\psi(X)$ and $\psi(Y)$ that guarantee the correctness of all marginal probabilities over single variables. In particular, we should assign the new auxiliary potentials $\psi(X)$ and $\psi(Y)$ so that the resulting model satisfies the following condition:

$$Pr'(X) = Pr'(Y) = \alpha\psi(X)\psi(Y) \tag{1}$$

where Pr' denotes the distribution induced by the simplified model. This condition states that after relaxing an equivalence constraint $X \equiv Y$, the marginals $Pr'(X)$ and $Pr'(Y)$ (and the marginals constructed from the new potentials) should at least be equivalent in the simplified model, a weaker notion of equivalence [7,9].

In a tree, every equivalence satisfies the desired assumption (that it splits a model into two independence components) and, hence, this compensation scheme leads to exact node marginals in this case. But when applied to arbitrary models, one is no longer guaranteed correctness (which is to be expected). The surprise, however, is that if *all* equivalence constraints are relaxed from an arbitrary model (see Figure 4), the approximations returned under this compensation scheme correspond precisely to the ones computed by the influential algorithm of loopy belief propagation [7,9].

The weaker notion of equivalence given by Equation 2 happens to be equivalent to the following local property on the parameters $\psi(X)$ and $\psi(Y)$ introduced for the compensation:

$$\psi(X) = \alpha\frac{\partial Z'}{\partial\psi(Y)} \quad \text{and} \quad \psi(Y) = \alpha\frac{\partial Z'}{\partial\psi(X)} \tag{2}$$

where Z' denotes the partition function (normalizing constant) of the compensated model, and α is a normalizing constant for the parameters $\psi(X)$ and $\psi(Y)$. Equation 2 can also be viewed as update equations, suggesting an iterative method that searches for parameters $\psi(X)$ and $\psi(Y)$ [7]. Starting with an initial approximation at iteration $t = 0$ (say, with uniform parameters), we can compute parameters $\psi_t(X)$ and $\psi_t(Y)$ for an iteration $t > 0$ by performing exact inference in the approximate network of the previous iteration $t - 1$, computing the right-hand sides of Equation 2. We repeat this process until all of our parameter updates converge (if ever), in which case we have a model satisfying Equation 2, and equivalently Equation 1.

In Bayesian Networks. As we described for pairwise Markov random fields, we can introduce and then relax equivalence constraints to simplify a Bayesian network. In particular, we can replace any edge $U \to X$ with a chain $U \to \hat{U} \to X$, where $U \to \hat{U}$ denotes an equivalence constraint $U \equiv \hat{U}$.

To *compensate* for the relaxation of an equivalence constraint $U \equiv \hat{U}$ (i.e., the deletion of the edge $U \to \hat{U}$), we first add an observed variable $\hat{S}$ as a child of U. We then need to specify the CPTs $\Theta_{\hat{U}}$ and $\Theta_{\hat{S}|U}$ for variables $\hat{S}$ and $\hat{U}$, so that the resulting network satisfies a weaker notion of equivalence. A condition analogous to the one given in Equation 1 will also produce an approximation corresponding to loopy belief propagation, but for Bayesian networks [7].

In Factor Graphs. We can introduce and then relax equivalence constraints in factor graphs as well. For a factor graph with a factor $\psi(\mathbf{X})$, we can replace a variable X in the set $\mathbf{X}$ with a clone $\hat{X}$, and then introduce a factor $\psi(X, \hat{X})$ representing an equivalence constraint $X \equiv \hat{X}$. When we now relax this equivalence constraint, we are effectively disassociating the factor $\psi(\mathbf{X})$ from the variable X, simplifying the topology of the factor graph. To compensate for this relaxation, we can introduce auxiliary factors $\psi(X)$ and $\psi(\hat{X})$, which we use to enforce a weaker notion of equivalence like the one given in Equation 1. In this case, we again identify an approximation corresponding to loopy belief propagation, now for factor graphs.

In Weighted CNF Models. The same approach to approximate probabilistic inference can be applied to tasks in logical reasoning as well. Consider for example the following weighted CNF over three variables A, B and C:

$$\{(a \vee b, w_1), (\bar{b} \vee c, w_2), (\bar{c} \vee d, w_3)\}.$$

where each clause is assigned a non-negative weight w_i. It is also straightforward to augment such models to an equivalent one where equivalence constraints can be relaxed. For example, we can replace the variable C appearing as a literal in the third clause with a clone variable C', and add an equivalence constraint $C \equiv C'$, giving us:

$$\{(a \vee b, w_1), (\bar{b} \vee c, w_2), (\bar{c}' \vee d, w_3), (C \equiv C', \infty)\}.$$

Here, the equivalence constraint $C \equiv C'$ is a hard constraint (having "infinite" weight) that ensures C and C' take the same value. When we remove, in this example, the equivalence constraint $C \equiv C'$, we have a relaxed formula composed of two independent models: $\{(a \vee b, w_1), (\bar{b} \vee c, w_2)\}$ and $\{(\bar{c}' \vee d, w_3)\}$.

We can introduce four auxiliary clauses into the relaxation:

$$\{(c, w_4), (\bar{c}, w_5), (c', w_6), (\bar{c}', w_7)\}$$

with four auxiliary weights that we can use to compensate for the relaxation of the equivalence constraint $C \equiv C'$. How we compensate for the relaxation of course depends on the query that we are interested in. In the case of weighted Max-SAT, it is possible to specify a weaker notion of equivalence so that the weighted Max-SAT solution of the simpler, compensated model is an upper-bound on the weighted Max-SAT solution of the original [13].

3.3   Recover

Now that we have discussed the *relaxation* and *compensation* components of this framework — what about *recovery?*

As described thus far, our framework leaves out the question of which equivalence constraints to relax. Answering this question intelligently typically requires inference, which is not possible — otherwise, we would not be thinking about relaxing equivalence constraints to start with. Instead of thinking about relaxing constraints, however, our framework calls for thinking about recovering them. That is, we can start by relaxing too many equivalence constraints, to reach, say, a tree model. We can then perform inference on the resulting compensated model to try to identify those equivalence constraints whose relaxation has been most damaging, and then *recover* these constraints. The recovery process can be incremental. That is, as we recover more and more equivalence constraints, we expect our approximate model to improve, leading to better decisions about which equivalence constraints to recover. This incremental process stops when we have recovered enough constraints to make the model inaccessible to exact inference algorithm.

We have proposed a number of recovery heuristics in previous work [7,11,10,9]. In the following, we highlight a few of these heuristics. The heuristics that we do highlight have been designed for the particular form of compensation based on the condition of Equation 1, which characterizes loopy belief propagation when we have relaxed enough equivalence constraints to simplify the model to a tree [7]. Thus, when we start with a tree model, we start with loopy belief propagation as a base approximation, hopefully identifying improved approximations as we recover equivalence constraints.[6] We shall also introduce a new heuristic that was developed for and successfully employed at the latest evaluation of approximate inference systems conducted by UAI'10 [23].

---

[6] Each time we recover constraints, we update the compensation so that the resulting network again satisfies Equation 1. In this case, the resulting approximations correspond to iterative joingraph propagation approximations [36,1,31,7]. From this perspective, our *relax, compensate and then recover* framework can also be seen as a way to find good joingraphs, and thus as a concrete way to design iterative joingraph and generalized belief propagation approximations.

Mutual Information. Remember the case where we relax an equivalence constraint $X \equiv Y$ that splits a model into two independent components: one containing variable X and the other containing variable Y. In this case, we can effectively compensate for the relaxation (by enforcing the weaker notion of equivalence in Equation 1), and guarantee the correctness of the marginal probabilities for each variable. Thus, we would see no benefit in recovering an equivalence constraint that had split a model into two independent components. On the other hand, if variables X and Y remain highly dependent on each other, after relaxing the constraint $X \equiv Y$, then our compensation scheme may in fact be over-compensating, since it expected that they would be independent.

Thus, we proposed in [7] to use the mutual information between variables X and Y as a way to *rank* equivalence constraints to recover. More specifically, we compute the mutual information between X and Y in the compensated model and recover first those equivalence constraints with highest mutual information. After recovering a few equivalence constraints, we can continue by re-scoring and re-ranking the other equivalence constraints, recovering them in an adaptive fashion. In [7], we found empirically that it was possible to identify a *small* set of equivalence constraints that can effectively improve the quality of an approximation without impacting much the complexity of inference.

Focused Recovery. The mutual information heuristic we just described is based on a property (that relaxing an equivalence constraint splits the model into two) that guarantees exact marginals for every variable in the model. This approach can provide good approximations (even exact) for many variables, but may still provide only poor approximations for others. One must then ask if this is the ideal approach when one is interested only in a particular query variable. Indeed, from query-to-query, ones focus may change from one submodel to another, while varying observations may render different parts of the model irrelevant. Ideally, one would like to target the approximation so as to maximize the accuracy of the queries one is truly interested in, giving less weight to those parts of the model that are only weakly relevant to the query at hand.

In [10], we proposed a more refined mutual information heuristic that focuses recovery on targeted query variables. It is based on simple independence conditions that can guarantee the exactness of a specific variable's marginal in the case where a single equivalence constraint is relaxed. This in turn leads to a more refined mutual information heuristic based on the query variable Q and the variables X and Y of the equivalence constraint $X \equiv Y$ relaxed. When used in an adaptive recovery process, we found empirically that a focused approach to approximation can indeed be more effective than an unfocused approach.

Residual Recovery. Finally, we introduce now a new heuristic that was critical to the success of a system based on this relax, compensate and then recover framework, at the UAI'10 approximate inference evaluation [23]. Our solver won first place in the most demanding categories of 20-second response time, for both probability of evidence and marginal probabilities. It also won second place in four other categories, for 20-minute and 1-hour response time (by a very thin margin). The system used was quite simple, as we have described thus far: relax enough equivalence constraints to reach a tree, and then incrementally recover equivalence constraints until the time allotted is up.

The recovery heuristic, which we refer to as "residual recovery", was inspired in part by the residual belief propagation algorithm [24]. Consider that the primary failure mode of loopy belief propagation is its failure to converge in certain cases. In these cases, even if loopy belief propagation is made to converge (using convergent alternatives), it has been observed that the quality of the approximation is often not good anyways; for more on loopy belief propagation and convergence, see e.g., [37,32,24]. On the other hand, when loopy belief propagation is able to converge naturally, then the quality of the approximation tends to be good, at least in practice.

Our "residual recovery" heuristic thus seeks to recover first those equivalence constraints that cause the most difficulty in the iterative process of compensation. Namely, we measure how close each equivalence constraint $X \equiv Y$ is to satisfying Equation 1, during the iterative process of compensation.[7] We then simply recover first the most problematic equivalence constraints, the ones that are furthest from convergence.

There are a number of advantages of the residual recovery heuristic:

- It encourages faster convergence during the iterative process of compensation (analogous to message passing in loopy belief propagation and iterative join-graph propagation). This translates directly into improved efficiency (fewer iterations required).
- Assuming that improved convergence behavior indicates improved approximation quality, we can expect our heuristic to have a positive impact on approximation quality as well.
- The heuristic is extremely efficient, and introduces little overhead to the overall relax, compensate and then recover process. In fact, the computations required to rank equivalence constraints are already required by the iterative compensation process to determine convergence.

The original mutual information heuristic we discussed still tends to identify better equivalence constraints to recover (in terms of the accuracy of the resulting approximation), but it is relatively expensive [11]. More efficient heuristics are preferrable however in time-constrained situations such as the strict 20-second response time categories that our system won in the UAI'10 evaluation [23].

4   Discussion

The performance of our system in the UAI'10 approximate inference evaluation was clearly a strong demonstration of the practical effectiveness of the *relax, compensate and then recover* framework. The latest public release of the SAMIAM system is available at http://reasoning.cs.ucla.edu/samiam/, which includes

---

[7] In the UAI'10 evaluation, we used a 3-way symmetric KL–divergence to measure how close an equivalence constraint was to converging.

an implementation of this framework based on the mutual-information recovery heuristic described earlier; the "residual recovery" heuristic used in UAI'10 will be included in an upcoming release.

The system we employed in the UAI'10 approximate inference evaluation used only standard jointree algorithms for exact inference in the simplified model. Since the *relax, compensate and then recover* framework requires only a black-box for exact reasoning in the simplified model, one can in principle employ other inference engines as well. The ACE system is particularly attractive for this purpose, given its strong performance in the UAI'06 and UAI'08 exact inference evaluations. However, to fully exploit this system, or other systems based on the same principle, in this framework for approximate inference, one requires some more advances that we are currently pursuing.

Consider for example our more recent efforts on knowledge compilation, based on a refinement of the decomposability property called *structured* decomposability [34,35]. The property allows for an efficient conjoin operation between knowledge bases that satisfy structured decomposability. The *relax, compensate and then recover* framework stands to benefit immensely from this conjoin operation, as recovery corresponds to a process where we conjoin equivalence constraints with an existing knowledge base. Thus, it allows one to smoothly recover equivalence constraints without having to re-initiate exact inference each time an equivalence constraint is recovered.

The suggested integration between the two inference approaches that we discussed in this paper could also admit more sophisticated and accurate approximations. Using a black-box inference engine that is exponential in treewidth, such as the jointree algorithm, limits one's ability to recover equivalence constraints as one is limited to approximate models that have low enough treewidth. On the other hand, one can direct the *relax, compensate and then recover* process towards approximate models that are efficiently *compilable* by systems such as ACE even if they have a large treewidth. This is the subject of current work.

References

1. Aji, S.M., McEliece, R.J.: The generalized distributive law and free energy minimization. In: Proceedings of the 39th Allerton Conference on Communication, Control and Computing, pp. 672–681 (2001)
2. Bilmes, J.: Results from the evaluation of probabilistic inference systems at UAI 2006 (2006),
   http://ssli.ee.washington.edu/~bilmes/uai06InferenceEvaluation/results
3. Chavira, M., Darwiche, A.: On probabilistic inference by weighted model counting. Artificial Intelligence 172(6-7), 772–799 (2008)
4. Chavira, M., Darwiche, A., Jaeger, M.: Compiling relational Bayesian networks for exact inference. International Journal of Approximate Reasoning 42(1-2), 4–20 (2006)
5. Choi, A., Chan, H., Darwiche, A.: On Bayesian network approximation by edge deletion. In: Proceedings of the 21st Conference on Uncertainty in Artificial Intelligence (UAI), pp. 128–135. Arlington, Virginia (2005)

6. Choi, A., Chavira, M., Darwiche, A.: Node splitting: A scheme for generating upper bounds in Bayesian networks. In: Proceedings of the 23rd Conference on Uncertainty in Artificial Intelligence (UAI), pp. 57–66 (2007)

7. Choi, A., Darwiche, A.: An edge deletion semantics for belief propagation and its practical impact on approximation quality. In: Proceedings of the 21st National Conference on Artificial Intelligence (AAAI), pp. 1107–1114 (2006)

8. Choi, A., Darwiche, A.: A variational approach for approximating Bayesian networks by edge deletion. In: Proceedings of the 22nd Conference on Uncertainty in Artificial Intelligence (UAI), pp. 80–89 (2006)

9. Choi, A., Darwiche, A.: Approximating the partition function by deleting and then correcting for model edges. In: Proceedings of the 24th Conference on Uncertainty in Artificial Intelligence (UAI), pp. 79–87 (2008)

10. Choi, A., Darwiche, A.: Focusing generalizations of belief propagation on targeted queries. In: Proceedings of the 23rd AAAI Conference on Artificial Intelligence (AAAI), pp. 1024–1030 (2008)

11. Choi, A., Darwiche, A.: Many-pairs mutual information for adding structure to belief propagation approximations. In: Proceedings of the 23rd AAAI Conference on Artificial Intelligence (AAAI), pp. 1031–1036 (2008)

12. Choi, A., Darwiche, A.: Relax then compensate: On max-product belief propagation and more. In: Proceedings of the Twenty-Third Annual Conference on Neural Information Processing Systems (NIPS), pp. 351–359 (2009)

13. Choi, A., Standley, T., Darwiche, A.: Approximating weighted Max-SAT problems by compensating for relaxations. In: Gent, I.P. (ed.) CP 2009. LNCS, vol. 5732, pp. 211–225. Springer, Heidelberg (2009)

14. Darwiche, A.: Decomposable negation normal form. Journal of the ACM 48(4), 608–647 (2001)

15. Darwiche, A.: Recursive conditioning. Artificial Intelligence 126(1-2), 5–41 (2001)

16. Darwiche, A.: A compiler for deterministic, decomposable negation normal form. In: Proceedings of the Eighteenth National Conference on Artificial Intelligence (AAAI), pp. 627–634. AAAI Press, Menlo Park (2002)

17. Darwiche, A.: A logical approach to factoring belief networks. In: Proceedings of KR, pp. 409–420 (2002)

18. Darwiche, A.: A differential approach to inference in Bayesian networks. Journal of the ACM 50(3), 280–305 (2003)

19. Darwiche, A., Dechter, R., Choi, A., Gogate, V., Otten, L.: Results from the probablistic inference evaluation of UAI 2008 (2008), http://graphmod.ics.uci.edu/uai08/Evaluation/Report

20. Darwiche, A., Marquis, P.: A knowledge compilation map. Journal of Artificial Intelligence Research 17, 229–264 (2002)

21. Dechter, R.: Bucket elimination: A unifying framework for probabilistic inference. In: Proceedings of the 12th Conference on Uncertainty in Artificial Intelligence (UAI), pp. 211–219 (1996)

22. Dechter, R., Rish, I.: Mini-buckets: A general scheme for bounded inference. J. ACM 50(2), 107–153 (2003)

23. Elidan, G., Globerson, A.: Summary of the 2010 UAI approximate inference challenge (2010), http://www.cs.huji.ac.il/project/UAI10/summary.php

24. Elidan, G., McGraw, I., Koller, D.: Residual belief propagation: Informed scheduling for asynchronous message passing. In: Proceedings of the 22nd Conference in Uncertainty in Artificial Intelligence (2006)

25. Geiger, D., Meek, C., Wexler, Y.: A variational inference procedure allowing internal structure for overlapping clusters and deterministic constraints. J. Artif. Intell. Res. (JAIR) 27, 1–23 (2006)
26. Jaakkola, T.: Tutorial on variational approximation methods. In: Saad, D., Opper, M. (eds.) Advanced Mean Field Methods, ch. 10, pp. 129–160. MIT Press, Cambridge (2001)
27. Jensen, F.V., Lauritzen, S., Olesen, K.: Bayesian updating in recursive graphical models by local computation. Computational Statistics Quarterly 4, 269–282 (1990)
28. Jha, A., Suciu, D.: Knowledge compilation meets database theory: compiling queries to decision diagrams. In: Proceedings of the 14th International Conference on Database Theory, pp. 162–173 (2011)
29. Jordan, M.I., Ghahramani, Z., Jaakkola, T., Saul, L.K.: An introduction to variational methods for graphical models. Machine Learning 37(2), 183–233 (1999)
30. Lauritzen, S.L., Spiegelhalter, D.J.: Local computations with probabilities on graphical structures and their application to expert systems. Journal of Royal Statistics Society, Series B 50(2), 157–224 (1988)
31. Mateescu, R., Kask, K., Gogate, V., Dechter, R.: Join-graph propagation algorithms. J. Artif. Intell. Res. (JAIR) 37, 279–328 (2010)
32. Mooij, J.M., Kappen, H.J.: Sufficient conditions for convergence of the sum-product algorithm. IEEE Transactions on Information Theory 53(12), 4422–4437 (2007)
33. Pearl, J.: Probabilistic Reasoning in Intelligent Systems: Networks of Plausible Inference. Morgan Kaufmann, San Francisco (1988)
34. Pipatsrisawat, K., Darwiche, A.: New compilation languages based on structured decomposability. In: Proceedings of the Twenty-Third AAAI Conference on Artificial Intelligence (AAAI), pp. 517–522 (2008)
35. Pipatsrisawat, K., Darwiche, A.: Top-down algorithms for constructing structured DNNF: Theoretical and practical implications. In: Proceedings of the 19th European Conference on Artificial Intelligence, pp. 3–8 (2010)
36. Yedidia, J.S., Freeman, W.T., Weiss, Y.: Understanding belief propagation and its generalizations. In: Lakemeyer, G., Nebel, B. (eds.) Exploring Artificial Intelligence in the New Millennium, ch. 8, pp. 239–269. Morgan Kaufmann, San Francisco (2003)
37. Yuille, A.L.: CCCP algorithms to minimize the Bethe and Kikuchi free energies: Convergent alternatives to belief propagation. Neural Computation 14(7), 1691–1722 (2002)
38. Zhang, N.L., Poole, D.: Exploiting causal independence in Bayesian network inference. Journal of Artificial Intelligence Research 5, 301–328 (1996)

Discovering Unconfounded Causal Relationships Using Linear Non-Gaussian Models

Doris Entner and Patrik O. Hoyer

Helsinki Institute for Information Technology, Finland
Department of Computer Science, University of Helsinki, Finland

Abstract. Causal relationships among a set of observed variables are often modeled using directed acyclic graph (DAG) structures, and learning such structures from data is known as the causal discovery problem. We here consider the learning of linear non-Gaussian acyclic models [9] with hidden variables [5]. Estimation of such models is computationally challenging and hence only possible when the number of variables is small. We present an algorithm for obtaining partial but in the large sample limit correct information about pairwise total causal effects in such a model. In particular, we obtain consistent estimates of the total effects for all variable pairs for which there exist an unconfounded superset of observed variables. Simulations show that the estimated pairwise total effects are good approximations of the true total effects.

Keywords: Causal Discovery, Latent Variables, Non-Gaussianity.

1 Introduction

In many fields it is essential to discover causal relationships among a set of variables. The preferred approach for this task is to perform controlled experiments, in which one or more variables are randomized and their effect on some other variables observed. However, such experiments might be technically impossible to perform, unethical, or simply too expensive. Thus, developing methods for inferring causal relationships from non-experimental data is an important research topic.

Much recent research on causal discovery from non-experimental data relies on probabilistic graphical models [8,11], typically directed acyclic graphs. In the case of continuous-valued variables and linear relationships among the variables these models are also known as linear non-recursive structural equation models (SEMs) [1].

In this family of models, it is common to assume that the variables follow a multivariate normal (Gaussian) distribution. With such an assumption, one need only concern oneself with the second-order statistics of the data (the covariance matrix), and conditional independence tests reduce to tests for zero partial covariance. A second common assumption is that the system of variables is causally sufficient, i.e. that all the relevant variables are observed and included in the model. However, even in this very restricted setting the data typically do not fully constrain the structure of the underlying graph, and additional background knowledge may be needed to fully identify the generating model. When relaxing the second assumption, i.e. allowing latent variables in the system, the degree of underdetermination is even greater. See [11] for details.

T. Onoda, D. Bekki, and E. McCready (Eds.): JSAI-isAI 2010, LNAI 6797, pp. 181–195, 2011.

In contrast, in [5,9] it was shown that for non-Gaussian data, the degree of underdetermination is much reduced. For causally sufficient systems, such linear non-Gaussian acyclic models are fully identifiable and can be estimated efficiently [9]. When latent variables may be present the system is not always fully identified [5], but the degree of underdetermination is much reduced from the Gaussian case. Unfortunately, in this case the existing algorithm to learn the full model only works for small variable sets.

One approach to simplify the problem is to learn only partial but (in the large sample limit) correct information about the causal structure from data generated by a linear non-Gaussian acyclic model including latent variables. In [7] an algorithm is presented (for a slightly modified model) which learns a causal order among *groups* of variables such that the causal effects among variables in different groups can be identified. In contrast, in this paper we introduce an algorithm to obtain partial information about the causal relationships among *pairs* of variables from data generated by such a model by searching for each pair for a superset of variables which *is* causally sufficient, for which causal effects can be consistently estimated.

2   Linear Non-Gaussian Acyclic Model

We consider the model introduced in [9], termed LiNGAM (for Linear Non-Gaussian Acyclic Model) which is defined as follows. Let $\mathbf{x} = (x_1, \ldots, x_N)^T$ denote a random vector that groups together the N observed variables, which we assume to be normalized to zero mean. The causal structure among these variables is represented by a directed acyclic graph (DAG), which implies that there exists a causal order, denoted by $k(i)$, such that no 'later' variable causes any 'earlier' one in the ordering. Furthermore, each variable is a linear function of its parents in the graph. The model is given by

$$x_i = \sum_{k(j)<k(i)} b_{ij}x_j + e_i. \tag{1}$$

where e_i, $i = 1, \ldots, N$, are mutually independent, non-Gaussian zero-mean (unobserved) disturbances or error terms corresponding to the observed variable x_i. By collecting the causal coefficients b_{ij} into an $N \times N$ matrix $\mathbf{B}$ and the error terms into an $N \times 1$ vector $\mathbf{e} = (e_1, \ldots, e_N)^T$ Equation (1) can be written as

$$\mathbf{x} = \mathbf{Bx} + \mathbf{e}. \tag{2}$$

Because of the acyclicity assumption of the model $\mathbf{B}$ is strictly lower triangular (i.e. all diagonal and all upper-triangular elements are zero) when the variables are arranged in a causal order $k(i)$. An example with $N = 7$ variables is given in Figure 1 (a).

As shown in [9], LiNGAM models are fully identifiable from non-experimental data as a result of the assumptions of acyclicity and non-Gaussianity of the disturbance terms, and a computationally efficient learning procedure can be obtained using independent component analysis (ICA, [6]). This can be seen by rewriting (2) into

$$\mathbf{x} = (\mathbf{I} - \mathbf{B})^{-1}\mathbf{e} = \mathbf{Ae} \tag{3}$$

with $\mathbf{A} = (\mathbf{I} - \mathbf{B})^{-1}$. This is the ICA mixing model with $\mathbf{e}$ being the independent sources, $\mathbf{A}$ the mixing matrix, and $\mathbf{x}$ the mixed signals. The inherent ambiguities of ICA (scaling, sign and ordering) can be solved by the acyclicity assumption of the model [9].

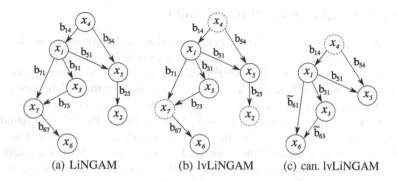

(a) LiNGAM   (b) lvLiNGAM   (c) can. lvLiNGAM

Fig. 1. Examples of the different models. Observed variables are represented by solid circles and hidden ones by dashed circles; the coefficients b_{ij} and $\tilde{b}_{ij}$ are all non-zero. The canonical lvLiNGAM model shown in (c) is obtained from the lvLiNGAM model in (b) with $\tilde{b}_{61} = b_{67}b_{71}$ and $\tilde{b}_{63} = b_{67}b_{73}$. The independent disturbances e_i of x_i, $i = 1, \ldots, 7$, are left implicit.

3   Linear Non-Gaussian Acyclic Model Including Latent Variables

One drawback of the basic LiNGAM model is the assumption of causal sufficiency, meaning that all variables $(x_1, \ldots, x_N)$ must be observed. While certain types of hidden variables (such as those without any observed descendants) can safely be omitted, in general hidden variables can *confound* the relationships among the observed variables, violating the assumption of mutual independence of the disturbance terms e_i. In such cases, estimation methods based on the standard model typically give biased estimates of the underlying causal effects.

This problem was tackled in [5] where an extended model, termed lvLiNGAM (for latent variable LiNGAM) was introduced. The model is similar to the LiNGAM model defined in Equation (2), however, only a subset of the variables $\mathbf{x} = (x_1, \ldots, x_N)^T$ may be observed. In Figure 1 (b) such a model is shown, derived from the LiNGAM model in Figure 1 (a) with variables x_2, x_4 and x_7 unobserved.

In most cases it is not possible to infer the existence of all the hidden variables from the observed variables. For example, in Figure 1 (b) the latent variable x_2 has no observed descendants and hence cannot be detected. Fortunately, such variables do not play a role in the causal discovery process. Thus, in [5] the authors showed that every lvLiNGAM model is causally equivalent to a *canonical* model in which all the hidden variables have no parents and at least two children. Hence, in what follows, we will restrict our analysis to lvLiNGAM models in such a canonical from. To illustrate, the canonical form of the latent variable model in Figure 1 (b) is given in Figure 1 (c).

The existing method for estimating lvLiNGAM models, proposed in [5], is based on estimating an overcomplete basis ICA model [6]. Unfortunately, this method is in practice only applicable when the number of variables is very small. Thus, in this contribution, we will suggest a method to estimate causal effects for pairs of variables which are unconfounded with respect to some given superset of variables. We will give some intuition of unconfounded sets as well as the basic idea of the algorithm in the next section, after which we present these concepts formally in Sections 5 and 6.

4   Intuitive Explanation of the Method

Consider the graph in Figure 1 (c) representing an lvLiNGAM model in canonical form.

First, we give some examples of confounding. Informally, a confounder is a variable that has effects on two or more other variables and is not taken into account in the analysis. For instance, the hidden variable x_4 acts as a confounder for the variable pair (x_1, x_5): Assume for the moment that we know that x_1 precedes x_5. We then can try to estimate the effect of x_1 on x_5 by regression: $x_5 = \hat{b}_{51} x_1 + \hat{e}_5$. In this case the confounder x_4 will typically cause a bias in the estimate $\hat{b}_{51}$ of the true effect b_{51}. Nevertheless, linear regression will leave $\hat{e}_5$ uncorrelated with x_1. In a Gaussian model linear uncorrelatedness is sufficient for statistical independence. However, in the non-Gaussian models considered here, $\hat{e}_5$ would necessarily be *statistically dependent* on x_1.[1]

The upshot is that, in the non-Gaussian setting, we are able to *detect* confounding, by detecting a statistical dependence between the residual and the regressor. In a similar way, x_4 is also a confounder for x_3 and x_5, and for x_5 and x_6.

Examples of unconfounded pairs are (x_1, x_3) and (x_1, x_6). Regressing the later one in the causal order on the earlier, assuming for now that we know this order, we get unbiased estimates of the total effect of one variable on the other. (Here, 'total' effect refers to the effect of one variable onto the other, possibly partly mediated by other observed variables.) For the first pair the total effect is given by b_{31}, for the latter one by $\tilde{b}_{63} b_{31} + \tilde{b}_{61}$. Again, note that in the non-Gaussian setting we cannot reject unconfoundedness, when checking whether the residual is statistically dependent on the regressor.

The variable pair (x_3, x_6) is confounded by the observed variable x_1. However, including x_1 in the regression leads to an unbiased estimate of the effect of x_3 on x_6, again assuming we know the causal order. Thus, in the set $S = \{x_1, x_3, x_6\}$ all three total effects can be consistently estimated by controlling for confounding as necessary. Such a set S will be called an *unconfounded set* and the pair (x_3, x_6) will be called unconfounded with respect to the set S.

The proposed algorithm will search iteratively for all pairs which have an unconfounded superset. First, it detects all those pairs for which the pair itself is unconfounded, finds the causal order among the pair and estimates the total effect of the earlier on the later. In our example model these would be the pairs (x_1, x_3) and (x_1, x_6) with total effects as above. Next, for any pair which is not yet part of an unconfounded superset, the algorithm tries to build up such a set by including (in addition to the pair itself) any node which is known to have an unconfounded non-zero causal effect on both variables of the pair (i.e. any potential confounder). For this step we need to assume that the distribution is *faithful* to the graph [11], implying that zero total effects are due to missing arcs and not canceling paths. In our case, for the pair (x_3, x_6) the variable x_1 is a cause of both (estimated in the previous step) and faithfulness ensures that $\tilde{b}_{63} b_{31} + \tilde{b}_{61} \neq 0$. Hence, this would yield the set $S = \{x_1, x_3, x_6\}$ which is unconfounded as discussed above. The algorithm continues the iteration as long as more pairs are added. In our specific example the algorithm would terminate after the next round.

---

[1] To see this, we first write $x_1 = b_{14} e_4 + e_1$, and $x_5 = (b_{51} b_{14} + b_{54}) e_4 + b_{51} e_1 + e_5$. Thus, $\hat{e}_5 = x_5 - \hat{b}_{51} x_1 = (b_{51} b_{14} + b_{54} - \hat{b}_{51} b_{14}) e_4 + (b_{51} - \hat{b}_{51}) e_1 + e_5$. By the Darmois-Skitovitch theorem [2,10], with non-Gaussian e_1 and e_4, we need to have $\hat{b}_{51} = b_{51}$ and $b_{14}(b_{51} - \hat{b}_{51}) + b_{54} = 0$ to obtain statistical independence between x_1 and $\hat{e}_5$, which is not possible except if $b_{54} = 0$.

5   Unconfounded Sets

To formalize the algorithm, and prove that it is both sound and complete, we need to properly define the concept of unconfounded variable sets.

For the remainder of the paper we will use the following notation. The DAG G of the underlying lvLiNGAM model is given by the vertex set of indices of the full set of variables (including all latents) and a set of ordered pairs of indices describing the edges: $G = (V, E)$ with $V = \{1, \ldots, N\}$, and $E \subset V \times V$. If $(i, j) \in E$ we write $i \to j$ and say that i is a *parent* of j, and j is a *child* of i. A directed path in G is denoted by a sequence of indices $(n_1, \ldots, n_k)$ such that for any two consecutive nodes the edge (n_i, n_{i+1}) is in the graph. We write such a directed path as $n_1 \to \ldots \to n_k$. If there is a directed path from i to j we say that i is an *ancestor* of j, and j is a *descendant* of i. The acyclicity property requires that there are no directed paths from any node to itself.

Definition 1. *Two directed paths in G starting at the same node n_1, given by $p_1 = n_1 \to \ldots \to n_k$, and $p_2 = m_1 \to \ldots \to m_l$ with $m_1 = n_1$, are* non-intersecting *if $n_i \neq m_j$ for all $i = 2, \ldots, k, j = 2, \ldots, l$.*

Definition 2. *A variable x_t is a* confounder *for a variable pair (x_i, x_j), with $i \neq t$, $j \neq t$, $i \neq j$, if there exist directed non-intersecting paths from x_t to x_i and x_j in G.*

Definition 3. *Let $S \subseteq V$ be a set indexing variables $\{x_s : s \in S\}$ and $s_1, s_2 \in S$, $s_1 \neq s_2$. The nodes x_{s_1} and x_{s_2} are said to be* unconfounded with respect to S *if there does not exist a confounder $x_t, t \notin S$, for x_{s_1} and x_{s_2}.*

Definition 4. *A set $S \subseteq V$ which indexes a set of variables $\{x_s : s \in S\}$ is called an* unconfounded set *of variables if all pairs (x_{s_1}, x_{s_2}), $s_1, s_2 \in S$, $s_1 \neq s_2$, are unconfounded with respect to S.*

Note, that Definition 3 implies that variables in S may be confounded by other variables in S but not by any variable outside S. Furthermore, from Definition 4 follows that an unconfounded set is a causally sufficient set. Examples were given in Section 4.

6   Algorithm

6.1   Motivation and Algorithm Details

A brief presentation of the basic idea of the algorithm, which finds all variable pairs that are part of an unconfounded set, was given by means of an example in Section 4. Here, we motivate and describe the algorithm in more detail.

First, we note that as the number of *all subsets* of variables grows exponentially in the number of variables, it is infeasible for all but the smallest problems to take the trivial approach of checking all subsets individually for confounding.

Fortunately, it is easily seen that unconfounded variable sets always have unconfounded subsets: Any unconfounded set of $k > 2$ variables also has an unconfounded subset of size $k - 1$, obtained by leaving out a sink in the DAG corresponding to the original set. Hence, one might consider an approach in which the goal would be to find

---

Algorithm 1. Pairwise lvLiNGAM

Input: A set of observed variables $\{x_1, \ldots, x_n\}$ and a set of samples over these variables.

Output: For each of the $n(n-1)/2$ variable pairs, an indication of whether that variable pair is part of an unconfounded subset of the observed variables, and if so the relative causal order and an estimate of the total effect of one on the other.

1. Initialize an $n \times n$ matrix $\mathbf{P}^{(1)} = \mathbf{0}$. The entries of this matrix will be interpreted as follows:

$$
P_{ij} = \begin{cases}
1, & x_i \text{ is an ancestor of } x_j \\
-1, & x_j \text{ is an ancestor of } x_i \\
2, & \text{No causal path from } x_i \text{ to } x_j, \text{ and vice versa} \\
0, & \text{No unconfounded subset has yet been found containing both } x_i \text{ and } x_j
\end{cases}
$$

   Furthermore, initialize an $n \times n$ matrix $\mathbf{T} = \mathbf{0}$. If $P_{ij} = 1$ then T_{ij} will contain the estimated total effect from x_i to x_j, otherwise it will be 0. Initialize $q = 1$ and $m = \text{TRUE}$.

2. repeat while $m = \text{TRUE}$
   a. set $m = \text{FALSE}$, $q = q + 1$, and $\mathbf{P}^{(q)} = \mathbf{P}^{(q-1)}$
   b. for each ordered pair (x_i, x_j), $i \neq j$, for which $P_{ij}^{(q-1)} = 0$:
      (i) Find the set S of indices for which $P_{si}^{(q-1)} = 1$ and $P_{sj}^{(q-1)} = 1$
      (ii) Test if the set $S^+ = \{i, j\} \cup S$ is unconfounded by fitting a LiNGAM model to S^+ and verifying if the empirical distribution matches the distribution implied by LiNGAM
         If S^+ is confounded continue with the next pair in step 2b
         Else, get the connection between x_i and x_j from the LiNGAM model and
         - If $x_i \overset{\alpha}{\to} x_j$ with $\alpha \neq 0$, set $P_{ij}^{(q)} = 1$, $P_{ji}^{(q)} = -1$, $T_{ij} = \alpha$ and $m = \text{TRUE}$
         - If $x_j \overset{\beta}{\to} x_i$ with $\beta \neq 0$, set $P_{ji}^{(q)} = 1$, $P_{ij}^{(q)} = -1$, $T_{ji} = \beta$ and $m = \text{TRUE}$
         - If $x_i \overset{0}{\leftrightarrows} x_j$, set $P_{ij}^{(q)} = P_{ji}^{(q)} = 2$ and $m = \text{TRUE}$

---

all *maximal* unconfounded subsets of variables. However, it can be seen that, for the worst-case graphs, even these may grow exponentially in number. Consider a graph with k distinct confounded pairs: $x_{2i-1} \leftarrow l_i \to x_{2i}$, with x_{2i-1}, x_{2i} observed, and l_i hidden variables ($i = 1, \ldots, k$). The biggest unconfounded subsets contain k variables (pick any one variable from each confounded pair) and there are exponentially many of those, namely 2^k. Thus, an algorithm designed to find all maximal unconfounded subsets would also necessarily have exponential worst case running time.

Thus, our approach, termed 'Pairwise lvLiNGAM', is instead simply to search for variable pairs which are contained in one or more unconfounded variable sets. Pseudocode is given in Algorithm 1. Step 1 is for initialization, while step 2 does the main work. In the first sweep of step 2 the algorithm tests each pair of variables for confounding (by fitting a LiNGAM model, see Lemma 1 below) and for every unconfounded pair finds the causal order and an estimate of the total effect of the earlier on the later variable. In every later sweep, in step 2b the algorithm selects each pair $\{x_i, x_j\}$ which is still confounded and re-tests it when taking into account the set S of all common causes of that pair which is formed in step 2b(i). If this set $S^+ = \{i, j\} \cup S$ is unconfounded the algorithm finds the causal order and the connection strength in step 2b(ii). (A more practical implementation for testing unconfoundedness is discussed in Section 6.3.)

6.2   Correctness of the Algorithm

In this section we prove that in the large sample limit and given the model assumptions Algorithm 1 is sound and complete. Soundness means that the algorithm never produces incorrect results: Variable pairs deemed part of an unconfounded subset are indeed unconfounded in this sense, and estimated total effects converge to the true total effects. Similarly, completeness means that *all* variable pairs that are part of an unconfounded subset will be discovered as such. Thus, the algorithm returns in the limit all and only the sought variable pairs. Towards proving these results we first state the following lemma.

Lemma 1. *Let* $\mathbf{x} = (x_1, \ldots x_N)^T$ *follow an lvLiNGAM model in canonical form. Let J denote the indices of the observed variables in* $\mathbf{x}$*, and let* $I \subseteq J$*. Then the set I is unconfounded if and only if the joint distribution over the variables* $\{x_i : i \in I\}$ *can be represented by a LiNGAM model.*

Proof: The proof of this and all subsequent lemmas and theorems are provided in the Appendix of this paper.

The above lemma formalizes and generalizes the notion, mentioned in Section 4, that it is possible to test for confoundedness: To test a set of variables for confoundedness (as required by step 2b(ii) of Algorithm 1), we can fit a LiNGAM model to those variables and then test whether the empirical distribution matches the distribution implied by the model by testing whether the residuals are non-Gaussian and mutually independent. If the match is rejected, the variable set is deemed confounded.

Using Lemma 1 we can prove the main result, which shows that the proposed algorithm is sound and complete.

Theorem 1. *Given a set of independent, identically distributed samples generated from an lvLiNGAM model, and assuming that the generated distribution is faithful to the model, in the large sample limit Algorithm 1 returns an estimate of the pairwise total effect for* $\{x_i, x_j\}$ *if and only if there exists an unconfounded set of observed variables* $S^+ \supseteq \{i, j\}$*, with* S^+ *a subset of the original variable set V. Furthermore, the estimated total effects are consistent estimates of the true total effects.*

6.3   Implementation

As shown in Lemma 1, we could use the standard LiNGAM algorithm combined with appropriate statistical tests to test for confounding in step 2b(ii). However, such an algorithm is both computationally wasteful and also prone to unnecessary re-testing. Hence, we here show how to avoid these problems using a simple regression-based analysis combined with statistical independence tests. First, we need the following result.

Lemma 2. *The set S defined in step 2b(i) of Algorithm 1 is unconfounded.*

The above lemma states that at any point in the algorithm, given a variable pair $\{x_i, x_j\}$, the corresponding set S is by construction necessarily unconfounded. This can be used to prove the following very useful result.

Algorithm 2. Replacement for step 2b(ii) in Algorithm 1

2b(ii)*   Call the subroutine below with parameters i, j, S, which returns (ind, γ), and
  - If $ind = 0$, $S^+ = \{i, j\} \cup S$ is confounded; continue with the next pair in step 2b
  - If $ind = 1$, set $P_{ij}^{(q)} = 1$, $P_{ji}^{(q)} = -1$, $T_{ij} = \gamma$ and $m = $ TRUE
  - If $ind = -1$, set $P_{ji}^{(q)} = 1$, $P_{ij}^{(q)} = -1$, $T_{ji}^{(q)} = \gamma$ and $m = $ TRUE
  - If $ind = 2$, set $P_{ij}^{(q)} = P_{ji}^{(q)} = 2$ and $m = $ TRUE

Input arguments: i: the index of the first variable in a pair, j: the index of the second variable in a pair, and S: the indices of a subset of variables to be included in the regressions. The subroutine performs two regressions: $x_j = \alpha x_i + \sum_{s \in S} c_s x_s + e_j$ and $x_i = \beta x_j + \sum_{s \in S} \tilde{c}_s x_s + e_i$ and returns

$$\begin{cases} (1, \alpha), & \text{if } e_j \perp\!\!\!\perp x_i \text{ and } e_i \not\!\perp\!\!\!\perp x_j \\ (-1, \beta), & \text{if } e_j \not\!\perp\!\!\!\perp x_i \text{ and } e_i \perp\!\!\!\perp x_j \\ (2, 0), & \text{if } e_j \perp\!\!\!\perp x_i \text{ and } e_i \perp\!\!\!\perp x_j \text{ and } \alpha = \beta = 0 \\ (0, 0), & \text{otherwise} \end{cases}$$

Lemma 3. *Given a set of independent, identically distributed samples generated from an lvLiNGAM model, and assuming that the generated distribution is faithful to the model, in the large sample limit the set $S^+ = \{i, j\} \cup S$ as defined in step 2b(ii) of Algorithm 1 is unconfounded if and only if when estimating the regression models $x_j = \alpha x_i + \sum_{s \in S} c_s x_s + e_j$ and $x_i = \beta x_j + \sum_{s \in S} \tilde{c}_s x_s + e_i$ one of the following statements holds:*

1. $e_j \perp\!\!\!\perp x_i$ and $e_i \not\!\perp\!\!\!\perp x_j$
2. $e_j \not\!\perp\!\!\!\perp x_i$ and $e_i \perp\!\!\!\perp x_j$
3. $e_j \perp\!\!\!\perp x_i$ and $e_i \perp\!\!\!\perp x_j$ and $\alpha = \beta = 0$

where, for any two variables y and z, $y \perp\!\!\!\perp z$ denotes independence and $y \not\!\perp\!\!\!\perp z$ dependence between the two variables.

Thus, we can use the above as a simple and computationally efficient alternative when testing for confoundedness. From these regressions we also get the causal order among x_i and x_j as well as the total causal effect: If the first statement holds then x_i is an ancestor of x_j and α gives an estimate of the total effect. Similarly, the second statement corresponds to x_j being an ancestor of x_i and the total effect is estimated by β. Finally, the last statement implies that x_i is independent of x_j given $\{x_s, s \in S\}$ and there is a zero total effect of one on the other. Furthermore, the estimated total effects converge to the true total effects in the large sample limit, since estimated (sample) regression coefficients converge to the population regression coefficients as the number of data samples grows without bound, and the independence tests ensure that the total effect is estimated in the correct causal order with no bias from confounding. Hence, we can replace step 2b(ii) of Algorithm 1 by the procedure given in Algorithm 2.

Independence Tests. In Lemma 3 and the corresponding step of the algorithm we need to test for a dependence between the residual and the regressor. There are several ways to carry out this test in practice. We will give two examples of such tests.

  The first one is to measure the correlation of some simple nonlinear function(s) of the variables. This is based on the well known fact that two random variables x and

y are independent if and only if $E\{g(x)h(y)\} = E\{g(x)\}E\{h(y)\}$ for all functions g and h. Of course it is not possible to test all functions g, h, but using some combinations can indicate whether two random variables are statistically dependent. In particular, the equation implies that the covariance between the transformed variables must vanish, i.e. $cov(g(x), h(y)) = 0$, for which a standard statistical test can be used.

The second approach, termed HSIC (Hilbert Schmidt Independence Criterion, [4]), is a recently developed kernel-based test for statistical dependency. While in the nonlinear correlation approach, when using any finite set of functions g and h, certain forms of statistical dependency may be missed, HSIC is provably universal in the sense that *any* statistical dependency will be detected in the large sample limit. The main drawback of HSIC is its computational complexity of $O(m^2)$, where m is the number of samples, which limits the number of samples that can be used and hence the power of the test.

7 Simulations

To evaluate our method we sample i.i.d. data from randomly generated lvLiNGAM models in canonical form with different numbers of observed and hidden variables and a variety of non-Gaussian error terms, and apply Pairwise lvLiNGAM with both nonlinear correlation (with $g(x) = \tanh(x)$ and $h(y) = y$) and HSIC as independence tests, as well as standard LiNGAM [9] as a reference, to the data of the observed variables. Pairwise lvLiNGAM yields estimates of the total causal effect for all those pairs which were deemed to be part of an unconfounded set whereas LiNGAM returns an estimate

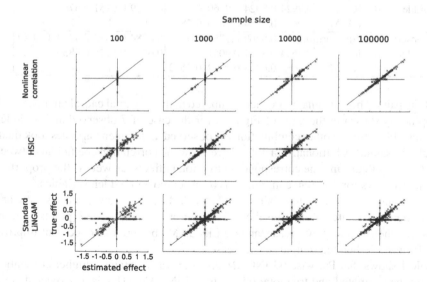

Fig. 2. Simulation results from 50 lvLiNGAM models with 7 observed and 3 hidden variables. The top row shows the results of Pairwise lvLiNGAM using nonlinear correlation as independence test, the middle row of Pairwise lvLiNGAM with HSIC as independence test, and the bottom row of standard LiNGAM. In the columns the results for different sample sizes are shown. In each of the scatterplots, the horizontal axis represents the estimated total effects while the vertical axis represents the true total effects, such that accurate estimates are on the diagonal.

Table 1. Simulation results of different choices of observed and hidden variables, and sample size. For each of the variable combination and each sample size 50 models were generated randomly and Pairwise lvLiNGAM with nonlinear correlation and HSIC as independence test as well as standard LiNGAM were applied (shown along the rows). The correlation between the estimated and the true total effects for the all sample sizes are given in columns 3-6, the proportion of pairs for which an estimate was found in columns 7-10. *The entry NaN for correlation occurs because the only estimated coefficients were 0. **The missing entries for LiNGAM are due to non-convergence in any of the sample runs.

		Correlation				Proportion of estimated effects			
		Sample Size				Sample Size			
		100	1000	10000	100000	100	1000	10000	100000
4 observed	nonlin. Corr.	NaN*	0.9646	0.9819	0.9783	0.4067	0.3867	0.5067	0.6367
1 hidden	HSIC	0.8884	0.9386	0.9912		0.6633	0.6767	0.6833	
	LiNGAM	0.6690	0.8337	0.8484	0.8481	1	1	1	1
7 observed	nonlin. Corr.	0.3235	0.9042	0.9637	0.9857	0.4924	0.4105	0.4667	0.5429
3 hidden	HSIC	0.8527	0.8994	0.9310		0.5943	0.6476	0.6238	
	LiNGAM	0.4986	0.8134	0.8294	0.8329	1	1	1	1
11 observed	nonlin. Corr.	0.1762	0.9203	0.9802	0.9785	0.5316	0.4189	0.4305	0.5265
4 hidden	HSIC	0.7892	0.9058	0.9325		0.5985	0.6629	0.6215	
	LiNGAM	-**	0.7911	0.8042	0.8108	1	1	1	1
15 observed	nonlin. Corr.	0.3165	0.9275	0.9727	0.9707	0.5867	0.4975	0.4834	0.5533
5 hidden	HSIC	0.8148	0.9101	0.9288		0.6057	0.6568	0.6322	
	LiNGAM	-**	0.7311	0.7932	0.8082	1	1	1	1
20 observed	nonlin. Corr.	0.1758	0.8828	0.9689	0.9635	0.6018	0.4352	0.3959	0.4453
8 hidden	HSIC	0.7924	0.8924	0.9160		0.6209	0.6251	0.5760	
	LiNGAM	-**	0.7254	0.7866	0.7828	1	1	1	1
25 observed	nonlin. Corr.	0.1955	0.8769	0.9759	0.9629	0.6384	0.4813	0.4233	0.4840
10 hidden	HSIC	0.7624	0.8901	0.9051		0.6323	0.6275	0.5839	
	LiNGAM	-**	0.6468	0.7482	0.7553	1	1	1	1

for all the pairs. These estimates are then compared to the true total causal effects, which is graphically shown in the plots of Figure 2 for the case of 7 observed and 3 hidden variables. (Plots for the other combinations of observed and hidden variables look qualitatively the same.) Additionally, in Table 1 we show the correlation coefficient between the estimated effects and the corresponding true total effects, as well as the proportion of estimated pairs for different combinations of observed and hidden variables.[2]

From Figure 2 we can see that Pairwise lvLiNGAM (top two rows) outputs more and more accurate estimates of the causal effect with growing sample size (points concentrate along the diagonal), whereas standard LiNGAM (bottom row) does not improve its performance when the sample size increases.

Table 1 shows that Pairwise lvLiNGAM also generally obtains a higher correlation between the estimated and true total effects than LiNGAM. This is as expected since LiNGAM does not take latent variables into account and hence gives a (in many cases biased) estimate for every pair. For our method, only the effects of pairs which are deemed to be part of an unconfounded subset (40% - 70% of all pairs) are estimated.

---

[2] An implementation of Algorithm 1 as well as code to replicate all the results in matlab can be found under http://www.cs.helsinki.fi/u/entner/PairwiseLvLingam/.

For small sample sizes Algorithm 1 performs much better with HSIC as independence test than nonlinear correlation: the correlation coefficient between estimated and true total effects is higher, and the proportion of estimated effects is bigger. For large sample sizes, HSIC is not applicable because of its complexity[3]. However, for large sample sizes nonlinear correlation as independence test seems to work well. The difference in the performance of the two independence tests is due to the characteristics of the tests as explained in Section 6.3.

Generally, the simulations confirm that the Pairwise lvLiNGAM algorithm is able to detect confounded variable pairs and hence biased estimates. However, more experiments are required to study its performance in a diverse set of circumstances.

Acknowledgments. Funding for this work was provided by the Academy of Finland.

References

1. Bollen, K.A.: Structural Equations with Latent Variables. John Wiley & Sons, Chichester (1989)
2. Darmois, G.: Analyse générale des liaisons stochastiques. RIIS 21 (1953)
3. Eriksson, J., Koivunen, V.: Identifiability, Separability, and Uniqueness of Linear ICA Models. IEEE Signal Processing Letters 11(7) (2004)
4. Gretton, A., Fukumizu, K., Teo, C.H., Song, L., Schölkopf, B., Smola, A.J.: A Kernel Statistical Test of Independence. In: Adv. NIPS (2008)
5. Hoyer, P.O., Shimizu, S., Kerminen, A.J., Palviainen, M.: Estimation of causal effects using linear non-Gaussian models with hidden variables. IJAR 49 (2008)
6. Hyvärinen, A., Karhunen, J., Oja, E.: Independent Component Analysis. Wiley Interscience, Hoboken (2001)
7. Kawahara, Y., Bollen, K., Shimizu, S., Washio, T.: GroupLiNGAM: Linear non-Gaussian acyclic models for sets of variables. arXiv:1006.5041v1 (2010)
8. Pearl, J.: Causality: Models, Reasoning, and Inference. Cambridge University Press, Cambridge (2000)
9. Shimizu, S., Hoyer, P.O., Hyvärinen, A., Kerminen, A.: A linear non-gaussian acyclic model for causal discovery. JMLR 7 (2006)
10. Skitovitch, W.P.: On a property of the normal distribution. DAN SSSR 89 (1953)
11. Spirtes, P., Glymour, C., Scheines, R.: Causation, Prediction and Search, 2nd edn. MIT Press, Cambridge (2000)

Appendix: Proofs

Proof of Lemma 1

First we show that if I is unconfounded then the distribution can be represented by a LiNGAM model (Equation (2)). Recall that the LiNGAM model can be rewritten as an ICA (independent component analysis) model given as $\mathbf{x} = \mathbf{A}\mathbf{e}$ (Equation (3)) with $\mathbf{x}$ the mixtures, $\mathbf{A}$ the mixing matrix, and $\mathbf{e}$ the independent sources. We now rely on a basic result in ICA [3]: If all the sources are non-Gaussian then the ICA mixing matrix

---

[3] Already for the sample of size 10000, subsampling (2000 samples) was necessary to perform the independence test with HSIC in reasonable time.

is identifiable from the joint distribution over the observed variables if and only if all the basis vectors (columns of the mixing matrix) are pairwise linearly independent. If two basis vectors are linearly dependent then in the identified ICA model the corresponding sources are combined into one.

Let $I = \{i_1, \ldots, i_K\} \subseteq J$ and $|I| = K$. The induced ICA model can be written as $\mathbf{x}_I = \mathbf{A}_I \mathbf{e}$ where $\mathbf{x}_I = (x_{i_1}, \ldots, x_{i_K})^T$, $\mathbf{A}_I$ is a $K \times N$ mixing matrix containing the rows with indices in I of the original mixing matrix $\mathbf{A}$ and $\mathbf{e}$ are the original error terms. We show that the mixing matrix $\mathbf{A}_I$ can be reduced (by combining parallel basis vectors) to a $K \times K$ mixing matrix $\tilde{\mathbf{A}}_I$, and we can form a new $K \times 1$ error term vector $\tilde{\mathbf{e}}_I$ with independent errors such that $\mathbf{x}_I = \tilde{\mathbf{A}}_I \tilde{\mathbf{e}}_I$.

We can assume that any x_j, $j \notin I$, is an ancestor of some x_i, $i \in I$, since the basis vector of any other x_j is a zero-vector and thus does not show up in $\mathbf{A}_I$. By the unconfoundedness of I we know that all directed paths from a given variable x_j, $j \notin I$, to variables x_k, $k \in I$, must pass through some single x_i with $i \in I$. Thus, the set of variables $x_i, i \in I$, define a partition of the full set x_j, $j \in V$, and their corresponding disturbances e_j. It is straightforward to show that any two basis vectors corresponding to disturbances e_{j_1} and e_{j_2} in the *same* partition are necessarily parallel, while any two basis vectors corresponding to disturbances e_{j_1} and e_{j_2} in different partitions are necessarily non-parallel. The basis vectors of each partition can thus be combined to obtain a $K \times K$ ICA mixing matrix, with the causal order induced from the generating lvLiNGAM model. This suffices to guarantee the reduction to a standard LiNGAM system.

Next we show, using a similar technique, that if the distribution over a subset of variables indexed by I can be represented by a standard LiNGAM model, then I is necessarily unconfounded. We do this by showing that if I was confounded, the mixing matrix would not be reducible to a square matrix but would necessarily be an overcomplete ICA model, implying that a LiNGAM model cannot represent the distribution.

We can assume without loss of generality that the causal order implied by the generating lvLiNGAM model among the variables in I is given by $(i_1, \ldots, i_K)$ and that the set I is only confounded by a single variable x_t, $t \notin I$, which is a root node in the generating lvLiNGAM model. Furthermore, x_t directly affects only two nodes in I, denoted by x_{i_p} and x_{i_q}, $i_p, i_q \in I$ and $i_p < i_q$. This implies that there are $|I| = K$ mixtures and $K + 1$ independent sources (error variables) and we can write the model as

$$x_I = (\mathbf{A}_t, \mathbf{A}_{i_1}, \ldots, \mathbf{A}_{i_K})(e_t, e_{i_1}, \ldots, e_{i_K})^T$$

with $x_I = (x_{i_1}, \ldots, x_{i_K})^T$, and $K \times 1$ dimensional vectors $\mathbf{A}_k$ containing the total effects of the error term e_k on x_I, $k = t, i_1, \ldots, i_K$. To prove that the mixing matrix $(\mathbf{A}_t, \mathbf{A}_{i_1}, \ldots, \mathbf{A}_{i_K})$ does not reduce to a square mixing matrix (and hence to a standard ICA model) we show that the columns $\mathbf{A}_k$, $k = t, i_1, \ldots, i_K$, are pairwise linearly independent.

This is clear for $\mathbf{A}_{i_1}, \ldots, \mathbf{A}_{i_K}$ since for each $k = 1, \ldots, K$ we know that (i) the kth entry of $\mathbf{A}_{i_k}$ is 1 and (ii) the entries 1 to $(k-1)$ are 0 (because the error term cannot affect any earlier variable due to acyclicity). Hence, $(\mathbf{A}_{i_1}, \ldots, \mathbf{A}_{i_K})$ form a lower triangular matrix with all ones on the diagonal. Clearly, the columns of such a matrix are pairwise linearly independent.

Now we show that also the effects of the confounder $x_t = e_t$ given in $\mathbf{A}_t$ on the variables in I are not proportional to the effects of any other error variable.

The vector $\mathbf{A}_t$ is given by $\mathbf{A}_t = (0, \ldots, 0, a_{i_p,t}, \ldots, a_{i_q,t}, \ldots, a_{K,t})^T$ with $a_{i_p,t} \neq 0, a_{i_q,t} \neq 0$ being the non-zero effects of e_t on x_{i_p} and x_{i_q}, respectively. A necessary condition for two vectors to be linearly dependent is that they have zeros in the same entries, which leaves us with only one candidate for being linearly dependent on $\mathbf{A}_t$, namely $\mathbf{A}_{i_p}$: For any $x_i, i \in I$, with $i < i_p$ (earlier in causal order than i_p) the ith entry of $\mathbf{A}_i$ is 1, whereas the ith entry of $\mathbf{A}_t$ equals 0. On the other side, for any $x_i, i \in I$, with $i > i_p$ (later in the causal order than i_p) the coefficient at the i_p^{th} entry is zero.

To see that $\mathbf{A}_{i_p}$ and $\mathbf{A}_t$ cannot be linearly dependent, we look at the entries in position i_p and i_q. For $\mathbf{A}_{i_p}$ we have that $a_{i_p,i_p} = 1$ and $a_{i_q,i_p} = \alpha$, where α denotes the total effect of x_{i_p} on x_{i_q}. For $\mathbf{A}_t$ we get $a_{i_p,t} = \beta$ with $\beta \neq 0$ the effect from x_t on x_{i_p}, and $a_{i_q,t} = \beta\alpha + \gamma$, with $\gamma \neq 0$ the direct effect of x_t on x_{i_q}. This means that $\mathbf{A}_{i_p} = (0, \ldots, 0, 1, \ldots, \alpha, \ldots, a_{i_p,t})^T$ and $\mathbf{A}_t = (0, \ldots, 0, \beta, \ldots, \beta\alpha + \gamma, \ldots, a_{K,t})^T$ and since $\gamma \neq 0$ these two vectors cannot be linearly dependent.

Proof of Theorem 1

First we note that the faithfulness assumption implies that an estimated zero total effect among a pair of variables is equivalent to (conditional) independence between the two.

If we obtain an estimate of the total effect for $\{x_i, x_j\}$ then there trivially exists an unconfounded superset S^+, because by point 2b(ii) in the algorithm if there does not exist an unconfounded superset, then there will not be an estimate.

To prove that the existence of an unconfounded superset S^+ for a pair always yields an estimate of the total effect of this pair we show that for every pair in S^+ the algorithm outputs an estimate. Let $|S^+| = K$. Because the unconfounded superset S^+ has an associated DAG, the variables in S^+ can be arranged in a causal order. We can assume that such a causal order over the K variables in S^+ is given by the labels $1, \ldots, K$. We will show by induction that after sweep $q = q'$, all pairs $\{l_1, l_2\}$ with $l_1 < q'$ and $l_2 \neq l_1$ are marked with a non-zero value in $\mathbf{P}$ (meaning that these effects are estimated). In the first sweep ($q = 2$), all pairs $\{1, l\}, l \neq 1$ are marked non-zero in $\mathbf{P}$ because there are no confounders outside the set S^+ (by assumption) and because x_1 has no parents in S^+ there are no confounders for these pairs within S^+ either. Next, assume that after sweep $q = q' - 1$ all pairs $\{l_1, l_2\}$ with $l_1 < q' - 1$ and $l_2 \neq l_1$ are marked with a non-zero value in $\mathbf{P}$. Consider a pair $\{q' - 1, l_2\}$ with $l_2 > q' - 1$. This pair may already be marked with a non-zero value in $\mathbf{P}$, but if it is not it will be marked in the current sweep $q = q'$, because there are no confounders outside the set S^+ (by assumption), and any variable in S^+ which is a potential confounder (has a non-zero total effect on both $x_{q'-1}$ and x_{l_2}) is included in the LiNGAM estimation for that pair. Hence, after sweep $q = q'$, all pairs $\{l_1, l_2\}$ with $l_1 < q'$ and $l_2 \neq l_1$ are marked with a non-zero value in $\mathbf{P}$.

Finally, we need to show that the estimates of the total effects converge to the true total effects in the lvLiNGAM model. We only estimate effects for pairs for which there is an unconfounded superset, and by Lemma 1 we know that a LiNGAM model fits to such a superset. Since the coefficients estimated by LiNGAM converge to the true effects, we have proved the theorem.

Proof of Lemma 2

For a set S with $|S| \leq 1$, the claim is trivially true.

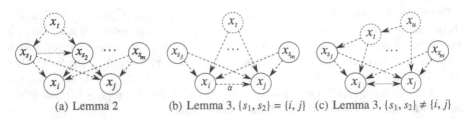

(a) Lemma 2   (b) Lemma 3, $\{s_1, s_2\} = \{i, j\}$ (c) Lemma 3, $\{s_1, s_2\} \neq \{i, j\}$

Fig. 3. Graphs for proofs of Lemma 2 and Lemma 3. The dashed arrows represent direct paths. Solid circles indicate variables in the set S^+, dashed circles confounders for S^+. In (a) the dotted arrow stands for either a directed path from x_{s_1} to x_{s_2} or no effect between the two variables. Similarly, in (c) the dotted bidirected arrow can be replaced by either arrow or left out.

If the set S contains at least two elements, we use a proof by contradiction to show that it is unconfounded. Assume that for an arbitrary pair (x_i, x_j) the set S defined in step 2b(i) is confounded. This means that there exists a confounder x_t, $t \notin S$, for variables x_{s_1} and x_{s_2} with $s_1, s_2 \in S$, $s_1 \neq s_2$. We can assume without loss of generality that in the underlying lvLiNGAM model x_{s_1} is in the causal order before x_{s_2}.

First we note that x_t must also be a confounder for x_{s_1} and x_i as well as for x_{s_1} and x_j. As depicted in Figure 3 (a) there are directed non-intersecting paths from x_t to x_{s_1} and x_{s_2} (by definition of a confounder) and directed paths from x_{s_2} to x_i and x_j (by construction of the set S in step 2b(i) of the algorithm) not containing x_{s_1}. Hence, there are non-intersecting paths from x_t to x_{s_1} and x_i, and to x_{s_1} and x_j.

Furthermore, also by construction of the set S, the pairs (x_{s_1}, x_i) and (x_{s_1}, x_j) are part of unconfounded sets $S^+_{s_1,i} := \{s_1, i\} \cup S_{s_1,i}$ and $S^+_{s_1,j} := \{s_1, j\} \cup S_{s_1,j}$, respectively, which where formed in step 2b(ii) in some previous iteration of the algorithm.

Since x_t is a confounder for x_{s_1} and x_i as well as for x_{s_1} and x_j we must have both $t \in S_{s_1,i}$, and $t \in S_{s_1,j}$, implying that $P_{ti} = 1$ and $P_{tj} = 1$, respectively. This however would mean that $t \in S$ which contradicts the assumption.

Proof of Lemma 3

As in Theorem 1, the faithfulness assumption allows us to conclude that zero estimated causal effects correspond to (conditional) independences.

First we show that if the set S^+ is unconfounded then one of the three statements must hold. For S^+ unconfounded we know by Lemma 1 that a LiNGAM model fits to S^+, and by construction of S^+ the variables x_i and x_j are the last in the causal order (since there is a causal effect from every x_s, $s \in S$, to both x_i and x_j). Hence, all confounders for x_i and x_j are included in the regression, and one of the 3 points must hold (which one depends on the causal relationship among x_i and x_j, as explained below Lemma 3).

To prove that S^+ is unconfounded if one of the three statements holds, we assume that one of the statements is true and that the set S^+ is confounded, and lead this to a contradiction. The latter means that there exists a confounder x_t, $t \notin S^+$, for variables x_{s_1} and x_{s_2} with $s_1, s_2 \in S^+$ and $s_1 \neq s_2$. We assume that the paths from x_t to x_{s_1} and x_{s_2} do not contain any other nodes from the set S^+ and prove the claim for different assignments of the indices s_1 and s_2: First we show that for $\{s_1, s_2\} = \{i, j\}$ we get a contradiction if one of the three statements holds. Then we prove for any other assignment of s_1 and s_2 that the existence of a confounder for x_{s_1} and x_{s_2} leads to the existence of a confounder for x_i and x_j and hence have a contradiction by the first part. As above, x_i and x_j are the last two variables in the causal ordering regarding the set S^+.

Let $\{s_1, s_2\} = \{i, j\}$. We know that there are non-intersecting paths from the confounder x_t to x_i and x_j which by assumption do not contain any elements of S.

First we assume that statement 1 holds. This implies that the regression into x_j fits the data, and the one into x_i does not. Thus, x_i is before x_j in the causal order of the underlying lvLiNGAM model and has a non-zero effect α on x_j (see Figure 3 (b)).

For simplicity, assume that x_t is the only confounder outside S^+ for x_i and x_j (essentially the same logic applies if there are more than one such confounder). Since $t \notin S$ and since there are directed paths from x_t to x_i and x_j not containing any nodes from S we get for the regressions $x_i = \sum_{s \in S} \tilde{c}_s x_s + c_{ti} x_t + e_i$ and $x_j = \alpha x_i + \sum_{s \in S} c_s x_s + c_{tj} x_t + \tilde{e}_j = \alpha x_i + \sum_{s \in S} c_s x_s + e_j$ with $e_j = c_{tj} x_t + \tilde{e}_j$, and $c_{ti} \neq 0, c_{tj} \neq 0$. The confounder x_t has a non-zero effect on both x_i and e_j, and hence the non-Gaussianity of x_t and the Darmois-Skitovitch theorem [2,10] imply that $x_i \not\perp\!\!\!\perp e_j$, contradicting the assumption that statement 1 holds.

A similar argumentation applies when statement 2 is assumed to be true.

If statement 3 holds, we see from $\alpha = \beta = 0$ that x_i and x_j are independent given $\{x_s, s \in S\}$. The graph is similar to the one in Figure 3 (b) with the arrow from x_i to x_j removed. Assuming again that x_t is the only confounder outside S^+ for x_i and x_j, we get for the regressions $x_i = \sum_{s \in S} \tilde{c}_s x_s + c_{ti} x_t + \tilde{e}_i = \sum_{s \in S} \tilde{c}_s x_s + e_i$ and $x_j = \sum_{s \in S} c_s x_s + c_{tj} x_t + \tilde{e}_j = \sum_{s \in S} c_s x_s + e_j$ with $e_i = c_{ti} x_t + \tilde{e}_i$, $e_j = c_{tj} x_t + \tilde{e}_j$, and $c_{ti} \neq 0, c_{tj} \neq 0$. From the non-Gaussianity of x_t and the Darmois-Skitovitch theorem [2,10] follows that neither $x_i \perp\!\!\!\perp e_j$ nor $x_j \perp\!\!\!\perp e_i$ holds which is in contradiction to statement 3.

We now assume that $\{s_1, s_2\} \neq \{i, j\}$, with $s_1, s_2 \in S^+$, and reduce it to the previous case by showing that in this case a confounder for x_i and x_j must exist.

First we note that $s_1, s_2 \in S$ (that means both s_1 and s_2 not equal to i or j) cannot occur since by Lemma 2 the set S is unconfounded. Thus, let $s_1 \in S$ and $s_2 \in \{i, j\}$. As we will see the order among x_i and x_j does not matter in the proof and we can without loss of generality set $s_2 = i$. Furthermore, as stated above, we assume that the path from the confounder x_t to x_i does not contain any elements of S.

By construction of the set S we know that x_{s_1} and x_i are part of an unconfounded set denoted by $S^+_{s_1, i} = \{s_1, i\} \cup S_{s_1, i}$. Since x_t is a confounder for x_{s_1} and x_i we must have $t \in S_{s_1, i}$, meaning that $P_{ti} = 1$ (i.e. we have estimated an effect of x_t on x_i).

Since $t \notin S$ and $P_{ti} = 1$, we also must have that $P_{tj} \neq 1$ (by step 2b(i) of Algorithm 1). Furthermore, since there is a directed path from x_t to x_j (via x_{s_1}) we get $P_{tj} \neq -1$ (by the acyclicity assumption) and $P_{tj} \neq 2$ (by the faithfulness assumption). Hence, $P_{tj} = 0$ implying that there exists a confounder x_u for x_t and x_j.[4] As depicted in Figure 3 (c), the path from the confounder x_u to x_j does not contain any nodes in S (otherwise x_u is also a confounder for two nodes in S which is not possible by Lemma 2).

Thus, there are directed non-intersecting paths from the confounder x_u to x_i (via x_t) and to x_j not containing any nodes from the set S. Particularly, x_u is a confounder for x_i and x_j as considered in first part of the proof, which was shown to lead to a contradiction and thus the lemma is proved.

---

[4] $P_{tj} = 0$ and no confounder for (x_t, x_j) is only possible in the first sweep of the algorithm before testing the pair, but since $S \neq \emptyset$ this situation will never occur in the first sweep.

Detection of Mutually Dependent Test Items Using the LCI Test

Takamitsu Hashimoto[1,2] and Maomi Ueno[1]

[1] University of Electro-Communications,
1-5-1 Chofugaoka, Chofu-shi, Tokyo, Japan
[2] National Center for University Entrance Examinations,
2-19-23, Komaba, Meguro-ku, Tokyo, Japan

Abstract. Item response theory (IRT) is widely used for test analyses. Most models of IRT assume local independence, meaning that when the ability variables influencing the test performance are held constant, an examinee's responses to any pair of items are statistically independent. However, many factors might cause local dependence among items. Consequently, conditional independence (CI) tests are needed among items given a latent ability variable. Hashimoto and Ueno (2011) proposed the latent conditional independence (LCI) test. While other CI tests are sensitive to dependencies of items aside from the targets, the LCI test is robust to such dependencies. However, when the two target items affect the same items, the LCI test might fail to detect local independency between the targets. The previous work of Hashimoto and Ueno (2011) is improved on to obtain a more accurate detection method.

Keywords: latent variable, conditional independence test, Bayesian network IRT.

1 Introduction

Tests of many kinds are implemented to assess, select, and predict. To analyze testing data, item response theory (IRT) is widely used. To formulate the basic constructs of the IRT, Lord and Novick [1] used a modern mathematical statistical approach. Since then, a great deal of research effort has been spent to develop their idea from different perspectives (e.g., statistical theory, parameter estimation algorithms). Many possible IRT models exist, differing in the mathematical form of the item characteristic function and/or the number of parameters specified in the model, e.g. the Rasch model [2], the normal ogive model [1], the two-parameter logistic model [3], and the three-parameter logistic model [4]. More general and well-known IRT models exist, such as the graded response model [5], the free response model [6], the partial credit model [7], and the nominal response model [8]. All IRT models incorporate one or more parameters describing the examinee's abilities. Also, most IRT models assume that when the abilities influencing the test performance are held constant, the examinee's responses to any pair of items are statistically independent. This conditional

T. Onoda, D. Bekki, and E. McCready (Eds.): JSAI-isAI 2010, LNAI 6797, pp. 196–209, 2011.

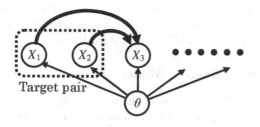

Fig. 1. Target items (X_1 and X_2) affecting the same item (X_3)

independence assumption is called "local independence". For this assumption to be true, an examinee's performance on one item must not affect, either positively or negatively, a response to any other item in the test. Regarding this local independence assumption, Yen [9] previously pointed out that actual situations often violate this assumption. Furthermore, many previous studies [10], [11], [12], [13] have shown that parameter estimation often fails when the local independence assumption is violated.

Consequently, conditional independence (CI) tests among items given an examinee's ability are necessary for applying IRT to test data. However, it is difficult to realize such a test because dependencies caused by the ability parameter must be controlled and the ability parameter is a latent variable. Several CI tests given a latent variable have been proposed for overcoming this problem. For example, Chen and Thissen's G^2 test [10], which is the most frequently used CI test given a latent variable, is a log-likelihood ratio test between an observed frequency and an expected frequency derived from an IRT model. This G^2 test integrates out the ability parameter and uses frequencies of only the two target items for the test statistics. Nevertheless, dependencies that are irrelevant to the target items cause inaccuracy in the test.

To solve this problem, Hashimoto and Ueno [14] proposed the latent conditional independence (LCI) test. The feature of the LCI test is that it assumes dependencies among all other items, and the test statistics are robust to dependencies of irrelevant items. In other words, conditional independence given all items except the targets is tested in the LCI test. However, when the two target items affect the same items (Fig. 1), the LCI test might fail to detect local independence between the targets. This problem has not been discussed by Hashimoto and Ueno [14] yet. This paper improves on their work [14] to obtain a more accurate detection method.

2   Item Response Theory

Since this paper discusses a problem in IRT, this section briefly introduces IRT. As an example of conventional models of IRT, a two-parameter logistic (2PL) model [4] is used. This section also explains local independence, which is assumed by conventional IRT models such as the 2PL model. When the local independence assumption is violated, the parameter estimation of conventional IRT models often fails. As an IRT model that relaxes this local independence assumption, Bayesian network IRT [15] is introduced.

2.1 Two-Parameter Logistic Model

Item response theory (IRT) represents the probability of an examinee answering an item correctly as a function of the examinee's latent ability variable. In the standard dichotomous response formulation of IRT, the correctness of the i-th item in a test is indicated by a random response variable taking a value of 1 for a correct response and a value of 0 for an incorrect response. An examinee's latent ability variable is denoted as θ. The two-parameter logistic (2PL) model [4], which is a conventional IRT model, links the probability that the j-th examinee correctly answers the i-th item to the examinee's own latent ability variable θ_j:

$$P(X_{ij} = 1|\theta_j, a_i, b_i) = \frac{1}{1 + \exp\{-1.7a_i(\theta_j - b_i)\}} \ , \tag{1}$$

where $X_{ij} = 1$ stands for the j-th examinee correctly answering the i-th item and $X_{ij} = 0$ stands for incorrectly answering it. Item parameters a_i and b_i are respectively designated the "discrimination parameter" and a "difficulty parameter".

The likelihood function of the 2PL model is

$$L(x_{ij}|\theta_j, a_i, b_i)$$
$$= \left[\frac{1}{1 + \exp\{-1.7a_i(\theta_j - b_i)\}}\right]^{x_{ij}} \left[1 - \frac{1}{1 + \exp\{-1.7a_i(\theta_j - b_i)\}}\right]^{1-x_{ij}} \ , \tag{2}$$

where x_{ij} stands for the j-th examinee's response to the i-th item, and it takes 1 or 0.

Equation (2) contains no parameter of the other items. Therefore, any pair of items is locally independent (Fig. 2). Statistically, local independence means that, for a given value of the latent ability variable θ, the joint probability of correct responses to a pair of items is the product of the probabilities of correct responses to the two items, as

$$P(x_i, x_i'|\theta, \xi_i, \xi_{i'}) = P(x_i|\theta, \xi_i)P(x_{i'}|\theta, \xi_{i'}) \ , \tag{3}$$

where ξ_i and $\xi_{i'}$ respectively denote item parameters of the i-th and the i'-th items.

In reality, as described in section 1, in educational assessment, many factors can cause local dependence among items. For example, Yen [9] pointed out the following causes of local dependence: external assistance or interference, speed, fatigue, practice, item or response format, passage dependence, item chaining, explanation of a previous answer, scoring rubrics or raters, and others.

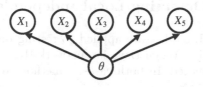

Fig. 2. Graphical expression of a locally independent structure

2.2   Bayesian Network IRT

Bayesian network IRT [15] is an IRT model that relaxes the local independence assumption. This model introduces different item parameters by responding to other items. An item with a response that changes the item parameter value of the i-th item is designated as a parent item of the i-th item. Consequently, the Bayesian network IRT model is regarded as an IRT model containing parent items. Details of this model are described below.

Let a certain examinee's response pattern to m items be

$$\mathbf{x} = (x_1, x_2, \cdots, x_i, \cdots, x_m)^t, \tag{4}$$

where

$$x_i = \begin{cases} 0 & \text{for an incorrect response} \\ 1 & \text{for a correct response} \end{cases} . \tag{5}$$

When B_s encodes the assertions of local independence in a model, the joint probability of scores is given as

$$
P(x_1, \cdots, x_m | \theta, \xi, B_s)
$$
$$
= \prod_{i=1}^{m} \prod_{j=0}^{2^{p_i}-1} \left\{ P(X_i = 1 | \theta, \xi_i, \tilde{\mathbf{X}}_{ij})^{x_i u_{ij}} P(X_i = 0 | \theta, \xi_i, \tilde{\mathbf{X}}_{ij})^{(1-x_i)u_{ij}} \right\} ,
$$
$$\tag{6}$$

where

$$
u_{ij} = \begin{cases} 1 & \text{for the } j-\text{th response pattern to parent items} \\ & \text{of the } i-\text{th item} \\ 0 & \text{for the other patterns} \end{cases}
$$

p_i : the number of parent items of the $i-$th item

$\tilde{\mathbf{X}}_{ij}$: the $j-$th response pattern to parent items of the $i-$th item

ξ_i : a parameter vector for $\tilde{\mathbf{X}}_{ij}$

$\xi = \left(\xi_1^t, \xi_2^t, \cdots, \xi_i^t, \cdots, \xi_m^t \right)$

B_s : structure

Bayesian network IRT can express a conditional item characteristic curve given a response to other items. Note that in Bayesian network IRT, the topological order of test items must be fixed, because the order affects parameter estimates. Therefore, we determined the topological order using the presentation order in the test.

3   Methods for Detecting Local Independence

When conventional IRT models are applied to testing data, locally dependent items must be eliminated. When Bayesian network IRT is applied, dependence structure must be estimated. In both cases, a method to detect local independence is required.

Several methods for testing local independence between items have been proposed. In such methods, the G^2 test developed by Chen and Thissen [10] is the most frequently used. For that reason, this paper introduces Chen and Thissen's G^2 test.

However, traditional methods such as G^2 test have a problem in that they are inaccurate when dependencies that are irrelevant to the target items exist. The LCI test developed by Hashimoto and Ueno [14] is robust to such dependencies. This paper uses the LCI test to detect locally dependent items. The LCI test is introduced after Chen and Thissen's G^2 test.

3.1   Chen and Thissen's G^2 Test

Chen and Thissen's G^2 test is conducted using the following procedure.

Let $N_{x_i x_{i'}}$ be the number of examinees whose responses to the i-th item X_i and the i'-th item $X_{i'}$ are x_i and $x_{i'}$ ($x_i, x_{i'} = 0, 1$), respectively; let N be the total number of examinees. Under a local independence assumption, the expected number of examinees whose responses will be x_i and $x_{i'}$ is calculated as follows:

$$E_{x_i x_{i'}} = N \int \hat{P}_i(\theta)^{x_i} \hat{P}_{i'}(\theta)^{x_{i'}} \left[1 - \hat{P}_i(\theta)\right]^{1-x_i} \left[1 - \hat{P}_{i'}(\theta)\right]^{1-x_{i'}} p(\theta)d\theta \ . \quad (7)$$

Therein, $\hat{P}_i(\theta)$ is the item characteristic curve in which item parameter estimates are substituted. The G^2 statistic is computed as

$$G^2 = 2 \sum_{x_i=0}^{1} \sum_{x_{i'}=0}^{1} N_{x_i x_{i'}} \log_e \frac{N_{x_i x_{i'}}}{E_{x_i x_{i'}}} \ . \quad (8)$$

To calculate G^2 statistic, $\hat{P}_i(\theta)$ and $\hat{P}_{i'}(\theta)$ in equation (7) require estimates of item parameters. Since these estimates are obtained under the local independence assumption (Fig. 3), when some items aside from the target items are locally dependent, G^2 is inaccurate.

3.2   Latent Conditional Independence Test

Hashimoto and Ueno [14] proposed the latent conditional independence (LCI) test. Whereas traditional methods for detecting local independence are not robust to dependencies that are irrelevant to the target items, the LCI test is.

Since any pair of items is dependent when a latent ability variable θ is marginalized out (Fig. 4), the LCI test assumes dependencies among all items (Fig. 5). Such a structure is designated as a completely dependent structure.

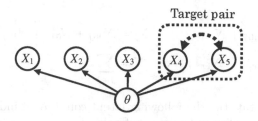

Fig. 3. Graphical expression of a locally independent structure of items aside from the targets

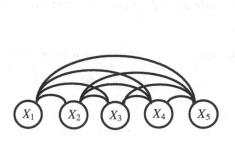

Fig. 4. Structure when a latent ability variable was marginalized out

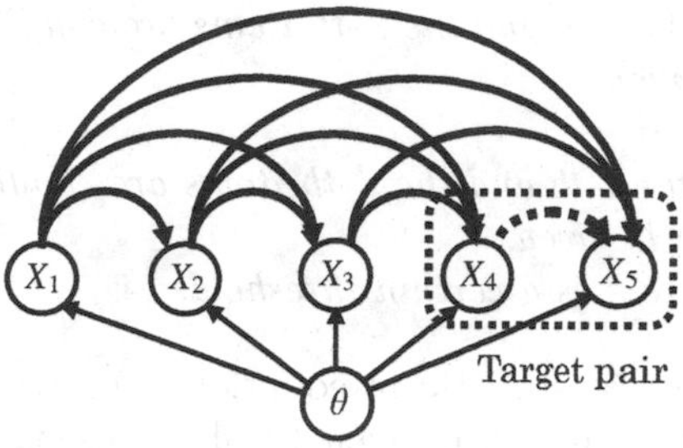

Fig. 5. Completely dependent structure given a latent ability variable

Although some extended IRT models that relax local independence assumption have been proposed, only Bayesian network IRT [15] can express a completely dependent structure given a latent variable. Therefore, the LCI test uses Bayesian network IRT model.

The test statistic of the LCI test is computed as

$$I(X_i; X_{i'}|\mathbf{X}^{\neg ii'}, \xi, B_s^c) = \frac{1}{N} \sum_{j=1}^{J} \sum_{x_i=0}^{1} \sum_{x_{i'}=0}^{1} N_{x_i x_{i'} j} \log_2 \frac{N_{x_i x_{i'} j} N_j}{N_{x_i j} N_{x_{i'} j}} , \quad (9)$$

where

X_i : i−th item

$X_{i'}$: i'−th item

$\mathbf{X}^{\neg ii'}$: all items except X_i and $X_{i'}$

J : number of observed response patterns to $\mathbf{X}^{\neg ii'}$

$\mathbf{x}_j^{\neg ii'}$: j−th response pattern to $\mathbf{X}^{\neg ii'}$ $(j = 1, \cdots, J)$

ξ : item parameters of the model

B_s^c : parent variable set of the i−thand i'−th items with a completely dependent structure

$N_{x_i x_{i'} j}$: number of examinees whose response pattern is $\mathbf{x}_j^{\neg ii'}$

and

$$N_{x_i j} = N_{x_i 0 j} + N_{x_i 1 j} \quad , \quad N_j = N_{00j} + N_{01j} + N_{10j} + N_{11j}$$

$$N_{x_{i'} j} = N_{0 x_{i'} j} + N_{1 x_{i'} j} \quad , \quad N = \sum_{j=1}^{J} N_j \quad .$$

Using this test statistic, the following latent conditional independence (LCI) test, given a latent ability variable, is definable.

Definition 1. *(latent conditional independence (LCI) test)*
If $I(X_i; X_{i'} | \mathbf{X}^{\neg ii'}, \xi, B_s^c) > \varepsilon$
→ the i-th and the i'-th items are conditionally dependent when a latent variable is given
else
→ the i-th and the i'-th items are conditionally independent when a latent variable is given,
where ε is a certain threshold.

The test statistic in equation (9) is the same as the conditional mutual information measure given to all items except the target items. According to the Neyman factorization theorem [16], an examinee's response pattern is sufficient for estimating his/her latent ability variable when the number of items is sufficiently large. Therefore, this statistic measures conditional dependency given latent variable asymptotically.

When two target items are parents of the same child items, the LCI test might detect local dependency between the targets even if they are locally independent. This is because the child items are also given in the test. In this case, when the child items are not given, the targets are locally independent. Therefore, as shown in the algorithm in Fig. 6, extra dependencies detected by the LCI test can be corrected.

4   Simulation Examinations

This section examines values of the LCI test statistics when two target items are parents of the same child item. Moreover, this section examines effectiveness of the correction algorithm shown in Fig. 6. In addition, a traditional G^2 test is applied to the same data, and results are compared.

4.1   Method

The following three structures are assumed. In structure (a), one item affects the difficulty of two other items (Fig. 7(a)). In structure (b), one item affects the difficulty of another item, and the affected item affects the difficulty of another item (Fig. 7(b)). In structure (c), two items affect the difficulty of one item (Fig. 7(c)).

---

input:

  X_i: a candidate of two parent items
  $X_{i'}$: another candidate of two parent item
  X_k: a candidate of a child item
  $\mathbf{X}^{\neg ii'}$: response pattern to all items except X_i and $X_{i'}$
  $\mathbf{X}^{\neg ii'k}$: response pattern to all items except X_i, $X_{i'}$ and X_k
  B_s^c: parent variable set of X_i and $X_{i'}$ with a completely dependent structure
  ε: threshold of local dependency
output: parent variable set B_s
main:

  1: $B_s \leftarrow B_s^c$
  2: **if** $I(X_i; X_{i'}|\mathbf{X}^{\neg ii'}, \xi, B_s^c) > \varepsilon$ **do**
  3:   **if** $I(X_i; X_{i'}|\mathbf{X}^{\neg ii'k}, \xi, B_s^c) \leq \varepsilon$ **do**
  4:     eliminate edge X_i–$X_{i'}$ from B_s
  5:     substituted the edges X_i–X_k–$X_{i'}$ by $X_i \rightarrow X_k \leftarrow X_{i'}$ in B_s
  6:   **end if**
  7: **end if**
  8: **return** B_s

Fig. 6. Algorithm of extra dependency elimination

All datasets have $10,000$ examinees and 7 items in order to observe sufficient samples for each response pattern. Parameters of items 4, 5, 6, and 7 are fixed to $(a_4, b_4) = (1.00, -1.0)$, $(a_5, b_5) = (1.00, 1.0)$, $(a_6, b_6) = (0.71, 0.0)$, and $(a_7, b_7) = (1.41, 0.0)$. Parameters of items 1, 2, and 3 differ among structures.

In structure (a), parameters of item 1 are $(a_1, b_1) = (1.00, 0.0)$. Discrimination parameters of items 2 and 3 are set as equal $(a_2 = a_3 = 1.00)$. When an examinee answers item 1 incorrectly, difficulty parameters of items 2 and 3 $(b_{2|X_1=0}, b_{3|X_1=0})$ become 1.5. When an examinee answers item 1 correctly, difficulty parameters $(b_{2|X_1=1}, b_{3|X_1=1})$ become -1.5.

In structure (b), parameters of item 1 are $(a_1, b_1) = (1.00, 0.0)$. Discrimination parameters of items 2 and 3 are set as equal $(a_2 = a_3 = 1.00)$. Difficulty parameters are $b_{2|X_1=0} = 1.5$, $b_{2|X_1=1} = -1.5$, and $b_{3|X_2=0} = 1.5$, $b_{3|X_2=1} = -1.5$.

In structure (c), parameters of item 1 and item 2 are $(a_1, b_1) = (a_2, b_2) = (1.00, 0.0)$. Discrimination parameters of item 3 are set as 1.00. When an examinee answers both items 1 and 2 correctly, the difficulty parameter of item 3 $(b_{3|X_1=1,X_2=1})$ becomes -1.5. Otherwise, the difficulty parameter of item 3 $(b_{3|X_1=1,X_2=0}, b_{3|X_1=0,X_2=1}, b_{3|X_1=0,X_2=0})$ become 1.5.

In every structure, 100 sets of data are generated, and the LCI test and Chen and Thissen's G^2 test are applied to them.

4.2 Results

Structure (a) contains two local dependencies: between X_1 and X_2, and between X_1 and X_3. Minimal LCI statistics of such pairs are larger than the maximum of

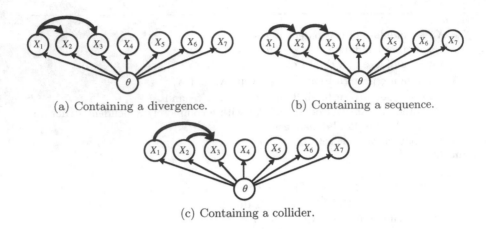

(a) Containing a divergence.   (b) Containing a sequence.

(c) Containing a collider.

Fig. 7. Item structures of simulation examinations

locally independent pairs (Table 1(a)). LCI statistics between X_2 and X_3, which are locally independent items, are as small as those of other locally independent pairs.

Structure (b) obtains results similar to those of structure (a). All LCI statistics of locally dependent pairs are larger than those of locally independent pairs (Table 1(b)).

In structure (c), items X_1 and X_2 have the same child X_3. LCI statistics between X_1 and X_2 are smaller than those of locally dependent pairs but larger than those of other locally independent pairs. However, when X_3 is not included in the parent item sets of X_1 and X_2, LCI statistics between X_1 and X_2 are as small as those of other locally independent pairs (Tables. 1(c)). Consequently, if the algorithm in Fig. 6 is applied, collider structure of X_1, X_2 and X_3 can be correctly detected.

According to Table 1, the appropriate value of threshold ε might exist between 0.03 and 0.07. Although many CI tests using conditional mutual information measure utilize chi-square distributions to determine a threshold, the LCI test statistic $I(X_i; X_{i'} | \mathbf{X}^{\neg ii'}, \xi, B_s^c)$ cannot. This is because when the number of items is insufficient, association caused by a latent variable is not fully controlled even if all items except targets are given. Therefore, how to determine ε remains an unsolved problem.

This paper also applies Chen and Thissen's G^2 test to the same data. If the two target items are locally independent, G^2 statistics are expected to follow a chi-square distribution with 1 degree of freedom. However, according to Tables 2(a) and 2(b), even the 5th percentile of G^2 between locally independent pairs exceed the 95th percentile of a chi-square distribution with 1 degree of freedom, 3.841. The result shows that when some items aside from the target items are locally dependent, G^2 test is inaccurate.

Table 1. Values of the LCI statistics

(a) Containing divergence

Item Pair	Mean	Minimum	Maximum
X_1-X_2, X_1-X_3	0.149	0.129	0.167
X_2-X_3	0.004	0.002	0.006
Other independent pairs	0.009	0.001	0.032

(b) Containing sequence

Item Pair	Mean	Minimum	Maximum
X_1-X_2	0.156	0.142	0.173
X_2-X_3	0.150	0.133	0.169
X_1-X_3	0.002	0.001	0.004
Other independent pairs	0.008	0.001	0.033

(c) Containing collider

Item Pair	Mean	Minimum	Maximum
X_1-X_3, X_2-X_3	0.249	0.231	0.276
X_1-X_2	0.070	0.061	0.080
Other independent pairs	0.010	0.002	0.027
X_1-X_2 (Without X_3)	0.016	0.011	0.022

Table 2. Values of G^2 statistics

(a) Containing divergence

Item pair	Mean	5 percentile	95 percentile
X_1-X_2, X_1-X_3	120.87	0.26	167.48
X_2-X_3	55.80	19.28	167.09
Other independent pairs	50.72	14.10	149.97

(b) Containing sequence

Item pair	Mean	5 percentile	95 percentile
X_1-X_2	156.20	131.59	191.99
X_2-X_3	153.01	6.99	201.31
X_1-X_3	30.70	14.19	39.84
Other independent pairs	51.51	15.97	144.02

(c) Containing collider

Item pair	Mean	5 percentile	95 percentile
X_1-X_3, X_2-X_3	185.40	153.95	275.76
X_1-X_2	251.36	226.69	276.66
Other independent pairs	39.27	0.25	102.80

In structure (c), G^2 statistics between X_1 and X_2 are as large as those of locally dependent pairs. G^2 test also detects local dependencies between parents that have the same children.

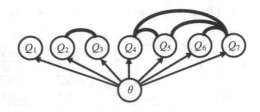

Fig. 8. Detected local dependencies of mathematics test items in Hashimoto and Ueno [14]

5   Application to Real Data

Hashimoto and Ueno [14] applied the LCI test to a mathematics test and detected dependencies as shown in Fig. 8. However, if locally independent items are parents of the same child items, local dependencies might be detected between such parents. This section applies the correction algorithm to a mathematics test and reconsiders the detected local dependencies. Moreover, a traditional G^2 test is applied to the same data, and results are compared.

5.1   Method

This test contained seven items and was taken by 367 freshmen from five national universities in Tokyo. Items Q1, Q2, and Q3 were questions about inequalities of the second degree, and Q3 required the correct response to Q2. Items Q4, Q5, Q6, and Q7 were questions about logical expressions. See the Appendix for details.

5.2   Result

Table 3 shows values of the LCI test statistics. According to the results of simulation examinations in section 4.2, an appropriate threshold of the LCI test might exist between 0.03 and 0.07. Therefore, 0.05, which is the midpoint of 0.03 and 0.07, was set as the threshold ε.

Table 3. LCI test statistics for seven items of a real test

items	Q1	Q2	Q3	Q4	Q5	Q6	Q7
Q1		0.012	0.012	0.005	0.017	0.000	0.019
Q2			0.159	0.009	0.022	0.004	0.031
Q3				0.029	0.032	0.018	0.048
Q4					0.066	0.020	0.053
Q5						0.010	0.052
Q6							0.056
Q7							

Table 4. G^2 test statistics for seven items of a real test

items	Q1	Q2	Q3	Q4	Q5	Q6	Q7
Q1		1.734	0.990	2.973	0.665	4.383	5.431
Q2			9.227	5.803	4.483	4.876	10.084
Q3				4.127	4.304	2.980	4.883
Q4					9.042	0.356	5.336
Q5						0.273	0.411
Q6							10.017
Q7							

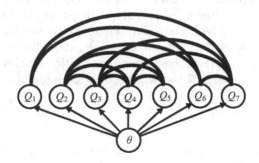

Fig. 9. Pairs for which G^2 statistics were greater than 3.841

Within items of logical expressions (Q4, Q5, Q6, and Q7), four pairs were judged to be locally dependent. Since Q4, Q5, and Q7 were mutually dependent, the correction algorithm in Fig. 6 was applied to them. However, no corrected LCI statistics were lower than ε $(I(X_4; X_5 | \mathbf{X}^{\neg 457}, \xi, B_s) = 0.076;$ $I(X_4; X_7 | \mathbf{X}^{\neg 457}, \xi, B_s) = 0.063;$ $I(X_5; X_7 | \mathbf{X}^{\neg 457}, \xi, B_s) = 0.062)$, and no collider could be found. Therefore, local independencies did not exist between Q4, Q5, and Q7. Items Q4–Q7 share the same alternatives, but each of those alternatives can be chosen several times. Consequently, such sharing of alternatives might cause mutual dependence.

Table 4 shows values of Chen and Thissen's G^2 test statistics, and pairs of items judged to be locally dependent are shown in Fig. 9. This G^2 test detects a lot of local dependencies, and the estimated structure is difficult to interpret.

6   Conclusions

This paper examined how correctly the LCI test detects local independencies when the two target items affect the same items. In addition, this paper improved the LCI test to obtain a more accurate detection method. Results show the following.

When two items were parents of the same child item, values of the LCI test statistics of these parents were larger than those of other locally independent pairs but smaller than those of locally dependent pairs. Moreover, when the common child item was eliminated from the parentsf set, the LCI test statistics became as small as those of locally independent pairs. These results revealed that when such a structure existed in a test, the LCI test could determine directions of local dependencies.

However, some problems remain unresolved. First, the number of examinees was fixed to 10, 000 in order to observe sufficient samples. If sample size is small, sampling errors might affect the LCI test. The amount of sampling error effects should be measured in the next study. Second, the critical point ε was set to 0.05 for the analyses described herein. The conditions were limited (10,000 examinees; seven items). Consequently, the LCI test should be applied to various conditions of data and more appropriate ε must be explored. Third, if a test does not contain a structure in which two items are parents of the same child item, direction of local dependency cannot be determined. Therefore, more detailed methods to decide the direction should be explored. Given the above limitations, conclusions drawn from the real-world data should be taken cautiously. However, when these problems are resolved, the LCI test will become more useful.

References

1. Lord, F.M., Novick, M.R.: Statistical Theories of Mental Test Scores. Addison-Wesley, Reading (1968)
2. Rasch, G.: An item analysis which takes individual differences into account. British Journal of Mathematical and Statistical Psychology 19, 49–57 (1966)
3. Birnbaum, A.: Efficient design and use of tests of a mental ability for various decision-making problems (Series Report 58-16, no.7755-23). USAF School of Aviation Medicine, Randolph Air Force Base, Texas (1957)
4. Birnbaum, A.: Some latent trait models. In: Load, F.M., Novick, M.R. (eds.) Statistical Theories of Mental Test Scores, pp. 397–424. Addison-Wesley, Reading (1968)
5. Samejima, F.: Estimation of latent ability using a response pattern of graded scores. Psychometrika Monograph (17) (1969)
6. Samejima, F.: A general model for free-response data. Psychometrika Monograph (18) (1972)
7. Masters, G.N.: A Rasch model for partial credit scoring. Psychometrika 35, 43–50 (1982)
8. Bock, R.D.: Estimating item parameters and latent ability when responses are scored in two or more nominal categories. Psychometrika 37, 29–51 (1972)
9. Yen, W.M.: Effects of local item dependence on the fit and equating performance of the three-parameter logistic model. Applied Psychological Measurement 8, 125–145 (1984)
10. Chen, W.H., Thissen, D.: Local dependence indexes for item pairs using item response theory. Journal of Educational and Behavioral Statistics 22, 265–289 (1997)
11. Reese, L.M.: The impact of local dependencies on some LSAT outcomes. Law School Admission Council Statistical Report 95(02) (1995)
12. Sano, M.: Detecting overestimation of discrimination parameter applying mutual information. Japanese Journal for Research on Testing 5, 3–21 (2009)
13. Sireci, S.G., Thissen, D., Wainer, H.: On the reliability of testlet-based tests. Journal of Educational Measurement 28, 237–247 (1991)

14. Hashimoto, T., Ueno, M.: Latent conditional independence test using Bayesian network item response theory. IEICE Transactions E94-D(4), 743–753 (2011)
15. Ueno, M.: An extension of the IRT to a network model. Behaviormetrika 29, 59–79 (2002)
16. Wilks, S.S.: Mathematical Statistics, 2nd edn., pp. 355–356. Wiley, Chichester (1962)

A   Test Used in Section 5

You are requested to answer from Q1 through Q7.

[1] In a rectangle ABCD, AB = CD = 8 and BC = DA = 12. For point P on side AB, point Q on side BC, and point R on side CD, the following relation holds.

$$AP = BQ = CR$$

Let $AP = x$ $(0 < x < 8)$.

Q1. The area of the trapezoid PBCR is $\boxed{\ ?\ }$.
Q2. The area of $\triangle$ PQR is

$$S = x^2 - \boxed{\ ?\ }x + \boxed{\ ?\ }$$

Q3. If $S < 24$ holds, then x must be in the range of

$$\boxed{\ ?\ } < x < \boxed{\ ?\ }.$$

[2] Fill in the boxes from $\boxed{\ \text{A}\ }$ through $\boxed{\ \text{D}\ }$, selecting one each from the options from ⓪ through ③ below. You may select the same options as many times as you wish.

Here, m and n are natural numbers. We set the following three conditions: p, q, and r.

p: $m + n$ is divisible by 2
q: n is divisible by 4
r: m is divisible by 2, and n is divisible by 4

Let the negation of the condition p be $\bar{p}$, and let the negation of the condition r be $\bar{r}$. Then,

Q4. p is $\boxed{\ \text{A}\ }$ for r.
Q5. $\bar{p}$ is $\boxed{\ \text{B}\ }$ for $\bar{r}$.
Q6. "p and q" is $\boxed{\ \text{C}\ }$ for r.
Q7. "p or q" is $\boxed{\ \text{D}\ }$ for r.

⓪ necessary and sufficient condition
① necessary but not sufficient condition
② sufficient but not necessary condition
③ neither necessary nor sufficient condition

Searching Optimal Bayesian Network Structure on Constraint Search Space: Super-Structure Approach

Seiya Imoto, Kaname Kojima, Eric Perrier,
Yoshinori Tamada, and Satoru Miyano

Human Genome Center, Institute of Medical Science, University of Tokyo
4-6-1 Shirokanedai, Minato-ku, Tokyo 108-8639 Japan
{imoto,kaname,perrier,tamada,miyano}@ims.u-tokyo.ac.jp

Abstract. Optimal search on Bayesian network structure is known as an NP-hard problem and the applicability of existing optimal algorithms is limited in small Bayesian networks with 30 nodes or so. To learn larger Bayesian networks from observational data, some heuristic algorithms were used, but only a local optimal structure is found and its accuracy is not high in many cases. In this paper, we review optimal search algorithms in a constraint search space; The skeleton of the learned Bayesian network is a sub-graph of the given undirected graph called super-structure. The introduced optimal search algorithm can learn Bayesian networks with several hundreds of nodes when the degree of super-structure is around four. Numerical experiments indicate that constraint optimal search outperforms state-of-the-art heuristic algorithms in terms of accuracy, even if the super-structure is also learned by data.

Keywords: Bayesian networks, Structural learning, Optimal algorithm, Constraint search space, Super-structure.

1 Introduction

Understanding the dependencies of a huge number of correlated variables has became an important problem in various kinds of research fields including sociology, medicine, biology, and so on. However, from a collection of raw data for such variables, it is hard to discover the structure of the dependencies. Therefore, several mathematical models including Bayesian networks have been used for unraveling networks of variables. In this review, we focus on the structural learning of Bayesian networks that represent joint probability distribution over the set of variables using a directed acyclic graph (DAG) to encode conditional independencies between them.

So far, various research directions have been explored through a numerous literature to deal with structure learning of Bayesian networks. Among them, defining a score function that represent a goodness-of-fit of a graph to the data and finding a graph that maximizes the score function over the space of DAGs is

T. Onoda, D. Bekki, and E. McCready (Eds.): JSAI-isAI 2010, LNAI 6797, pp. 210–218, 2011.

a promising approach towards learning structure from data [2]. A search strategy called optimal search (OS) have been developed [4,6,10,11] to find the graphs having the highest score (or global optima), however, it takes exponential time for the number of variables. Therefore, capability of existing optimal search algorithms is limited and small sized networks containing thirty nodes or less are only feasible. Hence, in a practical situation, some heuristic algorithms for Bayesian network learning have been used; the built structure is a local optimal and its accuracy strongly depends on the search strategy. On the other hand, independent test (IT) based approach [7] is another way to learn the Bayesian network structure; it uses statistical hypothesis testing that evaluates conditional independence between variables. A network from an IT approach is obtained as an undirected network and the direction of each edge will be determined by the properties of conditional independence, i.e., so-called v-structure, and acyclicity.

To improve HC, Tsamardinos *et al.* [13] proposed a hybrid approach, termed MMHC, that an IT approach first constructs an undirected network and a heuristic search algorithm, i.e., greedy-hill climbing (HC) search, is run on the undirected network that is a constraint for the space of DAGs. Some numerical comparisons show that MMHC outperforms HC in both accuracy and score of the resulting networks. However, MMHC is still a heuristic search and finds local optima networks.

Recently, Perrier *et al.* [9] considered an optimal search of Bayesian networks in the constraint search space called super-structure. A super-structure is defined as an undirected network and the score-based search is performed so that the skeleton of the resulting network become a sub-graph of the super-structure. Perrier *et al.* [9] theorized this idea and proposed a constraint optimal search (COS) algorithm. They showed that COS can be applied to larger networks than OS (with an average degree around 2.1, graphs having 1.6 times more nodes could be considered). Furthermore, by using a sound super-structure, COS can learn more accurate graphs than unconstrained optima.

To increase applicability of COS for larger networks, Kojima *et al.* [5] considered dividing super-structure into clusters and develop an optimal search algorithm called Extended Constraint Optimal Search (ECOS) that performs cluster-based search and finds an optimal Bayesian network given the constraint. For clustered super-structure, one may consider all patterns of directions for the edges between clusters and apply COS on each cluster for every pattern of directions independently and return the best result found. However, it is possible that a cycle straddling multiple clusters can be happened. Kojima *et al.*[5] derived the necessary and sufficient conditions that must be considered to find an optimal network under a given super-structure. ECOS extends the size of networks that we can consider by more than one order.

This paper is organized as follows: First, we introduce an optimal search algorithm in Section 2.1 and constraint optimal sesarch (COS) and its extension (ECOS) in Sections 2.2 and 2.3, respectively. Basic concept and fundamental mathematics for constraint optimal searches will be given together with some theoretical results. Discussion and concluding remarks are given in Section 3.

2   Algorithms for Constraint Optimal Search

In the rest of the paper, we will use upper-case letters to denote random variables (e.g., X_i, V_i) and lower-case letters for the state or value of the corresponding variables (e.g., x_i, v_i). Bold-face will be used for sets of variables (e.g., $\mathbf{Pa}_i$) or values (e.g., $\mathbf{pa}_i$).

Given a set $\mathbf{X}$ of n random variables, we would like to study their probability distribution P_0. To model this system, we will use Bayesian networks. Note that we will deal only with discrete probability distributions and complete data sets for simplicity, although a continuous distribution case could also be considered using our method. We will denote the set of the parents of a variable V_i in a graph G by $\mathbf{Pa}_i$, and by using the Markov condition, we can prove that for any Bayesian network, the distribution P can be factored as follows:

$$P(\mathbf{V}) = P(V_1, ..., V_n) = \prod_{V_i \in \mathbf{V}} P(V_i | \mathbf{Pa}_i).$$

We first present the algorithm of Ott et al. [6] for summarizing the main idea of OS. The constraint optimal search algorithms, COS and ECOS, are then explained in the following sections.

2.1   Optimal Search (OS)

Given data $\mathbf{D}$ for a set of random variables $\mathbf{V}$, learning an optimal Bayesian network using a decomposable score like BDeu involves finding a directed acyclic graph (DAG) N^* such that

$$N^* = \arg\min_N \sum_{V_i \in \mathbf{V}} s(V_i, \mathbf{Pa}_i; \mathbf{D}),$$

where $\mathbf{Pa}_i \subseteq \mathbf{V}$ is a set of parents for a vertex V_i in network N and $s(V_i, \mathbf{Pa}_i; \mathbf{D})$ is the value of the score function for V_i in N. From now we omit writing $\mathbf{D}$ when referring to the score function.

Ott et al. [6] defined the best local score, F_s, and the best parent set, F_p, for every V_i and every candidate parent set $\mathbf{A} \subseteq \mathbf{V} \backslash \{V_i\}$ by

$$F_s(V_i, \mathbf{A}) = \max_{\mathbf{B} \subseteq \mathbf{A}} s(V_i, \mathbf{B}),$$
$$F_p(V_i, \mathbf{A}) = \arg\max_{\mathbf{B} \subseteq \mathbf{A}} s(V_i, \mathbf{B}).$$

By initializing $F_s(V_i, \emptyset) = s(V_i, \emptyset)$, F_s can be obtained recursively on the size of $\mathbf{A}$:

$$F_s(V_i, \mathbf{A}) = \max(s(V_i, \mathbf{A}), \max_{V_j \in \mathbf{A}} F_s(V_i, \mathbf{A} \backslash V_j\})). \tag{1}$$

When considering an ordering of nodes, w, and defining w-linearity of the graph that is a property of the graph, G, satisfying $w(V_i) < w(V_j)$ for every directed edge $(V_i, V_j) \in G$, we can find the best w-linear graph G_w^*. Threrfore, to perform optimal search, we need to find an optimal w^*, which is an optimal topological ordering of an optimal DAG. To find an optimal ordering, a recursive formula was derived [6]. Suppose $M_l(\mathbf{A})$ is the last node of an optimal ordering on $\mathbf{A}$ and $M_s(\mathbf{A})$ is the best score of graphs on $\mathbf{A}$. Note that $\mathbf{A}$ is not empty, $M_s(\{V_i\}) = s(V_i, \emptyset)$ and $M_l(\{V_i\}) = V_i$ are set for initialization. The recursive formula can be represented by

$$M_l(\mathbf{A}) = V_{i^*} = \arg \max_{V_j \in \mathbf{A}} \{F_s(V_j, \mathbf{B}_j) + M_s(\mathbf{B}_j)\}, \tag{2}$$

where $\mathbf{B}_j = \mathbf{A} \backslash \{V_j\}$. M_s and M_l can be computed dynamically (M_s can be computed from eq. (2) directly) and an optimal ordering can be found in reverse order [9]. Hencer, the optimal search algorithm is summarized by:

Algorithm 1 (Optimal Search): (Ott *et al.* [6])

(a) Initialize $\forall V_i \in \mathbf{V}$, $F_s(V_i, \emptyset)$ and $F_p(V_i, \emptyset)$

(b) For each $V_i \in \mathbf{V}$ and each $\mathbf{A} \subseteq \mathbf{X} \backslash \{V_i\}$:
Calculate $F_s(V_i, \mathbf{A})$ and $F_p(V_i, \mathbf{A})$ using (1)

(c) Initialize $\forall V_i$, $M_s(\{V_i\})$ and $M_l(\{V_i\})$

(d) For each $\mathbf{A} \subseteq \mathbf{V}$ with $|\mathbf{A}| > 1$:
Calculate $M_s(\mathbf{A})$ and $M_l(\mathbf{A})$ using (2)

(e) Build an optimal ordering w^*

(f) Return the best w^*-linear graph $G_{w^*}^*$

It should be noted that the total time complexity of Algorithm 1 is $O(n \cdot 2^n)$ and the total memory usage of F function is $O(n^2 \cdot 2^n)$. Therefore, Algorithm 1 is feasible only for small n.

2.2   Constraint Optimal Search (COS)

Since the result of OS converges to the true graph in the sample limit, limiting search space in the true skeleton should be an efficient way to put structure constraint on Bayesian network learning. However, knowing the true skeleton is a strong assumption and learning it with high confidence from finite data is a hard task. We propose to consider a more flexible constraint than fixing the skeleton. To this end, we introduce a super-structure as:

Definition 1 (Super-Structure): (Perrier *et al.* [9])
An undirected graph $S = (\mathbf{V}, \mathbf{E}_S)$ is said to be a super-structure of a DAG $G = (\mathbf{V}, \mathbf{E}_G)$, if the skeleton of G, $G' = (\mathbf{V}, \mathbf{E}_{G'})$ is a subgraph of S (i.e., $\mathbf{E}_{G'} \subseteq \mathbf{E}_S$). We say that S contains the skeleton of G.

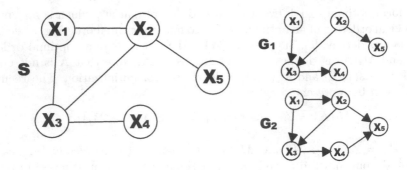

Fig. 1. Example of super-structure and possible DAG: In a search constrained by S, G_1 could be considered but not G_2. (Perrier *et al.* [9])

Considering a structure learning task, a super-structure S is said to be true or sound if it contains the true skeleton; otherwise it is said incomplete. In practice, the skeleton learned by MMPC (Tsamardinos *et al.* [13]) can be used as a super-structure. However, the super-structure learned by MMPC is not proven to be true or sound. Finally we propose to study the problem of model inference from data given a super-structure S: S is assumed to be sound, and the search space is restricted to DAGs whose skeletons are contained in S as illustrated in Figure 1.

Using a super-structure, the step (b) of Algorithm 1 (optimal search) and be revised as

(b*) For each $V_i \subseteq \mathbf{V}$ and each $\mathbf{A} \in \mathbf{N}(V_i)$
Calculate $F_s(V_i, \mathbf{A})$ and $F_p(V_i, \mathbf{A})$ using (2)

for realizing a constraint optimal search. Here, $\mathbf{N}(V_i)$ is the neighborhood of a variable V_i in S, i.e., the set of nodes directly connected to V_i in S. F functions still can be computed recursively since $\forall V_j \in \mathbf{A}$, the subset $\mathbf{A} \backslash \{V_j\}$ is also included in $\mathbf{N}(V_j)$, and its F value is already known. With this slight modification, the time complexity of computing F becomes $O(n^m)$, where $m = \max_{V_i} |\mathbf{N}(V_i)|$. The computation of M functions can also be simplified by considering connectivity of the super-structure. Let $\mathbf{C}_1, ..., \mathbf{C}_p$ be the maximum connected subsets of a subset $\mathbf{A}$ on the super-structure ($p > 1$). The computation of M can be represented as follows:

$$M_s(\mathbf{A}) = \sum_{i=1}^{p} M_s(\mathbf{C}_i),$$
$$M_l(\mathbf{A}) = M_l(\mathbf{C}_1).$$

Note that any $M_l(\mathbf{C}_i)$ is an optimal sink and could be selected, we chose $M_l(\mathbf{C}_1)$ since it is accessed faster when using the data structure proposed in Perrier *et al.* [9]. Let $Con(S)$ be the set of connected subsets of $\mathbf{V}$. Perrier *et al.* [9] stated a theorem for the validity of the algorithm: *A constrained optimal graph can be found by computing M only over $Con(S)$.*

The total computational complexity is in $O(n^m + |Con(S)|)$. Concerning the complexity of calculating F, $O(n^m)$ is in fact a large upper bound. Actually, its time complexity is upper bounded by $O(\gamma_m^n)$, where $\gamma_m < 2$ depends on the maximal degree m of S.

The true super-structure is rarely known and we need to determine by given data. In Perrier et al. [9], MMPC is used for getting a sound super-structure. However, since MMPC is a method based on an IT approach, the complexity of the given super-structure depends on the significant level for each hypothesis testing. If we use a loose significant level, i.e., 0.2 or so, the super-structure becomes dense and the probability that S contains the true skeleton increases. COS, however, sometimes cannot run on such dense S. On the other hand, strict significant level gives a sparse S and COS runs very fast. However, there exist missing edges in such a sparse S. In practice, it is better to use larger significant level that COS can run. However, Perrier et al. [9] considered using post-processing of the resulting graph of COS with HC, they called COS+. COS+ first performs COS with a strict significant level and HC then runs from the resulting graph of COS. The empirical study showed that COS+ works well in terms of both score and accuracy.

2.3 Extended Constraint Optimal Search (ECOS)

As Perrier et al. [9] showed, the constraint optimal search based on super-structure is a promising approach; the resulting networks from COS have higher accuracy than those from other heuristic algorithms. However, even for a sparse super-structure, i.e., the average degree of the super-structure is around 2, COS is feasible for networks with 50 nodes or so. Therefore, development of more efficient algorithm for constraint optimal search has a tremendous impact on researches associated with large size networks, including biological networks [1,3].

The key idea of Kojima et al. [5] is to divide given super-structure into clusters and run COS on each cluster. An intuitive way is to perform this strategy for all patterns of the direction of edges that connect between clusters and select the network that has the best score. However, by performing COS to each cluster separately, it is possible to occur a cycle that passes several clusters; the final network cannot be not guaranteed as a DAG. To ensure acyclicity, Kojima et al. [5] introduced the concept of ancestral constraints (ACs) and derive an optimal algorithm satisfying a given set of ACs. The necessary and sufficient sets of ACs to be considered for finding an optimal network under a super-structure were also theoretically derived. In this section, we briefly introduce basic idea of an extended constraint optimal search (ECOS).

We assume that we are given a set of edges $\mathbf{E}^- \subset \mathbf{E}$ such that the undirected graph $G^- = (\mathbf{V}, \mathbf{E} \backslash \mathbf{E}^-)$ is not connected. By defining a cluster as a maximum connected component of G^-, we can consider a pattern of directions of the edges in $\mathbf{E}^-$. We call this pattern of the directions a tentative direction map (TDM). Especially, let $C = (\mathbf{V}_C, \mathbf{E}_C)$ be a cluster. $\mathbf{E}^C \subset \mathbf{E}^-$ containing all and only the

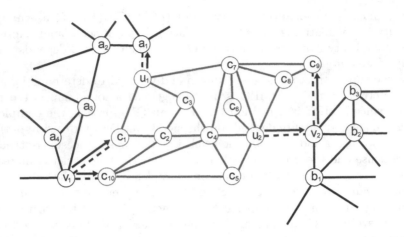

Fig. 2. An example of a super-structure to illustrate the definitions we have introduced. The edges of $\mathbf{E}^-$ are dashed and they define a cluster C (gray). δ indicated by arrows is one of the 32 TDMs possible over E^C that defines $\mathbf{V}_{C,\delta}^{in} = \{v_1, v_2\}$ and $\mathbf{V}_{C,\delta}^{out} = \{u_1, u_2\}$. (Kojima *et al.* [5])

edges incident to a vertex in V_C is called the set of cluster edges for C. A TDM is a set of pairs $\{(e,d), e \in \mathbf{E}^C$ and $d \in \{\leftarrow, \rightarrow\}\}$ such that for $\forall e \in \mathbf{E}^C$, there uniquely exists d such that $(e,d) \in \delta$. Formally, TDM can be defined as follows:

Definition 2 (in-vertex and out-vertex): (Kojima *et al.* [5])
For a cluster C and a TDM δ, we define the sets of in-vertexes and out-vertexes as

$$\mathbf{V}_{C,\delta}^{in} = \{v \in \mathbf{V} \setminus \mathbf{V}_C \mid \exists v_a \in \mathbf{V}_C, (\{v, v_a\}, \rightarrow) \in \delta\},$$
$$\mathbf{V}_{C,\delta}^{out} = \{v \in \mathbf{V}_C \mid \exists v_a \in \mathbf{V} \setminus \mathbf{V}_C, (\{v, v_a\}, \rightarrow) \in \delta\},$$

respectively.

Figure 2 illustrates the previously introduced definitions.

To keep the acyclicity, Kojima *et al.* [5] considered an ancestral constraint (AC) that is a pair (v, u) with $v \in \mathbf{V}_{C,\delta}^{in}$ and $u \in \mathbf{V}_{C,\delta}^{out}$ that is used to disable v as an ancestor of u. Mathematically, Kojima *et al.* [5] proved the necessary and sufficient sets of ACs, nested ACs called NACS, for the constraint optimal search. NACS is defined as follows.

Definition 3 (Ancestral Constraints): (Kojima *et al.* [5])
Let $\mathcal{A}$ be a set of ancestral constraints (ACS), and $\mathcal{A}(v)$ be the set of all out-vertices u_i such that $(v, u_i) \in \mathcal{A}$. We say that $\mathcal{A}$ is a NACS if and only if for any v_a and v_b in $\mathbf{V}_{C,\delta}^{in}$, $\mathcal{A}(v_a) \subseteq \mathcal{A}(v_b)$ or $\mathcal{A}(v_a) \supseteq \mathcal{A}(v_b)$ holds.

Kojima *et al.* [5] performed a theoretical analysis of the time complexity of the ECOS algorithm and evaluated maximum number of nodes that ECOS

Table 1. Values of $n_{max}(\tilde{m})$ of ECOS and COS for average degree of super-structure $\tilde{m}$. $n_{max}(\tilde{m})$ is the feasible size of the super-structure for computation. (Kojima et al. [5] (revised))

Algorithm	$\tilde{m}$	2	2.5	3	3.5
ECOS	$n_{max}(\tilde{m})$	355	273	151	93
COS	$n_{max}(\tilde{m})$	51	43	38	35

can handle. The random networks with several values of averaged degree were used in this empirical evaluation. By comparing with COS, ECOS can learn 355 nodes network when the super-structure is sparse (the averaged degree, $\tilde{m}$, is 2). This is a big improvement of COS, because the maximum size of the networks is estimated as 51 in COS. Even for a relatively dense super-structure, say $\tilde{m} = 3$, the feasibility of ECOS yields 151. The detailed results are summarized in Table 1. In the comparison of ECOS with other heuristic algorithms, MMHC and HC, ECOS showed outstanding performance.

3 Discussion

There are many algorithms proposed previously for learning Bayesian network structures. As explained before, there are mainly two types of strategies: One is to maximize a score function over the space of DAGs. The other is to use independence test based approach. In the research direction of the former method, optimal search algorithms have been investigated by several papers [6,4,10,11]. However, the size of networks is still limited to small. In fact, the largest optimal network was achieved by Silander and Myllymäki [10] and the size is 29. Recently Parviainen and Koivisto [8] investigated a trade-off between the speed of the algorithm and the space of the memory. From empirical results for a partial sub-problem, they predicted that their algorithm is computationally feasible for up to 31 nodes. On the contrary of time-space trade-off, Tamada et al. [12] established a parallel algorithm for the optimal search and achieved 32 nodes optimal network by using massively parallel computer.

Although the size of optimal network slightly increases, it is difficult to get a breakthrough; in practical situations, optimal search is sometimes infeasible due to the number of nodes we should considered. In this observation, constraining search space is a promising way to achieve accurate networks. COS and ECOS are pioner algorithms to do so, however, there are several points to be improved. For a dense super-structure, the feasibility of COS and ECOS strongly depends on the maximum degree of the super-structure. Even if the averaged degree is moderate, one big hub node prohibits the computation. As for the current feasibility of the COS and ECOS algorithms for a dense super-structure, the maximum size of the optimal search is a trivial upper bound. Therefore, it is possible to investigate a parallel algorithm for COS and ECOS like optimal search [12].

Also, some heuristics can be considered together with optimal search. A relevant example was shown in Perrier *et al.* [9]: they used HC after performing COS with a strict significant level (sparse super-structure). It can be considered that for a big hub node in given super-structure to use some heuristic trick.

To find a sound super-structure is very important. In COS and ECOS, MMPC is currently used. However, to obtain an undirected graph, there are several algorithms especially in statistics and machine learning. For example, graphical Gaussian model is a traditional one. To handle large number of nodes, combination of a graphical Gaussian model and sparse learning, e.g., lasso, elastic net, and so on, can be considered as a candidate.

Acknowledgments

Computational time was provided by the Supercomputer System, Human Genome Center, Institute of Medical Science, The University of Tokyo.

References

1. Friedman, N., Linial, M., Nachman, I., Peér, D.: Using Bayesian network to analyze expression data. J. Comp. Biol. 7, 601–620 (2000)
2. Heckerman, D., Geiger, D., Chickering, D.M.: Learning Bayesian networks: the combination of knowledge and statistical data. Machine Learning 20, 197–243 (1995)
3. Imoto, S., Goto, T., Miyano, S.: Estimation of genetic networks and functional structures between genes by using Bayesian network and nonparametric regression. In: Pacific Symposium on Biocomputing, vol. 7, pp. 175–186 (2002)
4. Koivisto, M., Sood, K.: Exact Bayesian structure discovery in Bayesian networks. Journal of Machine Learning Research 5, 549–573 (2004)
5. Kojima, K., Perrier, E., Imoto, S., Miyano, S.: Optimal search on clustered structural constraint for learning Bayesian network structure. Journal of Machine Learning Research 11, 285–310 (2010)
6. Ott, S., Imoto, S., Miyano, S.: Finding optimal models for small gene networks. In: Pacific Symposium on Biocomputing, vol. 9, pp. 557–567 (2004)
7. Pearl, J.: Probabilistic Reasoning in Intelligent Systems: Networks of Plausible Inference. Morgan Kaufman Publishers, San Mateo (1988)
8. Parviainen, P., Koivisto, M.: Exact structure discovery in Bayesian networks with less space. In: Proceedings of the 25th Conference on Uncertainty in Artificial Intelligence (2009)
9. Perrier, E., Imoto, S., Miyano, S.: Finding optimal Bayesian network given a super-structure. Journal of Machine Learning Research 9, 2251–2286 (2008)
10. Silander, T., Myllymaki, P.: A simple approach for finding the globally optimal Bayesian network structure. In: Conference on Uncertainty in Artificial Intelligence, pp. 445–452 (2006)
11. Singh, A.P., Moore, A.W.: Finding optimal Bayesian networks by dynamic programming. In: Technical report, Carnegie Mellon University (2005)
12. Tamada, Y., Imoto, S., Miyano, S.: Parallel algorithm for learning optimal Bayesian network structure (submitted for publication)
13. Tsamardinos, I., Brown, L.E., Aliferis, C.F.: The max-min hill-climbing Bayesian network structure learning algorithm. Machine Learning 65, 31–78 (2006)

The Role of Operation Granularity in Search-Based Learning of Latent Tree Models

Tao Chen[1], Nevin L. Zhang[2], and Yi Wang[3]

[1] Shenzhen Institute of Advanced Technology
Chinese Academy of Sciences
Shenzhen, China
tao.chen@siat.ac.cn
[2] Department of Computer Science & Engineering
The Hong Kong University of Science & Technology
Clear Water Bay, Kowloon, Hong Kong
lzhang@cse.ust.hk
[3] Department of Computer Science
National University of Singapore
Singapore 117417, Singapore
wangy@comp.nus.edu.sg

Abstract. Latent tree (LT) models are a special class of Bayesian networks that can be used for cluster analysis, latent structure discovery and density estimation. A number of search-based algorithms for learning LT models have been developed. In particular, the HSHC algorithm by [1] and the EAST algorithm by [2] are able to deal with data sets with dozens to around 100 variables. Both HSHC and EAST aim at finding the LT model with the highest BIC score. However, they use another criterion called the cost-effectiveness principle when selecting among some of the candidate models during search. In this paper, we investigate whether and why this is necessary.

1 Introduction

Latent tree (LT) models are tree-structured Bayesian networks where internal nodes represent *latent variables* while leaf nodes represent *manifest variables*. In this paper we assume that all variables are categorical. LT models were previously known as hierarchical latent class models [3]. They are interesting for three reasons:

1. They relax the local independence assumption of latent class (LC) models [4] and hence provide a more general framework for cluster analysis of categorical data. LT analysis can find meaningful classes along multiple dimensions while the LC analysis always clusters data in one single way.
2. LT analysis can reveal latent structures behind data. Using LT models, researchers have found interesting latent structures from stocks data [5], marketing data [6] and medical data [7].

T. Onoda, D. Bekki, and E. McCready (Eds.): JSAI-isAI 2010, LNAI 6797, pp. 219–231, 2011.
© Springer-Verlag Berlin Heidelberg 2011

3. LT models are computationally simple to handle and at the same time can model complex interactions among manifest variables [8]. Those two properties make LT models a good tool for estimating joint distributions of discrete variables [9].

This paper is concerned with the induction of LT models from data. A number of search-based algorithms have been developed. Some of them can deal with data sets with only a few variables [3]. The first algorithm that can handle dozens of manifest variables was published in 2004 and is called HSHC (Heuristic Single Hill Climbing) [1]. Recently [2] have published another algorithm called EAST (Expansion, Adjustment, Simplification until Termination) which, in comparison with HSHC, is conceptually simpler, yet is more efficient and finds better models.

Both HSHC and EAST aim at finding the LT model with the highest BIC score. However, they use another criterion called the cost-effectiveness principle when selecting among some of the candidate models during search. This is to deal with the issue of *operation granularity*, which refers to the phenomenon that, in search-based learning of LT models, some operations might increase the complexity of the current model much more than other operations.

However, it is not well understood whether and why it is necessary to use the cost-effectiveness principle. In this paper we seek to clarify the issue through empirical investigation.

2   Search-Based Learning of LT Models

Figure 1 (a) shows the structure of an example LT model. Let $\mathcal{D}$ be a data set on some manifest variables. To *learn an LT model* from $\mathcal{D}$ means to find a model m that maximizes the BIC score:

$$BIC(m|\mathcal{D}) = \max_\theta \log P(\mathcal{D}|m,\theta) - \frac{d(m)}{2} \log N,$$

where θ denotes the set of model parameters, $d(m)$ the number of independent parameters, and N the sample size.[1] It has been shown that edge orientations cannot be determined from data [3]. So we can learn only *unrooted latent tree models*, which are latent tree models with all directions on the edges dropped. An example is given in Figure 1 (b). From now on when we speak of LT models we always mean unrooted LT models unless it is explicitly stated otherwise.

2.1   Search Operators

The basic building blocks of a search-based algorithm are the search operators. We adopt with minor modification five operators from [1]. They are: *state introduction (SI), node introduction (NI), node relocation (NR), state deletion (SD),*

---

[1] Geiger *et al.* [10] argue that the BICe score should be used instead of the BIC score when latent variables are present. However, the BICe score is currently impractical to use due to the lack of efficient methods for computing effective dimensions of models.

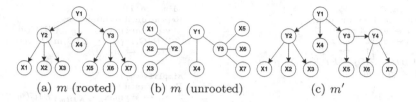

(a) m (rooted)   (b) m (unrooted)   (c) m'

Fig. 1. Rooted latent tree model, unrooted latent tree model and latent tree model obtained by the node introduction of $Y4$

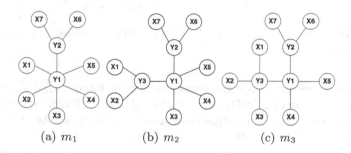

(a) m_1 (b) m_2 (c) m_3

Fig. 2. m_2 is a latent tree model obtained by applying NI to m_1. m_3 is a latent tree model by applying NR to m_2.

and *node deletion (ND)*. Given an LT model and a latent variable in the model, the *SI* operator creates a new model by adding a new state to the domain of the variable. The *SD* operator does the opposite. The *NI* operator involves one latent node Y and two of its neighbors. It creates a new model by introducing a new latent node Y' to mediate the latent variable and the two neighbors. The cardinality of Y' is set to be that of Y. In m_1 of Figure 2 (a), introducing a new node Y_3 to mediate Y_1 and its neighbors X_1 and X_2 results in m_2. For the sake of computational efficiency, we do not consider introducing a new node to mediate Y and more than two of its neighbors. The *ND* operator is the opposite of NI. The *NR* operator involves two latent nodes Y_1 and Y_2 and a neighbor Z of Y_1. It creates a new model by relocating Z from Y_1 to Y_2, i.e. removing the link between Z and Y_1 and adding a link between Z and Y_2. In m_2 of Figure 2 (b), relocating X_3 from Y_1 to Y_3 results in m_3.

The search operators can be divided into three groups. The NI and SI operators make the current model more complex and hence are *expansion operators*. The ND and SD operators make the current model simpler and hence are *simplification operators*. The NR operator rearranges connections between the variables and hence is an *adjustment operator*.

2.2 A Search Procedure

Figure 3 presents a search procedure for learning LT model [2]. Called EAST0, the procedure adopts the grow-restructure-thin strategy that has emerged from

EAST0($m, \mathcal{D}$)
Repeat until termination:
    $m_1 \leftarrow$ expand($m, \mathcal{D}$).
    $m_2 \leftarrow$ adjust($m_1, \mathcal{D}$).
    $m_3 \leftarrow$ simplify($m_2, \mathcal{D}$).
    If $BIC(m_3|\mathcal{D}) \leq BIC(m|\mathcal{D})$, return m;
    Else $m \leftarrow m_3$.

expand($m, \mathcal{D}$)
Repeat until termination:
    $m_1 \leftarrow \arg\max_{m' \in NI(m) \cup SI(m)} BIC(m'|\mathcal{D})$.
    If $BIC(m_1|\mathcal{D}) \leq BIC(m|\mathcal{D})$, return m.
    If $m_1 \in NI(m)$, $m \leftarrow$ enhanceNI($m_1, m, \mathcal{D}$);
    Else $m \leftarrow m_1$

adjust($m, \mathcal{D}$)
Repeat until termination:
    $m_1 \leftarrow \arg\max_{m' \in NR(m)} BIC(m'|\mathcal{D})$.
    If $BIC(m_1|\mathcal{D}) \leq BIC(m|\mathcal{D})$, return m;
    Else $m \leftarrow m_1$.

simplify($m, \mathcal{D}$)
Repeat until termination:
    $m_1 \leftarrow \arg\max_{m' \in ND(m)} BIC(m'|\mathcal{D})$.
    If $BIC(m_1|\mathcal{D}) \leq BIC(m|\mathcal{D})$, return m;
    Else $m \leftarrow m_1$.
Repeat until termination:
    $m_1 \leftarrow \arg\max_{m' \in SD(m)} BIC(m'|\mathcal{D})$.
    If $BIC(m_1|\mathcal{D}) \leq BIC(m|\mathcal{D})$, break;
    Else $m \leftarrow m_1$.

Fig. 3. EAST0 is the basic version of the EAST search procedure. It does not handle operation granularity.

the literature on learning Bayesian networks without latent variables (e.g., [11]). The search procedure of EAST0 has a number of rounds. Every round is divided into three stages: expansion, adjustment and simplification. At the expansion stage, EAST0 searches with the expansion operators until the BIC score ceases to increase. To understand the motivation, recall that the BIC score consists of two terms. The first term is the maximized likelihood, which measures model fit. The second term penalizes model complexity. Our objective is to optimize the BIC score. Suppose we start with a model that does not fit the data at all. Then improving model fit is the first priority at the initial phase of the search. EAST0 does so by searching with the expansion operators.

Note the a subroutine named **enhanceNI** is called after each application of the NI operator. This is to compensate for the constraint imposed on the NI operator. Consider the model m_1 in Figure 2. We can introduce a new latent node Y_3 to mediate Y_1 and two of its neighbors, say X_1 and X_2, and thereby obtain the model m_2. However, we are not allowed to introduce a latent node to mediate Y_1 and more than two of its neighbors, say X_1, X_2 and X_3, and thereby obtain m_3. To remedy the situation we consider, after each application of the NI operator, enhancements to the operation. As an example, suppose we have just applied NI to m_1 and have obtained m_2. What we do next is to consider relocating the other neighbors of Y_1 in m_1, i.e. X_3, X_4, X_5 and Y_2, to the new latent variable Y_3. If it turns out to be beneficial to relocating X_3 but not the other three nodes, then we obtain the model m_3. We use **enhanceNI**($m_2, m_1, \mathcal{D}$) to denote this subroutine.

After model expansion ceases to increase the BIC score, EAST0 enters the adjustment stage. At this stage, EAST0 repeatedly relocates nodes around in the model until it is no longer beneficial to do so. There are no definite conclusion on which of the likelihood term and the penalty term in the BIC score is improved. The intuition in the phase is that the search may make some mistakes in the expansion phase. For example, a variable is connected to a wrong parent. We correct such mistakes by relocating nodes. The BIC score is improved slightly in the resulting model. However, we come back to the right path to proceed. The adjustment stage is followed by the simplification stage. At this stage, EAST0 first repeatedly applies ND to the current model until the BIC score ceases to increase and then it does the same with SD. By considering ND and SD, we focus on the improvement of the penalty term in the BIC score. If model score is improved in any of the three stages, EAST0 repeats the circle with the best model obtained so far as the initial model.

2.3   Comparison with HSHC

EAST0 places no restriction on how far away a node can be relocated. Consequently it might need to evaluate a large number of candidate models, especially towards the end of the search process. Although expensive, unrestricted node relocation is necessary in EAST0 because model adjustment takes place after multiple expansion steps. Two nodes that should be neighbors might be located far away from each other after a series of NI operations and their enhancements. On the other hand, HSHC considers node relocation after each model expansion operation. It also considers more node relocations after a node has just been relocated. As such, it cannot afford to use unrestricted node relocation. So it restricts that a node can be relocated only one step away. Determining the pros and cons of the two options is another basic issue concerning search-based learning of LT models. In [12] we have shown that HSHC is more likely to end up at local maxima than EAST0. Hence we use EAST0 as the platform of study in this paper.

2.4   Efficient Model Evaluation

Each of the $\arg\max$ operators in EAST0 examines a list of candidate models and picks one of them as output. The BIC score is used as the objective function for the selection. To calculate the BIC score of a candidate model, one needs to maximize its likelihood function, which requires the expectation-maximization (EM) algorithm due to the presence of latent variables. EM is known to be computationally expensive. Hence it is prohibitive to compute the BIC scores of a large number of candidate models. Hence it is necessary to replace the BIC score with other objective functions that are easy to compute. In this section we present one such objective function. It is obtained from the BIC score by replacing its first term with what we call the maximum restricted loglikelihood.

Conceptually EAST0 works with unrooted LT models. In the implementation, however, we represent unrooted models as rooted models. Rooted LT models are BNs and their parameters are clearly defined. This makes it easy to see how the parameter composition of a candidate model m' is related to that of the current model m. Consider the models m and m' in Figure 1 (a) and (c). The latter is obtained from m by introducing a new latent variable Y_4 to mediate Y_3 and two of its neighbors X_6 and X_7. The two models share the parameters for describing the distributions $P(Y_1)$, $P(Y_2|Y_1)$, $P(X_1|Y_2)$, $P(X_2|Y_2)$, $P(X_3|Y_2)$, $P(X_4|Y_1)$, $P(Y_3|Y_1)$ and $P(X_5|Y_3)$. On the other hand, the parameters for describing $P(Y_4|Y_3)$, $P(X_6|Y_4)$ and $P(X_7|Y_4)$ are peculiar to m' while those for describing $P(X_6|Y_3)$ and $P(X_7|Y_3)$ are peculiar to m.

We write the parameters of a candidate model m' as a pair (δ_1, δ_2), where δ_1 is the collection of parameters that m' shares with m. Similarly, we write the parameters of the current model m as a pair (θ_1, θ_2), where θ_1 is the collection of parameters that m shares with m'. Suppose we have computed the MLE (θ_1^*, θ_2^*) of the parameters of m. For a given value of δ_2, $(m', \theta_1^*, \delta_2)$ is a fully specified BN. In this BN, we can compute $P(\mathcal{D}|m', \theta_1^*, \delta_2) = \prod_{\mathbf{d} \in \mathcal{D}} P(\mathbf{d}|m', \theta_1^*, \delta_2)$. As a function of δ_2, this will be referred to as the *restricted likelihood function* of δ_2. The *maximum restricted loglikelihood*, or simply the *maximum RL*, of the candidate model m' is defined to be

$$\max_{\delta_2} \log P(\mathcal{D}|m', \theta_1^*, \delta_2).$$

The *restricted likelihood (RL)* method for model evaluation replaces the likelihood term in the BIC score of m' with its maximum RL and uses the resulting function to evaluate m'.

There is another method for efficient model evaluation. It first completes the data set $\mathcal{D}$ using the current model (m, θ^*), where θ^* is the MLE of the parameters of m. Then it uses the completed data set to evaluate candidate models. Hence we call it the *data completion (DC)* method. Determining the pros and cons of the RL and DC methods for efficient model evaluation is also a basic issue concerning search-based learning of LT models. In [12] we have shown that the RL method is more accurate than the DC method and it results in better models. Hence we use the RL method in this paper.

3   Operation Granularity

Operation granularity refers to the phenomenon that some operations might increase the complexity of the current model much more than other operations. As an example, consider the situation where there are 100 binary manifest variables. Suppose the search starts with the LC model with one binary latent node Y. Applying the SI operator to the model would introduce 101 additional model parameters, while applying the NI operator to the model would increase the number of model parameters by only 2. The latter operation is clearly of much finer-grain than the former.

To deal with operation granularity, Zhang and Kočka [1] suggest that we choose between candidate models generated by NI and SI[2] using the so-called cost-effectiveness principle. Let m be the current model and m' be a candidate model. Define the *improvement ratio of m' over m* given data $\mathcal{D}$ to be

$$IR(m', m|\mathcal{D}) = \frac{BIC(m'|\mathcal{D}) - BIC(m|\mathcal{D})}{d(m') - d(m)}. \tag{1}$$

---

[2] Strictly speaking, operation granularity is also an issue for other search operators. However the issue is much less serious there and hence no special treatment is introduced for simplicity.

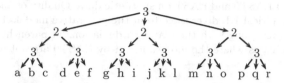

Fig. 4. One of the test models. Manifest nodes are labeled with variable names. All manifest variables have 3 states. Latent nodes are labeled with cardinalities.

It is the increase in model score per unit increase in model complexity. The *cost-effectiveness* principle states that among all candidate models generated by SI and NI, choose the one that has the highest improvement ratio. We use EAST to denote the algorithm that is the same as EAST0 except that it uses the cost-effectiveness principle for model selection in the expansion subroutine.

4 Empirical Results

We have conducted experiments on synthetic data to compare EAST0 and EAST. The data were generated using three manually constructed LT models that contain 7, 12 and 18 manifest variables respectively. The structure of the 7-variable model is shown in Figure 1 (a) and that of the 18-variable model is shown in Figure 4. The structure of the 12-variable model is similar to that of the 18-variable model. The parameters were randomly generated. Three data sets of sizes 1k, 5k and 10k were sampled from each of the three models. The three data sets for the 7-variable model are denoted by $\mathcal{D}_7(1k)$, $\mathcal{D}_7(5k)$ and $\mathcal{D}_7(10k)$. Similar notations are used for other data sets.

We analyzed the data sets using EAST0 and EAST.[3] Both algorithms started with the LC model with a binary latent node. The quality of a learned model is measured by the empirical KL divergence of the model from the corresponding generative model, an approximation to the true KL divergence that was computed based on 5k testing data. We report results that are averages over 10 runs, along with the standard deviations. The results are given in Table 1.

For convenience we will refer to models obtained by the EAST and EAST0 algorithms as EAST and EAST0 models respectively. Consider the models learned for the data sets $\mathcal{D}_{18}(10k)$, $\mathcal{D}_{18}(5k)$ and $\mathcal{D}_{12}(10k)$. The divergences of the EAST models from the generative models are 0.0047, 0.0148 and 0.0032 respectively, while those of the EAST0 models are 0.0207, 0.0326 and 0.0079. The EAST models are significantly closer to the generative models than the EAST0 models. So the EAST algorithm reconstructed the generative distributions better than the EAST0 algorithm.

---

[3] Both EAST0 and EAST have two parameters μ and ν that control a subroutine for model evaluation. We have run EAST under several settings to determine the impact of the parameters. The results reported in this paper were obtained under the setting $\mu = 8$ and $\nu = 40$, the highest setting that we tried.

Table 1. Results of EAST0 and EAST on synthetic data. Quality of a learned model is measured by its empirical KL divergence from the generative model. The numbers are averages over 10 runs, along with the standard deviations in parenthesis. Highlighted in boldface are the cases where the models found by EAST0 are not as good as those found by EAST.

	$\mathcal{D}_7(1k)$				$\mathcal{D}_7(5k)$				$\mathcal{D}_7(10k)$		
	KL	time (mins)	steps		KL	time (mins)	steps		KL	time (mins)	steps
EAST0	.0287(4.3e-6)	.7(8.5e-3)	0(0)		.0101(4.8e-5)	6.3(0.1)	2.0(0.0)		.0058(8.6e-5)	8.4(0.6)	2.0(0.0)
EAST	.0287(4.2e-6)	.7(1.3e-2)	0(0)		.0101(4.5e-5)	7.1(0.1)	2.0(0.0)		.0057(1.0e-4)	8.4(0.3)	2.0(0.0)

	$\mathcal{D}_{12}(1k)$				$\mathcal{D}_{12}(5k)$				$\mathcal{D}_{12}(10k)$		
	KL	time (mins)	steps		KL	time (hrs)	steps		KL	time (hrs)	steps
EAST0	.1017(1.8e-2)	17.1(1.8)	12.1(0.7)		.0311(1.3e-2)	1.0(0.1)	14.1(2.1)		**.0079(4.7e-3)**	1.5(0.1)	13(1.1)
EAST	.0999(1.2e-2)	17.2(2.2)	12.0(1.0)		.0310(4.9e-5)	1.4(0.0)	19.6(0.5)		**.0032(2.4e-4)**	2.6(0.2)	20.8(1.1)

	$\mathcal{D}_{18}(1k)$				$\mathcal{D}_{18}(5k)$				$\mathcal{D}_{18}(10k)$		
	KL	time (hrs)	steps		KL	time (hrs)	steps		KL	time (hrs)	steps
EAST0	.1865(6.3e-6)	.6(.01)	20(0)		**.0326(1.1e-2)**	4.4(0.9)	22.4(4.6)		**.0207(1.2e-2)**	10.4(1.7)	24.4(4.0)
EAST	.1865(7.5e-6)	.7(.02)	20(0)		**.0148(4.5e-3)**	6.0(0.6)	33.8(1.7)		**.0047(7.0e-4)**	18.4(3.9)	37.2(0.8)

To give the reader a concrete feeling about the models, we present in Figure 6 the structures of an EAST model and an EAST0 model for the data set $\mathcal{D}_{18}(10k)$. We see that the structure of the EAST model is almost identical to that of the corresponding generative model, while the structure of the EAST0 model is quite different. So the EAST algorithm reconstructed the structure of the generative model much better than the EAST0 algorithm. Moreover the BIC score of the EAST model is -115108, which is significantly higher than -115500, the BIC score of the EAST0 model.

In summary, the EAST algorithm learned better models for $\mathcal{D}_{18}(10k)$, $\mathcal{D}_{18}(5k)$ and $\mathcal{D}_{12}(10k)$ than the EAST0 algorithm. On the other six data sets, the two algorithms found models of similar or the same quality. The only difference between EAST and EAST0 is that EAST deals with operation granularity using the cost-effectiveness principle, while EAST0 does not. So the results imply that it is indeed necessary to deal with operation granularity and the cost-effectiveness principle is an effective method for doing so. We investigate the reasons in the next section.

5   Performance Difference Explained

We explain the differences in performance between EAST0 and EAST in four steps.

5.1   Early Use of SI Operations

Let us examine one run of EAST0 and one run of EAST on the $\mathcal{D}_{18}(10k)$ data set. Figure 5 (a) shows the change in model complexity over the search steps. We see that the curve for EAST0 increases quickly early in the search process. There are two big jumps, one at Step 1 and another at Step 7. A trace of the

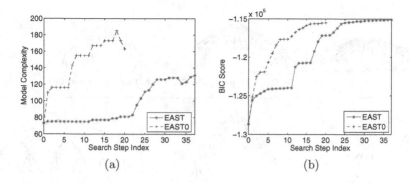

Fig. 5. Search processes on $\mathcal{D}_{18}(10k)$: Model complexity and score as functions of search steps

search path reveals that those are the steps where EAST0 applied SI operations. In contrast the curve for EAST increases slowly and has smaller jumps. The first jump occurred at Step 23. It was the first time where EAST applied the SI operator.

So EAST0 applied SI operations much earlier than EAST. This is true not only for the runs examined above, but also true for all runs on $\mathcal{D}_{18}(10k)$ and for all runs on $\mathcal{D}_{12}(5k)$, $\mathcal{D}_{12}(10k)$ and $\mathcal{D}_{18}(5k)$. We see from Table 1 that EAST0 took fewer steps than EAST to terminate on the four data sets. This is exactly because EAST0 took large steps by applying SI operation early, while EAST did not.

In general, EAST0 tends to apply SI operations early while EAST tends to apply them late. Here are the reasons. First, as discussed in Section 3, SI operations are often of larger-grain than NI operations at the early stage of search. Second, although a large-grain operation increases the penalty term of the BIC score more than a small-grain operation, it often increases the likelihood term even more early in the search process because model fit is usually poor at that time. So there are often SI operations with higher scores than NI operations at the early stage of search. Third, EAST0 selects model based on the BIC score. It would choose SI operations if they have higher scores than NI operations. Hence it often chooses SI operations over NI operations early in the search process. Fourth, EAST is not only concerned with the increase in model score, but also its "cost", i.e., the increase in model complexity. It tries to achieve maximum increase in model score with minimum increase in model complexity. As such, it is less likely than EAST0 to choose large-grain operations and hence tends to choose SI operations later than EAST0.

5.2   Fat Latent Variables

Three models from the aforementioned search path of EAST0 are shown at the top of Figure 6. We see that a latent variable with 4 states was created at Step 7,

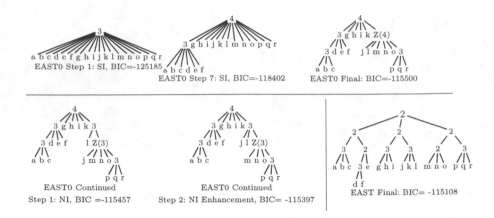

Fig. 6. Top Row: Three models from a search path of EAST0 on the data set $\mathcal{D}_{18}(10k)$. Bottom Row (Left): Continued search by EAST0 from the model that is obtained from the final EAST0 model by decreasing the cardinality of Z by 1. The search went on for 10 steps. Only two steps are shown here. Bottom Row (Right): Final model obtained by EAST.

after the second SI operation. Since the variable has more states than latent variables in the generative model, we call it a *fat latent variable*.[4] EAST0 introduced three other fat latent variables later. One of them was subsequently deleted and the cardinality of another was reduced by one. Two fat latent variables remain in the final model. On the other hand, EAST introduced no fat latent variables at all.

We say that a latent node is *well connected* if it is connected to, in a relative sense, a large number of manifest variables. To account for the interactions among those manifest variables, or even part of the interactions, the latent node usually needs to have a large number of states. If its cardinality is currently low, an increase in its cardinality would greatly improve model fit and hence greatly increase model score. Hence SI operations, if applied at all, tend to be applied on well connected latent nodes. Since search starts from LC model, there is only a few (maybe only one) well connected latent nodes at the early stage of search. EAST0 tends to apply SI operations at the early stage of search. Hence EAST0 tends to repeatedly increase the cardinality of well connected latent nodes and consequently tends to create fat latent variables. On the other hand, EAST usually applies SI operation late in the search process. At that time, a latent node is usually connected to a small number of manifest variables. Hence there is less chance to create fat latent variables.

---

[4] Intuitively, a fat latent variable is one whose cardinality is larger than necessary. For the case without a generative model, it can be defined with respect to the model that has the highest BIC score.

5.3   Local Maxima

Fat latent nodes do not necessarily lead to local maxima, but they do sometimes. Use m_{EAST0} to denote the final model obtained by EAST0. Its BIC score is -115500. In contrast the BIC score of the model found by EAST is -115108. So m_{EAST0} in Figure 6 is a local maxima. In the following we argue that one reason for EAST0 to be trapped at this local maxima is because Z is a fat latent variable.

A comparison of m_{EAST0} with the generative model suggests that it might be beneficial to introduce a new latent node to mediate Z and its neighbors j and l. However, EAST0 did not do this. The reasons, we argue, are as follows. In the generative model the interactions among the manifest variables m, n and o are accounted for by a latent variable with 3 states. However, the variable Z in m_{EAST0} has 4 states. This is more than enough to account for the interactions among m, n and o. In addition, it also accounts for, to some extent, interaction between j and l and correlations between the two groups of variables. Consequently there is no strong reason to introduce a new latent node.

To verify our argument, we decreased the cardinality of Z to 3 and searched further using EAST0 starting from the resulting model. The trace is shown at the bottom row of Figure 6. We see that, as expected, a new latent node was indeed introduced between Z and its neighbors j and l. The local maximum was escaped. Furthermore the new node is placed close to manifest variables g, h, i and k. This is ideal because in the generative model j and l are close to those variables.

Why didn't EAST0 decrease the cardinality Z as we did manually then? This is because Z is directly connected not only to m, n and o, but also j and l. To account for the interactions among m, n and o, three states are sufficient. However, to account for the correlations among all those 5 variables, three states are not sufficient. As a matter of fact, if the cardinality of Z is decreased from 4 to 3, the BIC score also decreases from -115,500 to -115,537. So this is a deadlock situation. To separate j and l from Z by introducing a new node, we need to first reduce the cardinality of Z; and to reduce the cardinality of Z, we need to first reduce the number of manifest variables connected to it. This deadlock would not have occurred had fat latent variables not been introduced.

5.4   Impact of Problem Size and Sample Size

Putting together the arguments presented above suggests that EAST0 is more easily than EAST to get trapped at local maxima. This explains why the models it found in our experiments are sometimes not as good as those found by EAST. One thing remains unexplained: Why the differences occurred only on the data sets $\mathcal{D}_{12}(10k)$, $\mathcal{D}_{18}(5k)$ and $\mathcal{D}_{18}(10k)$ that are more complex than the other data sets in terms of sample size and the number of manifest variables.

To understand the phenomenon, let o_{SI} be an SI operation and o_{NI} be an NI operation. Suppose the o_{SI} is of larger grain than o_{NI}. Then it increases the penalty term of the BIC score more than the latter. Further suppose that o_{SI} increases the likelihood term more than o_{NI}. Then which operation EAST0 ends up choosing depends on how the two terms balance out. It is well known that the likelihood term increases linearly with sample size, while the penalty term increase logarithmically. Therefore as the sample size increases, EAST0 would be more and more likely to choose o_{SI} over o_{NI}. This implies that EAST0 would be more and more likely to apply SI operations early in the search process and hence is more and more easily to get trapped at local maxima. This explains why, in our experiments, EAST0 performed worse and worse as we move from $\mathcal{D}_{18}(1k)$ to $\mathcal{D}_{18}(5k)$ and then to $\mathcal{D}_{18}(10k)$.

In our experiment, EAST0 performed worse and worse as we move from $\mathcal{D}_7(10k)$ to $\mathcal{D}_{12}(10k)$ and then to $\mathcal{D}_{18}(10k)$. We explain the phenomenon as follows. When the number of manifest variables increases, SI operations would be of larger and larger grain relative to NI operations. Consequently, EAST0 would be more and more likely to apply SI operations early in the search process and hence is more and more easily and get trapped at local maxima.

6   Conclusions

We have shown that operation granularity often results in local maxima if not dealt with. This is because that, at the early stage of search, SI operations are usually of larger grain than NI operations and often have higher BIC scores. If one simply uses BIC for model selection, then one tends to apply SI operations early, which often leads to fat latent variables, which in turn might result in local maxima. When the cost-effectiveness principle is used for model selection, on the other hand, SI operations are applied much latter. This reduces the chance of creating fat latent variables and hence the chance of local maxima.

One might suggest that we deal with operation granularity by introducing additional search operators. After reading Section 5.3 one might, for instance, suggest a composite search operator that first reduces the cardinality of a latent variable and then introduces a new latent node. This would complicate algorithm design and would significantly increase the complexity of the search process. In contrast the cost-effectiveness principle is a simple and yet effective way to deal with the issue.

Acknowledgements. Research on this work was supported by Hong Kong Research Grants Council GRF Grant #622408, the National Basic Research Program of China (aka the 973 Program) under project 2011CB505101 and the Shenzhen New Industry Development Fund #CXB201005250021A.

References

1. Zhang, N., Kočka, T.: Efficient learning of hierarchical latent class models. In: Proc. of the 16th IEEE International Conference on Tools with Artificial Intelligence (2004)
2. Chen, T., Zhang, N., Wang, Y.: Efficient model evaluation in the search-based approach to latent structure discovery. In: Proc. of 4th European Workshop on Probabilistic Graphical Model (2008)

3. Zhang, N.: Hierarchical latent class models for cluster analysis. J. Mach. Learn. Res. 5 (2004)
4. Lazarsfeld, P., Henry, N.: Latent structure analysis. Houghton Mifflin, Boston (1968)
5. Elidan, G., Friedman, N.: Learning hidden variable networks: the information bottleneck approach. J. Mach. Learn. Res. 6 (2005)
6. Zhang, N.: Discovery of latent structures: Experience with the coil challenge 2000 data set. In: Shi, Y., van Albada, G.D., Dongarra, J., Sloot, P.M.A. (eds.) ICCS 2007. LNCS, vol. 4490, pp. 26–34. Springer, Heidelberg (2007)
7. Zhang, N., Yuan, S., Chen, T., Wang, Y.: Latent tree models and diagnosis in traditional chinese medicine. Artificial Intelligence in Medicine (42) (2008)
8. Pearl, J.: Probabilistic reasoning in intellegent systems. Morgan Kaufmann, San Mateo (1988)
9. Wang, Y., Zhang, N.L., Chen, T.: Latent tree models and approximate inference in bayesian networks. Journal of Artificial Intelligence Research 32(879-900) (2008)
10. Geiger, D., Heckerman, D., Meek, C.: Asymptotic model selection for directed networks with hidden variables. In: Proc. of the 12th Conference on Uncertainties in Artificial Intelligence (1996)
11. Chickering, D.M.: Optimal structure identification with greedy search. J. Mach. Learn. Res. 3 (2002)
12. Chen, T.: Search-based learning of latent tree models. PhD dissertation, The Hong Kong University of Science and Technology, Department of Computer Science and Engineering (2009)

International Workshop on Innovating Service Systems

Service science has been raised, and coming to be established as a research domain all over the world. This workshop in Tokyo has been motivated by the systems-design dimension of the service science. We aim to share and discuss a progressive vision to develop methods for innovating systems of service resources where novel values are created and supplied sustainably. A "service system" here is an artificially organized or self-organized active integration of the following resources:

(1) Participants, i.e., providers and consumers of services, where a provider of a service may turn into a consumer in different contexts
(2) Money, or other entities representing value, and their active flows: An utterance of praise can be also this kind of entity
(3) Supply chains i.e., the chain of interactions from creators of service resources (products, information, food, etc) to consumers of services, and
(4) Tools (computers, robots, sensing devices, etc) aiding the activities of (1), (2), and (3)

In this workshop, we discussed methods for designing and realizing service systems and parts of a service system, with positioning resources of the four kinds above in the systems to be created. By this, we aim to respond to the social demand to design an environment for value-creative and dynamic interactions among participants via resources in the market, rather than merely passing existing products and services from providers to customers for predetermined prices.

We had 30 submissions, among which 13 papers has been chosen for presentation and 11 papers selected for this volume of post-proceedings. The submissions ranged from services of finance, medicine, manufacturing, retail stores, etc., which meant the strong expectation from businesses in all over the human society to this rising domain. We selected these papers from the aspect of the innovation of service systems, which lead us to meaningful discussions. We also invited David Bergner from NASA as plenary lecturer, and integrated services on the earth and his ideas on service innovations linked to/from spacecrafts, via the Innovators Market Game which is also a method of innovation created from the context of ISS. We desire readers working on different domains of sciences and services look in our content presented here, and join our future activities on systems innovations.

March 2011   Yukio Ohsawa, and Katsutoshi Yada

T. Onoda, D. Bekki, and E. McCready (Eds.): JSAI-isAI 2010, LNAI 6797, p. 232, 2011.
© Springer-Verlag Berlin Heidelberg 2011

Meandre Data-Intensive Application Infrastructure: Extreme Scalability for Cloud and/or Grid Computing

Bernie Ács, Xavier Llorà, Boris Capitanu, Loretta Auvil, David Tcheng,
Mike Haberman, Limin Dong, Tim Wentling, and Michael Welge

National Center for Supercomputing Applications
University of Illinois at Urbana-Champaign
1205 W. Clark Street, Urbana, IL 61801
{bernie,xllora,capitanu,lauvil,dtcheng,mikeh,lilydong,
wentling,welge}@ncsa.illinois.edu

Abstract. The volumes and velocity of data are growing at unprecedented rates, often physically distributed, have access constraints, and requirements to leverage the diverse computational fabrics like clouds and grids. The Meandre data-intensive component-based application infrastructure can leverage diversity and enables extremely scalable server clusters and applications to address these challenges. Data-intensive flows can: be web-services and/or computational tasks; co-locate processing with data; orchestrate cloud computing resources; and leverage grid resources with distributed execution. Meandre from a laptop to a cloud, grid, or server as analytical computational tasks and/or web-services in data-intensive flows made up of components that provide deployment and execution strategies for extreme scalability.

Keywords: data-intensive, components, dataflow, cloud, grid, Meandre.

1 Introduction

In an era where the volumes and velocity of data is growing at alarming rates the computational researchers, scientists, and analysts are forced to adopt traditional methods and functional approaches which is challenging. Innovations introduced and championed by commercial internet services like Amazon's EC2[1]/S3[2], Google Apps[3], and other service providers are influencing conceptual approaches to providing or using computational resources for research, analysis, and presentation to a world-wide community of users. The focus is on dynamic on-demand procurement, allocation, and distribution of computation services. This empowers consumers to self-manage an enterprise made up of one-to-many virtual machines and/or web-services. The approach segregates and helps to abstract hardware infrastructure management liabilities from those assumed by a consumer. Grid computational environments in contrast generally providing consumers with access to high-performance computing

---

[1] http://aws.amazon.com/s3/
[2] http://aws.amazon.com/ec2/
[3] http://www.google.com/apps/

T. Onoda, D. Bekki, and E. McCready (Eds.): JSAI-isAI 2010, LNAI 6797, pp. 233–242, 2011.
© Springer-Verlag Berlin Heidelberg 2011

resources with a batch scheduling system job submission and nodes that support a collection shared resources like high-speed interconnects, shared-disk space, and common software for compiling and/or scripting computational tasks.

There are some project efforts that attempt to merge the dynamic procurement, allocation, configuration, implementation, and disposition of virtual machines within the context of a grid environment and others that attempt to build and deploy virtual HPC clusters within the context of cloud computing platforms. Both of these approaches focus on the convergence of hardware technology deployment strategies that include facilitating dedicated interconnection, shared resources, and virtual machine technology rather than addressing the issues related to the underlying differences in software engineering strategies generally used in each environment. Cloud computing focus is on Service Orientated Architecture (SOA), web-service models (that may include load balancing techniques, and dynamic resizing of logical pool servers) to scale applications within a dynamically on-demand access to scalable resources paid for as they are used. On the other hand, grid applications generally focus on developing applications that use and/or create closely coupled machines that can leverage shared disk resources, high-speed low latency interconnects, and utilization of specialized techniques and machinery for parallel computing.

The objective of this document is to introduce the Meandre component-based data-intensive flow infrastructure as an innovative solution that can transparently leverage a variety of computational environments and the functional advantages they provide. In the remaining sections of this document we will briefly describe the component architecture to exemplify how the framework can be employed to develop applications that can be deployed in cloud environments. We will illustrate how the anatomy of this framework can be leveraged to orchestrate cloud computing resources using the Typica[4] (a java client library for a variety of Amazon web services). We will present a hypothetical example use case that demonstrates how a flow definition can be executed in a common cloud computing environment and then demonstrate how the same flow might be executed on the grid to leverage advantages of that environment.

2   The Component-Based Data-Intensive Flow Infrastructure

The Meandre component-based data-intensive flow infrastructure was initially developed for the Software Environment for the Advancement of Scholarly Research (SEASR)[5] project. Meandre is designed to: (1) provide a robust and transparent scalable solution that can be used on a single laptop or on large-scale high performance computation (HPC) clusters, (2) create a consistent and unified solution for batch processing models as well as supporting persistent interactive applications, and (3) encourage reuse and sharing of the functional component building-blocks. Meandre relies on semantic descriptors to define the anatomy of components: (1) data ports; (2) property values; (3) binary implementation; and (4) execution firing constraint. Flows are an aggregation of components that can be visualized as a directed multi-graph which can be cyclic or acyclic and are also expressed using semantic descriptors that define the flow anatomy as components with connectors.

---

[4] http://code.google.com/p/typica/
[5] http://www.seasr.org

The infrastructure depends on semantic descriptors to orchestrate and manage the flow of data movement between components. Executable components from the perspective of the service infrastructure are any executable binary code body that implements three required methods: (1) initialize; (2) execute; and (3) dispose. The service also provides an extended component model that is called a "WebUI" which has all the same characteristics as an executable component but adds additional required methods to be implemented which will receive redirected HTTP request from the execution engine. Since components can effectively perform any logical function or process (constrained only by the imagination of their creators) the infrastructure: (1) imposes only a simple interface; (2) expects components to consume data when invoked; and (3) allows components generate data output.

The infrastructure includes two essential server level functionalities: (1) an administrative server interface and (2) a flow execution engine. The administrative server interface supports management functions to: (a) access a "public" repository of components and flows; (b) access "private" user repository for their components and flows; (c) run flows and to view their runtime logs; (d) review archived logs for flows that have completed; (e) import/export repository content to/from an external location;(f) launch or abort data flow execution; and (g) to publish (make publically available) components and flows. The flow execution engine is invoked: (a) from the server's administrative interface; (b) used in context of a console scripting language called Zigzag; (c) as a standalone executable when a data flow and it's components are packaged into a Meandre Archive Unit (MAU); (d) from the Meandre Workbench Application; or (e) using the REST API. These essential server level functionalities are enabled by leveraging an embedded Jetty[6] Application server to provide the administrative server interface and the server-side mechanisms that enable the HTTP request/response functionalities exposed in the WebUI component type.

3   Data-Intensive Flows for Amazon EC2/S3 API Resource Use

Previous work, "A general approach to data-intensive computing using the Meandre component-based framework" [6], details how an application library or an API can be implemented as a family of components to allow flow developers to create web services and applications. This document introduces a family of components that wrap library methods from the Typica to enable Amazon EC2/S3 API compliant service environments like Eucalyptus[7] and Nimbus[8] to be interactively engaged within context of a Meandre flow adding an interesting dimension to potential scalability.

The family of Amazon EC2/S3 API compliant components being developed will allow Meandre flows to be constructed that could launch a virtual machine instance, open a session using ssh to configure the instance, perform computational task, and

---

[6] http://jetty.codehaus.org/jetty/
[7] http://open.eucalyptus.com/
[8] www.nimbusproject.org/

then dispose of the virtual machine instance freeing the resources allocated. Figure 3.1 shows this basic demonstration flow construct. Consider a scenario where the tasks being executed by the SSH Command component in the demonstrator flow transfers one or more preconfigured standalone MAU executable flow(s) from some network location and cause them to execute. This procured virtual machine resource could then potentially serve as a web-service end point for interactive processing or act as headless computational data-intensive flow acting upon some data-resource. The potential use-case could be further expanded to deploy multiple virtual machine instances to facilitate a highly available Linux service platform that implements a software load-balancer for HTTP requests. This type of software construct could allow for dynamic allocation of additional instance nodes to be included or removed from the load balancing service using Linux HA[9] (High Availability) software tools.

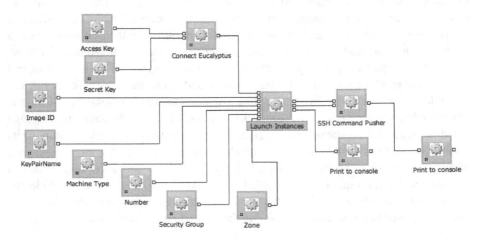

Fig. 3.1. Shows a flow excerpt where the connection attributes, Access Key and Secret Key, are pushed to the Connect Eucalyptus component which executes an API method to output an initialized connection object. The resulting object is then pushed to the Launch Instances component along with a number of other input attributes which allows the component to execute API methods that produces a running virtual machine instances and pushes appropriate values to a SSH Command component. Both the Launch Instances and SSH Command components print output to the console in this demonstrator flow.

A family of components engineered to wrap an API or library like Typica certainly would enable data-intensive flows to harness the power of dynamic cloud resource procurement and utilization where the Amazon EC2/S3 API is available. The potential for this kind of implementation is broader when considering another library like libvirt[10], a virtualization API that encompasses a wide range of virtualization platforms. This could enable another family of components to leverage the full spectrum of private cloud resources in a data intensive flow.

---

[9] http://www.linux-ha.org/wiki/Main_Page
[10] http://libvirt.org/

4 Meandre 2.0: Scalable Server and Customize Execution Engines

The new emerging version of the Meandre (2.0.x) has been rewritten to segregate the server facilities into three essential divisions: (1) the administrative user interface and a new set of REST APIs implemented using Crochet[11]; (2) a messaging and broadcast service using Snare[12] to enable multiple instances of the server engine to act as a single cooperative community with a consistent view; and (3) the JENA[13] store is replaced with an externalized implementation of MongoDB[14] a highly-scalable and highly-available JSON[15] store. The new data store plays an important role for the Meandre 2.0 server cluster by providing a common and consistent image to all server members of the cluster. Other significant advancements include support for a job queue and complete externalization of the execution engine to enable full customization with a minimal set of operational expectations. In this section we will briefly present: (1) Crochet API Service Engine; (2) Snare Monitor Service Engine; (3) the Meandre 2.0 servers, jobs, external execution, and extreme scalability; and (4) customizable external execution engines and the operational paradigms that influence strategies for scalability of flow execution.

4.1 The Crochet API Service Engine

The Crochet was developed using the Scala[16] programming language that implements a lightweight web-service framework that provides quick prototyping, a REST API, and hides the repetitive programmatic tasks required to build HTTP request/responses handling. It allows implementations to define methods that respond to the basic HTTP methods (GET, POST, PUT, DELETE, HEAD, OPTIONS, and TRACE) and optional allows: (1) MIME types to be define for HTTP responses; (2) allows *guards* to enforce conditional logic to be defined for multiple method and paths; (3) allows custom *authentication/authorization* logic to be incorporated. Figure 4.1.1 contains a sample code fragment of a Crochet API service.

```
import crochet._
new Crochet {
    get("/message","text/plain") { "Hello World!" }
} serving "static_content" as "/static" on 8080
```

Fig. 4.1.1. Shows a Scala code snipplet that demonstrates a Crochet API definition that will respond to HTTP request in the form http://hostname:8080/message with the text "Hello World!" and enables "static_content" by pointing the browser to http://hostname:8080/static.

---

[11] http://wiki.github.com/xllora/Crochet/
[12] http://wiki.github.com/xllora/Snare/
[13] http://jena.sourceforge.net/
[14] http://www.mongodb.org/
[15] http://www.json.org/
[16] http://www.scala-lang.org/

4.2   The Snare Monitor Service Engine

The Snare monitor service engine is written in Scala and is designed to be attached to a running process to provide a notification end-point that can send messaging events as broadcast or to targeted point-to-point destinations which can be to report process status as a heartbeat or be intended to invoke an interaction with a receiver. The messaging fabric in the Snare monitoring service relies on a persistent instantiation of a MongoDB data-store that is accessible by a set of process peers participating in the notification scheme. The basic implementation model assumes that the MongoDB installation and configuration are outside the functional scope of the of the Snare service which makes no assumptions about how the back-end is implemented in terms of scale, distribution, replication, or sharding that may be in place. It does, however need to comply with authentication requirements when the back-end store is configured to enforce authorized user credentials for access.

Monitors are generally grouped into pools allowing them to be organized in a fashion where each individual monitor is uniquely identified and collections of individuals can grouped into collections by the pool names. The Snare monitor service imposes no limitation on the number of monitors that may be active nor does it place any limitation on the number of pools that may be present. However, there are limitations to this open-ended scalability which is constrained by the capacity of the back-end service provided by MongoDB. Informal scalability testing has shown that tens of thousands of monitors in a single pool could be effectively used with a single back-end instance running on commodity hardware.

When creating monitors a proper callback needs to be defined, it is expected to be a function that takes single input argument of the type BasicDBObject which is a MongoDB java object wrapping a JSON document. Any JSON document can be passed to this required function that is expected to return a Boolean value where true indicates that the notification was acted upon and false indicating that notification was ignored. Regardless of the return value generated by the function notifications they are only passed to monitors once and are considered completed when delivered. This function will be invoked when any broadcast (unaddressed) or peer-to-peer messages are received as a notification. Any monitor can originate a broadcast notification or it can address a notification to any other peer at any time.

4.3   The Meandre 2.0 Servers, Jobs, External Execution, and Extreme Scalability

The Meandre 2.0 server implements the functionalities provided by Crochet to serve the REST API which include the new Jobs API specification and the Snare monitor service backed-by MongoDB to allow a service instance to be made up of at least one server but it also enables many servers to cooperatively work together as a single-image service entity that share a common view of server peers, operational state of the cluster group, and enables dynamic server additions or reductions at runtime. Users submit flow execution requests (jobs) which are registered by a server into cluster job queue stored in the MongoDB service. Cluster servers actively poll the central job queue to acquire a request to service. When a job request is serviced by a server an appropriate external execution engine is launched in a separate java virtual machine (JVM). The server: (1) provides the flow descriptor as inputs to the execution engine along with any other initialization parameters; and (2) assumes responsible for capturing the console and log outputs from the execution engine for persistent storage in the MongoDB back-end. This enhanced approach to execution provides a more expressive flow life-cycle that includes the implicit ability to forcibly terminate job with no adverse impact on the server itself. The flow life-cycle includes seven transitional states where three are operational: (1) Submitted, waits for an available server; (2) Preparing, execution engine is readied; (3) Running, execution engine is active; the four remaining are termination states: (4) Done, execution completed successful; (5) Aborted, user request; (6) Failed, badly behaved or internal flow error; (7) Killed, infrastructure termination of flow. Figure 4.3.1 shows a logical diagram of a Meandre 2.0 server cluster.

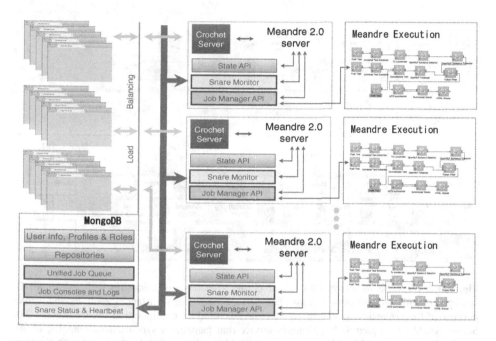

Fig. 4.3.1. Shows a Meandre 2.0.x server cluster and illustrates the relationship of individual servers, the Job Manager API, State API, Snare Monitor, Crochet Server, External Execution Engines and the central MongoDB service. External load-balancing of user interfaces and REST API end points can distribute request over the cluster of servers. All servers are equal peers and have a common view of cluster operational state that is collectively maintained in the MongoDB back-end store.

The Meandre 2.0 server cluster is configured (by default) to execute a single execution engine (job) on a member servers at a given point time. This is an indication the number of concurrent jobs that can be executed is equal to the number of member servers in the cluster. The central MongoDB service can be seen as the limitation to the potential scale of a Meandre 2.0 cluster of servers. However, since the MongoDB service is an external dependency of the cluster, the configuration options are open to site preferences. One of the options available is a highly-scalable distributed MongoDB configuration that leverages auto-sharding (partitioning) over many servers that addresses the scale limitations of a single standalone instance. Configuration options can also include replication for resilience and fault-tolerance of the critical centralized back-end service. Figure 4.3.2 shows a logical diagram of a MongoDB with sharding configured supporting the Meandre 2.0 cluster of servers.

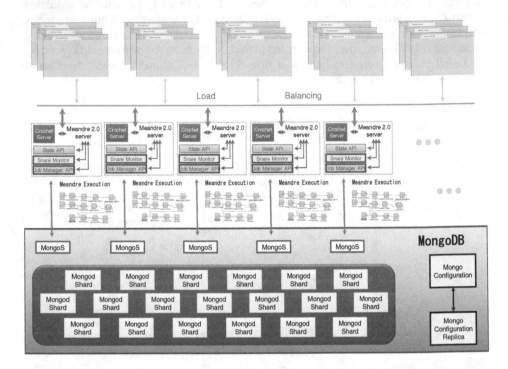

Fig. 4.3.2. Shows a Meandre 2.0.x server cluster that has a relationship with a MongoDB configured with the sharding feature. The service uses many instances each having some portion of the collective total data content. In this kind of configuration each Meandre 2.0 Server would be coupled with a MongoS service that manages a synchronized mapping of all shards. This allows the Meandre relationship with MongoDB to remain consistent with a single instance service model while providing sites with a transparent implementation path to extreme scaling of the back-end MongoDB service supporting their Meandre cluster of servers.

4.4   The Meandre 2.0 Customizable External Execution Engines

External execution engines are expected to read STDIN to receive the semantic descriptors for the flow definition and to provide two standard output channels: (1) STDOUT console output, generally informational outputs; (2) STDERR output that should be transcribed to a runtime log. Customized execution engines are free to interrupt flow descriptors as they need and are free to perform any processing actions before, during, or after a flow execution. Obviously, an implicit expectation to comply with the minimal component-level servicing exists.

The Meandre 1.4.x execution engine is a wrapped version of the same binary code set that provides execution for MAU packaged flows with minor hybridization to enable flow descriptors to be read from STDIN and to redirect outputs as expected. This engine provides the traditional Meandre data-driven mechanics and was designed for multi-core and multi-processor computational platforms. Figure 4.4.1 shows a hypothetical flow made up of a collection component that would be executed in a single JVM along with the two dedicated engine threads.

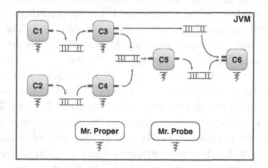

Fig. 4.4.1. Shows a hypothetical flow made up six distinct components, five distinct connectors, and two service-level threads indicative of a setup that reflects a Meandre 1.4.x execution engine scenario. This flow is executed entirely n a single JVM with eight threads allocated, six for component and two for the infrastructure interfaces.

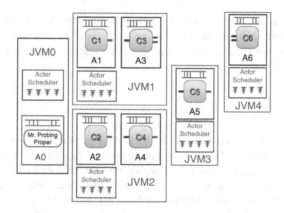

Fig. 4.4.2. Shows the hypothetical flow made up six distinct components distributed over five JVMs which could be on five different machines using Meandre 2.0.x snowfield execution engine. Notice two JVMs have multiple components and two others have a single component.

The Meandre 2.0 *Snowfield* execution engine is written in Scala and leverages the simple light weight concurrency model implemented in Actors which provides an efficient message passing functionalities. This approach is an abstraction that eliminates the relationship between dedicated threads and components which minimizes context switching. The main benefits gained from this new implementation are a simplified communications model and that it is trivial to distribute flow components over multiple JVMs that may be scattered over multiple hosts. Figure 4.4.2 shows same hypothetical flow distributed over five JVM hosts.

5 Conclusion

Throughout the narrative body of this document we have: (1) introduced briefly the Meandre data-intensive component-based application infrastructure; (2) described a component family that allow flows to be created that can orchestrate dynamic cloud resources; (3) described in some detail the anatomical features of the Meandre 2.0 enhancements that enable extreme scalability of the server infrastructure; and (4) the customizable external execution engine features it provides. These points help to exemplify how the infrastructure can be leveraged to create applications and computational processes that flexible and highly scalable.

The Meandre 1.4.x execution engine (provided for backwards compatibility) was developed with multicore multiprocessor computational platforms in mind which could include large single image machines (like Cobalt at NCSA). The Meandre2.0.x Snowfield execution engine represents the new generation that supports distributed execution of a flow over multiple JVMs and/or machine resources. This could be easily adopted: (1) for batch queue systems used in grid environments; (2) for specialized use of GPU hardware and models; (3) to distribute logical processing over grid and/or cloud computational fabrics; and is most applicable for large grid clusters (like Abe and Blue Waters) and/or elastic cloud platforms (like Amazon, Nimbus, and Eucalyptus). The Meandre data-intensive component-based application infrastructure provides for server clusters, flow execution, and strategies for extreme scalability.

Acknowledgments. We would like to thank The Andrew W. Mellon Foundation for support of this work through the SEASR project. Parts of this work have also been supported by National Center for Supercomputing Applications at the University of Illinois at Urbana-Champaign

References

1. Beynon, M.D., Kurc, T., Sussman, A., Saltz, J.: Design of a framework for data-intensive wide-area applications. In: HCW 2000: Proceedings of the 9th Heterogeneous Computing Workshop, p. 116. IEEE Computer Society, Washington, DC (2000)
2. Dean, J., Ghemawat, S.: MapReduce: Simplified Data Processing on Large Clusters. In: OSDI 2004: Sixth Symposium on Operating System Design and Implementation (2004)
3. Foster, I.: The virtual data grid: A new model and architecture for data-intensive collaboration. In: The 15th International Conference on Scientific and Statistical Database Management, p. 11 (2003)
4. Haller, P., Odersky, M.: Scala actors: Unifying thread-based and event-based programming. Theoretical Computer Science (2008), doi:10.1016/j.tcs, 09.019
5. Llorà, X., Àcs, B., Auvil, L., Capitanu, B., Welge, M., Goldberg, D.E.: Meandre: Semantic-driven data-intensive flows in the clouds. In: Proceedings of the 4th IEEE International Conference on e-Science, pp. 238–245. IEEE Press, Los Alamitos (2008)
6. Ács, B., Llorà, X., Auvil, L., Capitanu, B., Tcheng, D., Haberman, M., Dong, L., Wentling, T., Welge, M.: A general approach to data-intensive computing using the Meandre component-based framework. In: Proceedings of the 1st International Workshop on Workflow Approaches To New Data-Centric Science, Indianapolis, Indiana, June 06, pp. 1–12. ACM, New York (2010)

Agent-Based Simulation System for Supporting Sustainable Tourism Planning

Dingding Chao, Kazuo Furuta, and Taro Kanno

Department of Systems Innovation, Graduate School of Engineering,
The University of Tokyo
7-3-1 Hongo, Bunkyo-ku
Tokyo, 113-8656, Japan
{chao,furuta,kanno}@sys.t.u-tokyo.ac.jp

Abstract. The expanding tourism market, in particular of East Asia, has drawn great interests and has raised a series of significant issues for researchers and planners in sustainable development. Unsustainable tourism development caused problems such as loss of natural resources, conflicts between tourists and local residents, and so on. This research intends to understand the development process of Recreational Business Districts (RBDs) in tourism areas and to provide a framework for supporting sustainable tourism development by analyzing interactions between tourists and RBD. An Agent-Based Simulation (ABS) combined with Geographic Information System (GIS) provides planning supports to tourism bureaus and policy makers to help them assess possible future development plans in tourism under certain scenarios.

Keywords: sustainable tourism development, recreational business district; planning support architecture; agent-based simulation; GIS.

1 Introduction

Tourism has gained worldwide significance, becoming one of the largest industries in many countries (Clancy,1999). The rapid increase in the tourism market, in particular of East Asia, has drawn great interests and has raised a series of significant issues for researchers and planners in sustainable development. One of the most significant problems in tourism planning is its complex nature, and it makes the decision-making difficult. Clearly, new directions in tourism researches are required (Carter and et al., 2001) to support the accelerating demands for multi-disciplined studies in this field. Agent-Based Simulation (ABS) is a technique to deal with complex processes among various system components; it is expected to open the door for deeper understanding of tourism and the development of Recreational Business Districts (RBDs) (Malaka and et al, 2000) offering a way of linking multi-disciplinary theories. A planning support architecture based on a combination of ABS and Geographic Information System (GIS) can be used to examine and explore the spatial-temporal data at the macroscopic or individual level, which reflect patterns of changes and effects of tourists' activities as well as other potential aspects, to study a system of RBD. It also provides new perspectives for decision makers to evaluate different development plans.

T. Onoda, D. Bekki, and E. McCready (Eds.): JSAI-isAI 2010, LNAI 6797, pp. 243–252, 2011.
© Springer-Verlag Berlin Heidelberg 2011

A general term "sustainable tourism" is widely used among discussions on tourism these years. Accurately defining this term is difficult, however, due to its multi-dimensional nature. One of the most significant factors to affect sustainablilty of RBD is touirsts loads. In Bulter's widely accepted destination (RBD) life cycle model, the tourism destination follows a cycle in terms of the number of tourists visiting there. The turning point of the life cycle curve comes about, because the number of tourists exceeds the carrying capacity of the area and causes decline in environmental attractions. Other factors, such as interests conflicts between tourists and reidents, may also impact sustainable tourism (Carter and et al., 2001). The exsiting general models, however, are not sufficient to explain the complex nature of the tourism system, especially the interactions on the microscopic level were not substantial enough so that the theories may need further exploration before applied to practical tourism planning processes.

This research intends to understand the development process of RBDs in tourism areas and to provide a framework for supporting sustainable tourism development by analyzing interactions between tourists and RBD. Agent-based simulation combined with GIS under the framework provides planning supports to tourism bureaus and policy makers to help them assess possible future development plans in tourism under certain scenarios. Hakone is chosen as the target study area in this work, as it is one of the most famous tourism districts in Japan. The district, however, also faces some problems in environment preservation, contracting domestic market, and decrease of local population.

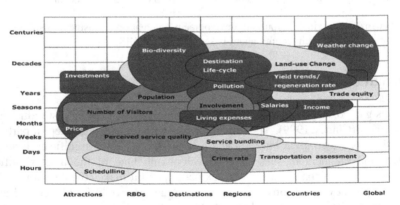

Space and Time Matrix for Sustainable Tourism Assessment

Fig. 1. Sustainable Tourism Indicators (After Becker, 1999)

2   Tourism System Framework

In order to simulate behavior of a tourism system and to assess development plans for sustainable tourism, understanding on the processes of both the macroscopic and the microscopic level is required, and appropriate indicators must be chosen for this purpose. The indicators can generally be divided into four groups: economic, environmental, social, and multi-dimensional indicators. The indictors were re-projected also according to their temporal and spatial scales into the matrix as shown in FIGURE 1 (Becker, 1999).

Hakone is a destination with a total area of 92.82km² and several RBDs. Its tourism development planning strategies are taken out on seasonal and yearly basis. According to the application domain of our study, Hakone, falls within the range of "RBDs-Destinations" and "Seasons-Years" so that the time scale and appropriate indicators are chosen from the matrix for the simulation: population of the local residents, number of tourists, land use change data, and the service quality perceived by tourists.

3   Simulation Model

3.1   Overview

The simulation model integrates ABS and GIS to explore phenomena of change in land useland use/cover, population of residents, and number of tourists in Hakone. Spatial and statistical data were processed using ArcGIS 9.3 (ESRI, 2008) and distributed into several layers of the model to represent the key features that the agents share and interact with. We obtained the original data of the land use, road network, and public facilities provided by National Land Information Office of Japan and converted them into different sub-layers: Land Type Layer, Transportation Layer, Tourist Spot and Public Facility Layer, and Tourists and Residents Layer. All the layers are re-projected onto the GIS grid plan and programmed in Netlogo 4.1 (Wilensky, U. 1999).

Many previous works have been done using agent-based models to study land useland use change (Parker, et al., 2002; Batty, 2005; Li and Liu, 2008), however, compared with the target study areas of the past researches, tourism destinations are usually more developed and have many constraints in future development. We adopted the model of a previous research on rural-urban land useland use change to capture the changes from preserved land to building lots (Li and Liu, 2008; Wu, 2002). Their model used ABM combined with GIS to examine the urban development patterns and predict the future trends. Although some componets of the tourism system are similar with their urban development system such as land use change and residents' assesment of the utility and movements, it differs from urban development in the following aspects : It is not nessessary that the residents in tourism system have to constantly moving from one place to another in order to find a satisfying one to live. Tourists are introduced into the system who have different behavior and standards for evaluation with the residents.The lands in tourism systems have more constrains to develop as the related laws and regulations in RBDs are stricter than thoses in common urben planning. Modifications of the model were made to reflect the differences between these contexts to better capture the characteristics of tourism system.

3.2   Agents

There are three major types of agents used in the simulation: tourist agents, resident agents and land agents, which are coupled with the corresponding spatial features in different layers. In addition, there is a government agent, which is an abstract agent and not coupled with any spatial features. Tourist agents distributed in the target areas evaluate the places of interests and select the most attractive one to visit. Resident agents located in the living districts evaluate their living environment and decide to stay longer or move away. Activities of these two agents will change the development potential of a certain location. The government agent will have much more determinate influence on change in land use, which is, however, subject to behavior of tourists and residents.

3.3   Agent Behavior

Tourist Agent

This research adopted the method of previous studies (Li and Liu, 2008; Wu, 2002) for calculating utility, attractiveness and development potential of lands. Their model is not for tourism development, however, but for urban development; some modifications have been added for applying it to the tourism domain. The tourist agent was introoduced into the system to interact with both the environemnt and the residents, and have different parameters to assess the attractiveness, differnt from those for ultilities assessment used by the residents.

Surrounding environment B'_{env}:
The tourist agent checks the patch of interest with its 8 surrounding neighbors and counts the number of patches B'_{env} that are classified as a lake or a forest B'_{env}
Availability of public facilities B'_{facil}:
The tourist agent checks if there is any "public facility" within a certain distance from the location of interest. Parameter B'_{facil} is the number of patches with facilities.
Availability of tourism spots B_{spot} :
The tourist agent checks if there is any "tourism spot" within a certain distance from the location of interest. Parameter B_{spot} is the number of patches with tourism spots.
Availability of transportation B'_{trans}:
The tourist agent checks if there is any "road" within a certain distance from the location of interest. Parameter B'_{trans} is the number of patches with roads.

Number of people B'_{ppl}:
The tourist agent counts the total number of tourists and residents B'_{ppl} in the patch of interest and its 8 surrounding neighbors.

The tourist agent evaluates the attractiveness of RBD by the following formula. For Tourist Agent n the attractiveness of Land i is:

$$A(n, i) = \sum_{i=1}^{N} B'_i * w'_i$$

where N is the number of attributes, w'_i is the weight for each attribute and

$$\sum_{i=1}^{N} w'_i = 1$$

The tourist agent then compares the attractiveness of other patches within a certain distance with the patch of its present location and decides to visit another place if its attractiveness exceeds the present position by 10%. The number of tourists will therefore decrease greatly in a patch where the attractiveness is of a local minimum.

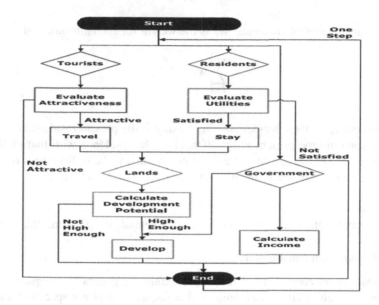

Fig. 2. Agents Behavior and Flow of the Program

Resident Agent

Each resident agent evaluates the utility of land agents within a certain distance from the following parameters.

Surrounding environment B_{env}:

The resident agent counts the number of patches B_{env} that are classified as a lake or a forestB_{env}

Availability of public facilities B_{facil}:

The resident agent checks if there is any "public facility" within a certain distance from the location of interest. Parameter B_{facil} is the number of patches with public facilities.

Availability of transportation B_{trans}:

The resident agent checks if there is any "road" within a certain distance from the location of interest. Parameter B_{trans} is the number of patches with roads.

Number of people B_{ppl}:

The resident agent counts the total number of tourists and residents B_{ppl} in the patch of interest and its 8 surrounding neighbors.

The resident agent evaluates the utility of residence by the following formula. The utility of Land j for Resident Agent m is:

$$U(m,j) = \sum_{j=1}^{M} B_j * w_j$$

where M is the number of attributes, w_j is the weight for each attribute and

$$\sum_{j=1}^{M} w_j = 1$$

The resident agent then decides whether to stay at the present residence or to leave there by comparing the present utility $U(m,i)$ of the residence with that of the past evaluation. $U(m,i)$ It decides to leave the present patch if the utility drops over 10%. When the resident agent leaves the present location, it leaves there forever.

Land Agent

The land agent calculates the development potential P (i) from the following parameters.

Land development constraint T :

The preservation conditions of lands in Hakone are generally categorized into 3 groups: business and living areas, preserved areas, and others not specified. Each has a certain level of development constraint. The conditions of each land agent, which is obtained originally from the land use data in FIG. 4.1, are assigned corresponding values at a 0 to 1 scale.

Distance to transportation D_t:

The land agent checks the distance to the nearest road, and D_t is a score evaluated from this distance.

Distance to public facility D_p:

The land agent checks the distance to the nearest public facility, and D_p is a score evaluated from this distance using the same scoring standards as D_t :

Percentage of developed lands in the neighborhood B_d

Parameter B_d is the percentage of developed land agents in the neighborhood of a certain distance.

Number of visitors B_v:

Parameter B_v is the number of tourists who visited the location. The development potential of a land agent is calculated from the following formula. $P^t(i) = \dfrac{1}{1+\exp[-(D_t * w_d + D_p * w_p + B_v * w_n)]} * T * B_d$

Government Agent

The government agent performs the following two tasks. It calculates the numbers of tourists and residents. The government agent observes the whole process and calculates the income from tourists and residents in each turn and decides whether lands can be developed. The government agent determines the construction rate R_{cons} of a land depending on the development potential. A higher development potential results in a higher construction rate.

4   Test Simulation and Case Study

The weights for evaluating the attractiveness and utility of lands were adopted first from the previous studies and then modified according to the nature of the target area of this study, Hakone. Some test simulations were then performed to adjust the model parameters so that simulation results of the average number of tourists per day and the average number of residents of year 2000-2009 well match the corresponding historical data.

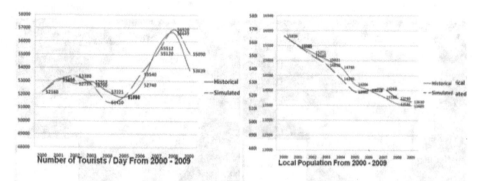

Fig. 3. Result of Test Simulation

4.1   Simulation Conditions

A case study of test simulation was performed to demonstrate the usefulness of the proposed ABS for sustainable tourism development planning. Two simulation scenarios (Plan-A and Plan-B) were set up to simulate different possible future developments of RBDs in Hakone. It is assumed that the government has different tolerance levels R_{cons} towards land use change.

All the other conditions were similar except the tolerance level for construction rate of the government agent, which affects the extent of development in RBDs allowed by the government. A higher tolerance level results in a higher possibility that the government would allow land agents to develop their lands for tourism business. Plan-A represents the conditions in the real world situation with a relatively low tolerance of 0.16; the government is very conservative in using land resources for new constructions. Plan-B is an imaginary plan that has a relatively high tolerance of 0.80; the government takes a more aggressive position for development of RBDs. The time-span of the both cases is 100 steps, and tourist and resident agents have 30 turns of actions in each step. Each action represents agent's behavior in one day of the real time; 100 steps correspond to 3,000 days. The tourist agent can choose three different places to visit in a day, while the resident agent can have one chance to decide whether to stay or leave the present residence. In 2009, 13,489 residents lived in Hakone and the total number of tourists was 19,649,000. As most of the tourists were one-day visitors, it is assumed that the tourists will not stay longer than 24 hours. It means therefore about 53,839 people visited Hakone per day. The number of tourist agents was set 5,384 in the both cases, which means each tourist agent represents 10 real tourists. The number of resident agents was set 1,349, which means each tourist agent represents 10 real residents, correspondingly.

4.2   Simulation Results

FIGURE 4 shows the simulated result of land use change after taking Plan A and B. As expected, a higher tolerance level resulted in a higher development rate, greater changes in land use and loss of natural resources. It was observed also from the simulation that areas with a higher density of transportation and other tourism services developed faster than other areas, which well match the real world situation.

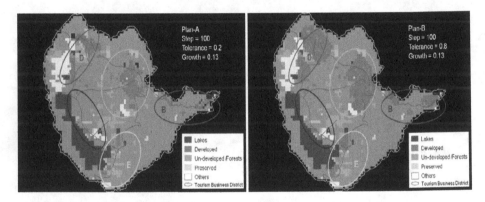

Fig. 4. Land use changes resulted from Plan A and B

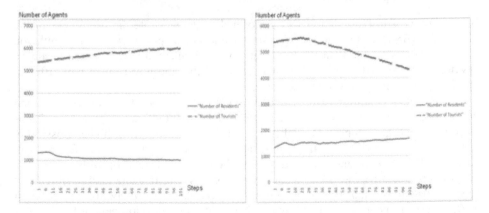

Fig. 5. Number of agents resulted from Plan A and B

FIGURE 5 shows the simulated results of the number of tourists and residents for Plan A and B. As a higher tolerance level resulted in a higher developing rate, it is expected that Plan B is likely to result in a larger capacity for tourists and to attract more people. However the numbers of tourists dropped after a short time of rising, reflecting that the "deterioration stage" of Butler's Tourism Life-Cycle is likely to happen for the over-developed tourism business districts. And residents have increased after the number of tourists starting to decrease, reflecting the phenomenon of the conflicts between tourists and residents in Tisdell's work.

4.3   Discussion

The simulation revealed that a high tolerance level for constructions resulted in intense conflicts between tourists and residents, which will largely influence the sustainability of RBDs. The residents and the tourists share the same environment but each has different expectations and evaluation criteria's of it. The tourism life-cycle can be reflected by the number of people (in case of the RBDs, including both tourists and residents) and the rising number of residents while the RBDs go to a "deterioration stage" reveals the possibility of a conflict between tourists and residents. From the case study the simulation results accented social aspects of sustainable tourism. Both tourists-residents conflicts and destination life-cycle exist during the development process of the destination, but not necessarily at the same time. The tourists-residents conflicts happen as a result of increasing number of tourists come to the RBDs and the living environment of the residents thus degrade the utilities of the land for the residents. Agent Based Simulation can replicate this interaction between tourists and residents to reflect the destination life-cycle on the macroscopic level.

5   Conclusion

Simulation has been demonstrated to reveal the influence of different development scenarios in the future of RBDs.The simulation reveals that the high tolerance of constructions will result in intense conflicts between tourists and residents, which will largely influence the sustainability of the Tourism Business District. In addition, from the result of the simulation, the social aspect of sustainable tourism is accented. To achieve sustainable developing, the conflict between tourists and residents should be reduced by better balancing the interests from both sides during the policy-making process. The research demonstrated that agent-based simulation approach can be applied to building the Planning Support System for sustainable tourism development. The problem of the vague definition of sustainability is avoided by well established pool of indicators and their corresponding time and spatial scale. The analysis on both macroscopic level and individual level are involved in the simulation to deal with the complexity of the tourism system.

References

Batty, M.: Cities and Complexity: Understanding Cities with Cellular Automata, Agent-Based Models, and Fractals. MIT Press, Cambridge (2005)

Becker, B.: Sustainability assessment: a review of values, concepts, and methodological approaches. In: Consultative Group on International Agricultural Research. The World Bank, Washington, D.C. (1997)

Butler, R.: The concept of a tourism area cycle of evolution: Implications for resources. Canadian Geographer 24(1), 5–12 (1980)

Carter, R.W., Baxter, G.S., Hockings, M.: Resource management in tourism research: A new direction? Journal of Sustainable Tourism 9(4), 265–280 (2001)

Clancy, M.: Tourism and development: Evidence from Mexico. Annals of Tourism Research 26, 1–20 (1999)

Tisdell, C.A.: Tourism Economics, the Environment and Development: Analysis and Policy. Edward Elgar Publishing, London (2001)

ESRI (2008): ArcGIS Desktop 9.3, http://www.esri.com/

Graham, S., Steiner, J.: TravellerSim: Settlements, Territories and Social Networks (2006), http://home.cc.umanitoba.ca/~grahams/Travellersim.html

Li, X., Liu, X.: Embedding sustainable development strategies in agent-based models for use as a planning tool. International Journal of Geographical Information Science 22(1), 21–45 (2008)

Malaka, R., Zipf, A.: DEEP MAP -Challenging IT research in the framework of a tourist information system. In: Fesenmaier, D., Klein, S., Buhalis, D. (eds.) Proceedings of ENTER 2000 Information and Communication Technologies in Tourism 2000, Barcelona. Springer Computer Science, pp. 15–27. Wien, New York (2000)

Parker, D.C., et al.: Multi-Agent Systems for the Simulation of Land use and Land-Cover Change: A Review. In: Special Workshop on Agent-Based Models of Land use, Irvine, California, USA, October 4-7 (2002)

Wilensky, U.: NetLogo, Center for Connected Learning and Computer-Based Modeling. Northwestern University, Evanston (1999), http://ccl.northwestern.edu/netlogo

World Tourism Organization: Tourism Vision 2020, http://unwto.org/facts/eng/vision.htm

Wu, F.: Calibration of stochastic cellular automata: the application to rural–urban land conversions. International Journal of Geographical Information Science 16, 795–818 (2002)

To Construct a Technology Roadmap for Technical Trend Recognition on Thin-Film Solar Cell

Tzu-Fu Chiu[1], Chao-Fu Hong[2], Leuo-hong Wang[2], and Yu-Ting Chiu[3]

[1] Department of Industrial Management and Enterprise Information,
Aletheia University, Taiwan, R.O.C
chiu@mail.au.edu.tw
[2] Department of Information Management,
Aletheia University, Taiwan, R.O.C
{cfhong,wanglh}@mail.au.edu.tw
[3] Department of Information Management,
National Central University, Taiwan, R.O.C
gloria@mgt.ncu.edu.tw

Abstract. To recognize technical trends is essential for the interested parties to understand the development directions of a technology at the industry level. Therefore, a research design has been formed for conducting technology roadmapping where association analysis is employed to measure the co-occurrence in the patent data sets and data crystallization is adopted to build the relations between clusters. Consequently, a technology roadmap for thin-film solar cell was constructed and relations between topics and subtopics were identified. Finally, according to the relations, the technical trends of thin-film solar cell were recognized and depicted.

Keywords: technology roadmapping, association analysis, data crystallization, thin-film solar cell, patent data.

1 Introduction

Technology roadmapping is one of the most promising approaches for the improvement of strategic technology planning, and the technology maps have been applied at the company, industrial sector, national, and international levels [1]. This study is attempted to emphasize on the industrial level to explore the trends of a specific technology so as to provide the R&D opportunities for companies and to grasp the developing directions of the industry. In the research design, the data mining methods, namely association analysis and data crystallization, are employed to analyze and visualize the patent data especially the textual Abstract and Claim fields. In addition, up to 80% of the technological information disclosed in patents is never published in any other form [2]. Therefore, it is plausible for this study to apply the technology roadmapping for exploring the potential trends of thin-film solar cell via patent data.

T. Onoda, D. Bekki, and E. McCready (Eds.): JSAI-isAI 2010, LNAI 6797, pp. 253–262, 2011.
© Springer-Verlag Berlin Heidelberg 2011

2   Related Work

As this study is aimed to explore the technical trends of thin-film solar cell using technology roadmapping, a research design needs to be developed via a consideration of association analysis and modified data crystallization. In order to handle the textual nature of patent data (especially the claim and abstract fields), association analysis is adopted to measure the frequency of a term and co-occurrence between terms, while modified data crystallization is employed to build the links between existing clusters and inserted terms. Subsequently, the research design will be applied to construct the technology roadmap of thin-film solar cell for exploring the technical trends. Therefore, the related areas of this study would be technology roadmapping, thin-film solar cell, association analysis, and data crystallization.

2.1   Technology Roadmapping

Technology roadmapping is a process that contributes to the integration of business and technology and to the definition of technology strategy by displaying the interaction between products and technologies overtime, taking into account both short- and long-term product and technology aspects [3]. There are several types of roadmaps including company, industrial sector, national, and international technology roadmaps [1]. Major objectives of these roadmaps are to provide a direction for the interested parties so that they can align their activities [4]. Recently, a technology roadmap by making use of patent information has been proposed by Suh and Park [5] and its main processes of technology roadmapping are: (1) to construct a patent map with initial keywords of technologies, (2) to evaluate technology's priority using the patent map, and (3) to build up a technology roadmap with the priority values of technologies. In this study, the technology roadmap will be constructed via the association diagrams and crystallized diagrams.

2.2   Thin-Film Solar Cell

Solar cell, a sort of green energy, is clean, renewable, and good for protecting our environment. It can be mainly divided into two categories (according to the light absorbing material): crystalline silicon (in a wafer form) and thin films (of other materials) [6]. A thin-film solar cell, also called a thin-film photovoltaic cell, is made by depositing one or more thin layers (i.e., thin film) of photovoltaic material on a substrate [7]. The most common materials of thin-film solar cell are amorphous silicon or polycrystalline materials (such as: CdTe, CIS, and CIGS) [6]. In recent years (2003-2007), total PV production grew in average by almost 50% worldwide, whereas the thin film segment grew in average by over 80% and reached 400 MW or 10% of total PV production in 2007 [8]. Therefore, thin film is the most potential segment with the highest production growth rate in the solar cell industry, and it would be appropriate for academic and practical researchers to contribute efforts to explore and understand the potential trends of this technology.

2.3   Association Analysis

Association analysis is a useful method for discovering interesting relationships hidden in large data sets. The uncovered relationships can be represented in the form of association rules or co-occurrence graphs [9, 10]. An event map, a sort of co-occurrence graphs, is a two-dimension undirected graph, which consists of event clusters, visible events, and chances [11]. An event cluster is a group of events with high frequency and high co-occurrence rate. The co-occurrence rate is measured by the Jaccard coefficient as in Equation (1), where e_i is the ith event in a data record (of the data set D).

$$Ja\left(e_i, e_j\right) = \frac{Freq\left(e_i \cap e_j\right)}{Freq\left(e_i \cup e_j\right)} \tag{1}$$

The event map is also called as association diagram in this study and will be employed with the crystallized diagram for technology roadmapping.

2.4 Modified Data Crystallization

Data crystallization, a technique of chance discovery, is used to detect the unobservable (but significant) events via inserting these unobservable events as dummy items into the given data set [12]. The unobservable events and their relations with other events are visualized by applying the event map. A generic data crystallization algorithm can be summarized as follows [11]: (a) event identification, (b) clustering, (c) dummy event insertion, (d) co-occurrence calculation: the co-occurrence between a dummy event and clusters is measured by equation (2), where DE_i is a dummy event and C is the specific number of clusters, and (e) topology analysis.

$$Co\left(DE_i, C\right) = \sum_{j=0}^{|C|-1} \max_{e_k \in c_j} Ja\left(DE_i, e_k\right) \tag{2}$$

Data crystallization was originally proposed to deal with unobservable events (i.e., dummy events) so as to emerge the hidden clues from existing circumstances via judging the unknown relations [12]. This method has been modified by the authors to insert extra data elements as dummy events into the initial data records so that the relations between the extra data elements and existing clusters could come out and be observed [13]. The modified data crystallization will also be used in this study.

3   A Research Design for Technical Trend Recognition

As this study is attempted to explore the technical trends, a research design for trend recognition, based on the association analysis and modified data crystallization, has been developed and shown in Fig. 1. It consists of five phases: data preprocessing, association analysis (I), association analysis (II), modified data crystallization, and technology roadmapping; and will be described in the following subsections.

3.1   Data Preprocessing

In first phase, the patent data of thin-film solar cell will be downloaded from the USPTO [14]. For considering the essential parts to represent a complex patent document, the claim, abstract, patent-no, and issue-date fields are selected as the objects for this study. Afterward, two processes, POS tagging and data cleaning, will be executed to clean up the source textual data. As the utilization of claim data is to glance the overall situation of a comparatively long period of time (e.g., ten years), the first sentence of claim field will be used to form the claim data set. Meanwhile, the abstract data set will come from the full content of the abstract field for grasping the detailed situation of a short period of time (e.g., two years). Therefore, the abstract data set (of the whole period) will be divided into 5 data subsets (i.e., 2000-2001, ..., and 2008-2009) in order to explore the technical trends successively.

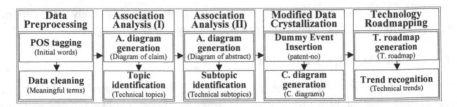

Fig. 1. A research design for technical trend recognition

(1) POS Tagging: An English POS tagger (i.e., a Part-Of-Speech tagger for English) from the Stanford Natural Language Processing Group [15] will be employed to perform word segmenting and labeling on the patent documents (i.e., the abstract and claim fields). Then, a list of proper morphological features of words needs to be decided for sifting out the initial words.

(2) Data Cleaning: Upon these initial words, files of n-grams, synonyms, and stop words will be built so as to combine relevant words into compound terms, to aggregate synonymous words, and to eliminate less meaningful words. Consequently, the meaningful terms will be obtained from this process.

3.2   Association Analysis (I)

Second phase is designed to conduct the association analysis on the claim data set via association diagram generation and topic identification so as to gain the outlined categories for understanding the overall technical situation of the whole period of time (e.g., ten years).

(1) Association Diagram Generation: In association analysis, an association diagram will be drawn via the meaningful terms of the claim data set, so that a number of clusters will be generated through the proper thresholds setting of frequency and co-occurrence.

(2) Topic Identification: According to the above association diagram, the clusters are regarded as technical topics in the overall situation and will be named using the domain knowledge.

3.3   Association Analysis (II)

Similar to the above phase, another association analysis is conducted on the abstract data subsets through association diagram generation and subtopic identification so as to acquire the detailed subcategories for perceiving the detailed technical situation of a segmented period of time (e.g., every two years).

(1) Association Diagram Generation: In this process, several association diagrams will be drawn from the abstract data subsets, so that a number of clusters will be produced through the proper thresholds setting of frequency and co-occurrence within each association diagram.

(2) Subtopic Identification: In accordance with the above association diagrams, the clusters are regarded as technical subtopics in the individual situation (of a segmented period) and will be named using the domain knowledge.

3.4 Modified Data Crystallization

Fourth phase, including dummy event insertion and crystallized diagram generation, is used to insert the patent-no into the preprocessed claim data set and abstract data subsets for generating the crystallized diagrams.

(1) Dummy Event Insertion: In order to perform the data crystallization, a dummy event (i.e., patent-no) needs to be inserted into the preprocessed data set of claim and data subsets of abstract.

(2) Crystallized Diagram Generation: After the dummy event insertion, data crystallization will be triggered to generate two kinds of crystallized diagrams for the technical topics (via claim data set) and technical subtopics (via abstract data subsets). Firstly, using the updated data set and data subsets, event maps will be drawn to show the clusters, dummy nodes, and individual nodes, and will be called as crystallized diagrams. Secondly, the clusters in crystallized diagrams will be regarded as topics or subtopics. Thirdly, the topics (or subtopics), dummy nodes, and links among them will be utilized to observe the relations within a topics (or subtopics) and among topics (or subtopics). Finally, these crystallized diagrams will be applied to form a technology roadmap.

3.5 Technology Roadmapping

Last phase is designed to construct the technology roadmap and to recognize the technical trends of thin-film solar cell, based on the crystallized diagrams of topics and subtopics.

(1) Technology Roadmap Generation: By integrating the crystallized diagram of topics and subtopics, a technology roadmap will be constructed via linking the relations from topics to subtopics through the patent-no.

(2) Trend Recognition: According to the above technology roadmap, the relations between topics and subtopics can be observed and the trends of technology can be recognized depending on the classification of topics. The technical trends of thin-film solar cell will be useful for the stakeholders to understand the developing directions of the technology.

4   Experimental Results and Explanation

The experiment has been implemented according to the research design. The experimental results will be explained in the following five subsections: result of data preprocessing, result of topic generation and modified data crystallization, result of subtopic generation and modified data crystallization, result of technology roadmap generation, and result of trend recognition.

4.1   Result of Data Preprocessing

As the aim of this study is to explore the technical trends, the patent documents of thin-film solar cell are the target data for this experiment. Mainly, the claim, abstract, patent-no, and issue-date fields of patent documents have been used in this study. Therefore, 160 issued patent documents during year 2000 to 2009 were collected from USPTO, using key words: "'thin film' and ('solar cell' or 'solar cells' or 'photovoltaic cell' or 'photovoltaic cells' or 'PV cell' or 'PV cells')" on "title field or abstract field". The partial content (i.e., the first sentence) of claim field and content of abstract field were used to form: a claim data set and an abstract data set. Furthermore, the abstract data set was then divided into 5 data subsets (i.e., 2000-2001, ..., and 2008-2009) for facilitating the exploration of the trends of thin-film solar cell; each data subset contained 44, 44, 22, 31, and 19 records respectively. In addition, the POS tagger was triggered and the data cleaning process was executed. Consequently, the claim data set and abstract data subsets during year 2000 to 2009 were cleaned up and the meaningful terms were obtained.

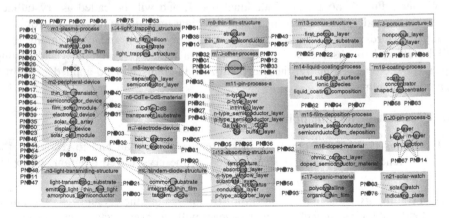

Fig. 2. A crystallized diagram of technical topics of Claim data

4.2   Result of Topic Generation and Modified Data Crystallization

Using the meaningful terms from data preprocessing of claim data set, an association diagram of claim data was drawn via 'association diagram generation'. In the diagram, twenty-one clusters were found while the number of consisting nodes of a cluster was set to no less than two, except cluster m2 and m10. According to the domain knowledge, the clusters were named and classified into four types as follows:

Process (m1-plasma-process, m10-other-process, …, and m20-pin-process-b), Device (m2-peripheral-device, m5-layer-device, m7-electrode-device, and m21-solar-watch), Structure (m3-light-emitting-structure, m4-light-trapping-structure, …, and m18-porous-structure-b,), and Material (m6-CdTe-CdS-material, m16-doped-material, and m17-organic-material). These named clusters were regarded as technical topics. Afterward, using the same claim data set with inserted dummy event (i.e., patent-no), a crystallized diagram of claim data was drawn via 'data crystallization' (in Fig. 2), showing the relations between topics and patent-no.

4.3   Result of Subtopic Generation and Modified Data Crystallization

Using the meaningful terms from the data preprocessing of abstract data subsets (from 2000-2001 to 2008-2009), five association diagrams of abstract data were drawn via 'association diagram generation' successively.

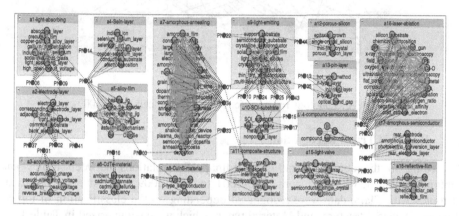

Fig. 3. A crystallized diagram of technical subtopics of Abstract data for 2000-2001

Taking the diagram of 2000-2001 as an example, eighteen clusters were found while the number of consisting nodes of a cluster was set to no less than four. According to the domain knowledge, the clusters were named as follows: a1-light-absorbing, a2-electrode-layer, …, and a18-reflective-film. These named clusters were regarded as technical subtopics. Afterward, using the same abstract data subsets with the inserted dummy event (i.e., patent-no), five crystallized diagrams of technical subtopics were drawn via 'data crystallization', showing the relations between subtopics and patent-no. Fig. 3 is an example for year 2000-2001.

4.4   Result of Technology Roadmap Generation

By integrating the 'crystallized diagram of technical topics' and five 'crystallized diagrams of technical subtopics (2000-2001 to 2008-2009)', a technology roadmap for thin-film solar cell (in Fig. 4) was constructed via linking the relations from topics to subtopics upon the same patent-no nodes. On the map, four types of topics (i.e., Process, Device, Structure, and Material) linked successively to the subtopics of 2000-2001: a2-electrode-layer, a5-alloy-film, …, and a17-amorphous-semiconductor;

to the subtopics of 2002-2003: b1-polycrystalline-film, b2-anti-reflection, ..., and b13-light-transmission; to the subtopics of 2004-2005: c1-thermal-budget, c2-organic-light-emitting, and c7-absorber-layer; to the subtopics of 2006-2007: d1-sulfur-compound, d2-organic-thin-film, ..., and d10-amorphous-silicon-film; and finally to the subtopics of 2008-2009: e2-aromatic-enediyne and e5-defective-region. This technology roadmap was then used to recognize the technical trends.

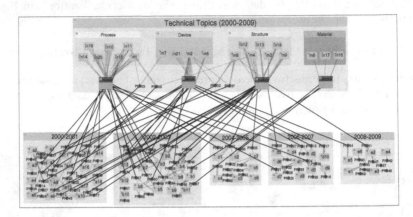

Fig. 4. A technology roadmap for thin-film solar cell (2000-2009)

4.5   Result of Trend Recognition

According to the above technology roadmap, the relations between topics and subtopics could be observed from 2000-2001 to 2008-2009 successively. The trends of topics with Claim data were recognized depending on the classification of topics: Process, Device, Structure, and Material types, which were summarized in Table 1.

Table 1. Technical trends of topics with Claim data

	2000-2001	2002-2003	2004-2005	2006-2007	2008-2009
Process type	m1-plasma-process, m11-m20-pin-process, m10-other-process (amorphous-annealing)	m1-plasma-process, m11-m20-pin-process, m19-coating-process	m15-film-deposition-process	m11-m20-pin-process, m10-other-process (organic-laser)	
Device type	m2-peripheral-device, m7-electrode-device	m2-peripheral-device, m21-solar-watch		m2-peripheral-device	m2-peripheral-device
Structure type	m3-light-trapping-structure, m8-tandem-diode-structure, m13-m18-porous-structure	m4-light-trapping-structure, m12-absorbing-structure, m13-m18-porous-structure	m12-absorbing-structure	m9-thin-film-structure	m9-thin-film-structure
Material type		m16-doped-material, m6-CdTe-CdS-material	m17-organic-material		

The trends of topics with Abstract data were also recognized depending on the classification of topics: Process, Device, Structure, and Material types, which were summarized in Table 2 (taking Process and Device types as examples).

Table 2. Technical trends of subtopics with Abstract data

	2000-2001	2002-2003	2004-2005	2006-2007	2008-2009
Process type	a07-amorphous-annealing, a09-light-emitting, a10-SOI-substrate, a11-composite-structure, a12-porous-silicon, a13-pin-layer, a14-compound-semiconductor, a16-laser-ablation, a17-amorphous-semiconductor	b2-anti-reflection, b3-consumable-electrode, b4-plasma-CVD-method, b5-polysilicon-pin, b6-thermal-emissive-coating, b7-SOI-layer, b8-porous-structure, b12-liquid-coating	c1-thermal-budget	d2-organic-thin-film, d3-organic-laser-diode, d4-Zn-compound, d5-conductive-layer, d7-SiGe-material	
Device type	a07-amorphous-annealing, a08-CuInS-material, a09-light-emitting, a11-composite-structure, a15-light-valve	b1-polycrystalline-film, b2-anti-reflection, b3-consumable-electrode, b6-thermal-emissive-coating, b7-SOI-layer, b13-light-transmission		d1-sulfur-compound, d2-organic-thin-film, d10-amorphous-silicon-film	e5-defective-region

From the above Table 1, the technical trends of topics via Claim data could be depicted as follows.

Process-type topics: moved from "plasma-process", "pin-process", and "other-process (amorphous-annealing)" of 2000-2001, to "plasma-process", "pin-process", and "coating-process" of 2002-2003, to "film-deposition-process" of 2004-2005, and finally to "pin-process" and "other-process (organic-laser)" of 2006-2007.

Device-type topics: moved from "peripheral-device" and "electrode-device" of 2000-2001, to "peripheral-device" and "solar-watch" of 2002-2003, to "peripheral-device" of 2006-2007, and lastly to "peripheral-device" of 2008-2009.

Structure-type topics: moved from "light-trapping-structure", "tandem-diode-structure", and "porous-structure" of 2000-2001, to "light-trapping-structure", "absorbing-structure", and "porous-structure" of 2002-2003, to "absorbing-structure" of 2004-2005, to "thin-film-structure" of 2006-2007, and finally to "thin-film-structure" of 2008-2009.

Material-type topics: moved from "doped-material" and "CdTe-CdS-material" of 2002-2003, then to "organic-material" of 2004-2005.

On the other hand, from the above Table 2, the technical trends of subtopics via Abstract data could be described as follows. Taking Process-type subtopics as an example, it moved from "amorphous-annealing", "light-emitting", "porous-silicon", "compound-semiconductor", "laser-ablation", and "amorphous-semiconductor" of 2000-2001, to "anti-reflection", "plasma-CVD-method", "polysilicon-pin", "thermal-emissive-coating", and "liquid-coating" of 2002-2003, to "thermal-budget" of 2004-2005, and finally to "organic-thin-film", "organic-laser", "Zn-compound", "conductive-layer", and "SiGe-material" of 2006-2007.

5   Conclusions

The research design of association analysis and data crystallization for technology roadmapping has been formed and applied to explore the trends of thin-film solar cell using patent data. The experiment was performed and the experimental results were obtained. A technology roadmap was constructed through integrating the crystallized diagrams of technical topics and subtopics. The topics of thin-film solar cell during 2000 to 2009 were classified into: Process, Device, Structure, and Material types. The technical trends during 2000 to 2009 have been recognized every-two-year depending on the classification of the topics, which would be helpful for the interested parties to understand the developing directions of the technology on the industry level.

In the future work, the product data and marketing information can be included so as to focus on a specific product area and shift a technology roadmap to the company level. Additionally, the patent database can be expanded from USPTO to WIPO or TIPO in order to explore the technical trends of thin-film solar cell widely.

Acknowledgments. This research was supported by the National Science Council of the Republic of China under the Grants NSC 99-2410-H-156-014.

References

1. Gindy, N., Cerit, B., Hodgson, A.: Technology roadmapping for the next generation manufacturing enterprise. Journal of Manufacturing Technology Management 17(4), 404–416 (2006)
2. Blackman, M.: Provision of Patent Information: A National Patent Office Perspective. World Patent Information 17(2), 115–123 (1995)
3. Groenveld, P.: Roadmapping Integrates Business and Technology. Research-Technology Management 50(6), 49–58 (2007)
4. Daim, T.U., Oliver, T.: Implementing Technology Roadmap Process in the Energy Services Sector - A Case Study of a Government Agency. Technological Forecasting and Social Change 75(5), 687–720 (2008)
5. Suh, J.H., Park, S.C.: Service-Oriented Technology Roadmap (SoTRM) using Patent Map for R&D Strategy of Service Industry. Expert Systems with Applications 36, 6754–6772 (2009)
6. Solarbuzz, Solar Cell Technologies (2010), http://www.solarbuzz.com/technologies.htm
7. Wikipedia, Thin film solar cell (2010), http://en.wikipedia.org/wiki/Thin_film_solar_cell
8. Jager-Waldau, A.: PV Status Report 2008: Research, Solar Cell Production and Market Implementation of Photovoltaics. JRC Technical Notes (2008)
9. Tan, P.N., Steinbach, M., Kumar, V.: Introduction to Data Mining. Addison-Wesley, Reading (2006)
10. Ohsawa, Y., Benson, N.E., Yachida, M.: KeyGraph: Automatic Indexing by Co-Occurrence Graph Based on Building Construction Metaphor. In: Proceedings of the Advanced Digital Library Conference (IEEE ADL 1998), pp. 12–18 (1998)
11. Maeno, Y., Ohsawa, Y.: Human-Computer Interactive Annealing for Discovering Invisible Dark Events. IEEE Transactions on Industrial Electronics 54(2), 1184–1192 (2007)
12. Ohsawa, Y.: Data Crystallization: Chance Discovery Extended for Dealing with Unobservable Events. New Mathematics and Natural Computation 1(3), 373–392 (2005)
13. Chiu, T.F.: Applying KeyGraph and Data Crystallization to Technology Monitoring on Solar Cell. Journal of Intelligent & Fuzzy Systems 21(3), 209–219 (2010)
14. USPTO: the United States Patent and Trademark Office (2010), http://www.uspto.gov/
15. Stanford Natural Language Processing Group, Stanford Log-linear Part-Of-Speech Tagger (2009), http://nlp.stanford.edu/software/tagger.shtml

Development of Service Performance Indicators for Operations Management in Airline

Toru Gengo[1], Kazuo Furuta[1], Taro Kanno[1], and Katsuya Fukumoto[2]

[1] Department of Systems Innovation, The University of Toky,
7-3-1 Hongo, Bunkyo-ku, 113-8656 Tokyo, Japan
{gengo,furuta,kanno}@sys.t.u-tokyo.ac.jp
[2] All Nippon Airways, Co. Ltd.
3-3-2 Haneda-kuukou, Ota-ku, 144-8515 Tokyo, Japan
k-fuku@ana.co.jp

Abstract. Reliable and efficient operations are essential for successful service business, and Performance Indicators (PIs) are useful tools for assessing appropriateness of service operations and providing cues to remedy flawed performance. Performance indicators should be based on objective data on operation performance, derivable by concrete and simple calculation rules, and exhaustively related to business goals. Development of such PIs is not an easy task, and this work tries to propose a framework for developing PIs using an application example of operations management in an airline. The proposed scheme of development is so general that it is applicable also to services other than airline business.

Keywords: performance measurement, performance indicators, airline business, flight operations management.

1 Introduction

Performance measurement and feedback of its result to remedial actions are getting more and more important for business management in every industry including services. Lots of ideas have been proposed for measurement and grading of business performance [1][2]. The balanced score card is a performance measurement framework popular in business management that includes strategic non-financial performance measures as well as traditional financial metrics to give managers and executives a comprehensive view of organizational performance [3]. But the balanced scorecard is a strategic tool and it is too heavy to be used in everyday service operations. Many methods of business performance measurement including the balanced scorecard are focused more on financial goals than others, because they are of main interests for corporate executives. This work, however, is concerned about management in sections closer to service frontlines and tries to propose a framework for developing PIs that is useful for assessing everyday operations in such sections. For this purpose, various aspects other than financial goals are to be considered in equal.

T. Onoda, D. Bekki, and E. McCready (Eds.): JSAI-isAI 2010, LNAI 6797, pp. 263–272, 2011.
© Springer-Verlag Berlin Heidelberg 2011

In this study a grading scheme of service performance will be proposed for flight operations management in an airline as an example of service operations. The Operations Management Center (OMC) is in charge of flight operations management in an airline, but no concrete measures exit at present to judge whether or not the performance of everyday operations was satisfactory. The highly competitive business environment of airline business, however, makes it inevitable for an airline to evaluate service operations performance, while the rapid increase of air traffic demands will result in more complicated flight operations management. In addition, transfer of skill and knowledge from experienced managers who are going to retire to younger generations is another issue [4].

From the above backgrounds, a new scheme of performance measurement of flight operations management is now desired. Performance Indicators (PIs) are useful tools for assessing appropriateness of service operations and providing cues to remedy flawed performance. In development of PIs it is desirable to obtain a set of PIs that are independent each other, complete and compact in terms of business goals, and practically derivable from measured data without any ambiguity. Development of such PIs, however, is not an easy task, and this work tries to propose a systematic method for developing PIs for flight operations management in an airline.

2   Development Method of PIs

Performance Indicators should be based on objective data on operations performance, derivable by concrete and simple rules, and exhaustively related to business goals. This study will propose to develop PIs by six phases as shown in Fig. 1.

(1) Identification of PIs

Each performance indicator is some measure that represents to what extent a particular business goal has been achieved. Performance indicators are identified first that correspond to business goals of fulfilling major stakeholders' requests in the target service business. Firstly, relevant stakeholders and then requests by each stakeholder are to be identified.

Brainstorming sessions participated by field staff in the business will be carried out for identifying relevant stakeholders and their requests. Brainstorming is a group technique to generate new ideas following four guide rules of critique free, restriction free, quantity rather than quality, and combination of ideas recommended. Cards are popular supporting tools used for idea generation and communication in brainstorming.

Since business goals are sometimes interdependent, they are organized in a hierarchical structure of goal-mean relations. Analytical techniques of systems engineering are applicable for this purpose. In this study, the KJ method [5][6] and Interpretive Structural Modeling (ISM)[7] have been adopted. The KJ method is a naïve but systematic technique of grouping idea cards generated by brainstorming in a hierarchical structure by group discussion. In applying ISM, goal-mean relations between goal pairs are identified based on expert judge by the field staff, and then mathematical analysis on the pair-wise relations can reveal the hierarchical structure of a goal-mean graph.

(2) Task Analysis
In order to reflect PI grading for improving service operations, service processes are categorized and looked into. Having analyzed the service processes by some approach of task analysis, the results are described by service blueprinting. A service blueprint is a diagram that represents all activities relevant to the service processes and their interrelations along the time axis [8][9].

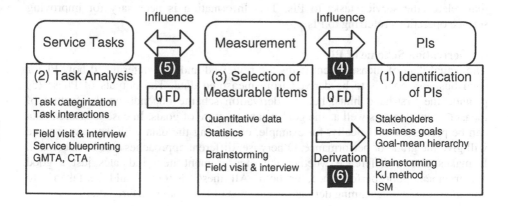

Fig. 1. Framework of PIs development process

For drawing service blueprints, visit and observation of the fields of service operations and interview to the field staff will be necessary in addition to collecting information written in documents. There are various methods of task analysis to reveal logical structure of tasks in the service processes, such as Goal-Mean Task Analysis (GMTA)[10] and Cognitive Task Analysis (CTS)[11].

(3) Service Performance Measurement
Concrete quantitative items are selected that is measurable in everyday service operations and affected by the performance of service tasks. The outputs of each task raised in Phase (2) are identified, and then how these outputs are related to the quantitative data or statistics is considered that will be available in the field of service operations. Consultation to the field staff will be necessary also in this phase.

(4) Relating PIs and Measurement
The performance indicators that were selected in Phase (1) and the quantitative measures in Phase (3) are to be interrelated and evaluated. The outputs of this phase provide clues for considering how PIs are to be derived from measured data, but it is unnecessary to consider exact scheme of PI derivation here.

Quality Function Deployment (QFD), which is a technique to translate customer needs into function requirements in products design, was applied in this study [12]. The results of this phase can be described as a QFD matrix that has PIs in columns and quantitative measures in rows. Cells of the matrix contain semi-quantitative scores that represent the degree of influence.

(5) Relating Service Tasks and Measurement

The service tasks that were identified in Phase (2) and the measurement on service operations in Phase (3) are to be interrelated: cause-consequence relations between the two are searched for and evaluated. The results can be described as a QFD matrix that has service tasks in columns and quantitative measures in rows. Cells of the matrix contain semi-quantitative scores that represent the degree of influence.

Combining the both QFD matrix from Phase (4) and (5), another matrix is obtained that relates the service tasks to PIs. This information is necessary for improving service operations referring to PIs.

(6) Derivation Scheme of PIs

The actual data of measurement items are reviewed and it is determined how PI for each business goal is to be derived from measured data. The outputs of Phase (3) provide the first-hand hints, but the derivation scheme depends on the feature of measurement items as well as the goal-mean structure of goals. In case measured data can be processed statistically, for example, comparing the data with the past average will give the grade of performance. Otherwise, different approaches will be necessary. It makes also a difference whether the measurement item indicates just a good performance, poor performance, or both. All these factors should be taken into consideration in determining derivation schemes of PIs from measured data.

3   PIs Development for Flight Operations Management

In this chapter, PIs development for flight operations management in an airline is presented following the framework presented in the previous chapter. We developed PIs for the domain in cooperation with an airline and many field staff of the company joined the development.

3.1   Stakeholders and PIs

Eight members of the Operations Management Center (OMC) and six ordinary people representing passengers joined brainstorming sessions. The KJ method was used for brief categorization of cards with business goals. As a result of brainstorming, six major stakeholders were identified in terms of the works in OMC: staff of OMC, staff of other parts of the airline, corporate executives and shareholders, passengers, government and society, and business partners.

Business goals requested by each stakeholder were then identified and organized by ISM. Table 1 shows the result, where requests from corporate executives and shareholders were judged inclusive of those by government, society, and business partners.

3.2   Service Tasks in OMC

Task analysis was performed for OMC in reference to operation guidelines, operation manuals, field observation, and staff interview. Service blueprinting was done and blueprints as shown in Fig. 2 were drawn separately for five different situations:

normal condition, meteorological irregular condition before/after departure, and organizational irregular condition before/after departure. A few members of OMC checked the service blueprints, and then necessary modifications were made.

Table 1. Business goals requested by each stakeholder

Stakeholder	Goals
Passengers	Amenity Utility Safety Reliability
Non-OMC Staff	Safety Work environment
Executives & shareholders	Business potential Profitability Transparency
OMC staff	Work environment Motivation

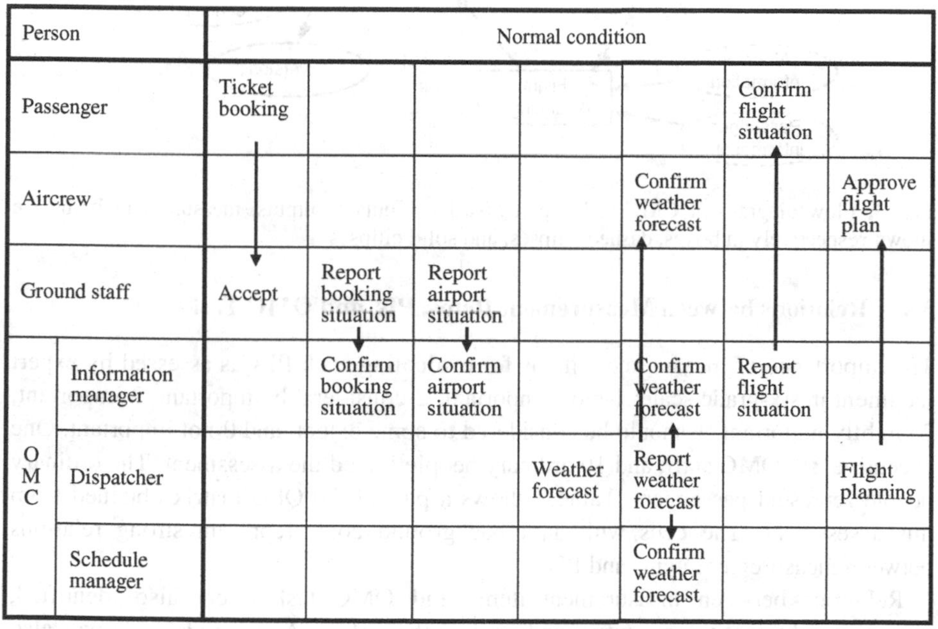

Person		Normal condition						
Passenger		Ticket booking					Confirm flight situation	
Aircrew						Confirm weather forecast		Approve flight plan
Ground staff		Accept	Report booking situation	Report airport situation				
O M C	Information manager		Confirm booking situation	Confirm airport situation		Confirm weather forecast	Report flight situation	
	Dispatcher				Weather forecast	Report weather forecast		Flight planning
	Schedule manager					Confirm weather forecast		

Fig. 2. Service blueprint for normal condition

3.3   Service Performance Measurement

In order to measure service performance, it is required to know what quantitative data have been or can be obtained in everyday operations in OMC and how service tasks affect these measures. Firstly inputs and outputs of each service task in OMC were identified and the results were described as task flow diagrams as shown in Fig. 3. Secondly measurable items as the final outputs of tasks were identified. Service performance measurement will be done on these items. This analysis was done for every task in OMC found in the previous section.

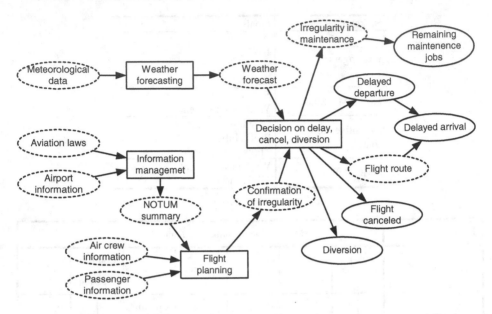

Fig. 3. Flow diagram of OMC tasks (part). Tasks, inputs / outputs, measurement items are shown respectively in boxes, dashed ellipses, and solid ellipses.

3.4   Relations between Measurement Items, PIs, and OMC Tasks

The importance of measurement items for evaluating each PI was assessed by expert judgment in six-grade scale: 1-most important, 2-considerably important, 3-important, 2-slightly important, 1-should be considered to some extent, and 0-not important. One executive, six OMC staff, and 10 ordinary people joined the assessment. The ordinary people represent passengers. Table 2 shows a part of the QFD matrix obtained from this assessment. The cells with dark background color represent strong relations between measurement items and PIs.

Relations between measurement items and OMC tasks were also identified, participated by just the executive and staff of the airline. A six-grade scale was also used: 5-most influential, 4-considerably influential, 3-influential, 2-slightly influential, 1-maybe influential, and 0-not influential. The result was also obtained as a QFD matrix similar to Table 2.

Combining the two QFD matrices, the weight of contribution from each OMC task to a particular PI was evaluated as a percentage.

Table 2. Relations between measurement items and PIs

Stakeholder	Passenger			
PI	Safety	Amenity	Utility	Reliability
Departure delay	0	0	5	4
Arrival delay	0	0	5	4
Maintenance suspension rate	1	0	0	0
Sway in flight	5	5	0	4
Unsafe incidents	5	0	0	4

3.5   Derivation Scheme of PIs

Finally derivation scheme and grading criteria were determined for each PI. The result of PI grading is given by 7-grade scale from AAA (excellent) to E (unacceptable). There are two types of grading criteria depending on the type of measurement item.

Table 3. Upgrading and downgrading criteria of PI. δ and σ are respectively deviation from the past average and the standard deviation of the past data.

(a) Upgrading

Grade	AAA (excellent)	AA (very good)	A (good)	B (normal)
Criteria	Conditions for both AA and A obtain	$\delta > 3\sigma$ or $< -3\sigma$ in more than 1% cases	$\delta > 2\sigma$ or $< -2\sigma$ in more than 5% cases	Conditions for neither AA nor A obtain

(b) Downgrading

Grade	B (normal)	C (poor)	D (very poor)	E (unacceptable)
Criteria	Conditions for neither C nor D obtain	$\delta > 2\sigma$ or $< -2\sigma$ in more than 5% cases	$\delta > 3\sigma$ or $< -3\sigma$ in more than 1% cases	Conditions for both C and D obtain

Table 4. Grading criteria for departure delay

Measurement item	Departure delay
Relevant PIs	(Passengers) Utility, reliability (Managers) Business potential, profitability
Method of measurement	Ratio of flights per month that delayed more than the acceptable period of time
Critical values	Average: 5.0 min. (2008 record) Standard deviation: 15.2 min. (2008 record)
Grading direction	Downgrading
Factors to be considered	Meteorological conditions

In case the measurement item stands for occurrence of any unfavorable event, like serious incident, that has not experienced before or that is unacceptable, the frequency of the event over the grading period directly results in the grade of PI. If no events occurred, the grade is judged B (normal); once, twice, or three times of occurrence gets C, D, or E grade.

Otherwise, grade judgment is determined by comparing the measured value with the normal level of data; the average and the standard deviation from the past statistics are used as the basis in grading PI of this type. There are two criteria: upgrading and downgrading. The upgrading corresponds to the case where deviation from the normal level stands for good operations performance, and downgrading to poor performance. Table 3 shows the grading criteria for the both. In some cases, grading of the both directions is possible.

Table 4 gives an example of grading criteria adopted for a measurement item of departure delay. Factors to be considered are potential causes that are not attributable to OMC task performance but can affect PI. In the above example, OMC can do nothing to change meteorological conditions but bad weather will cause departure delay of flights and a poor grade of the PI. Such factors should be eliminated when considering countermeasures against poor PIs.

4   Application Trial of Developed PIs

The PIs developed in this study was applied to the actual record on OMC operations in September 2008. The application was done in the flowing scheme.

(1) Performance grading following the developed PIs and grading criteria,
(2) Cause analysis of poor PIs,
(3) Identification of OMC tasks relevant to poor PIs,
(4) Identification of flights with problems,
(5) Identification of OMC tasks with potential problems.

Table 5 shows the final result of performance grading. Cells with hyphen '–' represent PIs that were not derivable at present due to lack of necessary data. A poor PI grade was observed for the amount of remained fuel, which is a subsidiary PI of safety for passengers and aircrew. From Fig. 3, the relevant tasks of the PI are weather forecasting, flight planning, and decision on delay, cancel, or diversion.

Two flights were found that caused the poor PI grade. One flight on August 25, 2008 from Haneda to Kansai delayed 2 hours and 5 minutes due to equipment trouble. The other on August 26, 2008 from Kochi to Haneda delayed 48 minutes due to traffic restriction by the air traffic control. Since the both of them were caused by unforeseen events after departure, neither weather forecasting nor flight planning could improve the performance. It can be recommended, therefore, that the processes of decision on delay, cancel, or diversion must be reconsidered, if similar events may repeat in the future.

Table 5. Result of application trial of performance grading (part)

PI	Contribution	Measurement item	Grade
(Passengers) Safety	5	Unsafe incidents	–
	4	Sway in flight	–
		Satisfaction of OMC staff	–
		Compliance	–
	3	Precision of information (internal)	B
		Amount of remained fuel	D
(Passengers) Amenity	5	Sway in flight	–
	3	Number of diverted flights	B
		Precision of information (external)	B
		Claims from customers	–
		Balance	–
(Passengers) Utility	5	Departure delay	B
		Arrival delay	B
		Canceled flights	B
		Diverted flights	B
	4	Precision of information (external)	B
		Speed of information delivery (external)	B
	3	Rescheduling frequency	B

5   Conclusion

Performance Indicators (PIs) are useful tools for semi-quantitatively assessment of service performance, but it is a nontrivial issue for developing practical and effective PIs. This work proposed a development method of PIs for flight operations management in an airline as an application domain. The developed PIs were applied to actual data of airline operations, and it was demonstrated that performance grading with PIs is useful for detecting potential problems in service operations.

The result of application trial was presented to field staff of airline operations, and their comments were obtained that the result did not conflict with their intuitive sense of expertise and seemed adequate and that PIs would be useful for pointing out problems in OMC operations.

The proposed architecture of development heavily depends on opinions, expertise, and ideas obtained from field staff, and it does not rely on any presumed task model of the application domain. We believe, therefore, it is applicable to various service business domains in general other than flight operations management of an airline. It is expected that PIs contribute finally to improvement in financial performance of a company. Exhaustive identification of stakeholders and elaborated decomposition of business goals are essential for achieving this goal. Actual demonstration of such contribution, however, will require a long period of trial use, because it is often necessary to monitor a long-term performance in service business.

Acknowledgments. The authors express their thanks to the staff of All Nippon Airways, Co. Ltd. who participated in the brainstorming sessions and interviews.

References

1. Neely, A., Gregory, M., Platts, K.: Performance measurement system design: A literature review and research agenda. Int. J. Operations & Production Management 25(12), 1228–1263 (2005)
2. Neely, A.: Business Performance Measurement: Unifying Theory and Integrating Practice, 2nd edn. Cambridge Univ. Pr., Cambridge (2007) (japanese translation)
3. Kaplan, R.S., Norton, D.P.: The Balanced Scorecard: Translating Strategy into Action. Harvard Business School Pr., Boston (1996) (japanese translation)
4. International Air Transport Association, http://www.iata.org/index.html
5. Kawakita, J.: Method of Idea Generation - For Creativity Development. Chuo Koron Pr. (1967) (japanese)
6. Scupin, R.: The KJ Method: A Technique for Analyzing Data Derived from Japanese Ethnology. Human Organization 56(2), 233–237 (1997)
7. Watson, R.H.: Interpretive Structural Modeling - A Useful Tool for Technology Assessment? Technological Forecasting and Social Change 11(2), 165–185 (1978)
8. Shostack, L.G.: How to Design a Service. Eur. J. Marketing 16(1), 49–63 (1982)
9. Shostack, L.G.: Design Services that Deliver. Harvard Business Review 84115, 133–139 (1984)
10. Hollnagel, E.: Human Reliability Analysis: Context and Control. Academic Pr., New York (1993)
11. Hoffman, R., Militello, L.: Perspective on Cognitive Task Analysis. Taylor & Francis, Abington (2009)
12. Akao, Y.: Introduction to Quality Deployment. Nikka Giren Pr. (1993) (japanese)

The Impact Factors in Remedial English E-Learning Instruction

Chia-ling Hsu

Tamkang University, Graduate Institute of C&I, Associate Professor.
151, Ying-chuan Road, Tamsui, Taipei County, 25137, Taiwan
clhsu@mail.tku.edu.tw

Abstract. Technology is one of the powerful media in education. Especially, the remedial instruction by computer technology is widely used from K-12 to higher education. This study applied the grounded theory approach analyzing data with visual association map to find the impact factors in English remedial e-learning instruction. The significances of this paper are proposing the results with visual representation and with an event scenario to instructors or instructional designers. The results indicated that the engineer school, science school, management school and concrete-sequential learning style were the main factors in learner characteristic perspective. With these learner characteristic impact factors, the instructional factors appeared in remedial English e-learning course. Future studies are needed.

Keywords: Instructional Design, e-learning, Chance Detection, Remedial Instruction, Teacher Professional Development.

1 Introduction

Educational technology is wildly used in individual learning. One good example is the computer assistant instruction (CAI). Because learners learn the material with their own pace; therefore, CAI became one of the powerful media for remedial instruction. Since Web 2.0 made the technology change radically, the instructional design in using educational technology appeared different. E-learning is a new trend in education. Although the technologies change very fast, the elements of education theories still make a lot of efforts in remedial instruction. Although the education reform policy changes the school environment, the remedial instruction is still one of the important issues. Many projects have been undertaken in education system, for example, "Every child matters in the curriculum" in England, "No child left behind" in the United States and "After school alternative program" in Taiwan [1][2][3]. Would there be difference in remedial instructional design when the technologies are different? What would be the important elements in remedial e-learning? This study examined an English remedial e-learning course to create a scenario for instructors and instructional designers showing the relationship among the elements derived from the learners' point of views.

Learner characteristics, learning material, teaching strategies and evaluation are the essential elements in education. Some research focus on learner characteristics, such

T. Onoda, D. Bekki, and E. McCready (Eds.): JSAI-isAI 2010, LNAI 6797, pp. 273–282, 2011.

as, gender difference and learning style. Some studies focus on such learning material as topics of the passage and length of the article. In addition, studies on teaching strategies are also interesting issues to researchers. The teaching activity is one of the teaching strategies. However, most studies investigated these elements independently. This study applied the grounded theory approach to investigate the interaction among these factors.

2   Relative Literature

This study evaluated the remedial English e-learning course with attention, relevance, confidence, and satisfaction (ARCS) model in order to provide a scenario for instructional design. The related literature is illustrated below.

2.1   Instructional Design

Accordingly, the practice of instructional design is to target specific learners, select specific approaches, contents, and strategies, and make an effective teaching policy [4]. Instructional design is often presented and explained through models [5].

2.2   ARCS Model

Keller proposed the attention (A), relevance (R), confidence (C) and satisfaction (S) motivation model in order to solve motivational problems for instructional designer [6][7]. There are two main issues facing with the ARCS model: one is attitude, and the other is evaluation. The evaluation for the motivation is not to evaluate the learning efficiency but to evaluate the motivation character of the learning motivation in the instructional design model [8]. The ARCS Model identifies four essential components for motivation instruction:

Attention: strategies for arousing and sustaining curiosity and interest
Relevance: strategies that link to learners' needs, interests and motives
Confidence: strategies that help students develop a positive expectation for successful achievement
Satisfaction: strategies that provide extrinsic and intrinsic reinforcement for efforts.

3   Research Method

This study was to analyze the students' motivation and preference in a remedial English e-learning course. Although the traditional ARCS questionnaire was applied, this study employed a new technology with a view to acquiring more information in learners' motivation. In addition, this study intends to combine the data of ARCS motivation with learner characteristics, interesting study materials, and teaching activities to formulate a possible teaching plan. The participants, instrument, and scoring system were expressed as follows.

3.1   Participants

A remedial English e-learning in a university for graduate students who did not achieve the graduation required level of English tests such as TOEIC, TOEFL and

GEPT. 186 students enrolled in this class. At the end of the course, students filled out an online questionnaire voluntarily. Hence, 179 questionnaires were collected. Table 1 showed population of the students.

Table 1. Population of the students

School	Number of students
Engineer	104
Science	32
Management	21
Business	9
Education	5
Liberal Arts	3
others	5
Total	179

3.2 Instrument

The ARCS questionnaire contains 34 items. The Attention factor contains item 1, 4*, 10, 15, 21, 24, 26*, and 29. The items marked with * mean the inverse items. The Relevance factor contains item 2, 5, 8, 13, 20, 22, 23, 25, and 28. The Confidence factor contains item 3, 6*, 9, 11*, 17*, 27, 30, and 34. The Satisfaction factor contains item 7, 12, 14, 16, 18, 19, 31*, 32, and 33. The score is calculated for each item by 5 scale points, from non-agree to very agree.

Besides, two more questions were asked. One was a multiple-choice question about the material types. The other was an open question about the material topics.

4   Data Analysis

Data analysis was conducted by the research model which was based on the grounded theory approach. The reason of using grounded theory approach was to identify the impact factors in learners and then let the instructional situation appeared by the data without any experiment. That iterative process of moving back and forth between data and analysis and that examining different explanations for the empirical findings are similar to the ground theory approach. The analysis steps are as follows.

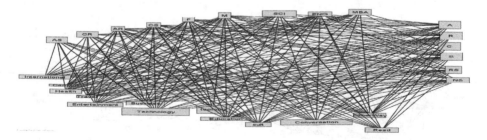

Fig. 1. The total impact factors in remedial English e-learning course

• Step 1: Screen the whole data

Screen the whole data to understand the whole impact factors in remedial English e-learning course. The results were shown in figure 1. Figure 1 indicated that learner characteristics (gender, school, and learning style) and instructional design (teaching material and methods) all affected learners who showed their feelings about the remedial English e-learning course.

• Step 2: Choose one aspect, learner characteristics

Choose one aspect, the learner characteristics to understand the factors affected the course evaluation. The result was shown in figure 2. Figure 2 indicated that gender difference, learning style difference or school difference would affect the course evaluation, the motivation of course learning.

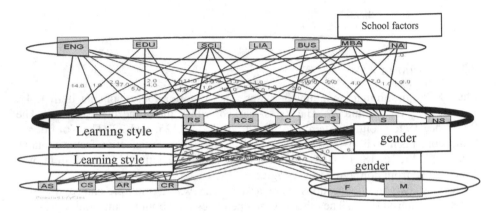

Fig. 2. The association of the course evaluation, ARCS, and the learner characteristics

• Step 3: In learner characteristics, examine gender factors

Examine each gender factor: The results of male and female were shown in figure 3 and figure 4.

• Step 4: Compare the differences between the male and female factors

Comparing figure 3 and figure 4, the two maps indicated that the learning style emerged both in the male map and female map. In this case, the gender factor was affected by schools.

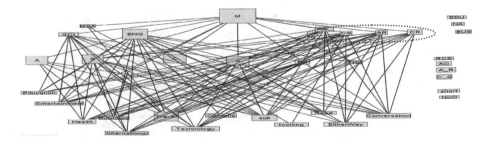

Fig. 3. The association of the factors in Male factor analysis

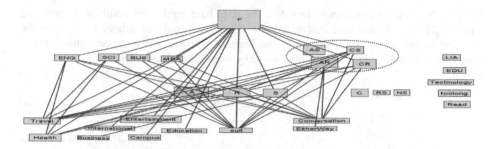

Fig. 4. The association of the factors in Female factor analysis

• Step 5: Zoom in gender factors

Go back to the original data base and zoom in the male factor and female factor without the learning style factor. The results were shown in figure 5 and figure 6.

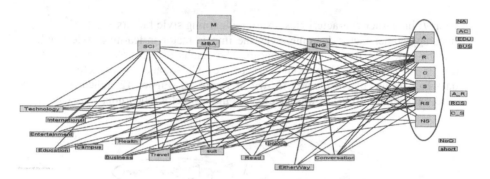

Fig. 5. The association of the ARCS and the Male gender factor

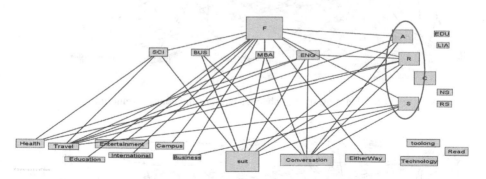

Fig. 6. The association of the ARCS and the female gender factor

• Step 6: Select impact factors from the evaluation in gender factors

Without the learning style factor, the gender factor was affected by school factor. Hence, checking with the different gender by the evaluation, the maps showed that there were A, R, C, S, RS, NS in male factor map and there were A, R, S in female factor map. Comparing figures 5 and 6, the differences were C, RS, and NS. Then, from the objective

(C, RS, NS, and school factor) to select the data base again, the result was shown in figure 7. Figure 7 indicated that in gender factor, the engineer school factor was the affected impact factor. In other words, the learners who were in engineer school would affect the remedial English e-learning course by examining the gender factors.

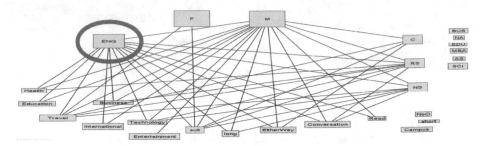

Fig. 7. The association of the ARCS and the gender factor

• Step 7: In learner characteristics, examine learning style factors

Choosing another factor, learning style, the impact factor in learning style would be selected by repeating from step 3 to step 6. The results of processing were shown in figure 8, 9, 10, 11 and 12. Then, from the objectives (C, NS, and school factors) to select the data base again, the result was shown in figure 12. Figure 12 indicated that, the concrete-sequential (CS) factor was the affected impact factor in learning style factor.

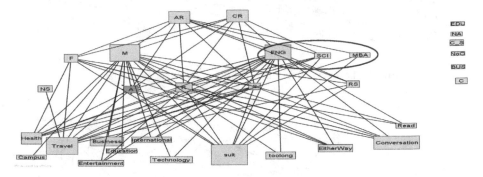

Fig. 8. learning style of abstract-random and concrete-random

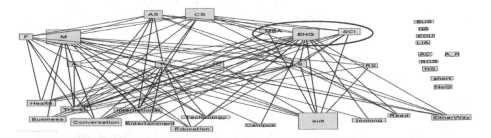

Fig. 9. Learning style of abstract-sequential and concrete-sequential

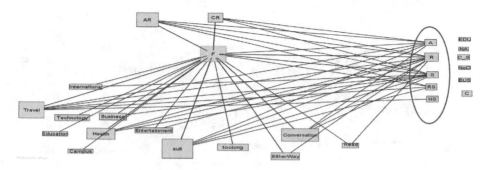

Fig. 10. The association of the ARCS and random learning style factors

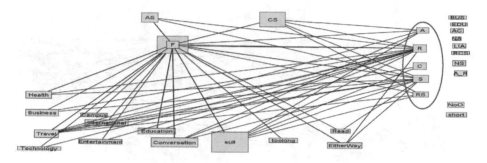

Fig. 11. The association of the ARCS and sequential learning style factors

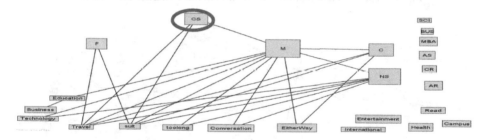

Fig. 12. The association of the ARCS and the learning style factors

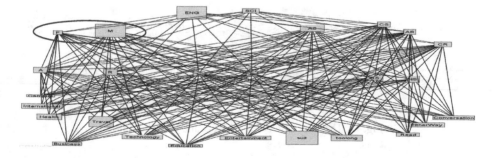

Fig. 13. School factor of engineer and science school

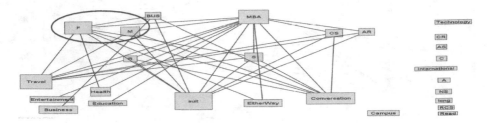

Fig. 14. School factor of business school and management school

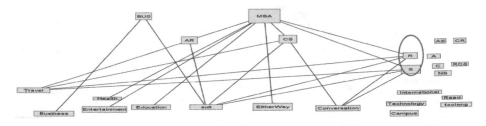

Fig. 15. The association of the ARCS and engineer–science school factor

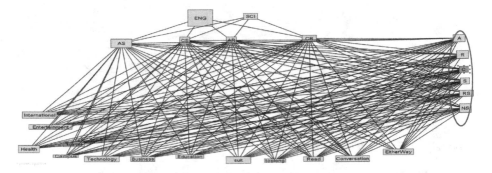

Fig. 16. The association of the ARCS and business–management school factor

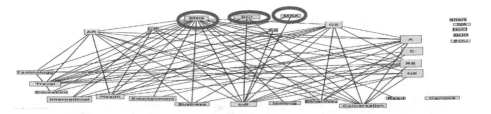

Fig. 17. The association of the ARCS and the school factor

• Step 8: In learner characteristics, examine school factors

Repeat from step 3 to step 6 again and choose the school factor. The results of processing were shown in figure 13,14,15,16 and 17. From the objective (A, C, RS, NS, and learning style factors) to select the data base again, the result was shown in figure 17. Figure 17 indicated that in school factor, the engineer, science and management school factors were the affected impact factors.

Following the grounded theory approach and repeating the analyzing data by zooming in and zooming out procedure, the impact factors tended to emerge. Using gender, learning style and school factor as triangulation evaluations for learner characteristics aspect, the impact factors for remedial English e-learning course emerged. The impact factors were engineering school, concrete-sequential learning style, and science school and management school that were indicated by fig. 7, 12 and 17 in red bold circles.

5   Results and Suggestions

As soon as the impact factors emerged, a scenario of the remedial English e-learning course would be generated.

5.1   Results

This study investigated the impact factors in remedial English e-learning course. With the iterative process of data and analysis approach in GTM, the impact factors in the learner characteristics were detected. With the examining the possible theoretical explanations such as learner characteristics, course evaluation(ARCS) and teaching strategy, a scenario of the remedial English e-learning was appeared in figure 18.

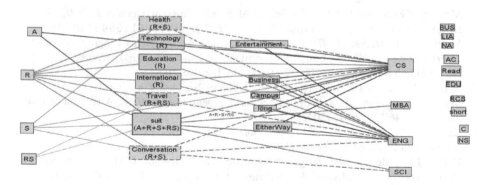

Fig. 18. A scenario of the impact factors in remedial English e-learning course

The results indicated that the impact factors in learner characteristics affected the course evaluation with ARCS by the factors in teaching perspective in figure 18. In other words, learners who were in management school, engineer school, science school, or with concrete-sequential learning style felt that the course would draw their attention, relate to their needs, and satisfy their efforts. The internal factors were the topics of health, technology, education, international, and travel. In addition, the topics of teaching materials and the suitable length of articles were also very important factors when learners evaluated the course. The teaching method was by means of conversation.

5.2   Suggestions

From the scenario, some suggestions to instructional designers or teachers were proposed as follows.

- When the majority of learners are male in engineer school, the remedial English e-learning course should take the length of reading material into consideration as figure 18 indicated.
- Although the topics of reading passages will affect the participants' course evaluation, the length of reading passages is a more important factor.

This study finds such impact factors as engineer school, science school, management school, and concrete-sequential learning style in the aspect of learner characteristics. Base on these learner characteristics, a scenario of instructional strategies is appeared. More studies are needed.

Acknowledgments. We would like to thank Dr. Hong, C. F. and Dr. Chiu, T. F. from Aletheia University for their support of computer system. The e-learning course was supported by Tamkang University and Dr. Wang was the instructor in the remedial English course.

References

1. Ministry of Education (2006), After School Alternative Program (October 2, 2009), http://163.19.64.10/handweb/data/files/200801110545520.doc
2. Ministry of Education (2007), Promote Educational Priority Areas Program (October 2, 2009), http://163.25.130.2/advedu/download/96eduplan.doc
3. No Child Left Behind Act of 2001 (2002), Public Law No. 107-110
4. Smith, P.L., Ragan, T.J.: Instructional design. Macmillan, New York (1993)
5. Michael, T., Marlon, M., Roberto, J.: The third dimension of ADDIE: A cultural embrace. TechTrends 46(12), 40–45 (2002)
6. Keller, J.M.: Motivation and Instructional Design. A Theoretical perspective. J. Instructional Development, 26–34 (1979)
7. Keller, J.M.: Motivational design of instruction. In: Reigeluth, C.M. (ed.) Instructional Design Theories and Models: An Overview of Their Current Status. Erlbaum, Hillsdale (1983)
8. Visser, J., Keller, J.M.: The Clinical Use of Motivational Messages: an Inquiry into the Validity of the ARCS Model of Motivational Design. J. Instructional Science 19, 450–467 (1990)

Surgical Workflow Monitoring Based on Trajectory Data Mining

Atsushi Nara[1], Kiyoshi Izumi[2], Hiroshi Iseki[3], Takashi Suzuki[3],
Kyojiro Nambu[4], and Yasuo Sakurai[3]

[1] Center for Spatial Analysis, University of Oklahoma.
3100 Monitor Avenue, Norman, OK 73072, USA
atsushi.nara@ou.edu
[2] School of Engineering, The University of Tokyo & PRESTO, JST.
7-3-1 Hongo, Bunkyo, Tokyo, Japan
kiyoshi@ni.mints.ne.jp
[3] Institute of Advanced Biomedical Engineering and Science,
Tokyo Women's Medical University.
8-1, Kawada-cho, Shinjuku-ku, Tokyo, Japan
{hiseki,takashi_suzuki,yasuo.sakurai}@abmes.twmu.ac.jp
[4] Research and Development Center, Toshiba Medical Systems Corporation.
1385 Shimoishigami, Otawara-shi, Tochigi-ken, Japan

Abstract. This research aims at investigating intermediate-scale workflows using the surgical staff's movement pattern. In this study, we have introduced an ultrasonic location aware system to monitor intraoperative movement trajectories on surgical staffs for the workflow analysis. And we developed trajectory data mining for surgical workflow segmentation, and analyzed trajectory data with multiple cases. As a result, in 77.18% of total time, a kind of current operation stage could be correctly estimated. With high accuracy 85.96%, the estimation using trajectory data was able to distinguish whether a current 5 minutes was transition time from one stage to another stage or not.. Based on these results, we are implementing the surgery safe support system that promotes safe & efficient surgical operations.

Keywords: Surgical Workflow, Surgical Management, Trajectory Analysis

1 Introduction

Nowadays an operating room in a hospital confronts problems include personnel shortages such as nurses, anesthesiologists, surgeons, and technicians; inefficient, ineffective, and redundant procedures for scheduling and supply management; and fragmented communications and isolation [2]. Especially, workflow issues are central to the efficiency of the operating room and in response to today's continuing workforce shortages. Surgical workflow monitoring and analysis in the operating room are an emergent topic for better designing and management of surgical operations.

The surgical workflow has different levels of granularity, and existing studies presented various monitoring methodologies and workflow analyses mostly focusing

T. Onoda, D. Bekki, and E. McCready (Eds.): JSAI-isAI 2010, LNAI 6797, pp. 283–291, 2011.
© Springer-Verlag Berlin Heidelberg 2011

at a scale of either operating room (coarse-scale) or operative field (fine-scale). A coarse-scale approach identifies the broad surgical phases such as the start and end of an operation by monitoring when a patient enters and leaves the operating room using patient's vital signs [10] and video imageries [1]. On the other hand, a fine-scale approach detects surgical procedures based on detail actions at the operative field; for example, dissecting, clipping, and detaching a diseased site using instrument signals [7] and exchanging surgical instruments between a surgeon and a scrub nurse from video imageries [6].

For better understanding of the surgical workflow, this paper presents a new approach that fills the gap between two scales. Our approach is based on the analysis of staff's trajectories since movement behaviors differ from staff's roles as well as surgical phases. The research objective is to identify distinct surgical events from the trajectory database, which helps the middle-scale surgical workflow segmentation. To trace a human movement in a surgical room, we developed an ultrasonic location aware system that continuously tracks 3D positions on multiple surgical staffs in the operating room. For identifying distinct surgical events, we employed a trajectory data mining technique, which includes two procedures, trajectory partitioning and trajectory clustering.

2   Operation Environments and System Architecture

2.1   Operation Environment

The operating room, where the ultrasonic location aware system was installed, is used only for neurosurgical operations. As a distinct feature of the room, an operation is performed under the open MRI to increase the tumour resection rate. During an operation, several intraoperative MR images are taken using the open-MRI scanner to confirm brain deformation caused by surgical procedures and tumour situation. A surgery in this room consists of surgical stages (preparation, craniotomy, tumor resection, replacement & suturarion, and recovery) illustrated in Fig. 1

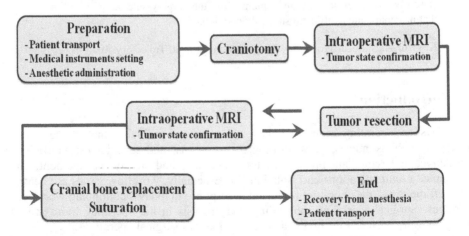

Fig. 1. A typical workflow of a neurosurgical operation with the intraoperative MRI process

Table 1 shows averages of total time and duration of each stage hours in 10 operations that we measured. We selected similar 10 neurosurgical operations with general anesthesia, but the total time varied among operations from 5.5 hours to 10 hours.

Table 1. Total time and duration of each stage (10 cases' average)

	Total	Preparation	Craniotomy	Tumor resection	MRI	Suturation	End
Average	8:24:11	1:12:46	1:23:49	2:48:41	1:19:33	1:00:22	0:39:00
Standard deviation	1:20:52	0:10:48	0:37:42	0:47:51	0:14:25	0:07:07	0:24:56
Max	10:17:14	1:25:54	2:42:22	3:50:45	1:34:55	1:08:47	1:39:26
Min	5:37:35	0:53:16	0:49:30	1:10:18	0:53:43	0:49:54	0:06:58

2.2 Surgical Management System

We have developed the ultrasonic 3D location aware system for collecting continuous staff's trajectories in the operating room during a neurosurgery. The location aware system has been built up on a surgical management system (SMS) proposed by Nambu and Iseki [5]. As an ongoing project, the SMS aims to real-time support of an operation by observing and recording surgical process, supporting decision making, and supporting communication between surgeons and an operating team. SMS consists of two sub systems, the operating room system and the surgical strategic desk. In the operating room system, there are three functional systems: 1) operating room monitoring system; 2) Surgical Information Analysis System; and 3) Surgical Information Visualization System. The ultrasonic location aware system presented in this paper belongs to the operating room monitoring system, which collects real-time multi-dimensional information including video captured images, audio data, surgeon's vital signs, medical device' audit logs, and staff's trajectories.

The Surgical Information Analysis System takes collected dataset and conducts workflow analyses for each dataset. The multi-dimensional analytical results will be sent to the surgical strategic desk, where a general manager, typically an expert surgeon, is permanently stationed. The manager evaluates the analytical result, and when necessary, the strategic desk like an air traffic control tower navigates an operation based on patient records, collected multi-dimensional surgical information, and evaluated results. Both the operating room system and the strategic desk own the surgical information visualization system so that all acquired information is shared among the staffs in the operating room as well as at the surgical strategic desk.

2.3 Ultrasonic 3D Location Aware System

We installed the ultrasonic 3D location aware system in the OR (5.8m (width) x 4.8m (depth) x 2.9m (height)) at the Tokyo Women's Medical University (TWMU), Japan (Fig.2). It consists of control units (Fig.2a), receivers (Fig.2b), and tags (transmitters)

(Fig.2c). The receivers receive ultrasonic pulses emitted from multiple tags. The control units identify each tag's identification and detect associated 3D positions. Because of delicate tasks during a surgical operation, a single tag is hooked on surgical clothes around the nape of surgical staff's neck for the purpose of minimum disturbance (Fig.2c). For 3D position estimation, the system records the time-of-flight, which is the travel time of the signal from transmission to reception. Based on more than three time-of-flight results, the system computes 3D position using the trilateration method using the robust estimation algorithm known as random sample consensus (RANSAC) [3].

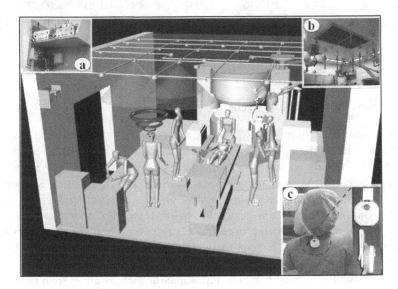

Fig. 2. The ultrasonic 3D location aware system

3   Trajectory Analyses and Workflow Estimation

3.1   Trajectory Data Mining Method

By the ultrasonic system, about 200,000 position data are measured per hour, and over 1,500,000 position data are totally acquired by one operation. In order to extract moving patterns relevant to characteristic work from such huge position data, we developed the following trajectory clustering method based on [4].

The ultrasonic location aware system collects a set of trajectories from multiple surgical staffs {Trajectory Set: $TR_{set} = TR_1, TR_2, TR_3, ..., TR_i$, where i denotes the number of surgical staffs} during a surgical operation. Each trajectory is composed of a sequence of 4-dimensional points {{ $TR_i = p_1, p_2, p_3, ..., p_j$, where j denotes the number of points in the trajectory i}, { $p_j = x, y, z, t$ }}. To extract distinct surgical events for the surgical workflow segmentation, we employed the trajectory data mining technique, which includes two procedures, trajectory partitioning and trajectory clustering (Fig.3).

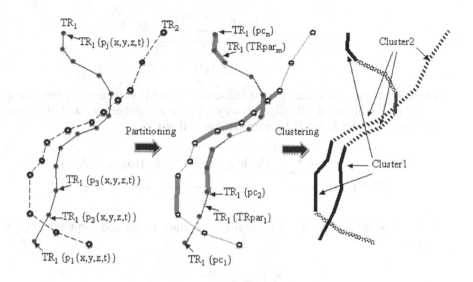

Fig. 3. Trajectory data mining; partitioning and clustering

1. *Trajectory partitioning*:
    The trajectory partitioning process partitioned an entire trajectory of a surgical staff during a surgery into trajectory partitions (sub-trajectories). This step finds the points where the behavior of a trajectory changes rapidly, called as characteristic points (pc). Each characteristic point partitions a trajectory into trajectory partitions and each partition is represented by a set of line segments between two consecutive characteristic points {TRi = TRpar(1){pc(1) pc(2)}, TRpar(1){pc(2) pc(3)}, ..., TRpar(m){pc(n-1) pc(n)}, where m denotes the number of trajectory partitions and n denotes the number of characteristic points (m = n-1)}. The optimal partitioning of a trajectory is achieved by two contradictory properties, preciseness and conciseness. Preciseness refers to the minimization of the difference between a trajectory and a set of its trajectory partitions, whereas conciseness refers to the minimization of the number of trajectory partitions. The optimal trade-off between preciseness and conciseness is approximated based on the minimum description length (MDL) principle.

2. *Clustering sub-trajectories*:
    For each trajectory partition, we obtain multi-dimensional vectors to characterize the partition trajectory. The vector values include total distance (x-y axes), distance between start and end nodes (x-y axes), total distance (z axis), and time duration. Based on normalized values of these vectors, we run the k-mean cluster analysis (group average method). A number of clusters K for each role was determined such that IGRC, Information Gain Ratio for Clustering [8], was maximized.

$$IGRC(K) = \frac{Ent(C) - \sum_{k=1}^{K} \frac{|C_k|}{|C|} Ent(C_k)}{-\sum_{k=1}^{K} \frac{|C_k|}{|C|} \log_2 \frac{|C_k|}{|C|}},$$

where $Ent(C)$ is a base entropy (no clustering), $Ent(C_k)$ is an entropy for cluster k, $|C|$ is a number of all sub-trajectory, $|C_k|$ is a number of sub-trajectories assigned as cluster k. $Ent(C_k)$ is calculated as follows.

$$Ent(C_k) = \frac{-\sum_{i=1}^{|C_k|} \sum_{j=1}^{|C_k|} (S_{ij} \log_2 S_{ij} + (1 - S_{ij}) \log_2 (1 - S_{ij}))}{|C_k|^2}.$$

S_{ij} is a similarity between sub-trajectory i's feature vector and sub-trajectory j's vector.

$$S_{ij} = \frac{\sum_{m=1}^{M} \left(1 - \frac{a_{im} - a_{jm}}{\max a_m - \min a_m} \right)}{M}.$$

a_{im} is a value of m-th dimension in sub-trajectory i's feature, $\max a_m$ is a maximum value of m-th dimension among all sub-trajectories, $\min a_m$ is a minimum value, and M is a number of dimensions of the feature vectors.

3.2 Extracted Trajectory Clusters

Using our method, we analyzed 10 cases' trajectory data for each role (surgeons, anesthetists, scrub nurses, and circulating nurses). As a result, moving patterns relevant to characteristic work were obtained. Fig. 4 shows trajectory clusters for circulating nurses. The upper figure shows the occurrence of 10 clusters through time. The bar chart on top of the figure is the reference of surgical workflow segmentation based on the direct observation. Images on the bottom exhibits trajectories associated with their cluster ID.

Trajectories in cluster 1 have large vertical movement and medium horizontal movement. For example, this moving pattern is related to line arrangement under surgical bed and checking values on medical devise under surgical bed & surgical table. Trajectories in cluster 7 have large vertical movement and large horizontal movement. This pattern represents the circulating nurse behaviour to bring surgical instruments for MRI process stored in a shelf in the operating room.

3.3 Workflow Estimation Using Trajectory Data

It is important that it is common in an advancing situation by an operation entire team also including the remote staff that is in front of a strategic desk. The method of estimating the current operation stage from the trajectory data was developed. We used the trajectory data because specific clusters tended to appear before transition of stages, as illustrated in Fig. 4.

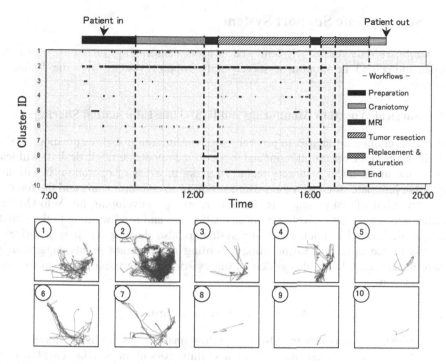

Fig. 4. Results of trajectory data mining for circulating nurses (K=10). Appearance patterns (above) and sample trajectories of each cluster (below).

First, trajectories of each role in the latest 5 minutes are classified into trajectory clusters that are extracted from trajectory data in past operations using our trajectory clustering method in Section 3.1. Next, total duration (sec) of sub-trajectory assigned as each cluster in the latest 5 minutes is calculated. We estimated a current stage by decision tree algorithm J48 [9] with these duration data of all clusters of all roles and elapsed time. Using trajectory data in the 10 operations in Section 2.1, we tested the decision tree by 10-folds cross validation. Table 2 shows results of the test. In 77.18% of total time, a kind of current operation stage could be correctly estimated. With high accuracy 85.96%, the estimation using trajectory data was able to distinguish whether a current 5 minutes was transition time from one stage to another stage or not.

Table 2. Percentages of correctly estimated time in 10 opearions. Estimation of stages' kinds (left) and whether transion or not (right).

	Stage (%)	Transition (%)
Average	77.18	85.96
Standard deviation	6.77	4.34
Max	87.96	91.82
Min	64.77	77.97

4   Surgery Safe Support System

By Surgical Management System and sensor data-mining technology, we are implementing and developing a surgery safe support system with the following functions.

4.1   Surgical Workflow Monitoring and Real-Time Information Sharing

We are developing a function to present various information such as position data on both displays in the operation room and those on the remote strategic desk. It will lead that all the members of a surgery team can grasp progress of operation. It will also support appropriate work with the sufficient timing as an entire team, and the forecast and prevention of risky situations. Moreover, we are developing an Auto-On-Call system, which automatically detect unusual situations and send warning to the remote strategic desk. And a quick reviewing system is also developing. It summarizes a progress of the operation to this time according to important points suggested by sensor data mining. Using this system, a supervisor can determine degree of risk in a risky situation.

4.2   Surgical Workflow Analysis and Standardization

Not only real-time supports but also a workflow analysis system using stored data is under development. Information about a certain patient or similar cases can be retrieved by this system. This information can support decision of staffs about arrangement of required equipments and staffs efficiently. Moreover, the function of an automatic workflow segmentation system by the above-mentioned trajectory data mining is under development. By accumulating operation data with workflow segmentation, standard duration of each operation stage can be extracted under various conditions. The standardization of workflow can help extraction of special knowledge and know-how about operations. And it also supports detection of unusual cases and potential sources of risks by examination of cases deviated from a standard case.

5   Conclusion

In this study, we have introduced an ultrasonic location aware system to monitor intraoperative movement trajectories on surgical staffs for the workflow analysis. And we developed trajectory data mining for surgical workflow segmentation, and analyzed trajectory data with multiple cases. As a result, the MDL approach is the best to correctly segment an entire surgery into intermediate workflows. Based on these results, we are implementing the surgery safe support system that promotes safe & efficient surgical operations. At the same time, we are developing a method to merge position information with other information such as videos available at the Surgical Management System. By the integration of various types of information, we aim to support feed-forward controlled operation management.

Acknowledgments. This research was partially funded by NEDO (New Energy and Industrial Technology Development Organization) through the Intelligent Surgical Instruments Project. And this research was partially supported by PRESTO, JST. We thank for Dr. Takashi Maruyama, Dr. Masahiko Tanaka, and other staffs of the Tokyo Women's Medical University for participating in data collection.

References

1. Bhatia, B., Oates, T., Xiao, Y., Hu, P.: Real-time identification of operating room state from video. In: Proceedings of Innovative Applications of Artificial Intelligence, pp. 1761–1766 (2007)
2. Cleary, K., Chung, H.Y., Mun, S.K.: OR 2020: The operating room of the future. Laparoendoscopic and Advanced Surgical Techniques 15(5), 295–500 (2005)
3. Fischler, M.A., Bolles, R.C.: Random sample consensus: A paradigm for model fitting with applications to image analysis and automated cartography. Communications of the ACM 24(6), 381–395 (1981)
4. Lee, J.-G., Han, J., Whang, K.-Y.: Trajectory clustering: A partition-and-group framework. In: Proceedings of the 2007 ACM SIGMOD International Conference on Management of Data, pp. 593–604 (2007)
5. Nambu, K., Iseki, H.: Surgical Strategic Desk and Surgical Safety Support System. Japanese Society for Medical and Biological Engineering 44(2), 257–264 (2001)
6. Ohnuma, K., Masamune, K., Yoshimitsu, K., Sadahiro, T., Vain, J., Fukui, Y., Miyazaki, F.: Timed-automata-based model for laparoscopic surgery and intraoperative motion recognition of a surgeon as the interface connecting the surgical and the real operating room. International Journal of Computer Assisted Radiology and Surgery 1, 442–445 (2006)
7. Padoy, N., Blum, T., Essa, I., Feussner, H., Berger, M.-O., Navab, N.: A boosted segmentation method for surgical workflow analysis. In: Proceedings of Medical Image Computing and Computer-Assisted Intervention, pp. 102–109 (2007)
8. Shoda, R., Matsuda, T., Yoshida, T., Motoda, H., Washio, T.: Graph Clustering with Structure Similarity. In: Proceedings of the 17th Annual Conference of the Japanese Society for Artificial Intelligence (2003) (in Japanese)
9. Witten, I., Frank, E.: Data Mining: Practical Machine Learning Tools and Techniques, 2nd edn. Morgan Kaufmann, San Francisco (2005)
10. Xiao, Y., Hu, P., Hu, H., Ho, D., Dexter, F., Mackenzie, C.F., Seagull, F.J., Dutton, R.P.: An algorithm for processing vital sign monitoring data to remotely identify operating room occupancy in real-time. Anesthesia and Analgesia 101(3), 823–829 (2005)

Discover the Used Innovativeness of the Early Adopters

Chao-Fu Hong[1], Chien-Jen Huang[1], Tzu-Fu Chiu[2],
Hsiao-Fang Yang[3], and Mu-Hua Lin[3]

[1] Department of Information Management
[2] Department of Industrial Management and Enterprise Information,
Aletheia University, No.32, Zhenli St., Danshui Dist., New Taipei City 251, Taiwan R.O.C.
{au4076,norman,chiu}@mail.au.edu.tw
[3] Department of Management Information Systems, National Chengchi University,
No.64, Sec. 2, Zhinan Rd., Wenshan Dist., Taipei City 116, Taiwan R.O.C.
{hfyang.wang,kikalin}@gmail.com

Abstract. From the innovative diffusion theory, it is known that the early adopters have the characteristic of being liable to accept new products and generate new value from using new products. Through their social networks, they also transmit information about new products to the early majority. Moreover, from the use and gratification theory, if a new product provides users with usability of information, social value or entertainment, it is likely that this new product will be accepted because users' physical/mental need is fulfilled. Based on the above two principles, this study thereby develop a Human-Computing Grounded System. Expert first divides data as technical specification or value induced by early adopters, grounded theory analysis is then performed interactively. Results in this study indicate the new value induced by early adopters using new products which supported by new technology embedded in the new product. Meanwhile, inferred from the use and gratification theory, it is easier for the majority to accept a new product if this product offers more new values. By integrating multi-type of values conceived by the early adopters, our research model shows that indeed products with more and new values attract more majority.

Keywords: Innovation Diffusion, Chasm, Qualitative Chance Discovery, Rare Associative Analysis.

1 Introduction

In today's fast shifting business world, when to push a product into the market and which product to be promoted is always a critical problem to all companies, a tough decision but every company has to face it from time to time to survive in the competing business environment. It is thus an important research issue, to analyze and understand the future trend of a line of upcoming products.

Moreover, whether it is the chasm [7] caused by consumers' different characters or the percolating vulnerable cluster of early adopters proposed by Duncan [10], they all indicate that to cross the chasm, product characteristics and early adopters'

T. Onoda, D. Bekki, and E. McCready (Eds.): JSAI-isAI 2010, LNAI 6797, pp. 292–301, 2011.

percolating vulnerable cluster are all important to the product diffusing effect in the consumer market. But previous studies did not stress the search of the percolating vulnerable cluster (early adopters); thereby, this research tries to analyze the traits of early adopters, which in turn help judging the maturity of new product for the enterprise in searching for the right timing to enter the market.

To show the feasibility of this research, the technical function of the innovative netbook is selected and the user of netbook's marketing time is set to be the early adopters. The key word "experience in netbook" is then entered into Google blog to search for related articles. These articles present the feelings and criticisms of the early consumers about their netbooks. New functions and new values derived from the product are also criticized by these users. Behavior model of the early adopters can be constructed from this type of articles; furthermore, multiple life styles conveyed from the new functions are also found in these articles. Using this concept, early adopters can be divided into different groups. From the discrepancies between different groups, behavior consistency can be recognized among the early adopters. More consistent behavior indicates emerging percolating vulnerable cluster is noticeable and hence, more likely to cross the chasm.

2   Literature Review

2.1   Percolating Vulnerable Cluster

In his Small World concept [10], he mentioned that the percolating vulnerable cluster (early adopters) decides the global cascades. When the percolating vulnerable cluster locates in an environment where nodes have high connectivity but have high transmitting threshold, information fast forecasts to large area because each node has high connectivity. But high transmitting threshold actually restricts the diffusion to local area. On the contrary, in low connectivity and low transmitting threshold environment, the percolating vulnerable cluster diffuses slowly initially, but the low transmitting threshold actually helps the diffusion process and improves connectivity. Once the node connectivity passes certain threshold, diffusion of global cascades is likely to occur.

The above section describes how to find the percolating vulnerable cluster (early adopters) and activate global cascades, an important factor in crossing chasm. But one important issue in this topic, how to search for the percolating vulnerable cluster in the real world, is still overlooked. In the following section, the possibility of searching for early adopters using data mining technique is explored.

2.2   Behavior Analysis: Weak Tied Cluster and Strong Tied Cluster

Holak proposed a new product adoption model to categorize the users according to their consuming traits, where innovators and early adopters form one group; early majority and late majority form another group [3]. Studying the consuming behavior of these two groups, he found both the function of the new product and the consuming habit would affect consumer's decision. People in the first group are willing to take chances and enjoy new experience; on the other hand, people in the second group accept new product mostly because their friends already do so. This phenomenon matches the chasm concept proposed in tornado by Moore [7]. In other words, in between early adopters and early majority, there is a big gap called chasm causing delay or interruption of diffusion, which is illustrated in figure one followed. He also pointed out not all new products can cross the chasm; this means it is crucial that early adopters have a special view about the new product. If early adopters hold same attitude, then they can influence many people to form early majority, and the chasm is crossed. Based on this principle, to obtain behavior rule among different objective groups, we have to divide data into different groups and expect to get behavior rules from different data groups. The following section discusses cluster analysis method using data mining.

Strong tied cluster, after data has been collected, data mining technique such as Apriori algorithm is then applied [1]. Apriori algorithm is a well-known algorithm for mining the association rules from a transactional database, which satisfies the minimum support and confidence levels specified by users. Using this algorithm, the extracted association rules can represent the meaningful customers' behaviors. Since association rules are useful and easily understood, there have been many successful business applications, including finance, telecommunication, marketing, and retailing so on. But from the experiment result [3], we find that some scarce data actually come from groups with innovative adventure nature, and they could create new fashion in the future. Their consuming behavior data is thus important. But their consuming behavior data would be neglected because traditional association rules mining uses higher support to filter out noise, and treats the lower support items as noise, thus, unable to analyze the future trend of the weak tied cluster.

Weak tied cluster, consider the association mining problem where we need to determine if there is an association between buying a food processor and buying a cooking pan [6]. The problem is that both items are rarely purchased in a supermarket. Thus, even if the two items are almost always purchased together, the association may not be found. It seems that the rare association data mining has a lower support but higher confidence searching method; therefore, the problem is solvable.

From the above discussion we can see that Data Mining and Rare Association Analysis are similar in terms of analysis method, but they differ on the definition of the threshold value of support level and confidence level. This discrepancy makes them search for different objects. For locking on rare innovative data, Rare Association Analysis may be able to process data of any purpose, but it lacks the flexibility which helps expert to find rare but interesting data for further analysis. This article applies grounded theory to help solve this problem.

2.3   Grounded Theory

Strauss and Corbin think the grounded theory is built from data [9], but the essence of grounded theory is a strategy to value innovative idea besides analytical skills. In grounded theory, innovative idea plays an important role in its research method per se, but its actual power dwells in the following: a researcher conceptualizes collected data and names it during preprocess the researcher then conceives of some problems worth thinking freely. Using the data analysis technique built in grounded theory consisting of the elements of open coding, axial coding and selective coding, we conceptualize the raw data, and accordingly, categorized and interesting scenario are gradually formed. At the final stage, by cross examination and verification with original data, new order established from old data and new theory is firmly set up.

We believe that grounded theory can be used to integrate the concept of Rare Association Analysis to construct a human-computing grounded system. This system not only helps the expert focus on finding the early adopters of new technology and scarce concept, but also releases his pressure of data processing and concentrate on the timing research of chasm crossing.

3 Methodology: Discover Global Cascade of Percolating Vulnerable Cluster

Roger's innovation diffusion model divides population into five groups according to their timing of accepting new innovation [8]. Additionally, small world experiment also explains how the early adopters transmitting information through social networks to affect early majority. Concluding the above discussion, we propose an innovative diffusion model to integrate these two concepts as shown in the following graph. This model illustrates how the early adopters transmit information through social networks and how new products cross chasm. But as pointed in the small world experiment, mutual consensus of the early adopters is an important indicator if the chasm is to be crossed. The higher the value is, the easier the chasm will be crossed.

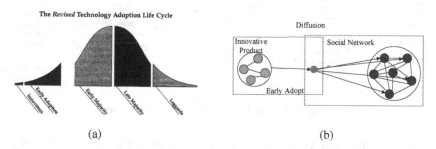

The *Revised* Technology Adoption Life Cycle

Innovators Early Adopters Early Majority Late Majority Laggards

Diffusion

Innovative Product

Social Network

Early Adopt

(a)   (b)

Fig. 1. (a)Chasm between early adopters and early majority, (b) Social network of early adopter

Although previous research shows good result in explaining how to cross the chasm, they did not explain how to search for the percolating vulnerable cluster. From Technology Acceptance Model's experiment (TAM) [2] we can see that the acceptance of the majority depends on two factors: 1. Can the new product improve work efficiency or save time? 2. Is the new product user friendly? We hereby present the following system to discover traits of the early adopters (percolating vulnerable cluster).

4   Human-Computing Grounded System and Case Study

4.1   New and Rare Data

In year 2007, manufacturer in Taiwan presented an innovative concept of notebook computers: netbook computers. From year 2008 to year 2009, the sale volume of netbook computers rise from 7% to 14% of total netbook computers, increasing by twofold. In fact, netbook computers have gained focus worldwide under the effect of financial tsunami. How can they get consumers' attention in such a short time? After we examine the specification of the ASUS netbook EeePC901, we find the followings: low power consumption Intel Atom N270 CPU, WLAN: 802.11n Bluetooth, resolution 1.3 mega, Dolby sound effect, shockproof SSD and 8 hour battery. To make ASUS EeePC901 more shining and eye grasping, Asus even provide six bright colors and four kinds of decorative pattern. All of this information indicates that after June 1, 2008, besides serving its practical purpose, netbook computer has reached the state of art in computer technology.

Therefore, ASUS EeePC901 is regarded as an innovative product in this research. Because ASUS is a Taiwan base company, the subject early adopters is restricted to Taiwan area. To give users enough time to appreciate this new product, data is collected from blog listed by Google in the time frame October 1, 2008 to December 31, 2008, four months after the marketing time of EeePC901. After entering the key word "experience in netbook" into Google, 63 articles are collected and 7 of them are accepted as related articles after being scrutinized by experts.

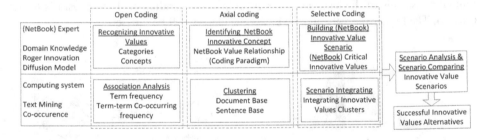

Fig. 2. Human-Computing Grounded System

4.2   Converting New Technical Function to Useful and Easy Using Life Style: Human-Computing Grounded System

In order to search for interesting innovative diffusion trends, expert accords to the innovation diffusion model to discover the created innovative value of new products by early adopters, and invests them into how to use their social networks to transmit the innovative value and new product to the early majority for consolidating their social position. In this study, we propose a human-computing grounded system, it includes two parts; one is the human (expert) and computing [4]. A system based on the expert's domain knowledge and innovation diffusion model integrates the grounded theory and computing technology, as shown in Fig. 2.

Phase 1: Open Coding

The netbook computer is a product of technology. Expert applying the usability and easy-to-use of TAM model [2] to analyze if increasing work performance or saving time can help users in accepting new technology. But how to evaluate the value or usability brought by the new product? To answer this question, Expert studies how the early adopters create innovative value by using new technology concept (portability and wireless network). Through the conversion from new technology to new value, early adopters transmit the new product and innovative value to the majority for their acceptance of the new product as well as innovative value.

1h) Defining research domain and related keywords: "Experience in netbook" is designated by experts as keywords, and time frame is set to be 2008/10/1~2008/12/31.

1c) Data searching: Google blog is used to search for related articles. As a result, 63 articles obtained.

2h) Word separation and concept analysis: After reading the content of these articles, 7 articles are regarded by the expert as related articles and proceeded to article coding stage. Next, after examining sentences closely, expert must sift out meaningful terms. He then conceives the concept embedded in each term and defines the name for each concept. Based on the meaning of a concept, a term is set to be part of a concept if its meaning is related to the concept. Afterwards, the concept is inserted as part of the term. New value in this research is actually created by the early adopters after they have used new products. So, just as Value Focused Thinking [5] where new service value is generated by focusing on new functions of a new product, we separate users' experience to two concepts: 1. The functionality of a new product 2. The new value derived from a new product.

2c) Computing term frequency and associative value

$$assoc(W_i, W_j) = \sum_{s \in D} \min\left(\left|W_i\right|_s, \left|W_j\right|_s\right)$$
(1)

Where i and j denote the ith term and jth term, s is a sentence in all documents (D).

3c) Visualizing document data: Associative analysis is used to generate associative graph.

3h) Category analysis: In the previous stage, different concepts among the early adopters are sorted out as: 1. functionality of a new product, 2. new value derived from a new product. The associative map is divided according to different concepts as: the upper half stands for new value concept and the lower half stands for new function concept. This kind of division helps expert find out interesting category condition of the early adopters, concept of real time movement: technical slick outlook and portability (i.e. light, thin, small, easy to use, pretty outlook, etc.) and wireless network capability. With the realization of this concept, the early adopters can do the followings: text creative work at anytime and anyplace, entertainment by oneself or with friends, wireless network capability with the help of blue tooth and cell phone. With the above functions, the early adopters can discuss and share information with classmates or coworkers anytime and anyplace.

4h) Concept of different categories: Helped by the above stimulation, experts begin to realize the association among mobility, real-time and multiple life styles. Experts also realize that new life styles have emerged within the early adopters and expect to find them out, life style(s) that will affect or even change the social life style of the majority.

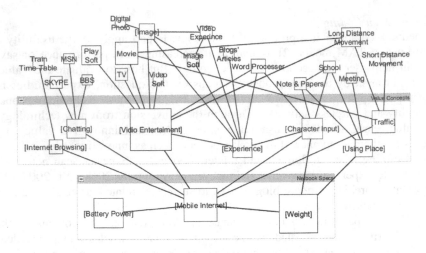

Fig. 3. Open coding

Phase 2: Axial Coding

The subject in this research, netbook computer, is a product of technology. Expert applied the usability and easy-to-use of TAM model to analyze if increasing work performance or saving time can help users in accepting new technology. But how to evaluate the value or usability brought by the new product? To answer this question, we study how the early adopters create high value (valuable output) by using new technology concept (portability and wireless network.) Through the conversion from new technology to new value, the analysis if majority accept the new technology is thus applicable. We collect data of the early adopters, new and scarce data, and attempt to construct its value. The process of the analysis is described as follows:

5h) Defining concept of axial partition: from portability and wireless network, the expert recognizes the concept of real time movement, as shown in Fig. 3, which shows that more creative or innovative daily values are generated, such as long distance movement, chatting, etc.

4c) Axial computing: We compute from the first innovative value (long distance movement) to the last innovative value (accessing web page), and then stop.

6h) Define keyword of coding paradigm: Expert decides the key word set of the new event and related words of the new product.

5c) Collecting valid sentence: Based on the definition of new event, system searches all information in the database. If a sentence contains a word related to a new event, it will be collected in the data set of that new event.

6c) Association analysis: The associative value of two terms is computed based on their co-occurrence in the same sentence as Eq. (2):

$$assoc(W_i, W_j) = \sum_{s \in vss} \min\left(\left.|W_i|\right._s, \left.|W_j|\right._s\right) \tag{2}$$

Where i and j denote the ith term and jth term, s is a sentence in the valid sentences set (*vss*).

7c) Information visualization: A line is drawn between two terms if they are associated. The scenario graph of an innovative product is thus generated, then go to 4c.

From Fig. 3, experts realize netbook computers have special functions of real time communication and portability. Comparing with traditional notebook computers, the early adopters of netbook computers have more innovative performance in mobile information, entertainment and social communication. Besides, from long distance movement, experts also see the need of real time scenario, so long distance movement is set to be the core concept and related document/sentence is selected. Figure two shows the category of long distance movement using associative analysis. Some interesting netbook applications have drawn researchers' attention such as real time social talk, real time mind writing and real time web page browsing. According to the above procedure, real time axial chart is constructed shown as Fig. 4.

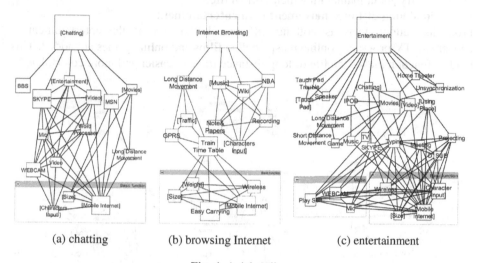

| (a) chatting | (b) browsing Internet | (c) entertainment |

Fig. 4. Axial coding

Phase 3: Selective Coding

In phase 2, expert recognizes how the early adopters use the netbook's portability and wireless Internet access to create their daily innovative value. After analysis, expert focuses on long distance movement, such as the travel, and then he tries to integrate some of the all innovative values into a bigger innovative value. For example, treating long distance movement as a core category, expert further explores the entertaining, social and informative scenarios of the early adopters.

7h) Constructing storyline: Storyline is constructed according to the need in real life long distance movement. Sentences are gradually gathered together to form the pleasant life scenario of netbook applications. These sentences contain information about entertaining, social and informative applications of netbook computer. The process is as follows:

8c) Collecting valid sentence: Accumulate all valid sentences to form valid sentence set.

9c) Scenario construction: Building a meaningful scenario association map.

Scenario comparing

Using the above analytical procedure, experts construct three story scenarios: long distance movement with chatting, long distance movement with web page access and long distance movement with entertainment. They are described as follows:

Scenario of long distance movement with chatting

From its outlook there is nothing different, but more tools such as Skype, BBS are added. Meanwhile, webcam and microphone are treated as standard equipment. Actually, Skype alone can provide online phone or video phone, the communication capability is enhanced largely. The users of netbook computers always can reach out and touch someone no matter where they are.

Scenario of long distance movement with web page access

From its outlook there is nothing different, but web page browsing capability enables the users gets real time information no matter where on earth they travel. They never have to worry about maintaining their normal life.

Scenario of long distance movement with entertainment

From its outlook there is nothing different, but as far as the entertainment is concerned, TV programs, online music, online films and online games are added. This kind of function makes the life of long-distance traveler easier and more colorful.

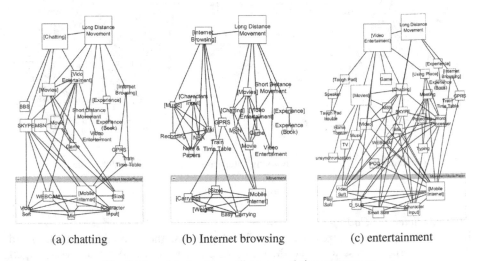

(a) chatting   (b) Internet browsing   (c) entertainment

Fig. 5. Three kinds of long-distance real-time movement

Previous summary discussing results represents that our human-computing grounded system is a useful system. For even during travelling, the customers can communicate real time with their family and friends to share their travel life just as they do at home. Of course, he can enjoy the videos and audios entertainment to forget lonely travel, too. Finally, when meeting the unexpected event, they can real time and easily change their travel program by accessing the train time table.

5   Conclusion

In this research, a Human-Computing Grounded System has been proposed. Case study has been performed to verify the feasibility of this model. Given that evidence that the early adopters are liable to accepting new products, this research intends to observe how they use social networks to cross chasm and transmit new value to the early majority. Applying the grounded theory, this research gathers new value information that is social, entertaining, or informative, and expects to fulfill the physical, mental or social need of the early majority. A Human-Computing Grounded System is used to analyze the early adopters' netbook experiences, some useful innovation applications have emerged. In the study of new value, three practical long distance real-time movement scenarios have been discussed: chatting, Internet browsing and entertainment. Results in this research show that the new value integrated from the experience of different types of early adopters is more complete and valuable. If this new value is to be diffused by the early adopters' social networks, it is more likely that the early majority accept the new product under public praise. In the future, case studies of different types of innovative products are to be performed to verify this model.

Acknowledgment

This research have been supported by National Science Council of Taiwan, ROC (NSC 99-2632-H-156 -001 –MY3).

References

1. Agrawal, R., Imielinski, T., Swami, A.N.: Mining Association Rules between Sets of Items in Large Databases. In: SIGMOD Conference, pp. 207–216 (1993)
2. Davis, F.D.: Preceived Usefulness, Perceived Ease of Use, and User Acceptance of Information Technology. MIQ Quarterly 13(3), 319–340 (1989)
3. Holak, S.L.: Determinants of Innovative Durables Adoption an Empirical Study with Implications for Early Product Screening. Journal of Product Innovation Management 5, 50–69 (1988)
4. Hong, C.F.: Qualitative Chance Discovery - Extracting Competitive Advantages. Information Sciences 179(11), 1570–1583 (2009)
5. Keeney, R.L.: Value-Focused Thinking: A Path to Creative Decisionmaking. Harvard University Press, Cambridge (1992)
6. Liu, B., Hsu, W., Ma, Y.: Mining Association Rules with Multiple Minimum Supports. In: Proceedings of the 1999 International Conference on Knowledge Discovery and Data Mining, pp. 337–341 (1999)
7. Moore, G.A.: Crossing the Chasm: Marketing and Selling Technology Products to Mainstream Customers. Harpercollins, New York (1991)
8. Rogers, E.M.: Diffusion of Innovations. Free Press, New York (1995)
9. Strauss, A.C., Corbin, J.M.: Basics of Qualitative Research: Techniques and Procedures for Developing Grounded Theory. Sage Publications, Inc., Thousand Oaks (1990)
10. Watts, D.J.: A Simple Model of Global Cascades on Random Networks. Proceedings of the National Academy of Sciences of the United States of America 99(9), 5766–5771 (2002)

Early Diagnosis Service for Latent Patients of Incurable Diseases

Yoko Nishihara[1], Yoshimune Hiratsuka[2], Akira Murakami[3], and Toshiro Kumakawa[2]

[1] Department of Systems Innovation, School of Engineering, The University of Tokyo,
7-3-1, Hongo, Bunkyo, Tokyo 113-8656, Japan
nishihara@sys.t.u-tokyo.ac.jp
[2] Department of Management Science, National Institute of Public Health,
2-3-6, Minami, Wako, Saitama 351-0197, Japan
[3] Department of Ophthalmology, Juntendo University, School of Medicine,
2-1-1, Hongo, Bunkyo, Tokyo 113-8421, Japan

Abstract. It is considered that many people are struggling with diseases that are difficult to cure. In general, it takes a long time to diagnose and to cure such diseases. In Japan, methods for curing 56 incurable diseases have been studied. However, methods for early diagnosis of incurable diseases have not been studied. To make early diagnoses for incurable diseases improves the quality of life of patients. This paper proposes a new service system that supports latent patients of incurable diseases by early diagnosis. For using this system, users have to prepare a text in which episodes about patients' experiences that have been caused because of their diseases are written. The system takes such a text as input, and then the system extracts common factors among episodes, i.e., keywords appearing in several episodes. The system output the extracted keywords as keywords relating to symptoms of an incurable disease. We experimented the system and extracted keywords relating to the symptoms of retinitis pigmentosa which was one of the incurable eye diseases. Most of the symptoms relating to the extracted keywords were not known even by medical doctors. Some of them indicated symptoms in the early stage of the disease. The experiment brought us one step closer to the early diagnosis of incurable disease as one of the service systems.

Keywords: service system of early diagnosis, incurable diseases, keyword relating to a symptom of incurable disease.

1 Introduction

There are many people who are struggling with diseases that are difficult to cure. According to the United Nations, at least four million people worldwide are suffering from Parkinson's disease [1]. In general, it takes a long time to diagnose and to cure such diseases. In Japan, methods for curing 56 incurable diseases have been studied [2]. However, methods for early diagnosis for such incurable diseases have not been studied.

T. Onoda, D. Bekki, and E. McCready (Eds.): JSAI-isAI 2010, LNAI 6797, pp. 302–310, 2011.
© Springer-Verlag Berlin Heidelberg 2011

For general curable diseases, IBM and Mayo Clinic have studied a method for early detection of aneurysm in the brain [3]. The system uses a plenty amount of data sets collected at hospital, Mayo Clinic, and identifies the presence of a disease by pattern recognition of images. Medical doctors usually discover aneurysm in the brain by seeing brain images of patients obtained by MRI. Though the accuracy of the detection has been about 70% by visual check by a medical doctor, the system proposed by IBM can detect aneurysm in the brain with the accuracy of about 85%.

Other methods also use a plenty amount of data for detecting diseases by matching patient's data to each data in their databases[8, 9]. However, people can not detect any incurable diseases by using the system because they do not have enough data sets of incurable diseases to make diagnoses. They need another new system that can detect the presence of incurable disease even if they have only few data sets.

Previous investigations on information science have proposed many data mining methods. Some of the methods can extract rare but important data from huge data sets. For example, Yamanishi, et al. has proposed a method for detecting invasions in large database system [4]. This method can extract important events for decision making in a various communications. However, even medical doctors may not discover significant data from large data sets by using these methods, because a plenty amount of noisy data is included in the sets. Therefore, new methods for extracting useful data from noisy data are required.

This paper proposes a new system that supports latent patients of incurable diseases by early diagnosis. For using this system, users have to prepare a text in which episodes about patients' experiences that have been caused by their diseases are written. The system takes such a text as input, and then the system extracts common factors among episodes, i.e., keywords appearing in several episodes. The system output the extracted keywords as keywords relating to symptoms of the incurable disease. People may be able to obtain keywords relating to symptoms in the very early stage of incurable disease by using the system.

1.2   Framework of the Proposed System as a Service System

This section instructs you the framework of the proposed system and how to use the system as one of the service systems (shown in Figure 1). The stakeholders in this system are latent patients (including their families), medical doctors, and researchers who try to list up symptoms of incurable diseases. The researchers extract symptoms of incurable diseases from patients' episodes to make checklists for identifying the presence of incurable disease. The lists are released on the Web. The latent patients download the lists to check them up by themselves. If a latent patient discovers a symptom which matches his/her own symptom, the patient will go to an appropriate hospital for obtaining a diagnosis by a medical doctor. In this way, the early diagnosis of incurable disease will be realized.

The system realizes not only the alleviation of mental burden of patient, but also the alleviation of body burden of medical doctor because he/she does not need to see inadequate patients.

This service system allows stakeholders to revise the checklist on the Web when new information from patients is obtained. If a patient looking at the checklist finds matched symptom to his/her own symptom, he/she goes to hospital for obtaining his/her diagnosis. Medical doctors at hospital question their patients about their symptom and histories. If new information is obtained from the questions, researchers in the service system can use the information for updating the checklists to a better one. The checklist made from a little amount of data can get chances for becoming a better one by being released to the public on the Web. Such service systems are often seen on the Web. For example, Wikipedia known as an encyclopedia/thesaurus at free has a service style in which individuals can revise information for providing better information to the public.

The proposed system may be one of the service systems defined in a previous study [7]. The service system can not earn financial benefit explicitly for the real society. This is the different point from general service systems. General service systems such as customer service, room service at hotel, and delivery service request compensation for using their services. Requesting compensation enables to flow money in the society. However, the use of the service system enables to reduce wasteful spending. If latent patients use the service system, they easily recognize which hospital they have to go. Speedy decision for choosing hospitals reduces transportation cost and therapy cost in wandering many hospitals. Medical doctors also obtain benefits. If latent patients go to appropriate hospitals, medical doctors are asked to see limited patients who are the targets for them.

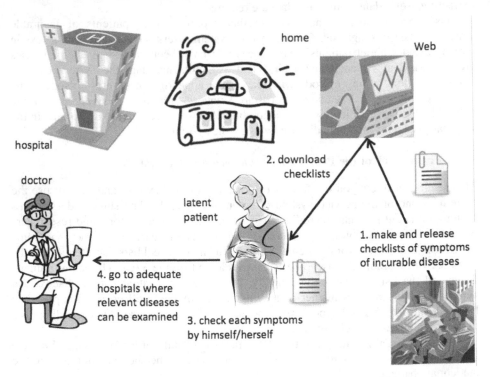

Fig. 1. The outline of the proposed system as one of the service systems. The stakeholders are latent patients (including their families), researchers, and medical doctors. When new information about symptom is obtained from patients, researchers can revise the checklist at needed.

2   Proposed Method

We explain the proposed system (Figure 2). A user of the system prepares a text in which episodes about patients' experiences are included. Five examples are shown in Table 1. Then, a user input a text into the system to extract words appearing in several episodes as keywords relating to symptoms of incurable disease. The system uses the algorithm of KeyGraph®[1], which has been invented by Yukio Ohsawa, to extract keywords [5]. We can extract rare but important keywords from a text by using the algorithm of KeyGraph.

The relationships of words in a text are described as a graph by KeyGraph. Black nodes denote words of high frequency. Clusters of black nodes denote topics in a text. White nodes connecting clusters denote words which are rare but important in a text. In this research, the white nodes obtained from the algorithm of KeyGraph are the candidates of keywords relating to symptoms of an incurable disease that have been hidden in daily lives.

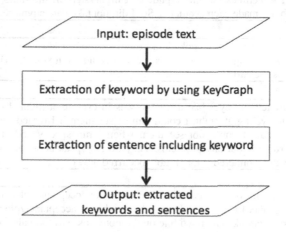

Fig. 2. Outline of the proposed method

2.1   Algorithm of KeyGraph

The algorithm of KeyGraph is very simple and versatile. The algorithm can extract keywords which are rare but important for decision making. The relationships of words in a text are described as a graph by using KeyGraph. In the graph, words of high frequency in a text are described as black nodes. Groups of black nodes connected by black edges are described as clusters. Words of low frequency connecting clusters are described as white nodes. Clusters can be considered as topics in a text.

By applying the algorithm to our research, we can understand the relationships of words in a text of episodes like as Figure 3. If we input a text in which episodes from patients are written into the algorithm of KeyGraph, words of high frequency are

---

[1] KeyGraph has been registered by Yukio Ohsawa in the University of Tokyo since 2011.

described as black nodes, episodes which are common among patients are described as clusters of black nodes, and words of low frequency connecting episodes are described as white nodes. The white nodes correspond to symptoms of an incurable disease.

In this research, we extract keywords evaluated as white nodes, and we also extract episodes including the extracted keywords from the input text. By using the extracted episodes, we make a checklist of incurable disease.

Table 1. A part of text in which episodes about patients' experiences are included. Five examples are shown. Original texts were written in Japanese. The authors translated them into English.

Example 1:
I could not see anything in the dark at three to four years old. For example, lights were not enough for illuminating streets because of the old day. Children could walk in the dark though I could not. I understood my ability of eye-sight. I always took a seat at the 3rd line in front of the black board in a classroom. After obtaining my employment, I sometimes fell into a puddle at night, step off the stairs, and so on. I think my attributes made such accidents. So, I did not take care anymore.
Example 2:
In studying, I always read textbooks in a little dark room. I always used a desk light whose power was stronger than my sister's one. I could see textbooks. However I felt it was hard too see clearly.
Example 3:
The first time I felt my eyes had a trouble was in cycling at night. I could not see street gutters in cycling at night. I could almost see them if I turned light of bicycle into the gutter side. I could not see them when I run speedy and straight. Other friends could run without any problems. They do not speak about any troubles such as I experienced. I wondered if the trouble occurred only on me.
Example 4:
When I was on business about counting the number of acceptance/placement orders, I made a fatal mistake. In counting, I input the number of acceptance/placement orders in each cell on notebook. The ruled line on the notebook was too pale for me. I could not follow the same ruled line. As a result, I input numbers in non-appropriate cells. In that case, I felt my eyes might has some troubles.
Example 5:
In my high school ages, I have experienced many times to crush into lower bushes. I could not understand why I could not see such bushes. In my junior high school ages, I have sometimes step off the stairs.

3   Evaluation

We experimented the proposed system and verified whether the proposed system worked efficiently or not.

3.1   Experimental Procedures

We prepared a text about episodes of patients. Then we extracted keywords from the text by using the proposed system. We extracted 75 words as black nodes, and 30 words as white nodes at maximum.

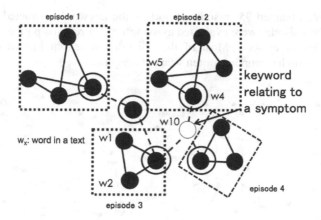

Fig. 3. Application of the algorithm of KeyGraph to our research

We focused on one of the incurable diseases, retinitis pigmentosa. This disease is an inherited eye disease. One of the 3,000 to 4,000 people will get the disease in Japan. Night-blind and visual field loss are known as the main symptoms. Now, Japan has 23,000 patients of the disease (from the surveillance by Health, Labour and Welfare Ministry in 1990 [6]).

In this experiment, we asked five patients as subjects to give us episodes. We transcribed recorded voices to a text with unifying words and phrases.

Evaluation was done with the help of an eye medical doctor. We asked the medical doctor to see episodes including keywords extracted as white nodes, and to evaluate whether or not each episode showed a symptom of retinitis pigmentosa. We counted the number of keywords and the number of episodes which were judged as symptoms of retinitis pigmentosa.

Table 2. Extracted keywords relating to the symptoms of retinitis pigmentosa. Keywords written in italic style were evaluated as the keywords relating to the symptoms of retinitis pigmentosa.

	Keyword
Verb	*step off*, go, connect, give, accept, touch, end
Noun	*consciousness*, police, license, *commute, bean, ruled line*, winter, *junior high school, parallel*, air conditioner, loss, *character*, individual, suction, *ball*
Adjective	strictly, *inappropriate, pale*, near
Adverb	surely, *at first*

3.2 Experimental Results

Figure 4 shows the relationships of words obtained by KeyGraph. Table 2 shows keywords which are shown as the white nodes in Figure 3. The 28 keywords were extracted as the white nodes. The 13 keywords written in italic style in Table 2 were evaluated as the keywords by the eye medical doctor relating to symptoms of retinitis pigmentosa. We obtained 95 episodes including the keywords extracted as the white nodes. 30 of the episodes were evaluated as symptoms of retinitis pigmentosa. Table 3 shows examples of episode. Most of the episodes were not known even by the medical doctor who has worked for ten years at hospital.

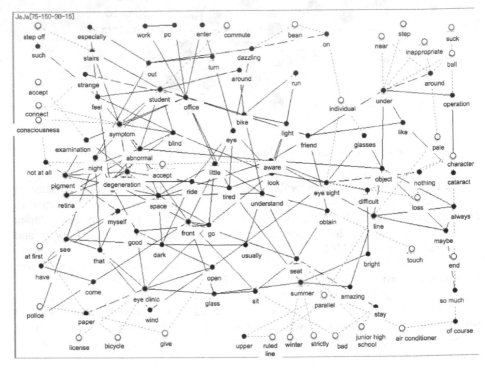

Fig. 4. The relationships of words obtained by KeyGraph. Five texts obtained from five patients were used for making the above graph. We used a text written in Japanese for the experiment. We translated Japanese keywords into English keywords by manually.

Table 3. Episode examples about the symptoms of retinitis pigmentosa

Keyword	Episode
Commute	- The patient could not see anything in commute to school by bicycle at night.
Step	- The patient step sucking tubes unawareness in lessons of surgical operation
	- The patient step objects on the floor unawareness.
Pale	- The ruled lines were too pale to see.
Ruled line	- The ruled lines were too pale to see.
	- The patient could not write characters on the ruled lines with parallel.
Parallel	- The patient could not write characters on the ruled lines with parallel.
	- The patient could not trace rows in tables with parallel.

4   Discussions

The 13 of 28 extracted keywords as the white nodes were judged as keywords relating to symptoms of retinitis pigmentosa by an eye medical doctor. From the result, we verified that the proposed system could extract keywords relating to symptoms of incurable disease.

Most of the episodes shown in Table 3 were related to patients' lives in schools and in offices. Especially, we obtained seven episodes about experiences in junior high school. This result indicates that patients have experienced a various symptoms before they recognized their diseases.

The episodes shown in Table 3 can be leveraged as a checklist of retinitis pigmentosa right now. For example, if a child always writes his/her notes leaning over a desk, he/she can not see ruled lines in a notebook. That is to say, his/her eye sights may be lost because of getting the disease. In this way, latent patients can be identified in the early stage of the disease.

The retinitis pigmentosa is a one of the inherited eye diseases. The developments of the disease, however, vary between individuals. Some of the patients have felt their symptoms in early childhood, and the others have felt them over 20 years old. We also obtained several symptoms in several ages shown in Table 3. This result indicates that we need to make several checklists by age.

5   Conclusion

This paper proposes a new service system for early diagnosis of incurable disease. To use this system, a user prepares a text in which episodes about patients' experiences that have been caused by their diseases are written. The system takes such a text as input, and then the system extracts common factors among episodes, i.e., keywords appearing in several episodes. The system output the extracted keywords as keywords relating to symptoms of the incurable disease. We experimented the system and extracted keywords relating to the symptoms of retinitis pigmentosa as one of the incurable diseases. The result verified that the proposed system could extract keywords relating to the symptom of retinitis pigmentosa. Most of the symptoms including the extracted keywords were not known even by a medical doctor. Moreover, some of them indicated symptoms in the early stage of the disease. The experiment brought us one step closer to the early diagnosis of incurable disease.

As the future work, we will make checklists for early diagnosis by clustering the obtained episodes by ages. We will also apply the proposed system to the other diseases.

References

1. Lozano, A.M., Kalia, S.K.: New Movement in Parkinson's. Scientific American 293, 68–75 (2005)
2. Japan Incurable Diseases Information Center, http://www.nanbyou.or.jp/
3. IBM Press room,
   http://www-03.ibm.com/press/us/en/pressrelease/29250.wss

310   Y. Nishihara et al.

4. Yamanishi, K., Takeuchi, J., Williamas, G., Milne, P.: On-line Unsupervised Outlier Detection Using Finite Mixtures with Discounting Learning Algorithms. Data Mining and Knowledge Discovery Journal 8(3), 275–300 (2004)
5. Ohsawa, Y., Benson, N.E., Yachida, M.: KeyGraph: Automatic Indexing by Co-occurrence Graph based on Building Construction Metaphor. In: Proceedings of the Advances in Digital Libraries Conference, pp. 12–18 (1998)
6. National Center for Biotechnology Information, http://www.ncbi.nlm.nih.gov
7. Karni, R., Kaner, M.: An engineering tool for the conceptual design of service systems. In: Spath, Fahnrich (eds.) Advances in Service Innovations. Springer, NY (2006)
8. Cohn, J.N., Finkelstein, S., McVeigh, G., Morgan, D., LeMay, L., Robinson, J., Mock, J.: Noninvasive Pulse Wave Analysis for the Early Detection of Vascular Disease. Hypertension 26, 503–508 (1995)
9. Farrington, C.P., Andrews, N.J., Beale, A.D., Catchpole, M.A.: A Statistical Algorithm for the Early Detection of Outbreaks of Infectious Disease. Journal of the Royal Statistical Society 159(3), 547–563 (1996)

Innovators Marketplace: Process of Service Innovation with Communication Games

Yukio Ohsawa and Yoko Nishihara

Department of Systems Innovation, School of Engineering, The University of Tokyo,
7-3-1, Hongo, Bunkyo, Tokyo 113-8656, Japan
{ohsawa,nishihara}@sys.t.u-tokyo.ac.jp

Abstract. The Innovators Market Game (IMG) has been proposed as a tool for aiding innovative thoughts and communication, coming after our 10-year experiences in chance discovery where tools of data visualization have been applied in cases of decision making of business teams. This game enabled to run and accelerate the process of innovation, as well as to train human's talent of analogical and combinatorial thinking. In this paper, we compare the effects of IMG as table game and a Web-based environment of communication where the fundamental features of IMG are imported. The effects of these two agorae, one on the table and the other on the Web, are compared. It is shown that there are some aspects of innovative communication we can enhance, some on the table and some on the Web. This directs us to future work merging the two in one process as a generalization of IMG.

Keywords: Innovators Market Game, Innovators Marketplance, Communication, Web-mediated Communication,

1 Introduction

One century is passing since Schumpeter suggested the concept *innovation* as a creative activity by which the economy jumps up to a new state, and that this creativity may come out as the fruit of novel combination of industrial resources [1]. It is noteworthy that this concept was originally presented as including not only creativity in technologies but also of ideas for manufacturing, logistics, and services, in the age Henry Ford I just established his company and introduced belt conveyer systems as a part of business process.

After half a century, Rogers [2] pointed out that some leading consumers play the role of *innovators*. That is, an important idea cannot become an innovation without these innovators on the side of consumers. And, the recent book by von Hippel *Democratizing Innovation* casted a revolutionary message: There are leading consumers who invent, not only use and diffuse, new ideas and technologies [3]. For example, some technologies for producing mountain bikes have been invented by leading users who continue thinking about new designs for solving his daily problems.

Thus, innovation came to be a term referring to the interaction of stakeholders in the market, involving inventors in companies, sensitive and communicative

T. Onoda, D. Bekki, and E. McCready (Eds.): JSAI-isAI 2010, LNAI 6797, pp. 311–320, 2011.

consumers, and even also consumers who invent. In other words, innovation means the value creating process of a system running on human-human interactions and individual human's thought for innovation, that have been modeled both socially and computationally [4]. We now are reaching the consensus that the combination and cross-disciplinary transplantation of existing methods/resources of business to new problems are basic engines of innovation.

The Innovators Market Game we show in this paper is a simple but powerful method for realizing the systematic process of innovation, i.e., combinatorial and analogical thoughts, involvement of stakeholders in the market, and their interdisciplinary communication and interaction. Here we are succeeding Schumpeter's point that an interdisciplinary combination of business actors and resources, possibly with the appearance of new actors, triggers innovation. And, our new actors include consumers and even stock investors.

2   Innovative Thoughts and Communications

First let us review a small portion of the Geneplore model of human's creativity, presented by Finke [5]. The process is, in short, the spiral of (1) generating an imaginary structure of invention, (2) exploration and interpretation of products made by the imaged structure, and returning to (1) the generation. This is a spiral in that the generated imaginary structure at each time is linked implicitly or explicitly to a newer function/product to be created. Thus, more complex and novel fruits are generated sustainably from this process. Meanwhile constraints are desired, rather than declined, for enriching the creativity both in quantity and quality of the imaginary structure. Especially, the number of basic images which are to be the building bricks for creating a complex product, and the target problem to be solved by the created idea, should be constrained artificially in order to create meaningful fruits. Also Finke pointed out that the building bricks should come from one's own imagination rather than borrowed from others or imported from external sources of knowledge.

In order to enable a group of collaborators in business and also the customers who may utilize the fruit to realize creativity, let us focus on the following two conditions for innovative communications.

Condition I: Representing one's own basic concepts
The bricks to be combined for creating something valuable should be the creator's own brainchild, i.e., the image from his/her own mind, according to the experiments of Finke. The preparatory basic ideas for innovation, therefore, should be presented by oneself, or by themselves if a group of collaborators aim to create a product or a service.

Condition II: Reasoning with combinations and analogy
One or both of the following ways of thought should be executed:
-   Combination of basic, i.e., existing and established ideas (or technologies).
-   Transplantation of basic ideas to a new application i.e., target domain, normally by changing minor parts, for the reason that the basis (a problem for which the

basic ideas worked previously) and the target (the present problem in the new application domain) have a similarity in some sense.

The combinatorial thoughts in the former pattern in Condition II can be regarded as a kind of abductive/inductive reasoning. That is, a combination

$$B_1, B_2, ..., B_m => C \tag{1}$$

where B_i is the i-th basic idea and C is a new one generated by combining $B_1, B_2, ...,$ B_m, means one of (a), (b), or (c) below:

(a) $X_i, B_i -> Y_i$ for all i of [0, m], of which a chain of equivalence is generated between X_{i+1} and Y_i for all i in [0, m]. That is, the state transitional formulae

$$X_1, B_1 \qquad \qquad -> \qquad \qquad Y_1,$$
$$X_2 (=Y_1), B_2 \qquad -> \qquad \qquad Y_2,$$
$$X_3 (=Y_2), B_3 \qquad -> \qquad \qquad Y_3,$$

$$...$$

$$X_m (=Y_{m-1}), B_m \qquad -> \qquad Y_m (=Y_n). \tag{2}$$

stand, where $X_1, B_1 -> Y_1$ means idea B_1 applied in state X_1 turns the state into Y_1. Thus C, the RHS of Eq.(1), means an idea of action to turn state X_1 finally into Y_n.

(b) $X_0, B_i -> Y_i$ for all i of [0, m], and the combination of $Y_1, Y_2, ...Y_m$ realizes a new state Y_n. Idea C means thus generated action, which changes the state from X_0 into Y_n. Here, X_0 is the same pre-state for applying B_i for all i of [0, m]. For example, given that B_1 is the technology for a producing water-proof chain, B_2 is a quick-reaction break, and B_2 is a slip-free tire of MTB. Then the bike made of these parts is expected to attract users working in the rain, such as bikers for delivery service. In this case, X_0 may be "user has to work even on rainy days" and C is to provide the user with the bike made combining these parts.

(c) A mixture of (a) and (b): Some new states emerge at the end of the chain as in (a), and will be combined with other new states, to compose a new state as in (b).

Because the states created by idea C should fit the changing demand of human(s) rather than become a compulsory supply of a created service, it is desired that C appears not at the end of the whole process of a purely bottom-up thought (i.e., only deductive combination of basic ideas). Rather, C should emerge by being called by human's requirements in the real life via interactions with the human's memories or life in the real world. Therefore, the elements in the LHS i.e., X_i and B_i for i of [$k+1, m$] where k ($< m$) is the number of basic ideas which have been in hand since the initial moment of thought, are supposed to appear abductively, i.e., deriving the pre-states and ideas to change the states, in all cases (a), (b) and (c) above, or inductively generalizing the states to obtain X_0 as in cases of (b). That is, the states X_i and the basic ideas for changing the states should be acquired via interacting with external opinions which mention about $Y's$ i.e., the desires.

And, the analogical reasoning in Condition II can be positioned as a sub-process of the abductive reasoning because analogy plays an essential role in creating a new hypothesis for achieving a new goal [6, 7]. For example, suppose

$$X_1, B_1 \qquad \rightarrow \qquad Y_1,$$
$$X_2, B_2 \qquad \rightarrow \qquad Y_2,$$
$$\cdots$$
$$X_m, B_m \;\rightarrow\qquad Y_m. \qquad\qquad (3)$$

stood in previously applying basic ideas B_i's, and the proposed idea C means to create a new state Y_n from a state where states $X_{a1}, X_{a2}, \ldots X_{aq}$ co-occur. If we can find lines $b_1, b_2, \ldots b_q$ and k, by searching the lines of Eq.(3), where

➤ the pre- and post-states are similar to $X_{a1}, X_{a2}, \ldots X_{aq}$ and Y_n respectively in the sense that an operation p changes from X_{ai} to X_{bi} all i in $[1, q]$ and Y_k to Y_n, and

➤ there are rules in lines of Eq.(3) which derives Y_k from $X_{b1}, X_{b2}, \ldots,$ and X_{bq}, deductively in the manner as in (a), (b), and (c) above,

then we can derive

$$X_{a1}, X_{a2}, \ldots X_{aq}, B_{a1}, B_{a2}, \ldots B_{aq}, \; p \rightarrow Y_n. \qquad\qquad (4)$$

Because p is an operator for the transition from known (basic) to the current (target) preconditions, Eq. (4) means analogical reasoning for coping with desire Y_n. Here, the desired states denoted by Y's and some pre-states and ideas by X's and B's should be acquired via interactions with opinions in the market. Thus, a process of thoughts and communication wth analogy and combination is based on abductive/inductive reasoning to obtain X's and B's, as well as deductive to obtain Y's, are expected.

From Conditions I and II, we should pay attention to the following types of thoughts and communications. Here, the solutions (I) and (II) roughly correspond to Conditions I and II above respectively. (III) below can be positioned as a branch of (II).

(I) *Meta Cognition, for externalizing basic factors (items, states, events, knowledge, and ideas) hidden in mind*: One needs a workplace for talking and showing ideas to oneself, so that the hidden dimensions of own value may be externalized. For example, basic items in daily life such as fresh water and trees may come out in self-talking, as basic factors composing healthy life, and be reflected to creating a new idea to order a picture of a lake in woods for exhibiting in the house. This simple idea may be used afterwards for creating a house-design business and accepted by a large-scale market. In this manner, the feeling that one can think and talk to oneself is an important factor for realizing an environment of thoughts for innovation.

(II) *Abductive and inductive reasoning via questions*: To the progress of these two types of reasoning, three methodologies for communication are expected to contribute. The first is meta-cognition in (I), because it enables to externalize hidden but significant factors, as seeds of important events at present and in the future of daily life. Thus, hidden parts of B's, X's, and p stated previously are to be externalized. The second is question asking. According to Eris, two categories of questions i.e., Generative Design Question (GDQ) urging divergent thoughts and Deep Reasoning Question (DRQ) urging convergent thoughts, play an essential role for making a group work innovative [10]. For example, the question about how a certain goal can be enabled is a Generative Design Question (GDQ), whereas a question for understanding causal antecedent of an occurred event is a Deep Reasoning Question (DRQ).

However, this categorization does not mean the interviewee *must* create a large number of scenarios for answering a GDQ or just one causality for a DRQ. It is possible to consider multiple sequences of causality where each sequence takes the form of Eq.(2), for explaining one present event by DRQ. On the other hand, if one searches an idea C for realizing state Y_n, the abductive and inductive reasoning for achieving Y_n may be triggered by a GDQ but converge to one optimal solution involving basic ideas B_i's, conditional states X_i's, and the operator p for analogy.

(III) *Negative and empathetic utterancens* to the presented proposals of new ideas, for urging the reasoning. As abstracted in [11], the empathetic communication means to talk with understanding other participants' context. As far as this kind of empathy is sustained in communication, the negation of others' comments tends to improve the quality of ideas and of the communication [12]. This effect of negation has been also known as a method for requirement acquisition [13]. Here, a necessary condition X_1 for realizing goal Y_1 with method B_1 is put as:

$$X_1, B_1 \quad \text{->} \quad Y_1, \tag{5}$$

(e.g. X1: the electricity works in my house, B1: I turn on the switch of the room light, Y1: The room gets lit up). Humans tend to interpret (or misunderstand) Eq. (5) as

$$B_1 \quad \text{->} \quad Y_1, \tag{6}$$

i.e., the light turns on if switched on. However, humans tend to notice the existence of X_1, if Y_1 is negated, i.e., if one faces a situation where the following stands:

$$B_1 \quad \text{->} \quad \neg Y_1, \tag{7}$$

i.e., the light is still off although the switch is on. Facing this situation, one notices

$$B_1, X \quad \text{->} \quad Y_1 \tag{8}$$

was really correct where X represents an ordinary situation but is not always true. By searching an event or a condition which is normally true but is violated at present, one notices "X_1: the electricity is connected to my house," was the entity of X, and that the electricity has been disconnected from the house. In other words, negation triggers the contextual shift in explaining the target events.

Thus, in general, let us call a process for innovation, where analogical/combinatorial thoughts based on abductive/inductive/deductive reasoning, and negative empathetic conversations with oneself or others in the market are involved, an *innovators marketplace*. In the remainder, one approach for realizing a innovators marketplace is defined and exemplified.

3   Innovators Market Game on the Table

Innovators Market Game (IMG) (see [15] for its original version) is a game for realizing innovators marketplace, which has been developed as a workplace for conversation to create innovative ideas, i.e, not only novel but also socially acceptable ideas. The players of the game are:

A) *Dealer*: The organizer, who distributes the money first, and sells prepared basic ideas on the demands of inventors. Also guides players to follow the rule.

B) *3 or 4 inventors*: Represents virtual innovative companies, buy cards on which basic ideas(/knowledge) are described, and combine useful basic ideas in order to create new ideas. Attach the colored post-it with writing the created idea, on the game board and explain it to the others. Wins if earns the largest amount of money by lending ideas to other innovators and by selling ideas/stocks to players in C below.

C) *4 or more investors, or users (consumers) of ideas*: If an investor, one evaluates the ideas presented by innovators, by buying the stocks of the promising inventors. If a user (/consumer), one pays money to buy an idea and obtains the right to use it for one's own life or business.

As in figure 1, the players share the visual and touchable graph showing the relations among the basic ideas. The links I this graph show the latent relevance between ideas which may be combined. This graph is obtained with KeyGraph applying Data Crystallization [16,17], in order to visualize latent possibilities for combining events existing in the data via contexts which are not explicitly included in the data but may affect events in the data. Hereafter, let us call this IMG on the table the "Table IMG" shortly. Note that the Table IMG is an approximate realization of innovators marketplace where stakeholders of the aimed innovation meet.

Fig. 1. A scene of Innovators Market game (IMG) on the table: Inventors, investors, and users continue conversations actively by creating, suggesting, and evaluating ideas for 2 hours. The small nodes in the bottom part of this figure are parts of the graph visualized by KeyGraph.

4   Innovators Marketplace on the Web

Although IMG can be regarded as a method for efficiently realizing the process of chance discovery [14], we still have problems when applied to real business. That is, ideas created by members of a real company with IMG based on their basic ideas (patents, existing techniques, current business models, etc) are sometimes rejected when proposed as a business plan in the company. We can say that Table IMG, which is once again an approximation of innovators marketplace (IM hereafter), is not strictly an IM, in that stakeholders who miss the opportunity to join the game are not involved in the process of innovation and may reject the obtained ideas afterward. From experiences, we learned the rejections have been due to the violation of financial or technological (prior) constraints and posterior constraints due to the conflict between the created ideas and the intentions of the missed stakeholders.

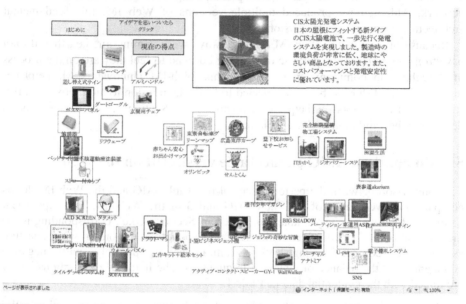

Fig. 2. The interface of Web IM: The new ideas are presented on the Web and are discussed on the bulletin board

In order to solve this problem, several approaches have been considered. In [18], we introduced a "tsugological" approach in IMG for creating realistic strategies for the management of aging problem of atomic power plants. Here, stakeholders relevant to the aging problem in atomic power plants, e.g., the national government, electric power companies, manufacturers of reactor and components, citizens, mass media, prefectural governments, universities, etc. described their *tsugoes* defined as the sets of {intention, action, pre-constraint, post-constraint} in making basic cards of IMG. The actions they described at this preprocess of IMG correspond to B_i's or C in the previous section. The pre-constraint of the action in an idea B corresponds to X described on the basic card of B, and the post-constraints correspond to Y's which may be aimed or events which may disturb the realization of Y's when the action of B is executed. And, the intention means to realize Y from X via the action of idea B. In other words, the tsugological approach aimed to be prepared for the deductive, abductive, and inductive reasoning presented in Section 2.

In [18], the players combined the basic ideas in the game, so that novel and acceptable ideas have been observed to come out. However, other constraints also turned out to be critical – the time of about 2 hours was much less than sufficient for enabling the thought, communications, or the survey of relevant knowledge from external sources. Thus, the site for extended communication has been developed on the Web, in order to compensate for this defect of the Table IMG.

Figure 2 shows the outline of Innovators Marketplace on the Web (Web-IM hereafter shortly): Each inventor creates an idea by looking at the display where basic ideas are visualized, positioned the created ideas close to relevant basic ideas. Then, the presented and posted new ideas appear also on the bulletin board, where the ideas will be discussed with other participants participating from other places linked to the network. Although we produced multiple versions of Web IM, this fundamental architecture is common to all versions.

Because players of the Web-IM do not always wear gaming air, i.e., they do not pay strong attention to the purpose of winning but tend to feel they are on the process of thoughts and communication, we call this Web-IM (Innovators Marketplace) instead of Web-IMG. Web-IM is expected to fulfill its mission to aid innovation, if it works as an innovators marketplace as mentioned in Section 2. The next section is devoted to the validation of this enablement.

5   Comparison: IMG on the Table versus IM on the Web

For comparison between the performances of the Table IMG and the Web IM, let us compare 3 conversations of the Table IMG and 3 of the Web IM. The experiment below are focused on the variables suggested in Section 2, i.e., corresponding to (I) meta-cognition, (II) deductive, abductive, and inductive reasoning with question asking, and context-focusing/shifting communication possibly with negative comments, and the balance of utterance frequencies. The itemized descriptions below are linked with the evidential data in Table 1.

Feeling of deep thought by oneself: Corresponds to the meta-cognition in Section 2. We asked 6 players who played both Table IMG and Web IM, whether or not they felt they could think deeply with his/her own brain. They first played on the table, and second on the Web the next day. The time of both has been fixed to 2 hours. Strictly speaking this is not a fair manner of experiment, because subjects may have been biased in some way due to playing first on the table. However, the result was that the 4 or the 6 players mentioned, after playing both games, that the Web-IM was better for thinking deeply by oneself without external interruptions. This is against the simple expectation that the players who had been biased by the ideas presented on the table may feel disturbed from concentrating on the Web IM. Thus, we here present the Web IM as a better environment for thinking and talking with oneself as a part of meta-cognition.

Questions: We counted the number of meaningful questions, considering their correspondence to Eris's categorization of DRG and GDQ (see Section 2), although we could not classify the questions into these two. As a result, the number of questions tends to be more frequent in the case of Web IM, than in the case of Table IMG, as in Table 1. Thus, well-designed products and socially acceptable comments are expected to come out from Web IM via question-asking conversations. In fact, the message-reply relations between utterances were more clearly observed in the log of communication of Web IM, whereas such reactions were not explicit according to the conversation log on the Table IMG.

Negative comments: We counted the number of negative comments, including those not explicitly negative as far as we find from the superficial expressions, but inferred to be negative. For example, "isn't it scary?" to a safe lifestyle in a tunnel means a negative impression, and urges the presenter of the idea to reconsider the idea for improvement. The Table IMG tends to show higher rate of negative comments than the Web IM. Thus, hidden factors ruling the accomplishment of players' fruit are expected to be mined on the table via negative comments.

Table 1. The comparison of Table IMG versus Web IM

	Table IMG				Web IM		
	Case 1	Case 2	Case 3		Case 4	Case 5	Case 6
Feeling of thought by oneself	16.7 (1 of 6)				83.3 (5 of 6)		
Excitation (%)	66.7(4 of 6)				33.3 (2 of 6)		
Questions (%)	5.6	6.2	7.8		10.8	14.1	9.1
Negative comments	5.6	4.6	2.9		3.2	3.1	2.3

6   Conclusions and Future Work

In summary, although the Table IMG has been invented as an approximate realization of and the improvement (with introducing the feeling of entertainment) of the process of chance discovery, its weakness has been the less consideration of deep background factors due to the short time and the air of the game. Here we introduced the Web IM, in order to cope with this weakness.

According to the experiments, the Table IMG serves as a system for enhancing communication among market participants, where participants dare negate others' comments. On the other hand, the Web IM has been found to be a strong place for accelerating meaningful questions. Because both features of communication are important paths to creating useful ideas, we here finally propose a process where players combine the IMG on the Table and the IM on the Web. The design of the process, i.e., whether participants play first on the table and then on the Web, or in the opposite order, or continue both to compose an endless spiral of value sensing process.

The comparison in this paper focused on the quality of communications and ideas presented in the game. However, the pre- and the post-processes are important as well. For example, the personal trust and mutual understanding among participants should be established in advance for enabling a sustainable environment for elevating the creativity for chance discovery [19]. In the future work, we shall extend the presented methods to a generalized framework of innovators marketplace, so that the collection of basic ideas and relevant knowledge (pre-process) and its extension to a prolonged serious discussion (post-process) are combined in one process.

References

[1] Schumpeter, J.A.: Theorie der wirtschaftlichen Entwicklung. Leipzig, Duncker & Humblot, Berlin (1912); Schumpeter, J., Backhaus, U.: The Theory of Economic Development. Transaction Publisher (1983)

[2] Rogers, E.M.: Diffusion of Innovations. Free Press, New York (1st edn. 1965, 5th edn. 2003)

[3] Hippel, E.V.: Democratizing Innovation. The MIT Press, Cambridge (2005)

[4] Goldberg, D., Sastry, K.: Genetic Algorithms: The Design of Innovation. Springer, Heidelberg (1st edn. 2002, 2nd 2010)

[5] Finke, R.A., Ward, T.B., Smith, S.M.: Creative Cognition: Theory, Research, and Applications. The MIT Press, Cambridge (1996)

[6] Abe, A.: Abduction and Analogy in Chance Discovery. In: Osawa, Y., McBurney, P. (eds.) Chance Discovery, ch. 16, pp. 231–248. Springer, Heidelberg (2003)

[7] Magnani, L.: Creative abduction and hypothesis withdrawal in science. In: International Congress on Discovery and Creativity, Belgium (1998)

[8] Nara, Y., Ohsawa, Y.: Tools for Shifting Human Context into Disasters Chance Discovery and Management session. In: Proc. Fourth International Conference on Knowledge-Based Intelligent Engineering Systems & Allied Technologies, KES 2000 (2000)

[9] Metcalfe, J., Wiebe, D.: Intuition in insight and noninsight problem solving. Memory & Cognition 15(3), 238–246 (1987)

[10] Eris, O.: Effective Inquiry for Innovative Engineering Design. Kluwer Academic Publishers, Boston (2004)

[11] Ohsawa, Y., Abe, A., Nakamura, J.: Chance Discovery as Value Sensing with Analogical Thinking. International Journal of Organizational and Collective Intelligence 1(1), 44–57 (2010)

[12] Nishihara, Y., Ohsawa, Y.: Analysis focusing Negative Utterances in Combinatorial Thinking Games, vol. 25(3), pp. 485–493 (2010)

[13] Kushiro, N., Ohsawa, Y.: A scenario acquisition method with multi-dimensional hearing and hierarchical accommodation process. New Mathematics and Natural Computation 2(1), 101–113 (2006)

[14] Ohsawa, Y., McBruney, P.: Chance Discovery. Springer, Heidelberg (2003)

[15] Ohsawa, Y., Nishihara, Y.: Niche of Idea Activations as Source of Social Creativity: a Finding from Innovation Game. In: The 2009 IEEE Int'l Conf. on Systems, Man, and Cybernetics, Texas, USA (October 2009)

[16] Ohsawa, Y.: Data Crystallization: Chance Discovery Extended for Dealing with Unobservable Events. New Mathematics and Natural Computation 1(3), 373–392 (2005)

[17] Horie, K., Maeno, Y., Ohsawa, Y.: Data Crystallization Applied to Desinging New Products. Journal of Systems Sciences and Systems Engineering 16(1), 34–49 (2007)

[18] Ohsawa, Y.: Tsugology: Structuring of Intentions and Constraints for Innovative Communication. In: The 11th International Symposium on Knowledge and Systems Sciences, Xi'an (2010)

[19] Oehlmann, R.: The Function of Harmony and Trust in Collaborative Chance Discovery. New Mathematics and Natural Computation 1(4), 69–83 (2006)

Multiscale Service Design Method and Its Application to Sustainable Service for Prevention and Recovery from Dementia

Mihoko Otake, Motoichiro Kato, Toshihisa Takagi, Shuichi Iwata,
Hajime Asama, and Jun Ota

Research into Artifacts, Center for Engineering, Science Integration Program -
Humans, the University of Tokyo / Fonobono Research Institute,
5-1-5 Kashiwa-no-ha, Kashiwa City, Chiba, 277-8568, Japan
otake@race.u-tokyo.ac.jp
http://www.race.u-tokyo.ac.jp/~otake/

Abstract. This paper proposes multiscale service design method through the development of support service for prevention and recovery from dementia. Proposed multiscale service model consists of tool, event, human, network, style and rule. Service elements at different scales are developed according to the model. Firstly, the author proposes and practices coimagination method, which is expected to prevent the progress of cognitive impairment. Coimagination support system and program were developed as "tool" and "event". Then, Fonobono Research Institute was established as a "network" for "human" who studies coimagination, which is a multisector research organization including older adults living around university campus, companies providing welfare and medical services, local government, medical institution, researchers of the University of Tokyo and Keio University. The institute proposes and realizes lifelong research as a novel life "style" for older adults, and discusses second social system for older adults as an innovative "rule" for social system of aged society.

Keywords: multiscale service design, prevention and recovery from dementia, aged society, coimagination method, fonobono research institute.

1 Introduction

There is a hypothesis that activation of three cognitive functions which decline at mild cognitive impairment (MCI) is effective for prevention of dementia[1, 2]. The cognitive functions include episode memory, division of attention, and planning function. Interactive communication activates above three functions as well as intellectual activities and basis of social network. Novel method named coimagination has been proposed by the authors supporting interactive communication for activating three cognitive functions[3–5]. Methods are effective when they are practiced in the real world. In order to develop services based on arbitrary methods, we propose multiscale service design method. Then we show how to implement the service for prevention and recovery from dementia from scratch via multiscale service design method.

T. Onoda, D. Bekki, and E. McCready (Eds.): JSAI-isAI 2010, LNAI 6797, pp. 321–330, 2011.

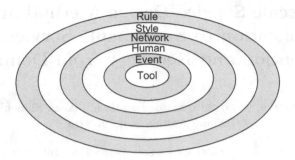

Fig. 1. Mutiscale Service Model

2 Multiscale Service Model

If we compare methods to seeds, services are seedlings. In order to grow such technical seeds to social seedlings, we propose multiscale service design method. It is known that amplifier of service consists of tool, circumstance, and social system[6]. For implementation, we devide circumstance for event and human. We also classify social system as network, style, and rule. In summary, we model that services consist of tool, event, human, network, style and rule (Fig. 1). Then, each element is implemented concurrently. Tool is designed which supports embodiment of method. Event is conducted utilizing the tool. Human resource development program is provided so as to grow human who can conduct events with the supporting tool. Network of humans and organizations is emerged through the series of event and training program. Lifestyle or philosophy is required for ogranization of network. Rule is also required for effective embodiment of lifestyle. We propose multiscale service design method which enumerate six elements of services, namely, tool, event, human, network, style and rule, and implement concurrently. In this paper, we show how to utilize this multiscale service design method with the case study of service for prevention and recovery from dementia.

3 Coimagination Method for Prevention and Recovery from Dementia

The aim of the coimagination method is to support interactive conversation for activation of episodic memory, division of attention, and planning function, which decline for early stage of mild cognitive impairment. Following is the description of coimagination method with cognitive functions which are expected to be activated for each step.The coimagination method is a method that supports interactive communication through the expression of feelings about images according to a theme. Allocated time periods and turns for each participant are predetermined so that all participants play the roles of both the speaker and listener. The aim of the coimagination method is to activate three cognitive

Table 1. A typical script of conversation supported by Coimagination Method

Speaker	Content
A	This picture shows the Fuse Sarasvati Temple. It was my first visit. This is one of the famous three sarasvati temples in Kanto region. The building was newly built very well.
B	It's in my neighborhood.
A	People place a lot of eggs because the god enshrined there prefer them.
D	Have you ever visited the temple?
C	Yes, once or twice on New Year's Day. It was quiet, not so many visitors.

Fig. 2. Image Displayed during Coimagination Session

functions for prevention of dementia. Following is the description of coimagination method with cognitive functions which are expected to be activated: Preparing speech in an alloted time activates planning function; Preparing images for speech activaties episodic memory; Interactive communication activates division of attention.

Table 1 shows the interactive conversation of older adults using day care service supported by coimatinagion method. Fig. 2 is one of the images displayed during coimagination session, brought by one of the participants, participant A. Participants A is healthy older adults, and participants B and C are dementia patients. Host is refered to as D. It is difficult for participants B and C to communicate in daily life. In contrast, they gave comments during coimagination session, since images and statements of other participants might have helped participants to remember the episodic memories of the temple, and to participate in the conversation.

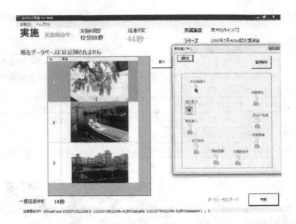

Fig. 3. Fonobono Panel: Coimagination Support System(Tool)

4   Multiscale Service Design Based on Coimagination Method

First of all, we summarize the definition of coimagination method. Coimagination method supports interactive communication through bringing feelings with images according to the theme. Allocated time for each subject is predetermined. Subjects take turns so as to play both roles of speakers and listeners. The themes of communication are examined considering the effects for social networking. Cognitive activities which require episodic memory, division of attention, and planning are measured by memory task. We describe developing service for prevention and recovery from dementia based on coimagination method, so that how to apply multiscale service design method to real-world problem.

4.1   Coimagination Support System (Tool)

There are four requirements for coimagination support system.

1. The system dynamically displays the images corresponding to the stories of subjects.
2. Users of the system easily register the images. The registered images are accumulated for each subject.
3. Operations of the system are logged so as to be analyzed afterwards. Questions for the memory task are generated from the registered data for display.
4. The system is accessible from all over the world, so that the results of coimagination program are accumulated.

We developed coimagination support system named "Fonobono Panel" which meets the above requirements. The system consists of a laptop computer which can communicate the remote web database for the chair of the session, a projector for displaying the images, and a screen.

Fig. 4. Coimagination Program for Older Adults Interested in Prevention of Dementia

Before starting the session, the chair of the session scans pictures into the computer and registers them for each subject. Once the session starts, the chair selects the images of the speaker. The initial window is shown in Fig. 3. On the right, icons of the participants are arranged according to the seating order. On the left, images of each speaker is displayed. In this case, three images of flowers, a bird, and a building are shown.

4.2   Coimagination Program (Event)

We designed coimagination program based on coimagination method. Typical coimagination program includes five series of sessions (Fig. 4). First four sessions are coimagination sessions. Last session is for memory task. Each session is held for an hour per week. Theme of each session is different. Average number of participants is six. There are two rounds for each coimagination session. The first round is for brief speech, and the second round is for questions and answers. Average allocated time is five minutes for each subject and round during first four weeks. On the fifth week, the session for memory task is held. Images of the series of four sessions are displayed one after the other. Subjects guess the owner and the theme of the collected images.

4.3   Human Resource Development Program of, by, to the Older
Adults (Human)

We propose human resource development program for coimagination program. Instructors of the program were older adults in Kashiwa city, Japan, who have been working with the inventor of the method. The curriculum of the program was designed so as to bring out social intelligence of the students. The program was divided into two parts. In the first half of the program, students participated in the coimagination program, and practiced interactive conversations. In the latter half of the program, students conducted coimagination sessions as moderators, score keepers, or reporters(Fig. 5). We found that social intelligence of the students improved through attending and conducting coimagination sessions during the program.

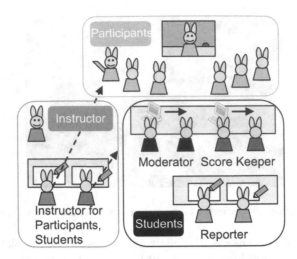

Fig. 5. Role of Instructors, Students, Participants of Human Resource Development Program

Fig. 6. Instructors and Students of Human Resource Development Program

Our first human resource development program aimed to train potential instructors with "social intelligence" started from fall 2008. It consists of 15 classes, each class for 2 hours with lectures and practices, and took about six months (Fig. 6). It was found that it was too long for two parties, both students and instructors. In order to solve the program, we designed a new short-term introductory course of coimagination, which is expected to bridge its graduated students with strong interests to a typical coimagination program.

Our first short-term introductory course of coimagination opened in fall 2009. It consists of 3 classes, each class for 1 hour and a half. Two of the classes are lectures, one of the class is a practice in order to learn through doing. In order to find and recruit motivated people among the students, we found our new method to be effective. In our newly designed course, a circulation of service receivers

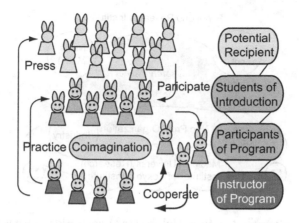

Fig. 7. Sustainable Delivery Method for Support Service for Prevention and Recovery from Dementia Organized

into service providers is expected, which ensures the sustainable human resource development(Fig.7). Currently in fall 2010, 5 among 36 graduates became citizen researchers or in training.

4.4 Fonobono Research Institute (Network)

In order to organize instructors of programs and to coordinate multiple sectors for implementation of services, we established "Fonobono Research Institute", a multisector nonprofit research organization including older adults living around university campus, companies providing welfare and medical services, local government, medical institution, researchers of the University of Tokyo and Keio University (Fig. 8). Research project of Fonobono Research Institute was established in July 2007. We establised an incorporated nonprofit organization of Fonobono Research Institute in July 2008 for running research project. Government and News Media involve in research project and not involve in an incorporated nonprofit organization for fairness. Older adults who are interested in prevention and recovery from dementia and social action program can participate an incorporated nonprofit organization rather than research project by membership system for supporters and instructors.

4.5 Lifestyle of Lifelong Research (Style)

Lifelong study is popular among retired people. However, learning is a consumption of knowledge whereas research is a production of knowledge. Older adults may contribute to society effectively if they are engaged in knowledge creation activities. Therefore, we propose the novel lifestyle of "lifelong research" rather than "lifelong study". Core members of the Fonobono Research Institute are named "citizen researchers"(Fig. 9). They embody the lifestyle of lifelong research through daily research and development activities of service creation.

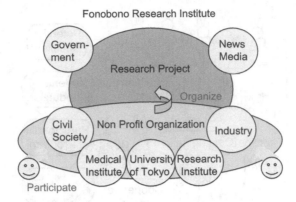

Fig. 8. Fonobono Research Institute: Multisector Organization of Civil Society, Industry, and Academia collaborating with Government and News Media

Fig. 9. Citizen Researchers and Director of Fonobono Research Institute

They develop and provide coimagination program, human resource development program, and organize Fonobono Research Institute. The citizen researchers presented their studies at the Annual Conferences of the Japanese Society for Artificial Intelligence every year in 2008, 2009 and 2010. Above all, the citizen researcher at the age of 84 presented in the first year of 2008, and encouraged other researchers through his spirit of challenge (Fig. 10).

4.6   Second Social System for Older Adults (Rule)

Older adults after retirement used to enjoy rest of their life with amusement and entertainment. It has been possible when the ratio of retired people in the society is vanisingly small. Recently, the percentage of people over 65 years old exeeded 20 %, and may become around 40 % in the year 2050 in Japan. Collapse

Fig. 10. Citizen Researcher who presented the Studies at the Annual Conferences of the Japanese Society for Artificial Intelligence in 2008

of social security system has become a real issue. The same situation may occur in developing countries as well as developed contries in the near future. However, retainment of older adults in the existing labor market narrows the opportuity of younger adults to enter into it. We propose that we develop the second social system and hopefully in the future, novel labor market consisting of older adults over 65 years old. With this innovative system, older adults and younger adults can coexist and co-prosper. Service for prevention and recovery from dementia is one of the prospective candidate for the second social system.

5   Discussion

The service which we are developing is bidirectional and co-creative. It amplifies through the interaction between service receivers and service receivers, as well as service receivers and service providers. In our service, service receivers attain service by actively participating communication, and influence other service receivers. Therefore, one service receiver plays a role of service provider for surrounding service receivers at the same time. If the design of the service system is successful and all service receivers are motivated, service receivers can receive service more than service providers prepared beforehand. Other service elements, tool, event, network, style and rule may help service receivers. We need to investigate the conditions so that all service receivers play roles of service providers as well to guarantee effectiveness.

It is reported that participatory approaches to research and evaluation is growing, particularly in public and social policy areas, and especially in relation to health and social care[7], and older adults are included in the whole processes of research[8]. In this study, older people play more innovative roles to both research and provide services concurrently.

6   Conclusion

In this paper, we proposed multiscale service design method which enumerate six elements of services, namely, tool, event, human, network, style and rule, and implement concurrently. We showed how to utilize this multiscale service design method with the case study of service for prevention and recovery from dementia based on coimagination method. Coimagination support system and program were developed as "tool" and "event". Then, Fonobono Research Institute was established as a "network" for "human" who studies coimagination, which is a multisector research organization. The institute proposes and realizes lifelong research as a novel life "style" for older adults, and discusses second social system for older adults as an innovative "rule" for social system of aged society. We successfully developed innovative service system from scratch utilizing the multiscale service design method. Future work includes service operating method for sustainable and evolving services which can meet future needs with uncertainty.

References

1. Rentz, D.M., Weintraub, S.: Neuropsychological detection of early probable alzheimer's disease. In: Scinto, L.F.M., Daffner, K.R. (eds.) Early Diagnosis and Treatment of Alzheimer's Disease, pp. 69–189. Humana Press, Totowa (2000)
2. Barberger-Gateau, P., Fabrigoule, C., Rouch, I., et al.: Neuropsychological correlates of self-reported performance in instrumental activities of daily living and prediction of dementia. Journal of Gerontology Series B: Psychological Sciences and Social Sciences 54(5), 293–303 (1999)
3. Otake, M., Kato, M., Takagi, T., Asama, H.: Coimagination method: Communication support system with collected images and its evaluation via memory task. In: Stephanidis, C. (ed.) UAHCI 2009. LNCS, vol. 5614, pp. 403–411. Springer, Heidelberg (2009)
4. Otake, M., Kato, M., Takagi, T., Asama, H.: Development of coimagination method towards cognitive enhancement via image based interactive communication. In: Proceedings of the 18th IEEE International Symposium on Robot and Human Interactive Communication, pp. 835–840
5. Otake, M.: Coimagination method: sharing imagination with images and time limit. In: Proceedings of the International Reminiscence and Life Review Conference 2009, pp. 97–103 (2009)
6. Yoshikawa, H.: Introduction to service engineering - a framework for dealing with services theoretically. Synthesiology 1(2), 111–122 (2008)
7. Kemshall, H., Littlechild, R.: User involvement and participation in social care: Research informing practice. Jessica Kingsley (2000)
8. Burholta, V., Nasha, P., Naylorb, D., Windlec, G.: Training older volunteers in gerontological research in the united kingdom: Moving towards an andragogical and emancipatory agenda. Educational Gerontology 36(9), 753–780 (2010)

Opinion Exchange Convergence Support System Using RFID Tags

Yoshifumi Shimizu and Wataru Sunayama

Graduate School of Information Sciences, Hiroshima City University,
3-4-1 Ozuka-Higashi, Asa-Minami-Ku, Hiroshima, 731-3194, Japan

Abstract. In our society, there are many opportunities to exchange opinions on decision. Problems may occur when we exchange opinions. It is desirable for solving problems to make an environment that can achieve a smooth opinion exchange. There are "divergence phase" and "convergence phase" in the opinion exchange for decision. The divergence phase is to enumerate various choices related to the subject, and to consider possibility. On the other hand, in the convergence phase, participants investigate alternatives arose in the divergence phase, and argue for making a single conclusion.

In this paper, we focus on the convergence phase, and propose a system that supports the process narrowing the listed alternatives by using RFID tags. That is, the system supports the smooth progress of opinion exchanges by controlling the time, the speech order, and the alternative evaluation for leading a single conclusion that many participants can accept.

Keywords: opinion exchange support, RFID tags, communication support, discussion convergence.

1 Introduction

In our society, there are many opportunity to exchange opinions to make decisions. There are many problems when multiple people exchange opinions such as derail from the theme, waste time by loops, settles conclusion for the conflicting opinions of each other, and blocks for honest opinions because of their relationships. Therefore, the environment that these problems are solved, and can establish smooth exchange of opinions is desired.

In exchanging opinions to make decision, there are two phases, the "divergence phase" and the "convergence phase". In the divergence phase, we associate alternatives with a wide range of themes, and consider about various possibilities. Then, in the convergence phase, we narrow the candidates after reviewing the alternatives listed in the divergent phase that determine the final conclusion. In many discussions, the final decision will be decided by agreement of the number of participants. Therefore, help the process to make a conclusion that many people can acceptable is significant.

In this paper, we focus on the convergence phase and support the process in the discussion to evaluate alternatives with using RFID tags. In other words, controls

T. Onoda, D. Bekki, and E. McCready (Eds.): JSAI-isAI 2010, LNAI 6797, pp. 331–340, 2011.

evaluation of alternatives with order to said time and said of participants for using RFID tags and a computer in discussion, supports the smooth progress of discussions to determine the conclusion that many participants can satisfied with.

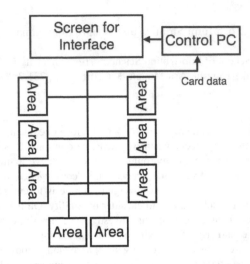

Fig. 1. Hardware Configuration of Opinion Exchange Convergence Support System

We suggest the tool that can support the process of discussion in unintuitive way with using cards with RFID tags. The following three points could be benefit for using RFID tags.

1. Participants can continue exchanging opinions without looking away from opportunities of discussion.
2. System can make order to say smoothly because participants can know who wants to say about what with observing another participant's behavior.
3. System can control order to say fairly by excluding any intentional ordering.

2   Configuration of Opinion Exchange Convergence Support System

In this section, we describe the detail of the opinion exchange convergence support system.

2.1   Problem Setting

In the discussion, there is the convergence phase after the divergence phase that participants consider and list alternatives.

This system supports the process "convergence phase" that narrow alternatives with initial states have been mentioned.

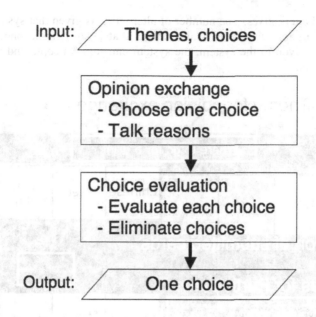

Input: Themes, choices

Opinion exchange
- Choose one choice
- Talk reasons

Choice evaluation
- Evaluate each choice
- Eliminate choices

Output: One choice

Fig. 2. Configuration of Opinion Exchange Convergence Support System

2.2 System Outline

Fig.1 shows the hardware configuration of the opinion exchange convergence support system. In this system, there are 8 areas that participants present their cards. The area read the ID number of the RFID tag attachment to card that presented by the participant, and send it to the computer with way of the host interface. The following 13 cards are used in the system.

- 8 Selection cards : 「Selection A」 「Selection B」 「Selection C」 「Selection D」
      「Selection E」 「Selection F」 「Selection G」 「Selection H」
- 1 Exit card : 「Exit statement」
- 4 Evaluation cards : 「Very good」 「Favor」 「Against」 「Strongly against」

"Selection cards" and "Exit card" are used when participants exchange opinion, and "Evaluation cards" are used when participants evaluate alternatives.

Fig.2 shows the trend of the opinion exchange convergence support system. First, enter the theme of discussion and alternatives that could be a conclusion of the theme to the system. Participants in the discussion describe the oral recommendation after acquiring the right to recommend alternatives. After the alternatives were issued, participants evaluate each recommended alternative and ultimately achieved the highest rated alternative will be the conclusion of the theme.

2.3 Input

Before the system starts the discussion, enter the theme and alternatives that could be a conclusion to the system. The alternatives are listed by participants in exchange, and given expected alternatives. The number of alternative is given that system can join 8 people for discussion, and up to 8 alternatives that push a single one. Less then 8 alternatives are given to the system, the system can join 8 people and each of them has a one opinion.

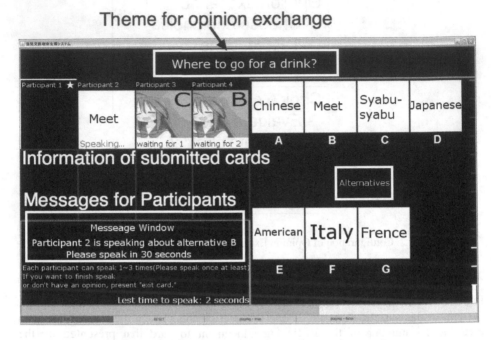

Fig. 3. Interface of Opinion Exchange Convergence Support System

2.4   Opinion Exchange Phase

In this section, we describe about the phase that reasons for recommending choices on the participants to recommend each other. In the opinion exchange phase, participants repeat two steps "presentation of views" that recommend alternatives, and "oral recommendation" that speak reason of recommendation. Each participant can speak "oral recommendation" more then once but less than three times. This phase will end if all participants speak "oral recommendation" three times or presents "exit card."

Next we describe the details of the "presentation of views" and "oral recommendation."

Presentation of Views. In order to recommend alternative opinions, each participant presents "selection card" to own area. Each choice in advance, participants have eight selection cards that assigned "A" to "H". In the order the card presented to dictate the nomination, and when their turn came around, they presented to dictate the nomination, and when their turn came around, they can describe in the next section "oral recommendation". Fig. 3 shows the interface of the opinion exchange convergence support system. When participants are waiting to speak, they can withdraw the card. And each participant can present "exit card" when he does not have any additional opinion if he spoke more than once in "oral recommendation."

Oral Recommendation. When the participant presents "selection card" and came turn to speak, he can speak the reason of recommendation in 30 seconds. Each participant can make up to three oral reasons to recommend at least once. At least having to speak to the participants to promote the idea of talking with the knowledge, the participants may have felt that each participant took part in discussions ultimately convincing to make the conclusion of thought required.

2.5   Evaluation Phase

In this section, we describe about the evaluation phase that narrows alternatives to one, and makes the conclusion that all participants accept. Each participant in this phase has four "evaluation cards" to choose the best evaluated alternative for the conclusion with narrowing low evaluated alternatives.

Next we describe the details of the "evaluation of alternatives" and "narrowing alternatives" in this phase.

Evaluation of Alternatives. Participants use "Very good", "Favor", "Against", and "Strongly against" four "evaluation cards." "Very good" card can presents only once and at least once because the system wants to show the most recommended alternatives for each participant to make easier between alternative's evaluations. Other evaluation cards "Favor", "Against" and "Strongly against" can present many times. At this time, not to know other participant's evaluation for each alternative, participant presents the card with reversed. Cards are assigned rating of four kinds of points, respectively, "Very good" with 2 points, 1 point in "Favor", "Against" the point -1, and -2 points in "Strongly against." After all alternatives were evaluated, the system begins narrowing alternatives.

Table 1. Themes and Alternatives of Discussion(seven each)

Themes	Alternatives
1: Who goes to buy a magazine?	Subjects
2: Who solve the puzzle people?	Subjects
3: Where to go for a drink?	Shops
4: Who decide where to go for a drink?	Subjects
5: What kind of song should be sung in front of everyone?	Songs
6: Who sing in front of everybody?	Subjects
7: How old is the ideal age gap of lover?	Difference of ages
8: Which character do you want to take a picture with?	Characters

Narrowing Alternatives. Based on the evaluation of each alternative given by all participants, the system narrows down remaining alternatives. This is one time as chosen by the favor-choice and evaluated, we reach the conclusion that many participants acceptable.

Negative rating alternatives (if all alternatives are negative rating, except the highest score) are removed by the system.

If more than one choice is left after narrowing alternatives, back to the evaluation of alternatives. Else, finish the evaluation phase.

2.6   Output

After narrowing the alternatives, the system outputs the left alternative as the conclusion by consensus of all participants, and finishes the discussion.

3   Evaluation Experiment: Results of Opinion Exchange Convergence Support System

In this section, we describe experiments to verify if we can get a mutually acceptable conclusion.

3.1   Experiment Description

We conducted an experiment by opinion exchanges with our proposed interface on the 7 themes shown in Table1 with 14 information science and graduate students. We divided 14 students into two groups by each subject, 7 for exchange views on using the system, and 7 for no verbal exchange views without the system. Grouping was conscious not to generate any significant bias prior knowledge of each theme. Also, if they make a verbal exchange, upon giving a good indication that leads to the conclusion that upon termination, timed in 15 minutes. In the theme 3 and the theme 7, author provided imaginable alternatives, and in the theme 8 and the theme 5, alternatives were listed by the each participant. In other themes, participants in the discussion were listed in alternatives.

Table 2. Questionnaires

Q1: Did you accept the decision what determined in the discussion?
Q2: Was the discussion smoothly?
Q3: Could you fully express your opinions?
Q4: How many participant's opinions could you hear enough?
Q5: Did you think numbers of participant's opinions were equal?

Table 3. Result of the Q1   (Consent to Conclude)

Alternatives	With the system	Without the system
Very acceptable	40	4
Acceptable	12	22
Rather unconvincing	4	28
Unconvincing	0	2

Table 4. Result of the Q2 (Smoothness of Discussion)

Alternatives	With the system	Without the system
Extremely smooth	23	6
Fairly smooth	28	22
Rather lacked smooth	5	25
Completely not smooth	0	3

The evaluation data for each subject and at times said the experiment, Table2 conducted questionnaire after experiment. Each question in the survey, Q1, Q2, Q3, Q5 were selected on a scale of 4, Q4 was the number of people had responded.

3.2 Experimental Result and Consideration

We cited for the proposed system and discuss the experimental results. Then, we describe the experimental results and discussion about the effectiveness of the proposed alternatives and evaluation of each phase of discussion. At last, we describe the qualitative effect of RFID tags.

Smooth of Discussion and Satisfy Level of the Conclusion. Table 3 shows the result of the Q1 that how much were you accepted with the result of the discussion. More than 70 percents of participants who used the system answered "Very acceptable", and half of the participants who performed the verbal exchange answered "Rather unconvincing". From these results, opinion exchange for this system was easy to make the conclusion that many people acceptable.

Table 4 shows the result of the Q2 that asked the smoothness of the discussion. In the questionnaire, most people had a smooth exchange of opinions with using the system. For this, we found that this interface could make the smooth discussion because the system narrowed alternatives mechanically.

Table 5. Result of the Q3 (Chance Remark)

Choices	With the system	Without the system
Could speak enough	24	4
Could speak fairly	29	27
Didn't said much	3	25
Not mentioned at all	0	0

Table 5, Table 6, and Table 7 shows the result of the Q3, Q4, and Q5 that opportunities for ourselves and others said. From Table 5, most of participants were able to express their opinion with the proposed system, and half of the subjects performed with verbal exchange, the opinions were not present. From Table 6, subjects using the proposed system indicated that respondents were able to hear the opinions of most other subjects. And from Table 7, subjects using the proposed system respondents were against equal opportunities for each other's remark, and half of the subjects performed a verbal exchange answered that little biased. For these results, the proposed system made the exchange opinions smoothly, and made the environment that participants could speak enough and heard the other participant's opinion. Table 8 shows the total number of cards in each subject for evaluation phase. The evaluation card "Very good" is most used in the discussion, but other evaluation cards were used as needed. For overall, it was easier to evaluate conclusions in favor of each subject repeated the evaluation led to the satisfactory conclusion. By using RFID tags, we could exchange opinions in a shared space. So we could discuss close as possible to form an oral exchange opinions.

4   Related Research

In this section, we review the related research of exchange support and the related research on the RFID tag based information control.

4.1   Communication Support

A study to rank the multiple-choice group, AHP decision support [1] was presented from old days that take time to compare a pair wise between all alternatives. In addition, the study do not approximate opinions with discuss directly each other.

The study aimed at building an environment that supports the exchange of real-time speech recognition on a specific speaker in order to get speech of the participants, morphological analysis, a process such as keyword extraction, and visualize the story structure [6], which aims to provide information to the participants. But the environment only to provide the information can not control the participant's action, it is possible to waste the time for some participant and conflict the discussion for relationships.

Table 6. Result of the Q4 （Another Opportunity to Say）

Choices	With the system	Without the system
six	37	9
five	16	13
four	2	12
three	1	15
two	0	7
one	0	0
zero	0	0

Table 7. Result of the Q5 （Equal Opportunity Statement）

Choices	With the system	Without the system
Equal	32	1
Fairly equal	17	24
Little biased	7	30
Very biased	0	1

Table 8. Number of Evaluation Card Used

Evaluation card	Number of used	Rate of used
Very good card	85	30.4%
Favor card	75	26.9%
Against card	61	21.9%
Strongly against	58	20.8%

Discussions that affect interpersonal relationships have been observed [2], as such research can solve the problem, regardless of language online exchange opinions with the participants showing research [3].

The brainstorming that includes limiting adverse opinion concludes the story [7], sometimes to exchange views on a clear goal. The presenter is not yet appropriate exchange views on progress and smooth talker limits, reach the conclusion that helps the environment have not been studied sufficiently.

In these studies, supports the process of making decision by majority vote the alternative for an equal footing all of the participants, but not done enough communication because of the words why the voting alternatives of each participant don't know. In our research, we create the environment that can control the time sequence and exchange opinions without power relations and relationships between participants with meeting exchanges of opinions.

4.2　Control Information with RFID Tags

Which RFID tags are attached to goods or for logistics, often used to treat movement history that people can be mobile. Recently, the environment people live and who shall be treated by attaching RFID tags to measure human behavior research [4][5] are also suffering. In our study, RFID tags attached to a tool to control and exchange tags in dealing with participants freely exchange the card, you automatically get intent of the participants.

5　Conclusion

In this paper, we focus on the convergence phase in the discussion that the process narrow the alternatives listed with the environment using RFID tags Experimental results show that the system helped determine participants satisfying conclusion with the smooth progress of the opinion exchange system.

In the future, we hope to expand the system to include the divergence phase of discussion that can support more discussion than the subject over the leg.

References

[1] Yoshiharu, Y., Manabu, S., Yamaki, N.: Group Analytic Hierarchy Process Based on Consensus Making Model. Journal of the Operations Research Society of Japan 40(2), 236–244 (1997)

[2] Dawar, N., Parker, P.M., Price, L.J.: A Cross-Cultural Study of Interpersonal Information Exchange. Journal of International Business Studies 27(3), 497–516 (1996)

[3] Tamura, Y., Yuuki, T., Sunayama, W.: Opinions Exchange Support System by Visualizing Input History. In: Setchi, R., Jordanov, I., Howlett, R.J., Jain, L.C. (eds.) KES 2010. LNCS, vol. 6278, pp. 235–243. Springer, Heidelberg (2010)

[4] Burgard, H.D., Fox, W., Fishkin, D., Philipose, K.M.: Mapping and Localization with RFID Technology. In: IEEE International Conference on Robotics and Automation (ICRA 2004), vol. 1, pp. 1015–1020 (2004)

[5] Hosaka, R.: Study for availability of patient identification in hospitalization ward by new UHF band RFID tag. Memoirs of Shonan Institute of Technology 44(1), 37–42 (2010)

[6] Conklin, J., Begeman, M.L.: gIBIS: A Hypertext Tool for Exploratory Policy Discussion. In: Proc. of the 1988 ACM Conference on Computer-supported Cooperative Work (CSCW 1988), pp. 140–152 (1988)

[7] Osborn, A.F.: Applied Imagination. Charles Scribner's Sons, New York (1953)

Author Index

Printed in the United States
by Baker & Taylor Publisher Services